The Cambridge Companion to
Medieval English Culture

The cultural life of England over the long period from the Norman Conquest to the Reformation was rich and varied in ways that scholars are only now beginning to understand in detail. This *Companion* introduces a wide range of materials that constitute the culture – or cultures – of medieval England, across fields including political and legal history, archaeology, social history, art history, religion, the history of education, and above all the literatures of medieval England in Latin, French, and English, plus post-medieval perspectives on the "Middle Ages." In a linked series of essays experts in these areas show the complex relationships between them, building up a comprehensive account of rich patterns of life and literature in this period. The essays are supplemented by a chronology and guide to further reading to help students build on the unique access this volume provides to what can seem a very foreign culture.

Andrew Galloway is Professor of English and Medieval Studies at Cornell University.

Cambridge Companions to Culture

The Cambridge Companion to
Medieval English Culture

Edited by
ANDREW GALLOWAY

CAMBRIDGE
UNIVERSITY PRESS

University Printing House, Cambridge CB2 8BS, United Kingdom

Cambridge University Press is part of the University of Cambridge.

It furthers the University's mission by disseminating knowledge in the pursuit of education, learning and research at the highest international levels of excellence.

www.cambridge.org
Information on this title: www.cambridge.org/9780521673273

© Cambridge University Press 2011

First published 2011

A catalogue record for this publication is available from the British Library

Library of Congress Cataloguing in Publication data
The Cambridge Companion to Medieval English Culture / edited by Andrew Galloway.
     p.   cm. – (Cambridge Companions to Culture)
Includes bibliographical references.
ISBN 978-0-521-85689-8 (hardback)
1. Great Britain – History – Medieval period, 1066–1485.   2. England – Intellectual
life – 1066–1485.   3. English literature – Middle English, 1100–1500 – History and
criticism.   4. England – Civilization – 1066–1485.   I. Galloway, Andrew, 1957–
DA185.C36   2011
942.03–dc22

2010044490

ISBN 978-0-521-85689-8 Hardback
ISBN 978-0-521-67327-3 Paperback

Contents

Illustrations

Contributors

DAVID R. CARLSON, Professor in the Department of English and formerly Adjunct Professor in the Department of Classical Studies of the University of Ottawa.

HELEN COOPER, Professor of Medieval and Renaissance English at the University of Cambridge.

DAVID N. DUMVILLE, Sixth-century Professor in History, Palaeography & Celtic at the University of Aberdeen.

ANDREW GALLOWAY, Professor of English and Medieval Studies at Cornell University.

RALPH HANNA, Professor of Palaeography in the English Faculty, University of Oxford.

DAVID A. HINTON, Emeritus Professor, University of Southampton.

PAUL HYAMS, Professor of History at Cornell University.

RICHARD W. KAEUPER, Professor of History at the University of Rochester.

LAURA KENDRICK, Professor and Director of the Humanities Department at the Université de Versaille.

REBECCA KRUG, Associate Professor of English at the University of Minnesota.

DAVID LAWTON, Professor of English, Washington University, Leverhulme Visiting Professor, University of Oxford 2009–10, and currently the Executive Director, New Chaucer Society.

CLARE A. SIMMONS, Professor of English at Ohio State University.

ELAINE TREHARNE, Professor of Early English, Florida State University, and Visiting Professor, University of Leicester.

SCOTT WAUGH, Professor of History and Executive Vice Chancellor and Provost at the University of California, Los Angeles.

Chronology

1066–87 King William I

1066   Battle of Hastings. King Harold II killed. Coronation
       of William I.
1078   White Tower (Tower of London) begun.
c. 1080   *Chanson de Roland* apparently written (earliest surviving copy
          c. 1150); other *chansons de geste* written.
c. 1086   "Domesday Book," surveying the goods and tenants of
          much of England.

1087–1100 William II "Rufus"

1091   600+ London houses destroyed by winds.
1098   St. Anselm, archbishop of Canterbury, writes *Cur Deus Homo*
       (*Why God became Man*) to define the justice of the Incarnation
       (Latin).

1100–35 Henry I "Beauclerc"

1101   Robert of Normandy, Henry's brother, invades England.
1114   Henry mounts expedition into north Wales, stopping Prince
       Gruffydd.
1127   Barons swear to accept Henry I's daughter Matilda as heir
       (but many later reject her).
c. 1135   Henry of Huntingdon, *History of the English*
          (Latin chronicle).

1135–54 Stephen versus Matilda

1135	Stephen elected by London citizens; Matilda claims throne; beginning of "the Anarchy" (civil war).
1138	Geoffrey of Monmouth, *History of the Kings of Britain* (Latin).
1147–49	Second Crusade.
c. 1100–50	Various copies of Old English homilies (e.g., Oxford, Bodleian Library, Bodley 343; London, British Library, Cotton Vespasian D.xiv etc.).
c. 1140–54	English chronicler makes final entries in the *Anglo-Saxon Chronicle* at Peterborough Abbey.

1154–89 Henry II "Curtmantel"

c. 1155	Wace, *Roman de Brut* (French translation of Geoffrey of Monmouth's *History of the Kings of Britain*).
c. 1158	Peter Lombard, *Sentences* (Latin: central text for university teaching).
1161	Canonization of Edward the Confessor.
c. 1160–80	Chrétien de Troyes (French poet) active at Marie de Champagne's court.
1160–75	Alan of Lille (Latin theologian and poet) active; *De planctu Naturae* etc.
1166	Assize of Novel Disseisin (new procedure to insure that heirs could remove hostile lords from lands due to them) and other new legal procedures for more efficient and just transmissions of property.
c. 1170	John of Salisbury, *Polycraticus*, *Metalogicon*, etc. (Latin).
1170	Thomas Becket killed in Canterbury Cathedral (canonized 1173).
c. 1180	Marie de France (French poet) active at Henry's court.

1189–99 Richard I "Coeur de Lion"

1190	Richard I leads Third Crusade to the Holy Land; massacre of Jews at York.
c. 1190	*Owl and the Nightingale*.

1199–1216 John "Lackland"

1204	Loss of Normandy.
1208	Founding of Cambridge University.
1208–13	England placed under papal interdict (no burials or masses allowed) because John refuses to accept Stephen Langton as archbishop of Canterbury.
1215	Magna Carta sealed. Fourth Lateran Council, adopting a range of new Church plans (from requiring annual confessions by all the laity, to formulation of doctrine of Transubstantiation, to sharper identification and treatment of Jews and heretics).

1216–72 Henry III

c. 1220	Layamon's *Brut*.
c. 1235	Guillaume de Lorris' *Roman de la Rose*.
1236	Henry marries Eleanor of Provence.
1238	Simon de Montfort, earl of Leicester, secretly marries king's sister, against king's wishes; barons take sides amid general baronial discontent with the king.
1250	Matthew Paris, Latin chronicler at St. Albans Abbey, ceases his *Chronica Majora* (*Great Chronicle*) since the present "age" of the world has reached its completion in round numbers (i.e., the Second Coming is at hand).
1251–59	Matthew Paris quietly resumes his chronicle, continuing it until his death.
1257–58	Crop failure and widespread famine.
1258	King forced to agree to Provisions of Oxford, giving power to fifteen barons, and insuring three parliaments per year.
1264	Henry captured by Simon's troops at battle of Lewes, giving counties representational power, substantially weakening royal power.
1265	Defeat of Simon of Montfort at battle of Evesham, where royal forces return to power, execute many rebellious barons.

1272–1307 Edward I "Longshanks"

1274	Death of Thomas Aquinas.
c. 1275	Jean de Meun's continuation of the *Roman de la Rose*.
1282–84	Conquest and settlement of Wales.
1290	Edward expels all Jews from England.
c. 1290	*Havelok, Guy of Warwick, Beves of Hamtoun* and other early English romances.
1290–92	Struggles over Scottish succession; Edward decides in favor of John Balliol as King of Scots.
1294	War between Edward and Philip IV of France.
1294–96	Welsh revolt of Madog ap Llywelyn.
1295	"Model" parliament; alliance formed between France and Scotland.

1307–27 Edward II of Caernarvon

1312	Execution of Piers Gaveston, favorite (presumed lover) of Edward.
1314	English defeat at Bannockburn.
1315–17	Widespread famine.
1320	Declaration of Arbroath (Scottish barons assert principle of popular sovereignty).
1327	Edward deposed and murdered by Queen Isabella and Roger Mortimer.

1327–77 Edward III

1328	Edward's claim to French throne (via his mother Isabella) is rejected in favor of Philip VI.
c. 1330–49	William of Ockham, radical critic at Oxford of "realism," writes commentaries on Aristotle and other authorities, and polemical works against papal authority over secular empire.
1340	Edward assumes title of King of France; English ships beat French ships at battle of Sluys; beginning of Hundred Years' War (1340–1453).

c. 1340–49	Richard Rolle, self-appointed hermit and mystic, writes Latin and English treatises evoking the "song" of his religious fervor.
1346	Scots defeated at Neville's Cross; Philip VI defeated at the battle of Crécy.
1348	Order of the Garter established, with mysterious and variously interpreted motto, *Honi soyt qui mal y pence* ("shame to anyone who thinks ill of this").
1348–49	Black Death (plague): 30–50 percent general mortality.
1351	Statute of Laborers, legislating penalties for laborers demanding higher wages.
c. 1352	*Winner and Waster* (alliterative poem): beginning of "alliterative revival."
1357	First record of Geoffrey Chaucer (as page to countess of Ulster).
1360	Peace of Bretigny between France and England.
c. 1360	*Prick of Conscience* (didactic English poem preserved in 114 copies, the most popular work in English of Middle Ages).
1362	Winds destroy thousands of trees.
c. 1362	*Piers Plowman*, A text.
c. 1370	Chaucer's *Book of the Duchess*.
1375	Widespread return of plague.
1376	"Good" Parliament; first Speaker elected for Commons; impeachment of king's mistress and financial associates; death of the Black Prince.

1377–99 Richard II

1377	Richard accedes to throne, age 10.
c. 1377	John Gower, *Mirour de l'Omme* (30,000-line French allegory of vices and virtues).
1378–1417	Great Schism: rival popes at Rome and Avignon.
c. 1378	*Piers Plowman*, B text.
1380	John Wyclif, inspirer of the Lollards, condemned for heresy at Blackfriars.
1381	Rebellion of "peasants" (and many others), June 12–15.

c. 1378–82	John Gower, *Vox clamantis* ("voice of one crying out") (30,000-line Latin poem satirizing a wide range of social estates and professions; after 1381 an opening dream-vision of the Rebellion in which the rebels appear as monstrous beasts was added).
c. 1385	Chaucer's *Troilus and Criseyde*.
c. 1385	Thomas Usk writes allegorical self-defense for charges of treason, *Testament of Love*.
c. 1387	John Trevisa translates into English Ranulph Higden's Latin universal chronicle, in which Trevisa declares that the English nobility no longer know French any more than "their left heel."
c. 1370–1400	John Gower: *Cinkante Balades* (fifty-one French ballads on love, dedicated in final form to Henry IV).
1388	"Merciless" Parliament, conviction and execution or exile of king's close advisors; Thomas Usk convicted and executed.
1389	Richard retakes control of government.
c. 1390	*Sir Gawain and the Green Knight* and other alliterative poems (e.g., *Siege of Jerusalem, Pearl, St. Erkenwald*).
c. 1392	John Gower, *Confessio Amantis* (English with Latin).
1394	Death of Queen Anne of Bohemia, Richard's queen; Richard destroys palace at Sheen (where Anne died). Richard begins rebuilding Great Hall of Westminster Palace.
c. 1395	Second version of the Wycliffite Bible.
1397	"Lords Appellant" convicted of treason.

1399–1413 Henry IV

1401	Statute *De Heretico Comburendo* (For the Burning of Heretics); William Sawtry burned for heresy (first Lollard burning).
1402–8	Glendower's revolt in Wales.
1405	Percy revolt; execution of Richard Scrope, archbishop of York.
1410	Lollard Disendowment Bill.

1413–22 Henry V

1414	Rebellion of the Lollards under Sir John Oldcastle.
1415	Henry's first expedition to France; battle of Agincourt.
1420	Treaty of Troyes between England and France; Henry marries Catherine of France and is recognized as heir to her father, Charles VI ("the Mad").
c. 1420	Margery Kempe's *Book* written.

1422–61 Henry VI

1422–37	Henry VI crowned as infant, England ruled by dukes of Gloucester and Bedford (to 1435).
1429	Joan of Arc defeats English; Charles VII crowned.
1431	Joan of Arc burned.
1431–38	John Lydgate, *Fall of Princes*.
1455	Reginald Pecock, bishop of St. Asaph and Chichester, writes English prose works against the Lollards, appealing to reason and Scripture.
1457	Reginald Pecock condemned for heresy in denying the primacy of Church authority and relying only on reason and Scripture; reprieved from burning by public recantation.

1461–83 Edward IV

c. 1470	*Wisdom, Mankind* (morality plays); Robert Henryson flourishes (Scotland).
1471	Former king Henry VI murdered.
1477	Blind Harry, *The Wallace* (Scottish verse historical epic).
1478	Thomas Malory, *Morte d'Arthur*.
1478	First print of *The Canterbury Tales* (William Caxton).

1483 Edward V

1483	Edward V accedes as king, but immediately opposed by Richard of Gloucester; Lord Rivers, Edward's guardian, is arrested and executed; Edward, lodged in the Tower, vanishes from records.

1483–5 Richard III

1485   Henry Tudor lands in Wales; Richard III defeated and killed
         at battle of Bosworth.

1485–1509 Henry VII

1487   Yorkist rebellion (defeated).
1497   Cornish rebellion (defeated).
1499   Skelton's *Bowge of Court*.

Abbreviations

CCSL   *Corpus christianorum, series latina* (Turnhout, 1953–)
DNB   *The Oxford Dictionary of National Biography,* eds. H. C. G. Matthew and
        Brian Harrison, 61 vols. (Oxford, 2004, and online edition 2004–)
EETS   The Early English Text Society; ES: Early Series; OS: Original Series
MS   manuscript
PL   *Patrologia Latina*, ed. J-P. Migne, 221 vols. (Paris, 1844–64, and online
        edition 1996–)

London is the place of publication unless otherwise stated.
References in notes with * are given in full in Guides to Further Reading.

ANDREW GALLOWAY

Introduction: medieval English culture and its companions

This "companion" is designed to introduce a range of materials deemed to constitute the culture (or, perhaps better, cultures) of medieval England, from approximately the Norman Conquest to roughly the Reformation. The fields presented here may offer a rather unusual fit with standard courses and disciplines, but the pressures on modern frameworks are intended. It is not unusual, however, for study of early periods to offer some combination of "literature," "history," "archaeology," "art history," or other fields. Studies in antiquity and the Renaissance do this regularly, and medieval studies from the outset was defined in an equally capacious framework. Partly this is because times more distant from our world make obvious the need for a more varied set of tools yet more synthetic angle of view. To be sure, the history of scholarship shows that studies in particular disciplines need the context of their own conversations, debates, and long-cultivated tools and strategies. But scholarly history also suggests that work in particular fields flourishes in an environment of other pursuits in the same period. Scholars and students in any one field need the companion-ship of others pursuing related kinds of work, to broaden perspectives and inspire new ways of carrying out particular endeavors, and to advance our understanding of how issues and materials that we treat separately were in their own period related.

A portable guide with such goals can only introduce and provoke, aiming for a significant variety of approaches, as well as a significant range of disciplines. The fields treated here include political and legal history, archaeology, social history, art history, religion, history of education, and, especially, the literatures of medieval England: Latin, French, and English. A general chronological sequence is followed but not rigorously divided; some chapters stress linear chronological developments, others center on issues or case studies. Their territories cannot and should not be simply merged with one another, and the goal of the overall arrangement is to suggest complex relationships – and the potential for further combinations of these fields – as well as set forth some new or reconsidered foundations for particular disciplines from the distinct points of view of a notable range of scholars.

The word "culture" – charged and laden as it is with its own history – is meant to help these pursuits, but as a challenge rather than a notion of some stable or unifying thing, which it can never be. "Culture," in Raymond Williams' view, is "one of the two or three most complicated words in the English language."[1] The term is a key that at best opens many locks, and its use in the title is intended to incite thought about ways of situating and connecting the fields surveyed in this volume (and others that are not). Williams mentions two senses of the word that are relevant. The older, but still available, sense of "culture" (and *Kultur, Cultur*, etc.) coined and developed in the eighteenth and nineteenth centuries refers to aesthetic, intellectual, political, and spiritual development or cultivation. This sense governs, for instance, Jacob Burckhardt's *Civilization of the Renaissance in Italy* (the English translation of Burckhardt's 1860 *Die Cultur der Renaissance in Italien*), a work foundational for the flexible and broad-ranging inquiry approach that we now consider "cultural history."[2] That meaning of *Cultur* – as "civilization" or "high culture" – carries an elite implication, conveying a particular threshold of social prestige in training or cultivation. Paradoxically (given its use as an index to very specific worlds and times), that sense can also purport to embody values that are transcultural and transhistorical, the "best" standards by which every artistic and social sphere or form should be measured. To avoid this, historical perspective is particularly important (as Burckhardt realized more than he is sometimes given credit for). In Burckhardt's presentation, those values were especially linked to distinctive individualism, as expressed in art, politics, and learning, and epitomized by a particular range of canonical forms of communication and particular (invariably monumentalized) artists and intellectuals. Other standards than individualism, of course, have sometimes prevailed in scholarly uses of the term. In any case, this sense of the word still refers to things of distinctive social value: "honor, morals, religion, and the law," as a scholar puts it in a recent volume on "the transmission of culture in early Modern Europe."[3]

A second and broader sense for the word has, however, overtaken the first in many uses today. This comprehensive if not all-inclusive meaning of the word "culture" insists on historical and circumstantial differences of values and meanings. This sense, emerging from anthropology, has touched all historical and literary studies. In this usage, "culture" refers to a materially and socially comprehensive range of human life, including kinship systems, trade patterns, structures of society and social power, and habits or modes of material production. People may strive to be "cultured" in the narrower, elite sense, but in the broader sense they are always already "cultured" – if, that is, they are to be even conceivable as members of the same world. These are the terms that the twentieth-century scholar and poet John Holloway invokes when he muses on his London childhood world and family of the 1920s and 1930s: "What – limited as we admittedly were – could we do? What did we know? What, perhaps one could ask, was our culture? By this I do not mean intellectual culture as I was later to know it, because of that we had none." Instead, Holloway shows that he means the "culture" made up of nursery rhymes, proverbs, holiday rituals, weather-lore, the small skills of making things, and imagining (or not) the prospects of social advancement and even the apocalyptic and religious end of the world. Some of the most difficult parts for him to see were the smallest ones. Confessing to the difficulty of capturing this range about a world that he himself inhabited, Holloway notes, "It is really quite difficult to unearth one's trivial skills. They feel almost like breathing, not part of a learned culture, and of course this whole account is very incomplete."[4]

There can be no doubt that, for much of the twentieth century, this sense of "culture" has been a productive strategy for connecting diverse fields. Currents of anthropological thought flowing into and, in turn, back out from literary and historical study represent perhaps the most important "trans-disciplinary" influence in the humanities. Highly influential has been anthropological work on the role of "games" and "deep play" in culture, often taking as a starting point Clifford Geertz's work.[5] Literary and historical scholars have both long drawn from the work of Pierre Bourdieu, whose concepts of "*habitus*," "symbolic capital," and the uses of language to deploy or manipulate social power extend the still important and stimulating work of Bronislaw Malinowski and others (though Bourdieu, opposing Malinowski, was opposed to a narrowly "functionalist" approach to the symbolic means of social life).[6] For Bourdieu, the general indoctrination of attitudes and "rules" supposedly defining social life mask the constant manipulations of such codes; thus, "culture" is no static system but instead unfolds from negotiations between the "symbolic" and material economies, in a *habitus* or dynamic system of values whose silences – the unspeakable or unthinkable – are as crucial yet as seemingly "natural" as those Holloway ponders. In these terms, scholarship has continued to extend "cultural" explanations across ever wider tracts of human life, including emotional, bodily, and even neurological features of human existence.

Yet at the same time, precise and sensitive pursuit of aesthetic issues is more important than ever. Literature's and art's formal properties are always at the center of pursuits by literary and art historians, and sometimes anthropologists as well. For those scholars, those properties provide the very reason to explore culture in any broader sense. There can be no full *a priori* or deductive account of a narrative or visual work: one must start inductively and by focused consideration, choosing contexts from the inside out, and only by following these strands can a larger picture emerge. Yet again, as Malinowski and other anthropologists remind us, there can be no meaning without context and use. The pursuit of both artistic and wider cultural history must go hand in hand.

Such theorizing is stimulating, but any historical and literary inquiry must treat particular conditions, traditions, and artifacts rather than general theories. Ideas of "culture" of any kind can dull as well as sharpen thought, and to carry out the latter, our suppositions and terms must be continually subjected to scrutiny. An example pertinent to this book might be the notion of "Anglo-Norman culture." Such a "culture" must be said to begin with the Norman Conquest of England in 1066, where this volume takes its general (though not categorical or impermeable) point of origin. That is a logical as well as a practical starting point. From the eleventh century on, Europe's political and intellectual life was transformed, with more widely connected interactions of thought, institutions, and goods, many more written vernacular literatures, and equally distinctive new political systems and emergent bureaucracies. Written French, German, Icelandic, and Italian literary traditions all take their start at this period, and English and Latin literatures both take new starts. A new range of diverse and interacting literary and other written materials emerges into view.

At the same time, however, Anglo-Saxon England did not simply cease to exist at the Conquest, though it was reframed, both as (to use Charles Taylor's term) a new "social imaginary," and in political, literary, and social realities.[7] As Elaine Treharne's chapter reminds us, much of what we identify as "Anglo-Saxon" prose is extant in copies from the century after the Conquest. Moreover, the Continental Norman culture that preceded the Norman Conquest of England possessed a range of political and ideological elements crucial not only for understanding what happened after the English Conquest, but also for how that Conquest and the spread of Norman rule elsewhere in eleventh- and twelfth-century Europe came to be. If one were to use "Anglo-Norman" as the main framework to define post-Conquest England, one ought to consider both the pre-Norman English culture, and the cultures of the Normans wherever those had already developed.

One might also want to consider whose views were being represented. Certainly, to many of those whose lands they conquered or threatened, the Normans seemed to possess a trademark style, if only of intimidation and exploitation. As the twelfth-century chronicler at Peterborough Abbey, last continuer of a tradition of writing in the *Anglo-Saxon Chronicle*, declared, in a unique English poetic epitaph to William the Conqueror, "Castelas he let wyrcean/and earme men swiðe swencean" ("He caused castles to be built/and wretched men oppressed").[8] The chronicler's judgment of William is mixed, but the perspective shows the beginning of the steady shift of English writers to that of outsiders to the new regime (with its new architecture and new patrons). Yet literary forms are already being mixed, and boundaries of those features of separate "cultures" blurred: the Peterborough chronicler's own verses on the Conqueror abandon the traditional alliterative style of Old English poetry, and instead use the form of rhyme that the Normans' French poetry thereafter influentially made available: "wyrcean ... swencean."

Capturing the *images* of other cultures, indeed, is as crucial to our understanding as determining any "real" boundaries or entities. As David Dumville's chapter here on Celtic (or, as Dumville pointedly insists, "celtic") visions of the English shows, past visions of a dominant or a subordinate "culture" open up the question of how valid any sweeping claim about a "culture" may be. Not that such visions of "cultures" are less real or not elements of history in themselves: they have their own meanings and traditions, passed down and among various historical communities. But modern scholarship should use such terms carefully, lest they replicate the social visions that the histories of such notions carry with them (what Bourdieu calls "complicit" analysis). The image of a struggle between "Anglo-Norman" and "English" literature and culture, for instance, has long lingered in medieval English literary history. It is fair to assume, as most scholars do, for instance, that the tradition of poetic English

writing that we think of as "classical Old English" poetry retreated well
before the Conquest, leaving a much less ascertainable range of forms
and traditions that depended on French forms, apart from such novel
poetic alliterative styles as that in Layamon's early thirteenth-century
Brut – eventually followed by the "triumph of English" with Chaucer and
his contemporaries and followers. But this literary historical narrative of
enslavement and liberation – which is also a cultural narrative, sometimes involving claims about a "true national spirit" – is too fully
wrapped up in nineteenth-century ideas of nationalism to be believable
as a complete guide to linguistic, much less to literary, intellectual, or
(proto-) national culture. Just as Old English did not cease to be read and
written for at least two generations after the Conquest, so the late-
medieval alliterative "revival" developed from its own, highly
Francophone contexts. True, the alliterative forms of Old English poetry,
and even more the rhythmic forms of Old English homiletic prose, may
have survived strongly enough to have shaped the finely (but quite
differently) crafted alliterative English poetry that appears as if out of
nowhere in the later fourteenth century, in works such as *Pearl*, *Sir
Gawain*, *Piers Plowman*, and others. Yet those works were profoundly
formed by the French literature that had developed in the meantime,
in England and on the Continent, to which those works often directly
responded and around which they were closely shaped.

As well as wondering what kinds of continuity really existed in such a
sudden resurgence of a long-buried vernacular literary style, we should
also ask what gains we seek by thinking – as scholars from the seventeenth century on have, as Clare Simmons notes in her chapter – of a
distinct "Anglo-Norman culture" or even a "Norman yoke" that was
somehow in continual struggle against and contradistinction to those
"true English" traditions. Part of the answer is that this division between
"Anglo-Norman" and "English" cultures and languages serves to bolster
a modern sense of the antiquity of English national and cultural identity.
But the English-only linguistic nature of that is a much more recent
invention, and a misleading one. It is easy to think, for instance, that in
the late fourteenth century, Chaucer both exemplified by his successful
production, and asserted by his various comments, that the French world
of Anglo-Norman culture was by his period of the late fourteenth century a lost cause, an elite game preserve. We might be tempted to think
this because he was and still often is seen to "found" English literature;
or simply by the deft and withering irony to which he subjects a prioress

who regularly speaks French but of the "scole of Stratford atte Bowe,/For Frenssh of Parys was to hire unknowe."[9] But the narrator's slyly patronizing ear belongs to someone who, unlike the prioress, discerns the "Frenssh of Parys" as different from the insular varieties, even the kinds from religious houses like Stratford atte Bowe of which she speaks so consummately. There is no "triumph of English" or death of French culture in England in this quietly satiric moment. On the contrary, this is a reminder that "Frenssh of Parys" was still a reference point for what Chaucer might, if he knew our terms, have earnestly called "culture" in the Burckhardtian sense.

This is also a reminder of the further late medieval social ideal of knowing many possible kinds and styles of speech, and having the ability to use them as occasion (including glancing satire) demanded, as opposed to those who could only excel at the provincial versions of such styles. The French of English varieties remained a frequent language of the English court, but at least some at that court had a continental ear and frame of reference as well (as the continental French style of Chaucer's associate John Gower shows well). The prioress has missed this crucial point, though she is said to take special pains "to countrefete cheere/Of court, and to been estatlich of manere" (lines 139–40). Immaculately careful but lacking a sense of "Frenssh of Parys," she will always be slightly less cultured than she thinks, a speaker instead of the kind of French that flourished in religious houses, rather than the kind of French that continued to be read in the deluxe copies of the *Roman de la Rose* and other continental French works that the nobility owned into the fifteenth century. So, too, other forms of "business" French persisted, as some records indicate, until the seventeenth century in England on the manors of the provincial nobility.[10] Hearing the social meanings in these differences is much harder for us than grasping the linguistic elements.[11] So fully is the *idea* of higher Parisian French "culture" (in the elite sense) assimilated into later medieval English literature that language as such is not the point. In *Sir Gawain and the Green Knight*, the elegant dinner conversation presented in alliterative English between the Cheshire household and Sir Gawain is called "frenkysh fare," a very high standard indeed (line 1116).

Our pursuit of culture must thus include the specters and images of culture – in every sense – from the period in question. As David Lawton's chapter makes clear, the *desire* in literary "voices" to constitute something other and more monumental than they really did is as much part of our object of inquiry as the empirical evidence of what languages were used (or abused), what texts actually made, what buildings actually built. As both Bourdieu the anthropologist and Holloway the poet stress, cultural history has to work both inside and outside its sources, and draw both critical awareness and historical sympathy wherever it can find it – be that in anthropology or in study of manorial records, or literary satire.

This volume begins with three essays that set the stage for the period and for the broad terms of life: political, legal, and material. The three chapters in this section stress the complexities of the boundaries between their disciplines even as they clearly indicate their outlines and riches. Scott Waugh opens with a magisterial overview of how politics at court and beyond developed in post-Conquest England. Here, the local as well as the wider social pressures on the royal power are interwoven. The same chronological starting point is used to frame Paul Hyams' detailed discussion of a very different social level, where literature and legal procedures mutually illuminate the transformations of culture in the twelfth and thirteenth centuries, marking the beginning of a lawyer-dominated world. As David Hinton's chapter on archaeology shows, further glimpses of everyday values, as well as the basis of literary meanings, are even more pervasively if sometimes elusively provided by the material evidence of life. Hinton's chapter pursues a range of social experience that moves smoothly between the high and the low senses of culture, and especially seeks to understand the undocumented creativity and endeavors of the mass of unlettered and rarely described common people.

Although all three opening chapters present broad settings indeed, all of them also make clear the importance of the local and the immediate. Waugh's study shows how highly particular patronage and intensely personal political strife shaped broader political history. Hyams' chapter suggests that maxims learned in childhood define one's outlook on law, wrong, and justice. Hinton's chapter reminds us that how people framed their houses depended on their region – although in this case, just what defined that particular regional boundary, as he shows, remains mysterious. Geography and region always matter, and much culture is local. Recent work has shown how regional studies, in fact, offer particularly rich opportunities for showing how several different kinds of "culture," rather than literature or society or art as such, must be considered as a unit and at the same time.

Other frameworks for social life than time or place allow us to pursue more widely shared views and concerns. The second section, therefore, considers a range of kinds and views of social relations – narrative or symbolic as well as lived – and the values and anxieties involved in those. This section is concerned with ideals and conflicts, while the focus moves forward somewhat in chronology. As Richard Kaeuper indicates in his chapter in this section, something like the beginnings of the idea of "the nation" are visible in Anglo-Saxon England, but the Norman Conquest imposed new forms of that notion, supported by new institutions for justice. Yet in a further development of that view, and continuing his consideration to the later centuries of the Middle Ages, Kaeuper makes the case that the later centuries reveal a real decline in public confidence in legal processes, a pervading sense of partisan interests, and a lack of credibility in the efforts by the powerful to serve the "common" good – an idea that emerged just as its fulfillment seemed unavailable. This is a question not only of chronological divisions in a culture, but of trans-formation of its broad assumptions about public institutions and key terms of experience and understanding.

No less complex and controversial are the assessments of how English medieval culture after the Conquest spread its values, and bigotries, into the neighboring islands and regions: modern Ireland, Wales, and Scotland, especially during the thirteenth-century expansion that has been called by the historian R. R. Davies "England's first empire." As Davies points out, "English advance was ultimately sustainable in depth and over a long period only in conditions which were sufficiently attrac-tive for intensive colonization and for the replication of conditions in which an English-type society and economy could flourish" – areas with somewhat similar preexisting social and economic features (such as parts of Scotland), or areas that could keep themselves intact and discrete from clearly segregated pockets of colonial English power and control (like Wales and Ireland). Beyond those areas, Davies suggests, assimilation into Wales, Scotland, and Ireland of English ways of life and authority was not likely or even imagined. "The incompatibilities of economic power, social custom, and political norms were simply too great."[12] Yet as a literary scholar, Michelle Warren, shows, a particularly rich and complex range of historical writing and literature about cultural author-ity – focused on the endlessly pervasive stories of King Arthur – emerges from these "borders of Britain."[13] These views may serve as general background to David Dumville's chapter in the present volume on "celtic" visions of England, which suggest that the incompatibilities were not simply material and political, but also stubbornly ideological. Images of the "Other" persisted and grew on both sides of the boundaries between England and its closest neighbors, and to some extent still govern social vision today. The question of values leads back to the question of whose values, and even whose values those are perceived to be, by others. As Dumville shows, the house of culture's mirrors can be complex.

Fundamental to medieval values is the desire for sanctity, and, indeed, the pull of religion as a whole is an unavoidably major element of medieval culture. Thus, closing the second section, Rebecca Krug provocatively charts both the desire for sanctity and some of the extraordinary deflections and survivals of it by way of the early fifteenth-century figure and (presumed) writer, Margery Kempe. The scale of the context in which Krug ultimately positions Margery is very large indeed. For Krug, *The Book of Margery Kempe* serves as a focus for the long history of the desire for sanctity in terms that occupy as broad a horizon for "culture" as Christianity itself.

Values lead logically to kinds of knowledge and literature and art, and these "literacies" are discussed in this volume's third section. Opening this section, the elucidation of the "textual" articulateness of visual art that Laura Kendrick's chapter surveys brings directly to the fore the issue of how to rejoin into a more meaningful unity the visual and the textual that are usually separated in modern scholarship. Seeing with "medieval eyes" is, as Kendrick shows, somewhat possible, with the right strategies, but it involves other assumptions than those we customarily make about the visual *and* the textual. So, too, as Ralph Hanna's following account of medieval schooling shows, the modes of medieval grammar education are unfamiliar to most of us. Such schooling was nonetheless central in inculcating participants into a range of complex levels of understanding and social discipline, and even in sensory training (by the ear rather than the eye). These are the unarticulated matters of schooling, the parts of learnedness as unnoticeable as breathing. The combinations of French and English that Elaine Treharne treats in her chapter – a key to any view of "Anglo-Norman" culture – offer another challenge to our common views: the basic assumptions of a single-language world, education, and literary production. Treharne offers that challenge through the most immediate kind of material encounter we still possess to access medieval language and literature: the manuscript, through whose physical display and details Treharne undertakes the same general pursuit of implicit codes of cultural meaning that Hinton applies to medieval house-frames and personal mirrors.

Cultural power resides in language as well as arms or castles, as David Carlson's following chapter on Latin literature shows. Yet as Carlson also emphasizes, the sweep of such a rich and "intimidating" tradition does not mean that such power and meaning were unchanging. Whereas Waugh's chapter discusses the center of authority and power in the political sphere, Carlson's chapter discusses the center of power and authority in the linguistic and literary sphere. Latin was the lifeblood not only of academic and theological writings in the Middle Ages, but also of political and cultural understanding on every level, as Carlson shows, from the (fabulous) chronicle accounts of King Arthur to the bombastic assertion that a king must be deposed.

The importance of all such non-English and non-literary materials and disciplines for understanding medieval English literature is implied, and sometimes directly indicated, throughout this volume. Treharne's and David Lawton's chapters offer this volume's most direct treatments of medieval English literature, though all the other chapters are more or less germane to the background, status, and development of medieval English literature.

Treharne and Lawton slice in very different ways through a series of concerns in order to raise broad questions about how medieval English and other writing can be appreciated and pursued within wider fields, as well as in minute formal literary details. Whereas Treharne's focus on Anglo-Norman and early Middle English is meticulously textual, for Lawton, the focus of inquiry is on the recuperation of the "voice" – and, even more, the desire for voicing – that late medieval written English literature presents. Lawton's chapter is thus focused on the historical treatment of a literary mode, one that is fraught with affect about its very basis of existence in texts. As well as the many other interests of this focus, it allows him to consider in small compass a host of major late medieval literary works, and a range of notoriously complex issues in late medieval English literature, which touch on a wide range of current medieval literary criticism. Those include the issue of the crafted or "real" persona of the vernacular author, the relation of an English translation to its (ostensibly more authoritative) source and tradition, and above all the evocation of or desire for "presence" in texts, cultivated and formed to suit a wide variety of administrative and religious purposes in the fourteenth and fifteenth centuries.

All the chapters in this volume show that the elements of "culture" – the "companions" of things found together – possess complex relationships, and are never as clearly distinguishable as they might have seemed from a distance (or in a library or bookstore section). The final section considers the relationships between the medieval and the post-medieval world, "us" and "them." The very name and endeavor of "medieval studies" asserts that the "Middle" ages ended, granting "us" (finally) our proper modernity. Helen Cooper's chapter surveys the adaptations as well as continuities in romance and many other fields of literature between the Middle Ages and the Renaissance, and Clare Simmons brings the focus on the appropriations of the Middle Ages up to the present. Just as literary historians have sometimes shown how important literature's visions of history are, so, as Cooper and Simmons show, the legacies and visions of the Middle Ages are central elements to later literary and wider culture. The final section of this volume is, therefore, a guide for rethinking the separation of the period in question from all later study and uses of it, demonstrating some of the extraordinary and varied importance of the Middle Ages from the sixteenth century to the present.

Every chapter and field in this volume is meant to help in the situating of something else. The volume seeks to present as "companions" a wide array of fields for whatever research and teaching scholars and students take up in the period. Not all possible fields and topics, of course, could be treated directly. Philosophy, music, and economics are not directly featured, though their presence is sometimes perceptible. Gender studies as such are also not directly explored. Women's circumstances and contributions are treated as parts of discussions rather than in the depth and detail that an adequate presentation would require; and the formation of masculine identity is treated only in passing (in Ralph Hanna's chapter on schooling). Other social and religious topics and groups, such as the Jews in England, receive some, but only passing, consideration (in David Hinton's chapter on archaeology). Questions of the nature of lordship may be pursued more fully elsewhere as well. These topics, however, have all received considerable attention in other studies and introductions, and suggestions for starting points on these and many other fields and issues appear in this introduction's Guide to

Further Reading, as well as throughout the Further Reading provided for the other chapters.

Notes

1. Raymond Williams, *Keywords: A Vocabulary of Culture and Society* (1983), p. 87.
2. Jacob Burckhardt, *Die Cultur der Renaissance in Italien* (Leipzig, 1860); *The Civilization of the Renaissance in Italy*, trans. S. G. C. Middlemore (New York, 1929, 1958, etc.).
3. Lawrence Stone, "Honor, Morals, Religion, and the Law: The Action for Criminal Conversation in England, 1670–1857," in Anthony Grafton and Ann Blair (eds.), *The Transmission of Culture in Early Modern Europe* (Philadelphia, 1990), pp. 276–315. The editors of that volume nowhere explicitly define their sense of "culture," but do so implicitly by aligning themselves with Burckhardt's work: see Anthony Grafton, "Introduction: Notes from Underground on Cultural Transmission," *Transmission of Culture*, pp. 1–7.
4. John Holloway, *A London Childhood* (New York, 1966), pp. 52, 63.
5. Clifford Geertz, *The Interpretation of Cultures: Selected Essays* (New York, 1973), including the influential essay, "Deep Play: Notes on the Balinese Cockfight," pp. 412–53.
6. Pierre Bourdieu, *Outline of a Theory of Practice* (Cambridge, 1977).
7. Charles Taylor, *Modern Social Imaginaries* (Durham, NC, 2004). A recent useful exploration of the post-Conquest views of the Anglo-Saxons is by Kenneth Tiller, *Layamon's Brut and the Anglo-Norman Vision of History* (Cardiff, 2007), especially pp. 39–96.
8. *The Peterborough Chronicle, 1070–1154*, ed. Cecily Clark, 2nd edn. (Oxford, 1970), s.a. 1087, p. 23; *The Anglo-Saxon Chronicle*, trans. Michael Swanton (New York, 1998), p. 220.
9. Chaucer, "General Prologue," lines 125–26, in *Riverside Chaucer*.
10. A. I. Doyle, "English Books In and Out of Court from Edward III to Henry VII," in V. J. Scattergood and J. W. Sherborne (eds.), *English Court Culture in the Later Middle Ages* (New York, 1983), pp. 163–82 (at 163–65); Richard Ingham, "Mixing Languages on the Manor," *Medium Ævum* 78 (2009), 80–97.
11. Ardis Butterfield, *The Familiar Enemy: Chaucer, Language, and Nation in the Hundred Years' War* (Oxford, 2010).
12. R. R. Davies, *The First English Empire: Power and Identities in the British Isles, 1093–1343* (Oxford, 2000), p. 193.
13. Michelle R. Warren, *History on the Edge: Excalibur and the Borders of Britain, 1100–1300* (Minneapolis, 2000).

Part One
_____

Theaters of culture: political, legal, material

1
_____

From court to nation

Throughout the Middle Ages, England was rife with politics: at every level of society individuals and communities waged contests to acquire, exercise, and retain power and authority. Wealthy peasant families dominated village society and used their wealth and prestige to hold sway over their lesser neighbors and maintain their economic grip on the village, while often vying with one another for ascendancy. In towns, oligarchies of wealthy merchants controlled urban courts and offices to protect and further their commercial and property interests, while trying to keep in check the retailers, artisans, and servants who made up the bulk of a town's population. Yet the oligarchs were no less competitive and scrambled among themselves for power and authority. The counties experienced similar levels of competition and conflict, stratified as they were among the wealthy lords whose property stretched across many counties, to knights who held one or more manors and thought of the county as their community, to smaller landholders who might not have had the wealth to break into the ranks of knighthood, but who had a proprietary interest in county affairs and who would in time become the "gentlemen" on whose shoulders the county community would rest. These men served on juries, became local officials, and had the loudest voice in meetings of the county court. They were bound into family groups by descent and by marriage, and they were also bound by ties of lordship and service to great magnates inside and outside the community. And individuals would not hesitate to call on such groups to help them in contests of power or property. Even within monastic communities, factions of monks could cause headaches for abbots and priors or end up in bitter feuds when asked to elect their successors.

At the level of the kingdom, politics could be no less contentious. English monarchs vied with neighboring rulers in Scotland, Wales, and

Ireland for territory and supremacy. The ruling family could itself split into competing factions, while coalitions of magnates, barons, and knights disgruntled by the king's actions or policies did not hesitate to take up arms to force the king to adopt policies more congenial to their interests. A dozen kings ruled England between the death of Edward the Confessor in 1066 and the accession of Henry IV in 1399, a period of just over three centuries. In that time, three kings were replaced and killed (Harold, Edward II, and Richard II), while strenuous efforts were made on at least one occasion to replace another five (William II, Stephen, Henry II, John, Henry III).

Furthermore, events at one level of the realm reverberated through others. After the Norman Conquest in 1066, English kings built on Anglo-Saxon precedents and developed a sophisticated network of officials, institutions, and practices that linked the crown to local communities and individuals. Those institutions, such as the hundred and county courts and the corresponding courts in towns and cities, and offices such as bailiff, coroner, sheriff, and mayor, helped to focus the identities of communities while simultaneously enabling the king to enforce laws and policies and to extract wealth from the realm. As a result of the interconnectedness of English government and communities, local political squabbles, especially in London, could bubble up into a national concern, while national politics, whether over questions of rivalry, policy, or ideology, almost always had repercussions in local communities.

Contemporary commentators, surveying the political scene, sometimes lamented the factiousness and quarrelsomeness of the English, declaring that their greatest liability was their inability to unite and get along. In the early thirteenth century, the biographer of a great nobleman, William Marshal, lamented that "there are no men in any land like those in England, each with a mind of his own," making it impossible for them to agree.[1] A hundred years later, another writer, surveying the lamentable state of politics in the reign of Edward II, laid the blame for political disorder on the ambitiousness and greed of the English, which led them to compete for status and wealth: "in almost every aspect of life the squire strains and strives to outdo the knight, the knight the baron, the baron the earl, the earl the king. Moreover when they cannot afford their expenses, because their inheritance is insufficient, they turn to pillage, they plunder their neighbours, fleece their tenants, and practice nefarious extortions upon the servants of God."[2] Observing these upheavals, another writer commented that "some people are of the opinion that the diversity of spirit among the English is the cause of their revolutions," while another stated that "it was no wonder" that they fought against one another "for the great lords of England were not all of one nation but were mixed with other nations," some Britons, some French, some Danish, and so on.[3]

This chapter summarizes how a political nation developed in medieval England between the Norman Conquest in 1066 and the ascension of Henry IV in 1400. It argues that this development rested on a critical paradox: in these three centuries, the royal government steadily expanded and became more sophisticated, involving a greater and greater proportion of the population, but at the same time the power of the king became more limited and the scope of royal action more constrained than it had been at the beginning. The development of a political nation will be followed through three central themes: court society and patronage; war, finance, and taxation; justice, administration, and political reform. These themes can help bring some intelligibility to the seemingly disordered fractiousness about which chroniclers lamented and show how England evolved from a courtly to a parliamentary, bureaucratic kingdom.

Any treatment as brief as this, however, cannot possibly do justice to the complexity of politics in medieval England or to the myriad ways that events at the national level influenced local conditions or vice versa. Similarly, it cannot do justice to the importance of developments within the other political communities who shared the British Isles with English kings. Indeed, one of the most noteworthy trends in the recent historiography of medieval politics has been the adoption of a "British" viewpoint, showing how kingdoms and principalities interacted as peers and how English kings attempted to subordinate their neighbors to their authority with more or less success.[4] A European perspective is equally critical, for England was entangled in a complex web of relations – political, diplomatic, familial, and commercial – that bound the kingdom and monarchy to countries and rulers across Europe as well as within the British Isles. All of these relations were important to English society and so deeply influenced politics.[5]

Court politics: kings, kingship, and nobility

At the highest level of the kingdom politics was above all about relations at the royal court, among those who surrounded the king either in the capacity of servants and officials or in the capacity of companions and lords. While court relations determined much of what happened in English politics throughout the Middle Ages and factionalism could erupt at any time, by the end of our period politics embraced a wider range of social and economic interests than it had at the beginning, and political leaders, including the king, appealed for support from segments of society beyond the court. Individuals and groups beyond the court had a voice in national affairs that had not been heard in the twelfth century and that called at the end of the fourteenth century for court reform.

It is important, therefore, to begin at the heart of politics, at the royal court. A literate courtier of the late twelfth century, Walter Map, confessed that in a "spirit of perplexity I may say that in the court I exist and of the court I speak, and what the court is, God knows, I know not."[6] His perplexity arose from his experience of the changing composition of the court over time and space, for the royal court was itinerant, always moving with the king as he traveled around his realm. In the twelfth century, when English kings devoted the majority of their time to fighting in France in order to defend their patrimonies, the composition of the court could change dramatically as it followed the king through one territory after another. Even when the king's movements were restricted to England, the court was constantly on the move and nobles did not ordinarily reside at court, but rather visited it. Yet, despite Map's lament, it is in fact possible to know something about the English court. The structure of the court comes partially into view as early as 1136 in the *Constitutio Domus Regis*, which laid out for the new government of King Stephen the offices of the king's household. These were the servants who made up the "downstairs" part of the court that ministered directly to the king's personal needs – his cooks, valets, and so on – distinct from the greater lords and knights who attended the king's court "upstairs."[7] As the king's household grew larger, more formal, and more powerful it periodically became an object of controversy and reform. Ordinances in 1279 and 1318 sought, for example, to regulate how the king's household should function, so that it was properly accountable for income and expenditures. The household, in fact, was an important accounting organization for the king, receiving and expending funds not only for the king's personal needs, but also for supporting royal armies. It functioned at times as a receiver, paymaster, and quartermaster. It also housed a significant military force – the household knights – that formed the core of the king's armies.

Unlike household officers and servants, the greater figures of the realm were not constantly in attendance, but they did appear on special occasions and the numbers at court swelled accordingly. Besides providing the king with logistical support, the court and household provided the setting for state occasions, feasting, ceremonies, diplomacy, and consultation. Chronicle accounts occasionally reveal the social activities and the personal relationships that brought the court to life. In February 1344, for example, Edward III established a Round Table at Windsor Castle "in the same manner and estate as the lord Arthur, formerly King of England, maintained it, namely to the number of 300 knights." The foundation was marked by three days of feasting and courtliness, attended by the king, his family, nobility, and knights, and included continuous joustings while "the best melody was made by the minstrels," who were munificently rewarded.[8] However splendid court society may have been, a long line of courtly critics stretching from Peter of Blois at the court of Henry II into the fourteenth century heartily condemned court life. One writer in the reign of Edward II acerbically asked "Who do you think is inflamed with greater malice against another than the courtier? While he is greatly puffed up with bitter ill-feeling he ignores his inferiors, despises his equals, and is always striving to equal his betters."[9] This critique reveals the kind of ambition, envy, and competition that underlay the bright ceremony of court displayed at the Round Table and that could at times undermine political order.

Records also reveal that between the *Constitutio* and the late fourteenth century, the royal household grew from about a hundred personnel to nearly 500.[10] The increase reflects the royal government's widening activities. It reflects as well the king's increasing wealth and desire for comfort. In contrast, upstairs, the number of courtiers fluctuated but did not display the same kind of growth. The nation's political elite was composed of the greater lay aristocrats – earls, barons, and knights – who largely derived their wealth from land and the products of lands and animals, and ecclesiastical lords – archbishops, bishops, and greater abbots – who occupied the most powerful offices in the Church. The king's greatest officials, such as the chancellor, treasurer, and others who were almost always in attendance, constituted another important element of the court. Most of these figures owed their power and influence to the king. He generally appointed his own officials, appointed or influenced the appointment of powerful churchmen, such as the archbishop of Canterbury, and could create new earls, though the title was heritable. These powerful men constituted not only the social core of the court, but also the king's closest counsel, who provided advice on policy and politics.

The court revolved around the king. "We courtiers are assuredly a number, and an infinite one, and all striving to please one individual."[11] As a result, the cohesion or stability of the court, and hence of the realm, depended to a great extent on the personality of the king, as well as on the mix of people at court. The king's personal influence can be seen in contrasting descriptions of two very different men: Henry II and Edward II. According to Gerald of Wales, Henry

> was a man easy of access and condescending, pliant and witty, second to none in politeness … a prince so remarkable for charity that as often he overcame by force of arms, he was himself vanquished through showing too great compassion. Strenuous in warfare, he was very prudent in civil life … When difficulties pressed hard upon him, none was more amicable, but none sterner once safety was regained. He was fierce towards those who remained untamed, but merciful to the vanquished, harsh to his servants, expansive towards strangers, prodigal in public, thrifty in private.

Gerald also pointed out that he was a consummate politician, ideally suited to lead a court, for though "he was daily set amidst a host of faces, he never again forgot anyone whom he had once closely scrutinized."[12] As another member of Henry's court, Walter Map, summed up, Henry "did naught insolently or pompously, but was temperate, moderate and virtuous, faithful and wise, liberal and victorious, bringing honor on all good men."[13] We must treat these passages carefully and with skepticism, for they may reflect the real Henry, but they certainly reflect ideals about good, courtly kingship that circulated at Henry's court.

Whatever measure of the real man these reflections might contain, they contrast starkly with the way men wrote about Edward II, a century and a half later. One author praised him being "fair of body and great of strength," but then condemned him for turning his back on "the company of lords" and turning instead "to harlots, to singers and to jesters, to carters and to delvers and ditchers, to rowers, shipmen and boatmen, and to other craftsmen."[14] He went on to condemn Edward for lightly revealing secrets, angering easily, spending lavishly on friends and entertainment, and displaying too much favoritism to those closest to him. The author of the "Life of Edward II" similarly admired Edward as "tall and strong, a handsome man with a fine figure" and noble ancestry, but also lamented that after six years of rule Edward "has achieved nothing praiseworthy or memorable."[15] Despite his gifts he "accepted the counsels of wicked men" and nearly brought the kingdom to ruin. Edward was therefore scorned and became the first king since the Conquest to be forced from the throne and then murdered. Family, inheritance, and physical endowments were important, but they could be undermined by character. The king's personality, bearing, and conduct were therefore of paramount importance in his ability to maintain the cohesion of the court and lead the nation.

Kings were judged not only on their personality, but also on their military ability. In an era when nobles and knights were trained as warriors, where the popular literature such as King Arthur extolled the virtues of martial prowess, and where territorial and economic interests had to be asserted and defended, the military image of kings was critical to their success. William the Conqueror, William II, Henry I, Henry II, and, above all, Richard I spent a significant portion of their lives in the field and gained honor and repute through their military command or their exploits on the battlefield. Edward I was likewise revered as a powerful commander, first on Crusade, then against the Welsh and the Scots. Edward III's wartime triumphs made him a hero to the military ranks and he consciously fostered a chivalric image and military comradeship through tournaments, Round Tables, and the creation of the Order of the Garter. In contrast to these "heroic" kings, those who were less bellicose, less able to lead, were judged harshly and found wanting. Henry III, for example, never developed any military skills and was never highly successful in battle, a shortcoming that strengthened the view of him as weak. Edward II's reputation was even worse, especially after his humiliating defeat at the hands of the Scots at Bannockburn in 1314. Richard II similarly failed to live up to the martial heritage of his father, the Black Prince, and his grandfather, Edward III. By the time he came to the throne, in fact, England had been exhausted by Edward's wars, and Richard's court was divided between pro-war and anti-war courtiers.

Whether a king was weak or strong, the office of kingship was endowed with an aura of religious sanction, as exemplified by the royal coronation, in part a religious ceremony that emphasized the lineage of kingship stretching back to the Old Testament kings and remodeled in Christ's image. As a Christian monarch, the king bore responsibility for justice and order, maintaining the law, and defending the weak – widows and orphans – from the powerful. By this Christian measure, the king was to be even-handed in all things, whether in judgment or favor, and had to rule with the good of his people always at the forefront of his policy. Reinforced in sermons and histories, this image of the Christian king was powerful in shaping people's perception of the quality of a king. Perceptions of the king were also influenced by the royal court itself. Writers around the royal court in the twelfth century borrowed from both traditions of Christianity and chivalry to create an image of a courtly king: one who was measured, reasoned, even-handed, affable, and generous.

As critical to the success of the court as the king may have been, it depended as well on those at court, especially those aristocrats who were seen as the natural leaders of the realm. Thus, according to the "Life" the barons "are the king's chief member, without which the king cannot attempt or accomplish anything of importance."[16] While English society experienced profound changes in the three centuries after the Conquest – a doubling or tripling of the population only to drop by a third to a half in the outbreaks of plague in 1349 and 1361; increased social stratification brought on by growing wealth and status consciousness; inflation and deflation; and expanding revenue from internal and overseas trade – the aristocracy did not change as dramatically. Fashions at court certainly changed, reflecting the growing wealth of its members who wanted to keep pace with fashion trends in France and Italy. And the ranks of the "natural lords," roughly native-born nobles, barons and knights, needed to be constantly replenished as landholders died without heirs, or their estates were divided among their daughters, or they forfeited their lands to the king for treason or rebellion. Ecclesiastical offices likewise turned over, bringing new faces to prominence at court and in society. Yet the upper portion of English society and the court remained relatively compact, dominated by a few families of nobles and wealthy knights, who never numbered more than 100 to 150. In these three centuries there was a more or less constant fluctuation at the level of individuals and families, but there was no tectonic shift in class structure producing a social revolution.

The most important force for change in the composition of the nobility was the king himself, who had the power "to raise men from the dust," in the memorable phrase of Orderic Vitalis writing about Henry I. Royal patronage was at once a powerful political tool and a controversial issue. Kings could ennoble and enrich individuals, and their patronage was much sought after. The king made it clear that he could ask any man to serve him: "it is the King's prerogative as chief of the executive that any man in the kingdom, if the King need him, may be freely taken and assigned to the King's service, whose man soever he be, and whomsoever he serves in war or in peace," as the Magister (master) tells the Student in the ruminatively edifying treatise on the workings of the Exchequer that has come down to us from the circle of ministers around Henry II in the second half of the twelfth century.[17] The king could also take away offices, as an angry Edward I did in 1297 when two earls refused to serve with his army overseas. Since "they would not obey his wishes, [they] were dismissed from their offices. And the king gave their offices to certain others who would serve him."[18] Kings similarly engaged in an ongoing tussle with the Church over the power to appoint church officers and very often got their way as a means of advancing their servants and friends, such as Thomas Becket. The king thus rewarded loyal service handsomely, and the royal court reflected his personal likes and dislikes as well as social and political tradition. The *Dialogus* on the Exchequer again: "The greatest of earthly princes, Henry II, is always striving to augment the dignity of those who serve him, knowing full well that the benefits conferred on his servants purchase glory for his own name, by titles of undying fame."[19] Though kings honored traditional ideals of the aristocracy in England, they also acted pragmatically to get the support they needed and did not hesitate to reach out beyond the ranks of the "natural lords" to entice into their service those lower down the social ladder or outside England altogether. In the thirteenth century, for example, Henry III brought around him members of his wife's Savoyard family, his own Poitevin relatives from his mother's second marriage, along with English lords and officials. Edward III favored his comrades-in-arms at the beginning of the Hundred Years' War with France, created six new earls in one year, and revived an old title – duke – to use in a new way to honor members of the royal family. Largesse was a salient characteristic of courtliness as it came to be defined in these centuries.

Royal patronage was thus an accustomed feature of court life, yet, precisely because everyone in the nobility expected to enjoy the king's generosity to some extent, patronage was seldom without political controversy. Within the hothouse atmosphere of the court, how the king's favor was evaluated depended to a great extent on personality, and the newly ennobled and traditionally noble elements of the court did not always mix well. A notorious example that illustrates how the court and royal patronage could become the focus of political rivalry was the rise and fall of Edward II's favorite, Piers Gaveston. Though Piers was non-noble and a foreigner, Edward showered gifts and wealth on him, married him to the heiress of an old English family and made him earl of Cornwall. His patronage and affection were excessive, but Piers made the situation worse through his arrogance.

> The earls and barons of England looked down on Piers because he was a foreigner and formerly a mere squire raised to such splendour and eminence, nor was he mindful of his former rank. He looked down on the earls and barons and gave them base nicknames [such as "Dog" or Horessone"]. He took offices and authority from others, and granted these at his pleasure to members of his household.[20]

Edward II's favoritism was particularly egregious and ultimately led to his downfall and murder, but the king's distribution of favor could become a divisive political issue at any time, and critics questioned the appropriateness of royal favor, demanding that the king reward only his "natural lords." Royal patronage, for example, provoked outrage and deep political challenges in the reigns of Henry III and Richard II.

What appears to be mere carping about the behavior of notoriously unpopular royal favorites should not obscure the serious, structural consequences of royal patronage. If the king's distribution of favors and rewards had the effect of heightening the sensitivity of interpersonal relations at court, it also had practical consequences affecting the English community as a whole. Whatever kings might have thought or wished, the English monarchy after the twelfth century was never financially independent. Its dependence occurred, in part, because the Norman conquerors and their Angevin successors gave away nearly all that they acquired. William the Conqueror and his sons – William Rufus and Henry I – gained control of an entirely new realm in addition to their patrimony in Normandy and almost completely dispossessed the Anglo-Saxon landlords. Yet the Domesday Book reveals that by 1089, only about 24 percent of the wealth of England was left to the royal family, while the rest was in the hands of lay and ecclesiastical lords and royal officials.[21] William's sons gave away even more to supporters as they struggled to gain the upper hand over one another. In raising men from the dust, Henry therefore may have gained loyal servants and cemented political alliances, but he also depleted his landed resources. More land was lost during the civil war between his successors – his daughter Matilda and his nephew Stephen – after his death. The creation of earldoms can serve as a simple measure of how wealth was transferred, even though they did not always involve gifts of land: between 1135 and 1154 the number of earldoms tripled. Henry II set out to recover this wealth by resuming unjust alienations of all kinds, but he could not resolve the underlying weakness of the landed base of the monarchy. Further erosion occurred under his son Richard I, whose ambitious plans for a Crusade and for defending his French territories demanded not only cash, but loyal followers, who expected to be rewarded for their service. Henry III built up a court party by lavishing gifts on his half-blood relatives from Poitou, his wife's family from Savoy, and Simon de Montfort. Edward II demonstrated lamentable prodigality in his favoritism and rewards to court favorites throughout his reign, while his son, Edward III, freely bestowed rewards on those who shared his military exploits in France. Only Edward I showed restraint, and was criticized for failing to display courtly generosity.

Because the landed wealth of the crown was so finite, kings had to find other resources to carry out their ambitions and to reward their friends and followers. For the latter, they relied heavily on wealth that came their way as a consequence of their position as feudal landlords. All the magnates and barons of the realm held their land of the king, and he could permanently acquire their lands if a tenant-in-chief (one who held directly of the king) died without any heirs at all (which was rare) or if a tenant-in-chief forfeited his or her land as a result of rebellion or dis-obedience (which was more common though irregular). The king also gained custody of land if the heir to an estate was a minor until the heir came of age (called a wardship, which was very common). If a tenant died leaving only unmarried daughters or sisters as his heirs, the king had the right of wardship until they married and then controlled their marriages as well. When ecclesiastical lords, whether archbishops, bish-ops, or abbots, died, kings took control of the estates held of the king (the temporalities) during the vacancy and sometimes prolonged the vacancy by not authorizing the appointment of a successor in order to prolong their enjoyment of the revenues from the estates. As might be imagined, vacancies annoyed and even aggravated churchmen, while abuses of wardships and marriage caused consternation among lay families. The seizure and re-distribution of the lands of the king's enemies was an easy way to reward loyalty in times of conflict, but it inevitably created competing claims to estates among the heirs and divisiveness among families at the highest level of society. All these measures could excite controversy, disgruntlement, and even outright opposition if not exercised with tact and sensitivity.

War and taxation

Patronage was not the only expense kings incurred. They needed money to attain other goals:

> kingdoms are governed and laws maintained primarily by prudence, fortitude, temperance and justice ... but there are occasions on which sound and wise schemes take effect earlier through the agency of money, and apparent difficulties are smoothed away by it, as though by skilful negotiation. Money is no less indispensable in peace than in war. In war it is lavished on fortifying castles, paying soldiers' wages and innumerable other expenses, determined by the character of the persons paid, for the defence of the realm.[22]

In a mildly ironic mode, the *Dialogue* thus underscores the costliness of war and its prominence as both a consequence and instrument of royal policy.

The best starting point for understanding the role of war in medieval English politics is the Norman Conquest, which had two long-lasting consequences that shaped royal policy for the following three centuries and beyond. The first was that it gave the king of England a landed stake in France and therefore bound England into a particular political relationship with the king of France. As a result of the Conquest, the duke of Normandy, a vassal of the king of France, became a sovereign king in his own right. In 1154, Henry II joined to this polity of England and Normandy his paternal inheritance of Anjou along with the territories he acquired through marriage to Eleanor of Aquitaine. Henry II and his sons Richard I and John thereby ruled over a huge conglomeration of lands and lordships stretching from Scotland to southern France. Though never unified into a single polity, the existence of such a powerful "empire" right in their backyard posed a challenge that French monarchs met by continually striving to wreck it. If French hostility were not enough, quarrels within the royal family over the right to rule could erupt into fully fledged civil war. As a result, English kings were almost constantly at war in the twelfth century. Not surprisingly, they spent most of their time on the Continent defending their French lordships and putting out fires rather than governing in England. Of the ten years that he was king Richard I was in England for less than six months.

This pattern of seemingly endless warfare changed after 1204, when Normandy, exhausted from continual fighting and suspicious of King John, fell to Philip Augustus, leaving only Aquitaine in English hands. To recover Normandy, John lavished vast sums on constructing a grand alliance to overwhelm Philip, but the scheme failed spectacularly when Philip defeated the coalition at the battle of Bouvines in 1214. The loss of Normandy had profound consequences: it radically reoriented the politics and political geography of France, it cut English aristocratic families off from their roots in France and forced many who still had lands in Normandy to choose allegiances, and it meant that English kings henceforth spent most of their time in England. War with France became less frequent than it had been in the twelfth century, but the king's desire to protect his stake in France remained strong, even after Henry III formally renounced most of his continental heritage in the treaty of Paris in 1259. The king of England still clung to his holdings in southwestern France, known as Gascony, which he held as a vassal of the king of France. French kings periodically demanded that their "vassal" swear fealty to them or appear at court in Paris to answer complaints against him from his French tenants; humiliating actions that the sovereign king of England was understandably loath to perform, though disobedience could result in judgments against him and the loss of his holdings.

A second long-term consequence of the Conquest was its incomplete nature; it left undetermined the fate of Scotland and Wales and, most importantly, the relationships among the rulers in the British Isles. English kings fancied themselves at least the overlords of their neighbors, and demanded obedience or fealty from them. Scotland and Wales, moreover, were politically very different, with far-reaching consequences not only for the Scots and Welsh, but for the English as well. Scotland early on developed a fairly cohesive kingdom, centralized under a single king. There might be disputes as to who should succeed to the throne, but the kingdom of the Scots appeared much like the kingdom of England and confronted English monarchs with a significant challenge. Wales was not so unified, and Welsh princes were as prone to fighting among themselves as fighting the English. Anglo-Norman aristocrats and their successors exploited this divisiveness to carve lordships out of Welsh territory, with the acquiescence of English kings. Nevertheless, when the Welsh did unite they could be formidable opponents, who, aided by the rugged territory of central Wales, proved difficult to defeat.

After John's reign, war was sporadic. Henry III largely used diplomacy to manage his relations with Wales and Scotland, and though he twice campaigned in France to secure his territory, England enjoyed much longer periods of peace than in the previous century. That interlude ended in the 1280s, and England entered into a new period of prolonged, costly warfare that lasted over a hundred years. Edward I, determined to be the master of his domain, undertook to subjugate the Welsh and succeeded in 1284 in conquering most of the country. He had far less success when he turned to Scotland with the same intentions in the 1290s. War between the two kingdoms raged on and off for more than a generation. Edward's son, Edward II, went to war only reluctantly and without much success, suffering a humiliating defeat at the hands of the Scots in 1314. Edward III radically changed policy after he came to the throne. Determined to remove the threat of the Scots in the north, he plunged into war and campaigned ceaselessly through the 1330s. Then he shifted the political ground against the French: whereas his grandfather and father – Edward I and II – fought to defend their French lordships, Edward III embarked on regime change. In 1337 he claimed to be the rightful heir to the kingdom of France and set out to re-conquer his heritage. The result was the start of the Hundred Years' War, a misleading title, since England had already been involved in wars in France for over two hundred years. But he initiated a new phase of fighting, and for the rest of the fourteenth century the king's wars in France were critical to shaping the political nation in England. War was a predominant feature of English policy as Edward not only tried to secure the French kingdom, but also fought to protect England's lucrative trading interests in Europe.

As the Dialog of the Exchequer implied, war was expensive, and the periods of greatest royal expenditure and revenue generation coincided with periods of war. War placed a huge burden on the king's finances, the royal administration, and local communities. Norman and Angevin kings resorted to various expedients to pay soldiers, allies, and suppliers for their ceaseless wars in France, setting precedents for their successors. They extracted as much as they could from traditional sources, especially royal lands, but they also raised taxes.

King John built on these precedents and collected more revenues than any of his predecessors except Henry I, but in so doing drove the country into rebellion. John had neither Richard I's military talent nor Henry II's political acumen. Suspicious of the motives of his barons and driven to recover the inheritance he had lost in France, he tightened the financial screws on the kingdom and ran roughshod over families and the Church, provoking a furious political reaction. In 1215, a coalition of magnates forced John to accept the Magna Carta. Magna Carta sought to place restrictions on the king's unfettered powers over the lands and marriages of his tenants-in-chief, over ecclesiastical property, and over the legal system. It also sharply curtailed his powers of taxation. The restrictions were a stinging rebuke of Angevin fiscal policies in general and John's political actions in particular. Above all, Magna Carta made it clear that no man, including the king, was above the law and that every free man could expect the protection of the common law. In fiscal matters, although some of the specific measures in Magna Carta were subsequently disputed, the king of England was forced to seek consent for any general taxation from the early thirteenth century onward. Magna Carta represented a watershed in English politics, and its terms resonated throughout the Middle Ages and formed the basis of subsequent efforts to curb royal government and policies.

Despite these limitations, royal revenues escalated under Edward I as he undertook to dominate Wales and Scotland and to protect Gascony. He levied taxes on the Church as well as on the laity, and secured a new, regular source of income by taxing the wool trade. Because he could not collect money as quickly as his armies needed it, he borrowed heavily and so died heavily in debt in 1307. Edward II climbed out of debt and amassed a sizable treasure, in part because he did not go to war as often as his father had. But whatever financial gains he made his son Edward III wiped away pursuing his military ambitions. Taxation of all kinds climbed to unheard of levels in the 1330s and remained high through the rest of Edward's reign. He tried every expedient he could to raise funds, by traditional taxes on wealth, manipulation of trade, and finally by a head tax that outraged nearly everyone in the kingdom. Edward's bellicose policies achieved stunning battlefield success – at Sluys, Crécy, Calais, and Poitiers – but their huge expense caused considerable hardship to his subjects.

Because escalating demands for money, soldiers, and supplies touched individuals down into village communities, they caused friction between the king and all his subjects. Debates over royal policy thus spilled out beyond the court to include a growing segment of the realm. Taxation quickly roused indignation and opposition, as Henry III discovered. He tried on more than fourteen occasions to get consent to tax the realm and succeeded only twice. The chronicles of Matthew Paris reveal the outrage his requests sparked. For example, when Henry wanted to campaign in France in 1242 to protect his inheritance and asked for taxes to defray his expenses, he was strongly rebuffed. Henry used the occasion to tell "prelates, earls, and barons, assembled at London" of his plans and to ask their consent to a tax.

> When, therefore, the king made known to them the irrevocable determination of his heart, namely to cross to the continent ... and with various arguments demanded pecuniary assistance from them, the nobles replied with great bitterness of spirit, that he had conceived this design without consulting them; that he was void of shame, to make such a demand; that he had so frequently harassed and impoverished his faithful subjects, demanding money from them as a matter of course, as if they were the basest slaves; and had so often extorted large sums of money from them, which was expended with no advantage; they therefore now opposed him to his face, and refused any more to be despoiled of their money to no purpose.[23]

Although hyperbolic, the passage illustrates baronial opposition to royal expenditures as well as taxation, and conveys a sense of the intimate atmosphere in which such negotiations were conducted in the twelfth and thirteenth centuries. The claim that taxation without consent led to slavery was heard again under Edward I in 1297, when a group of lords and knights said that "nothing sooner puts men in bondage than to redeem their own and to be [taxed] at will."[24] The wealth of such lords was hardly imperiled as they proclaimed, but the clash over the right to levy taxes generated a substantial part of the rhetoric that framed political debate in medieval England.

To overcome wariness about taxation, English kings tried to persuade their subjects of the necessity of taxes for the good of the realm. Edward III, who in contrast to Henry III was highly successful both in war and raising money, nevertheless cited melodramatic threats to the kingdom to gain support for taxation. In 1344 he cited "the many things attempted on the part of the enemy of our lord the king of France against the truce formerly taken in Brittany between our said lord the king and his said enemy ... and how his said enemy strives as much as he can to destroy our said lord the king, his allies and subjects, lands and places, and the English language." The rhetoric worked. Parliament "having had good deliberation and consideration thereon, and seeing clearly the threat to the land of England ... petitioned our said lord the king with great urgency that he would make himself as strong as he could in order to cross the sea in number" and granted a tax. While Edward was generally successful in raising the money he wanted – more so than any of his predecessors – the sensationalism of his pleas (more than once claiming that the French wished to obliterate the English language, a threat indicating the growing assumption of its propriety even among the French-speaking nobility) indicates how dependent the king was on the political process to raise large sums of money.

Government, opposition, and parliament

Beginning with Magna Carta, the king's opponents repeatedly attempted to limit royal power. These efforts were one of the most significant achievements of medieval politics and demonstrate how a political nation emerged. Calls for reform were often triggered by concerns about royal finances such as excessive demands for taxation or excessive patronage, but they were also a product of the interaction between the royal government and the population, especially in the realm of law and justice. One of Henry II's most admirable and enduring achievements was the development of a system of common law procedures and courts – resting on the use of juries – that brought legal remedies to an ever wider portion of the population. Most law and justice to that point had depended on the customs and practices of local courts, with little commonalty across the realm as a whole. Henry II, building on the precedents of his Anglo-Norman predecessors, changed that and made simple, uniform procedures available to all free men, a substantial part of the population. The reforms were so popular that the English came to expect as a matter of course that they could use the royal courts to protect their property and that any free man could enjoy due process of the law. The number of suitors lining up to have their pleas heard in the royal courts steadily mounted year after year and, as the business of the courts expanded, increasing numbers of local citizens were also brought into the judicial system through service on juries.

The king, moreover, insisted that his own tenants, the greater nobles and knights, adhere to the same principles of legal conduct that his courts practiced. And they, in turn, forced John to concede that the king had to behave according to the standards of law and justice that the country had come to expect.

> No free man shall in future be arrested or imprisoned or [dispossessed] of his [land], liberties or free customs, or outlawed or exiled or victimized in any other way, neither will we [the king] attack him or send anyone to attack him, except by the lawful judgment of his peers or by the law of the land. To no one will we sell, to no one will we refuse or delay right or justice. (Cap. 29)

Magna Carta enshrined the ideals that no one was above the law, including the king, and that due process and justice were the right of any free man.

The expansion of royal law, justice, and courts was but one part of a general and steady expansion of royal government in the three centuries after the Conquest. Building on Anglo-Saxon precedents, English monarchs expanded the scope of government, increased the number of officials, and touched every community in the realm. A considerable portion of this expansion can be attributed to the king's need to raise money and organize the country for war, but money was not the only motive. Sheriffs looked after the administration, land, and revenues in the county; coroners oversaw the king's legal prerogatives; and escheators supervised the king's feudal interests. In the realm of justice, two great courts were established centrally at Westminster – the King's Bench and Common Pleas – but the king also dispatched justices throughout the country to bring royal justice into the heart of county communities, in the form of eyres and assizes (royal justices commissioned to travel to all counties to hear cases, either of any kind or of particular kinds in which the king and royal law was deemed to have an interest). The inventiveness of royal justice stepped up in the fourteenth century, as the crown commissioned panels of officials to "hear and determine" specific complaints – oyer and terminer – and later relied on men of local importance to maintain law and order in their communities by appointing them as justices of the peace. Justices of the peace could both investigate crimes and pronounce judgment on those indicted. The crown relied heavily on individuals and panels specially commissioned to carry out a wide range of business locally: assess and levy taxes; raise supplies and troops;

conduct general inquiries; and care for the royal forests. By 1341, when the king ordered a general inquiry into the conduct of his local officials, the list was staggering:

> Escheators; sub-escheators; coroners; sheriffs; under-sheriffs; taxers; ... keepers and constables of the peace and of castles and land on the coast; takers and receivers of wool; assessors and receivers of the night and other subsidies ... keepers of forests, verderers, clerks and other ministers of forests, chases and parks; collectors and controllers of customs; troners, butlers and their substitutes; keepers of the king's horses and their grooms ... purveyors of victuals; purveyors for the king's household and its subsidiary households; keepers of gaols; electors, triers and arrayers of men-at-arms, hobelars and archers; bailiffs itinerant and other bailiffs and ministers.[25]

The returns to the inquiry in 1341 made it clear that corruption and malfeasance were rife within the ranks of local officials. The outcome of the growth of royal government – especially in the realm of law and justice – was therefore double-edged. It brought large numbers of ordinary people into governing and widely publicized ideals of justice, fairness, and the right to participate in government and justice. At the same time, it placed enormous power in the hands of those who occupied offices or who had the opportunity to influence who was appointed to hold office. The result was a potentially volatile tension between expectations of what royal government should do and how authority was actually exercised that underlay the day to day operations of government throughout these three centuries. The expansion of offices and functions, moreover, contributed to the expansion of royal authority and the ability of the king to marshal the resources of the kingdom, but it did so by placing considerable authority and power in the hands of the local landholders who occupied those offices and sat on ad hoc commissions. Depending on the circumstances, their loyalty and self-interest could be torn between the king and powerful nobles.

Complaints about corruption become better known during the fourteenth century, in part because there was a greater degree of record-keeping in private as well as royal administration. They also came to light and were encouraged by the development of parliament as an instrument of government and as a forum for interchange between the king and the community of the realm. From the beginnings of the Anglo-Norman kingdom, the crown had depended on consultation with the greater barons – lay and ecclesiastical – to settle difficult issues, whether judicial questions or policy issues, such as whether to go to war. Counsel was an inherent part of the bond between a lord and vassal: vassals were expected to attend their lords' courts when summoned and to provide counsel on those issues affecting them all. Kings secured such advice informally as part of court life, discussing issues with the officials who were constantly in attendance at court, but also formally, on ceremonial occasions such as when the king appeared in majesty wearing the crown at major feast days throughout the year. Councils were held often but irregularly during the twelfth century, and the expectation that the king should with consult with the greater lords on issues that affected the entire realm became well entrenched. One of Henry II's most significant pieces of legislation, the Assize of Clarendon, laid out procedures for the role of the crown in maintaining law and order in the realm. It was issued in 1166 and was "made by Henry II with the assent of the archbishops, bishops, abbots, earls and barons of all England." The idea that such assent was essential to governing was enshrined in Magna Carta a generation later. In reaction to the harsh fiscal demands of King John, Chapter 12 stipulated that taxes henceforth could be levied only "by the common counsel of our realm."

But who was to give that "common counsel"? Magna Carta gives a clue in a provision toward the end of the charter establishing a council of twenty-five barons, which was responsible for enforcing the provisions of the charter: "who with all their might are to observe, maintain and cause to be observed the peace and liberties" of England. Both provisions were dropped in subsequent versions of the charter, which was periodically reissued, but they indicate how deeply engrained the idea of advice and consent had become. The habit of consulting lay and ecclesiastical lords on matters of state was strengthened during the long minority of John's son, Henry, who was a child when John died. While Henry was incapable of ruling on his own, a council of barons around him made critical decisions with his consent. These great lords, therefore, represented the community of the realm and gave counsel to the king on its behalf.

In the next generation, the question of who should rightfully counsel the king and represent the community of the realm was hotly debated between Henry III and the barons. This debate grew out of Henry's financial weakness and his general political incompetence. Lavish to his family and friends, eager to be a major player on the

European stage, and determined to maintain the remainder of his French patrimony, Henry needed far more money than his traditional sources of revenue could provide, so he asked for taxation. Those requests, coupled with the perception that his ministers and local officials were corrupt, drove the barons to dig in their heels and to demand a stronger role not merely in counseling the king but in choosing his ministers. Tensions mounted and exploded after 1258 in a massive movement to reform the government. The enterprise was so thorough that Henry essentially lost his power to councils of nobles, who were supposed to exercise and supervise the principal functions of the monarchy as well as appoint the officials in his household. As part of this reform effort, the barons sought to obtain as much support as they could from the population at large, and therefore called on knights to represent local communities in these deliberations. As early as 1237 the term "parliament" was already being used officially to refer to an assembly summoned by the king to deliberate essential policies, and in 1254, for the first known time, representatives were summoned from the counties to widen the basis of consent. The term "parliament" became more commonly used as a result of the baronial reform movement after 1258, and it was becoming accepted that parliament should consist of representatives of towns and counties whenever taxation was at stake.

In the century after Henry III's reign, parliament became an established feature of English institutional and political life. Parliament sat only when summoned by the king, and kings increasingly found it a useful occasion to transact all kinds of business. During the reign of Edward I it met frequently, and after 1294 nearly always included representatives as well as the lay and ecclesiastical lords. Much of its work was taken up with justice and taxation, but discussions in parliament covered a wide range of topics. It became the accepted forum in which the king brought critical issues to the attention of the realm. That function broadened after 1278, when parliament began routinely to hear petitions from subjects and communities, so that it became an important channel through which individuals and communities could bring complaints, pleas, or requests to the attention of the king and his officials. In the fourteenth century, the representatives in parliament, the knights of the shire and the burgesses of towns collectively known as the commons, would present a common petition of their own, and the king's answers to these petitions formed the basis of the legislation that the king and parliament enacted.

As commons were more routinely summoned to parliament after 1300 and as consent to taxation and legislation were more firmly fixed, people began to view parliament as the embodiment of the community of the realm. Thus, the Ordinances of 1311 spoke of the "common assent of the baronage and that in parliament." The baronage – both the lay and ecclesiastical lords – still formed the core of parliament, along with the king. The king could summon whomever he liked to parliament, but in the fourteenth century, the list of those summoned gradually became fixed. Those who received individual summonses were distinct from the representatives of communities in the Commons and came to be known as peers or the peerage. They formed the House of Lords.

Thus, toward the end of the fourteenth century, after three centuries of political maneuvering and conflict, the English monarchy had grown in prestige, its bureaucracy had become more extensive and sophisticated, and it had developed new methods of tapping and deploying the resources of the kingdom. At the same time, the king's ability to generate and execute policies – to exercise his will – had become more limited than his Norman and Angevin predecessors' and politics had become more complex. Magna Carta enshrined the principle that the king was not above the law, political rebellion and reform had repeatedly demonstrated that it was dangerous for the king to attempt to rule arbitrarily, and the rise of parliament reminded the king that he could rule effectively and raise the money he needed only with the consent of the community of the realm. The political community was no longer limited to the king and nobility; it now stretched across the kingdom and through the ranks of society. Parliament embodied this new political reality. A document that probably dates from the early fourteenth century – the *Modus Tenendi Parliamentum*, or "The method of holding parliament" – depicted parliament as embracing the entire realm, with the king, his officials, the magnates, the clergy, and representatives from the counties (knights of the shire) and towns (burgesses). The court was still at the core of the community, with the king, household, and magnates, but other groups, especially the gentry in the counties and the burgesses from towns, had a significant stake in political questions. Parliament gave these latter folk the means to express their views and petitions on a more or less regular basis. The problem at the end of the fourteenth century was that the interests and aims of the different elements of the realm did not always pull in the same direction. Many of the political currents and issues visible in earlier periods converged in both familiar and novel ways to produce a lengthy period of political turmoil.

Richard II and the limits of politics and royal authority

In the 1350s and 1360s, Edward III had knitted together a highly successful political alignment within England. He had, in the words of one historian, made his personal quarrel with France a national policy, and to some extent it had been successful. Using a combination of fear-mongering and jingoism, Edward rallied the country to his wars, obtained unprecedented levels of taxation, and triumphed. He created a tight-knit, chivalric court by distributing honors and patronage widely among those who had served as his companions on the battlefield, and exalted martial ideals through tournaments, round tables, and the Order of the Garter.

Yet as Edward aged and grew senile, as the war in France dragged on inconclusively without showy victories, and as the community chafed under the endless financial burdens that war and the crown placed on it, the political unity fragmented into incompatible interests. Many of the nobility continued to advocate war with France, either to defend England, or to carry the battle to the heart of their old enemy, or to open new fields of conquest in Spain and Portugal. Still imbued with chivalric ideals, the nobility could not let go of Edward's ambitious vision. The Commons, however, yearned for peace. True, they wanted protection from French raids along the English coast, but above all they desired to have a stable political order inside the realm and beyond so that they could pursue their economic interests, which included trade with France, Flanders, and other countries across the Channel. They also wanted to be freed of the burden of taxation that war had imposed on them, and, while they could still see why they should pay for armies, they could not see why they should pay for the king's court, favorites, and patronage.

In the last decades of the fourteenth century, the Commons took the lead in voicing criticism of the court and taking action against those whom they perceived as wrongdoers, leading the king astray and pocketing unreasonable favors. They acted for the common good of the realm and articulated the concerns of the national community with regard to the court, law and order, finances, and the quality of local government. Thus, in the 1370s, a small clique of financiers and Edward's mistress,

Alice Perrers, accumulated great wealth from the vast amounts of money that changed hands in wartime and that Edward had accumulated, so gradually dominating Edward and his court. By the time of the Good Parliament in 1376, royal finances had become such a sensitive issue for the realm as a whole that the distribution of patronage at court was no longer a matter for debate just within the confines of court society and the aristocracy, but had become an issue of national concern debated in and investigated by parliament. The very first speaker of the Commons, Peter de la Mare, bemoaned the hardship caused by the king's levies and asserted that the king "has with him certain counsellors and servants who are not useful or loyal to him or the realm and they have taken advantage by their cunning to deceive our lord the king" and amass wealth for themselves. These accusations against Edward's courtiers gave birth to the action of impeachment, which the Commons wielded against those royal officials deemed not to be acting for the common good.

Things grew worse after Edward's grandson, Richard II, came to the throne the following year. Richard cherished the ideal of a powerful monarchy supported by loyal favorites and symbolic ceremony and display. Aged only 10 when he succeeded Edward, Richard first attracted to his court a crowd of non-noble favorites on whom he relied for advice. The glistening court life that Richard patronized in the 1380s attracted both Chaucer and Gower, who, though not directly supported by the court, moved in the outer circles of court life and wrote on courtly themes. Many nobles, however, were troubled by Richard's court and favorites, who earned the kind of contempt heaped on Henry III's foreign favorites and Edward II's courtiers. Parliament expressed its outrage at the "greed of the king's officers" who "were enriched beyond measure," while the rest of the kingdom was impoverished, and demanded their removal. Like Henry III, who staunchly defended his right to appoint any official he chose to his household, Richard declared that "he would not remove the meanest scullion in his kitchen from his office at [Parliament's] request." Once again, the convergence of court and courtiers, patronage, and finance fractured the political nation, pitting reformers against a king determined to exercise control over his household and government. This time, politics played out on the stage of Parliament. Parliament impeached and executed the most hated ministers, but while Richard was forced to retreat, he did not surrender and in the remaining years of his reign he attracted a new group of courtiers consisting of a younger generation of nobles, who shut an older generation out from power. Richard also increased the size of his household and his expenditures. He built up a retinue or affinity of Chamber knights who were his loyal bodyguard and who, like the men retained by nobles, wore the king's livery (robes) and his badge of the white hart.

English politics in the 1390s dramatized the limitations of both royal power and political opposition to the crown. On the one hand, the king was forced to live within the boundaries enshrined in Magna Carta, Parliament, and the long tradition of political reform. On the other hand, those opposed to the king had no mechanism for supervising him, his government, and his expenditures continuously. Three centuries of political conflict had not produced a lasting, institutional solution to the dilemma of how to curtail the royal will, but had engendered a wealth of political experiments turning on control of the royal council. Frustration and resentment were almost inevitable, and force became the only means of resolving the stalemate, as it had under John, Henry III, and Edward II. When Richard threatened the entire edifice of baronial power by unjustly confiscating the inheritance of the greatest lord in England, Henry of Derby – the son of John of Gaunt, Richard's uncle, who had transmitted to Henry the vast Lancastrian estates and who himself had some grounds by lineage for claiming the throne – the reaction was swift. Derby swept across England with an army, captured Richard, and had him deposed, becoming the first of the Lancastrian kings as Henry IV, but also beginning the series of disputed claims to the throne that spanned the fifteenth century.

Richard's reign and the rise of the Lancastrian monarchy further undermined the power of the king. By developing his own affinity, marked by robes and liveries, the king behaved as just any other nobleman: one power among others. The sense that the crown was but another baronial faction was intensified by the accession of Henry IV, who did not have, unlike Edward III in similar circumstances, a clear title to rule and who had been the head of the most powerful noble affinity in England under Richard. The prestige of the monarchy had suffered.

Notes

1. *History of William Marshal*, ed. A. J. Holden, trans. S. Gregory, historical notes David Crouch, 3 vols., Anglo-Norman Text Society, Occasional Publications 4, 5, 6 (2002–6), lines 18,041–3.
2. *Vita Edwardi Secvndi, The Life of Edward the Second*, ed. Wendy R. Childs (Oxford, 2005), pp. 98–99.

3. *Scalacronica by Sir Thomas Gray of Heton*, trans. H. Maxwell (Glasgow, 1907), p. 75; *The Brut, or the Chronicles of England*, ed. F. W. D. Brie, EETS, OS 131, 136 (1906–8), 2:220.

4. Interestingly, two volumes of the new *Oxford History of England* for the Middle Ages take opposing approaches. *Bartlett, *England under the Norman and Angevin Kings* (2000), adopts a "British" outlook, while *Prestwich, *Plantagenet England* (2005), steadfastly argues in favor of an "English" approach to political history. See also David Dumville, Chapter 5 below.

5. See *Matthew, *Britain and the Continent* (2005), and *Vale, *Origins of the Hundred Years War* (1996).

6. Walter Map, *De Nugis Curialium, Courtiers' Trifles*, ed. and trans. M. R. James, C. N. L. Brooke, and R. A. B. Mynors (Oxford, 1983), p. 3.

7. Malcolm Vale, *The Princely Court: Medieval Courts and Culture in North-West Europe* (Oxford, 2001), and Rita Costa Gomes, *The Making of a Court Society: Kings and Nobles in Late Medieval Portugal*, trans. Alison Aiken (Cambridge, 2003).

8. *English Historical Documents* [EHD], vol. 4, ed. A. R. Myers (1969), pp. 74–75, No. 25(i).

9. *Vita Edwardi Secundi*, pp. 98–99.

10. *Given-Wilson, *Royal Household and the King's Affinity* (1986), pp. 1–27.

11. *De Nugis Curialium*, pp. 2–3.

12. *EHD*, vol. 2, ed. David Charles Douglas and G. W. Greenaway, 2nd edn. (1981), pp. 405–7.

13. *EHD*, 2:410.

14. Roy Martin Haines, *King Edward II: Edward of Caernarfon, His Life, His Reign, and Its Aftermath, 1284–1330* (Montreal, 2003), p. 36, quoting John Trevisa's 1387 translation of Ranulf Higden's world history (*c*. 1350).

15. *Vita Edwardi Secundi*, pp. 68–69.

16. *Vita Edwardi Secundi*, pp. 48–49.

17. *Dialogus de Scaccario*, bk. 2, ch. iv; ed. and trans. Charles Johnson, with corrections by F. E. L. Carter and D. E. Greenway (Oxford, 1983), p. 84.

18. *EHD*, vol. 3, ed. Harry Rothwell (1975), p. 227.

19. *Dialogus de Scaccario*, bk. 1, ch. xiii, trans. Johnson, p. 61.

20. *Vita Edwardi Secundi*, pp. 4–9, 16–17.

21. William John Corbett, "The Development of the Duchy of Normandy and the Norman Conquest of England," in C. W. Previté-Orton, J. B. Bury, J. R. Tanner, and Z. N. Brooke (eds.), *The Cambridge Medieval History: Vol. 5* (Cambridge, 1957), p. 508.

22. *Dialogus de Scaccario*, Preface, trans. Johnson, p. 2.

23. *Matthew Paris's English History from the Year 1235 to 1273: Vol. 1*, trans. J. A. Giles (1889), p. 397.

24. *EHD*, 3:482.

25. Maddicott, *The English Peasantry and the Demands of the Crown 1294–1341* (1975), p. 3.

2

The legal revolution and the discourse of dispute in the twelfth century

European attitudes toward secular law and dispute regulation in general were transformed through a veritable legal revolution starting in the eleventh century, but with its main thrust coming only after about 1150. How cases were argued and processed before this date established the place and character of law within the political culture of the West with some permanence. A lawyer-dominated world came into being. The timing and manner of the professional's advent on the scene transformed the character of significant sectors in medieval life.

Law and dispute deserve a more prominent place in medieval culture than they usually receive, especially during the "long" twelfth and thirteenth centuries. Conflict always reaches into life's core, which makes the discourse with which we try to handle it culturally central too. Beyond this, the Francophone world rethought its law just when its most enterprising writers were rethinking fiction to create the romance. The two seminal transformations shared many stimuli and influences. Both homed in on psychology, intention, and motivation, privileging questions about *how* people act. We see in each a similar puzzlement concerning how we know what we think we know, and how in God's name to be sure. Faced by the twin challenges of proof and truth, both romancers and lawyers felt the lure of the miraculous to sort out the hard cases, magic potions, fairies, ordeals, and God's judgment. In the meantime, each plied his trade toward money and advancement by relying heavily on the gift of words. Rhetoric and grammar must have been quite as essential to lawyers as logic. A juxtaposition of texts from the two fields patently has much to offer to the decoding of each.

As numerous scholars have shown, literary sources can in fact provide unique insight into law and dispute in this pre-professional era, and guide us in the reading of other sources. This is so for several reasons. One concerns an atypical stage in the evolution of noble culture. Early medieval noblemen had long used force of arms to impress their women-folk and beat down their competition, on the battlefield or in the councils that framed their more violent activities. By the twelfth century other options had emerged. A gentleman could distinguish himself from his rivals by delivering a pretty plea in prose or verse directly to his lady, or cut a courtly figure by a variety of relatively peaceful means, such as demonstrating a new method of butchering deer after the hunt.[1] For a relatively brief period in the twelfth and early thirteenth centuries, he could also win admiration by his ability to plead in French the other kind of *conte*, a winning tale in some lawsuit. We see this best from entertainment literature, best of all from the literature in French (the medieval equivalent of today's fashion-leading American English) that – like new forms of law – took off in the course of the twelfth century.

Literary studies stand to gain too. Past studies by literary scholars frequently fail to convince historians, on the ground that they draw on assumptions abandoned by the specialists, concerning the workings of medieval law. We need to cooperate across disciplinary lines in order thereby to grasp better the expectations and goals of trials in the twelfth century and how people sought to implement them.

The trial as process

I start with some assumptions about the shape and thrust of the pre-twelfth-century trial. The aggrieved needed the opportunity to tell their tales of loss and harm to those with the power to grant the redress they sought, and do so in an effective manner to achieve their particular goals. They had to address not just the lordly figure at the center of the scene, but also many other people who moved on and off stage as they gathered information and formed views that developed into court judgments.

Proof was the structuring goal of trial process. One should first try to recover the ways in which contemporaries understood *proof*. Proof does not always refer to the final, conclusive demonstration of truth. The word often means something closer to mere evidence, that is, facts and argument controvertible by counterproofs adduced by the opposition. Yet not infrequently, discussion slides quietly and conveniently from the second meaning toward the first. In the twelfth century, Latin *probare*,

French *prover* and their derivatives show the same ambivalence. Their core sense of "test" can be ambiguous as to whether it is still to be faced or not. Since clear instances where such "proof" words denote conclusive proof in the strong sense seem rare, one must always be on the lookout for a weaker sense.

The vocabulary of proof presents further problems. Only in the course of the twelfth century did the Latin word *evidentia* (in classical Latin, "clearness of speech," "distinctiveness of language") cease to be a merely adjectival neuter plural participle and begin to function routinely as a substantive, "evidence." In this sense, it denoted the human side to a procedure that was, in principle or devout theory, attributed for the most part to omniscient God, who alone could deliver conclusive decisions in court, or for that matter on the battlefield. God's Judgment – in a form that favored their side – was the goal toward which all parties tried to move. It constituted a theoretical representation that certainly implied nothing precise about the actual degree and depth of religious belief and feeling among the actors. Within this framework, we find in the literary texts much highly instrumental action by all concerned.

One would think that a divinely omniscient judge would need no pleading of any kind. Certainly, we cannot yet expect anything like later rules of evidence. But human actors want to satisfy each other that they really know God's mind, in the hope that what they present as His judgment may end conflict. Human discomfort with uncertainty perhaps explains why the core notion underlying human proof is so visual. Humans can never know hearts and minds as God does. They have to make their decisions from surface appearances. Robert Grosseteste draws a proper conclusion from judgments "per faciem." Full truth is beyond human powers; only God, who sees into hearts and minds, can know intentions.[2] So, too, embedded within the word "evidence" is the notion of visibility, that only seeing is believing. Something similar is implicit in the Old French word *enseigne*, much used in the romances to denote something very like evidence, whose primary meaning is some kind of visual sign such as a banner or pennant.[3] Truth, it seems, should ideally be as easy to see as the heraldic identification that knights relied on to tell friend from foe on the field of battle. A champion in a judicial duel must normally swear to the truth of his principal's case by what he had personally seen or heard before taking arms for a duel.[4] In a criminal accusation, the most conclusive evidence (apart from a confession) was the eye-witness testimony of two witnesses, a principle that had started in Roman law but was adopted by the canonists and argued from a variety of biblical texts.[5] A central part of the court's function, therefore, was to commit its personnel to warrant what they had seen and done in the course of the lawsuit, which helps to explain why parties brought their supporters with them and courts were afforced with extra suitors for important cases.[6] One can see why the learned jurists of the thirteenth-century law schools in search of a test for the degree of vehement presumption on which to put a suspect to torture also fixed on a visual cue. The case must be, they said, *luce clarior*, clearer than the light of day.

The initial plaint, roughly equivalent to what lawyers today term a statement of claim, was often called *conte*, "tale," the word used for such other forms of storytelling as fairy tales and fables. This "count" (as it came to be called in law English) was met by a defense that was less formal and verbally rigorous than legally trained scholars have sometimes thought. One story met another. The focus of these pleas is worth close study. Literary pleading often centered less on the precise details of what happened than why and how. The parties sought to persuade their audience of their moral worth, that they were good people and in the right, as we might say. Rational argument was clearly part of the story. But the most convincing fictional examples tend not to come in the counts. Instead, authors often present the suitors – partisans of each side – as those who argue the merits of the case on the facts in the rational and logical fashion we think we might use (e.g., *Violette*, lines 5385–468, 6305–11). If they got their arguments from the parties and their counselors, this must have happened outside open court and beyond our gaze. Authors treated the counts as a kind of *mise-en-scène*, intended to direct the argument along routes favorable to the litigants' purpose and their own.

Each party sought an intermediate (*mesne*) judgment that awarded proof in a form that gave its side the best chance of success. Pleading in open court and much that went on behind the scenes was directed toward this *esgart* (award) or *iudicium*. This declared, in effect, both the issue, the question to be put to God for Him to answer, and the means by which this should be put. Since God was not available for cross-examination, the form of the question could be decisive. The *esgart* more or less declared the court's view of right and wrong, which therefore became most likely. Everyone present, suitor and spectator alike, knew that this allotment of proof would probably prove crucial. They had been vigorously discussing the issues for some time and were well aware of the differences between proofs, between, for example, a simple oath, and the terrifying prospect of carrying a hot iron which the ordeal required – proving innocence by a clean healing, and guilt by infection, and which they preferred. Fiction writers certainly exaggerated the frequency of ordeals, and even of judicial duels. But the oath was ubiquitous in both real and fictional trials. The underlying principle could be represented as the same. The swearer invoked the testimony of God or the saints on whose relics he swore to warrant (confirm and guarantee) his case, the premise being that God could then act to demonstrate truth or, in the event of perjury, rectify the situation. The debate among suitors on this *esgart* was therefore the real nub of the whole trial, all too rarely visible in charter narratives of actual lawsuits. Fiction authors, however, naturally press these debates into the foreground. Their assignment of set speeches to leading proponents of each side may make less historical than literary sense. But the issues and arguments have to be taken seriously as indications of genuine concerns of the day.

The organizing theme around which the disputants and their supporters debated their opposing stories was a notion of wrong. Before the late twelfth century there was no differentiation between crime and tort, criminal and civil offenses.[7] The complainant recounted events to explain the manner in which he had been wronged and to seek redress (e.g., *Violette*, lines 5128–49); his opponent's defense first denied the complainant's story, then customarily contended that the facts did not support it, sometimes challenging it as untrue, more often contending that the events did not occur in a genuinely incriminating manner. Much turned on "how" questions, matters of intention and style hard for humans to judge with certainty. The goal of the pleading exercise was to move a great man, some king or lord endowed with jurisdictional authority, to act on your behalf. It was a petition for the justice that good lords owed their followers. But complainants had more strident options than this. They might, for example, challenge their adversary to defend himself and his conduct physically in battle. The complaint behind this "appeal" shared the same underlying logic of wrong as was prominent outside the law courts, in feud and warfare. Here Old French *apel* denotes a summons of a special kind (not the modern concept of "appeal," a procedure to get an adverse judgment reconsidered): one "calls out" the enemy to physically defend his person and actions before all eyes and, more to the point, through the judgment of God. Direct vengeance was a further possibility. The quest to avenge wrongs, real and imagined, was a major theme of the literature and surely also of the general culture.

The first problem for the aggrieved wishing to sue in court preceded the storytelling. He had to persuade some court-holding lord to entertain his plea, a need shown by the seriousness by which "denial of justice" was regarded. There were several moves a complainant must make to gain a hearing. His first problem was to gain access to the great man. Old English laws confirm that this could be a challenge for anyone outside the charmed circle of royal intimates. Having gained his hearing and told his initial story, he must convince the great man of his seriousness and good faith. This is the reason for the offer of proof, by which one promised to do whatever the court deemed necessary or appropriate to establish the claim to justice (usually in a formulaic phrase at the end, such as "prest sumes del auerrer par quant la court e le Rey agarde" ["we are prepared to confirm (our plea) by whatever means the court and the king judge appropriate"],[8] or in plea-roll Latin something like "per legem et consideracionem curie"). Most important, by this means the complainant committed himself to suffer in the event of failure whatever penalties he had sought against his adversaries. Whoever sought an enemy's life and bodily members put his own on the line. This is the message behind the formal duel challenge. Since there were many opportunities to backslide, courts expected some kind of security that a complainant would appear on the appointed day to carry out his often onerous and risky obligations. The most dramatic manifestation of this was the throwing down of a gauntlet as gage (symbolic deposit) for their intentions, but one might have to offer, voluntarily or at the court's demand, friends as sureties, plus money or other guarantees that one would come on the day set. A person used as security was called in Old French *plege*, Latin *plegius*, modern English *surety*; for "pledge" in the sense of an inanimate object, Old French used *gage*, Latin *vadimonium* or *vadium*, and Old and Middle English *wed*.

The listening lord might still need persuading to adopt one's problem as his own. It was necessary to convince him not to turn a deaf ear. A smart complainant would seek to put his lord in a position where he could not afford to be inactive. The best strategy was to represent one's wrong as bringing shame and harm also to the lord. You were the lord's servant, like your father before you. The act that had harmed you was committed in breach of the lord's peace, in a manner that shamed him as well as you. Such lines of argument, easily documented from fictional trials, became enshrined in time as the formal methods by which thirteenth-century English plaintiffs gained a royal court hearing in the common law action of trespass, fossil memories of the way things were done before the advent of the new forms of law (e.g., *Rose*, lines 4744–90).

Success in litigation required the support or threat of coercive power. Recognition that one was in the right was an empty triumph if the opponent never turned up. The aggrieved needed the lord to issue or authorize a formal summons to bring into court on the appointed day an adversary who might simply refuse if he thought he could get away with it. Delay usually being in his interest, this summons was basic in the same kind of way that the "serving" of a writ over a debt or divorce may still be today. In thirteenth-century England, recipients of royal writs sometimes ostentatiously broke them to show their contempt.[9] There are cases of litigants actually being forced to eat the writs they carried – not as hard as it may seem, since from *c.* 1176, writs were sealed close, that is, folded up very small.

The appearance of both parties in court prepared to argue their case was the exception not the rule. Here both literary trials and the lawyers' leading cases convey a false impression. The force required to secure court appearance – a necessity in any legal system – had by the twelfth century mostly been tamed into the cluster of rules that lawyers call process and distraint. But even in the twelfth century, many a villain must simply have ignored unwanted summonses and citations to court. Secular lords and kings had on occasion to mount military expeditions to bring the recalcitrant to justice. Churchmen recognized their lack of this kind of coercive power all too well. They were, therefore, both among the first petitioners for royal assistance in twelfth-century England and very imaginative in the various, often supernatural, means by which they sought aid.

The need for coercive sanctions behind the legal process is shown at many other stages of trials too. This was equally true in cases settled by agreement, always the most desired outcome. Romance authors show little interest in these non-trials, disputes that never generated drama. They were drawn to the literary possibilities offered by forensic speeches. Much that they thought to find there differed greatly in character from what would be expected in, or indeed acceptable to, a modern court. The prudent man used all forms of persuasion available. The norms invoked in court covered moral and prudential matters, and even extended to proffers of money and other benefits, and blatantly political reliance on influence and power (e.g., *Rose*, lines 4874–77, 4914–46, 4922, 4954–55,

4976–77). In such situations, it is not clear that one can expect rules of evidence as such. Law school standards of appropriate discourse in court were slow to win acceptance. Courtholders had first to appoint judges inclined to take note of newfangled ideas from the professors, and let them assume the authority to make litigants conform.

To claim that courts should hear only argument that is in some sense "legal" in character entails that courtrooms merit special rules of behavior. There was little of this before 1150. A trial was an extraordinary occasion that excluded certain otherwise routine acts. There should be no weapons, for example, too close to the area marked for the proceedings (i.e., between the proverbial four benches). But secular trials had no special venue. They happened in the same halls and other locations (including the open air) that hosted other kinds of assembly. And some of the most important action took place out of the public eye. Unlike respectable case narratives, fictional accounts reveal the considerable amount of physical movement on and off the public stage, as it were, in the course of a trial. It is in the first place evident that much of the discussion from which the court made up its mind and formulated the issues of the cases took place in the intervals *between* formal court sessions. Nobody seems to have thought this inappropriate. Some procedural stages of the trial process that were taken for granted by contemporaries, but opaque to us – such as the "view" of disputed land and perambulation of boundaries – seem designed to facilitate informal negotiations within the community toward the verdict. The process did not end with public pleading in the trial proper. When the presiding lord or judge deemed the time ripe, he invited the suitors to consider their judgment and they would often, perhaps normally, leave the scene to generate and orally debate rival drafts in private. The aim was to facilitate free discussion. This is democracy of a kind, beyond the easy control of lord and judge.

The modern term "pleadings" is potentially misleading. Much court talk was conversation of a very informal nature in various locations. Yet the trial's progress was marked by a series of specific moments when the exact words used were clearly very important. One obvious example lies in the framing of oaths (discussed below). The general principle seems to be that all speakers were in their own way maneuvering toward an issue for God. The court had to decide on an issue more or less acceptable to all concerned. This determined the wording of oaths that might either be probative in themselves or simply define the questions to put to God through an ordeal or duel.

This was the decisive forensic moment. Though its structuring survived into later law, experienced (if not professional) lawyers now did much of the actual speaking in courts governed by carefully defined rules on the need for a litigant to ratify the commitments his pleader had entered on his behalf before the court would agree on the issue on which to decide the case. The explicit evidence for this comes from Edward I's reign, but the principle can be traced back to around the start of extant plea rolls, *c.* 1200, and surely derived from earlier practice. The mode of proof, mostly jury trial by that time, had changed more than a basic pattern originally of parties speaking for themselves.

After the argument and the proof, the court still had to perceive the result and implement it in such a manner that it would hopefully end conflict for good. Neither task was trivial. One reason for the growing preference for the duel over other ordeals was the apparent clarity of its denouement. A firm declaration of judgment might go far to determine future events, for life naturally continued after the trial.

These pivotal moments of verbal precision and commitment at proof and judgment were exceptional. This is a capital point. Fictional authors relished the opportunity to wring drama from a high-tension staging point, when their characters *must* tell the truth in the right way or come to grief. We can understand such passages without resorting to the kinds of interpretation of early medieval law in terms of procedural and verbal rigorism that once dominated learned discussion. One must resist the temptation to read back into the eleventh and twelfth centuries a verbal exactitude documented from the later professional literature, which was designed to train full-time lawyers in the increasingly written and complex law of the thirteenth century. Thirteenth-century English law generated a rich professional literature, mostly written in French. Both "practitioners' aids" and the Yearbook case reports that began slightly later convey an impression of little fluidity in the pleading of issues. Literary trials constitute a more reliable guide to the open pleading style of eleventh- and twelfth-century trials. There are no obvious signs of fear of verbal slips. Defenses do not seem, for example, to be "word for word" responses to the terms of the original complaint or *conte* (e.g., *Violette*, lines 2102–49). If verbal precision was required in actual trials, it is surprising that authors did not choose to highlight this in their fiction. The equivocal oath theme (discussed below) is a major exception here. Open pleading also better suits the more political nature of earlier law, and favors the kind of negotiation toward compromise that so often characterizes the style and content of legal argument in this period before professional lawyers.

A discourse of dispute

Francophone culture of the eleventh and twelfth centuries was full of conflict. Men, and often women too, had to argue their cases in court situations and justify their actions outside them. There has to have been a shared discourse of dispute, through which they declared, argued, opposed, interpreted, manipulated, and distinguished the norms by which they claimed to have acted.

Stephen D. White was the first legal historian to direct attention explicitly toward discourse, and his various studies are all required reading. But much remains uncharted. One of the most intriguing challenges for an alliance of literary and historical scholarship to tackle has to be the delineation of this discourse and its situation within the other overlapping discourses of the general culture. Clearly, the result will largely overlap with what White has called a "discourse of honor" that was in broad essentials common to both England and (at least) those areas of western France that were at various times politically linked to it.[10] Our guarantee of this is the degree to which the nobility read and listened to the same tales of justice meted out by King Arthur and evaded by Renart the Fox, then sat in each other's courts to advise on suits and their judgment. In such ways, they exchanged customary notions and brought their sometimes very different political and economic situations into some kind of linguistic unity. But "honor" alone is not the only term of common understanding. Compatible conceptions of justice and right circulated and set fashions throughout a Francophone world of Western Christendom whose bounds reached as far as Jerusalem. Not everything was done in the same way all over this area, but they understood each other's language in important ways.

Space precludes more than a few examples of shared discursive modes. One fundamental notion is the "undifferentiated" notion of wrong by which pleaders entered the discourse and maneuvered through it. Much of the argument lay between contested views of who had been wronged and in what way, moving on to consider how the wrongs might be removed or mitigated without excessive loss of face on either side. A full lexicographical study of Old French "wrong" words would likely demonstrate the ubiquity of this approach to justice. There is a striking absence of the distinction between criminal and civil law, between crime and tort, so deeply embedded in modern Western culture and as familiar to modern lay people as lawyers. It is a mistake to expect to read "crime" in the modern sense into twelfth-century literature.

This and other absences reflect the profound changes in European attitudes caused by the reintroduction into the West of the teaching of Roman law in the twelfth century, whose principles changed law in Italian cities as well as the Church's canon law, and which set entirely new standards for all secular laws.[11] It also introduced a series of distinctions, drawn in writing to a quite new degree. The most important of these for present purposes was that between law and fact, from then on a distinctive feature of Western law, which can be shown to have entered European political culture through the law schools about the middle of the twelfth century. This underpins today's influential myth that (lay) jurors are judges of fact, while the (professional) judge declares the law. Before this, we encounter a seamless mix of factual and moral-normative argument. It is not that people confused law with fact in the eleventh century; the distinction simply did not normally occur to them.

Foundational as this distinction is in principle, the actual transformation can be easily exaggerated. One can certainly find eleventh-century cases that turn on apparent factual issues. Nevertheless, one has to ask whether any case could ever turn on a "clear issue of fact" in any simple sense.[12] And is there any such thing? The apparently straight informational questions put to assize juries by the Angevin law reforms turn out on examination to be a mixture of normative and factual inquiry.[13] When twelve men of the neighborhood were asked to declare whether a deceased landholder had been seized of his holding "in demesne as of fee" (this is the assize of *mort dancestor*), they were being invited to say a good deal more than whether they had seen him in physical control of the land. Such factual seizin (crudely equivalent to our notion of possession) could easily have been wrongful and illicit, which was often the point of the complaint. The assize jurors were being asked for a preliminary opinion on the *right* to land, a question with more far-reaching implications that ultimately only God was thought capable of answering. This and other similar novel legal procedures drew on the old modes of inquiry, designed for an omniscient God, interested more in the maximization of salvation than the details of any particular incident, who neither needed nor recognized any law–fact distinction.

In early law, *lex* did not yet denote lawyer talk or any extraordinary discourse specific to the courts. In the thirteenth century, *factum* came to denote a deed, the document recording a property disposition or similar act. Not until at least the sixteenth century did it acquire the modern English meaning implied by analytical discussion of the law–fact distinction. One might wonder if we should not treat all apparently factual statements that arise in the course of trial narratives as "legally charged," in the sense that they were infused with meaning for the adjudication of the disputed issues.[14] Before the thirteenth-century distinction, there was no distinction. When it arrived, it seriously affected the general cultural balance of Western Europe, helping greatly to distance law and lawyers from ordinary people and the general culture.

Norms and legalitas

For many lay people, and some legal analysts, norms and rules constitute the very essence of Law. The classic account is H. L. A. Hart's *Concept of Law* (1961). Law requires and implies the existence of rules. The worst villains acknowledge this truth in their defenses. In the *Chanson de Roland*, the traitor Ganelon invokes norms in plausible fashion to support his case for remaining at peace with the Saracens (lines 72–73, 218–19). In what remains, I take up three basic points about norms that apply equally to literary and real twelfth-century trials. I ask first which of those cited in our trial narratives were distinctively legal, as a way to explore legal culture and assess how much autonomy to ascribe to its discursive space. I then seek to assess the degree to which we can expect our texts to make explicit the norms to which the actors refer. I close with a discussion of God's judgment and the phenomenon of the equivocal or ambiguous oath.

To what extent was there already in the eleventh century a domain of the legal? Very few people seem as yet to have felt that their law demanded its own autonomous sphere of action. It follows that, pending fuller inquiry, we should not be too quick to import modern legal parlance into either our translations of twelfth-century fictional trial scenes or our commentary on them. Non-lawyers today mostly believe that their law should be stated explicitly in writing somewhere, so that the courts can cite the rules on which they base their decisions. How explicitly this is done is one way to classify and rate a legal system. Norms could certainly be stated explicitly even in the eleventh century.

The Decalogue, a text all churchmen were supposed to know, is one excellent example. "Thou shalt not kill" is disarmingly direct and simple in form, but much more complicated in practice. The twelfth-century schools were busy deducing from their texts similarly direct rule statements; from the time of Pope Gregory VII, a genuinely learned literature of canon law (the Church's own legal system) emerged out of the schools to serve the Church's needs. Alongside, and at first largely in Italy, came the study texts essential to the revival of Roman law.[15] Individually and combined into the *ius commune* (law that took its principles directly from Roman and canon law), these collections and commentaries with their glosses gave the schools a standard by which to measure the law-ness, so to speak, of courtroom language. But references to actual laws or precedents are conspicuous by their absence from secular courts.

Yet most cultures make at least some rules explicit, and may deploy their norms with various degrees of explicitness according to circumstances.[16] A nice case in point is that of the treatise *Glanvill* (c. 1187–89), which should be recognized as the earliest French *coutumier*. Any reasonably careful reading reveals a whole range of rule statements from more or less direct quotation from recent royal legislation all the way to the fuzziest of statements of what we did last time. Here and in the references to judicial discretion as something to be carefully defined and constricted, I think we are seeing a new kind of secular lawyer starting to inject distinctions from the schools, and a new kind of rational order into secular courts.

We should not expect anything directly comparable to this from the softer customary world of earlier law and twelfth-century fictional trials. Yet the young need to acquire their norms somewhere, and there are normative texts available for rote learning: the proverb and its first cousin the legal maxim. These pithy statements of good and bad practice informed men and women in quite explicit terms about right behavior in different circumstances. Their overall message is never simple, for they had the exasperating habit of frequently coming in pairs, with one encouraging what the other prohibited. We know them only from written texts, which may distort, amend, or mistake originally oral messages by making them seem more authoritative and stable in form than they really were.

The corpus of legal maxims that continued in some measure to influence legal thought into the nineteenth century began to take on something like its lasting form in the twelfth century.[17] The history of proverbs at this time is less clear. The study of norms from both sources will greatly enrich our overall cultural understanding. Proverbs and maxims look as if they ought to have been used to educate the young. Otherwise, the most probable means of transmission was, with a pertinent exception treated below, largely experiential. Children imbibed their basic normative stock literally in their mother tongue along with the milk from their mothers or nurses. Later they might learn how to apply their norms to actual cases, by overhearing the discussions of their elders in between court sessions, or when permitted to accompany parents or other relatives to attend actual court sessions, as Hervey de Glanvill recalled doing in East Anglia early in the twelfth century.[18]

Here, as elsewhere, literature supplemented direct experience. Certain genres such as fable and *fabliau* encourage the direct statement of some normative moral at their close. More often, better writers took authorial pride in presenting lessons organically within their narratives, so their audiences might discover them for themselves. Our romances constantly reinforce simple normative lessons of right and wrong for their audience. Some authors problematized with relish the difficult questions, thus, signaling difficulties for sensible men to avoid in real cases by negotiated settlements. The literary debates round an *esgart* can show us not just the types of argument felt to be acceptable or persuasive, but something of the way the author believed suitors to deploy their norms in practice. In so doing, they figure among the most promising evidence for the general character of the legal culture assessed by the degree of explicitness with which it stated its norms.

Ami e Amile: a forensic and theological puzzle

This is one of many indicative points to emerge from any close reading of *Ami e Amile*, a twelfth-century French romance where the focus on friendship and sacrifice is sharpened by a trial.[19] Amile is a house-guest of Charlemagne's. One dark night Charlemagne's beautiful daughter, Belissant, steals quietly and unannounced into the chamber where he lies in bed. Her intentions, to secure him in marriage, were more honorable than her chosen means. Amile, unable to see who she is, all too easily reassures himself that she must be some serving wench, whose unsolicited offer he can safely accept and enjoy on a cash basis. Alas, the evil Hardré in the next room overhears what they are up to. Afterwards, when Amile realizes whom he has slept with, he is horrified. He is at once aware that he is likely to lose his head, even before Hardré shouts through the wall that he will tell ("conter") the emperor (lines 711–13). In the morning, Hardré tells Charlemagne what has happened and accuses Amile of having shamed his daughter in bed and invites him to burn the count at the stake (lines 726–27).

The author does not bother stating that fornication is wrong. Clearly, neither he nor his audience see anything wrong in sex with an unmarried girl of low rank lacking champions. Nor does he think to tell his readers that it is inadvisable to sleep with the king's daughter in an age when this could still be construed as a political act amounting to the staking of a claim on the realm itself. Such an act constituted a manifest but undefined offense, if only because of the way it shamed her and (more importantly) her royal father. There is evidence of conquerors laying claim to land and lordship by bedding heiresses before 1100; the 1352 statute that declared sleeping with the king's eldest daughter to be "treason" in England was certainly not making new law.[20] Disconcertingly, the label of traitor is reserved here for Hardré and never applied to Amile. The intention can only be to declare opposition to particular heinous acts. *Trahison* denotes an aggravated breach of trust in acts comparable with the killing or betrayal of a lord. The author gives no explicit statement of the relevant norms at all in this part of his story.

None of this helps Amile anyway. He was in trouble because he had been fooled, yet could not honorably save himself by explaining how. In a Church court, Amile might have pleaded that he had made a material error of fact, as in Gratian's *Decretum*, C. 22. 4, pt. III, and chapter 9 of the book of Joshua.[21] But this would have entailed a dishonorable accusation that shamed Belissant, whom he was slated to marry. In the subsequent confrontations with a very angry emperor, Amile staves off immediate death with great difficulty and gains only the right to defend himself in battle after a seven-month delay. This delayed disaster does little to set his mind at rest. Everybody, author, characters, and audience alike, seem to have taken for granted the existence of an active God who would do justice as He deemed best. The author never permits Amile to doubt that the outcome of the battle lay in God's hand, nor does he think to portray him as considering confession and prayer for that God's mercy. Our hero is left in dread of the outcome, not out of cowardice but because he knew he had done the deed, and thought himself guilty. He could not deny the deed, and so apparently saw himself as destined by God to be overcome in the duel. The possible defenses or pleas in mitigation (or even thoughts of flight) that we might harbor are simply beyond Amile's conception, ruled out of court, had they come to his mind, by contemporary notions of proper behavior. Escape, it seems, was impossible.

Only at this point does the audience receive an express norm statement, whose importance is signaled by aphoristic repetition: "Hom qui tort a combatre ne se doit" (lines 994, 1016). No man, we are warned, should knowingly fight a duel when he is in the wrong, or the consequences will be bad, which on this occasion meant, in addition to Amile's own end, the death of his sureties, Charlemagne's queen and her children. But the author has made abundantly clear where he wants his audience's sympathies to lie. Hardré is the traitor and called all the nastiest names, despite the factual accuracy of his accusation.

Tension is now acute, yet the eventual escape route is already perceptible. Amile has an identical twin, as it were. He and Ami, born to different parents in widely separated locations but at the very same hour, are impossible to tell apart. This is crucial, for an enraged Charlemagne denies Amile the usual rights of an accused nobleman to find himself a defender (lines 1023–26). Ami cannot, therefore, fight openly as Amile's champion. Oddly this might not have helped. The rules held that after the litigant's avowal, his champion became to all intents his exact equivalent. This ought to have prevented the verbal trick by which our author resolved his plot problem.

On the day Ami fools everybody, including the queen and Belissant, who are now in despair, seeing their only hope to lie in God's miraculous mercy. They know, however, that this is unlikely, since in order for God to pardon Amile it would be necessary for an innocent man (as they viewed the hated Hardré) to suffer shaming defeat and probably death. They think that their man, whom everyone believes to be Amile, is lying in the sight of God when he swears his oath, and that Hardré is telling the truth (lines 1434–40). The perjurer, should he even survive, must leave the field publicly shamed and ready to be hanged (lines 1392–93). His sureties will also die.

Our author stresses the seriousness of the occasion in the exceptionally stringent way he sets the scene for battle. The king, deeply wronged in everyone's eyes by a bootless offense that richly merits dismemberment and burning, will not ransom Amile for all the gold in the world (lines 1247–50; and compare *Rose*, lines 4884–901). There is to be no settlement (lines 1396–98). He solemnly calls for silence and forbids outside contact with the combatants until one of the pair cries "craven" (lines 1472–75). This proclamation may have been necessary to restrain hotheads among a highly partisan crowd.

The enemies then swear their oaths and declare in definitive form the issue for God to determine. Hardré sets up his ultimate demise by the terms of his oath. He clasps Ami by the right hand (and his left), an evocative gesture retained in late thirteenth-century English formularies that appear to have fixed forms of words. Hardré declares, "Hear now Charles son of Pippin and all of you great and small, so help me God and the saints who are here" (meaning the relics laid out before him) "and all the other confessors and martyrs, that I found *this man whom I hold here by the hand* naked together with Belissant as if they were husband and wife … So help me God that this is how it was" (lines 1415–24). Ami has no difficulty averring in response that he lied, that *he* has never slept with Belissant or felt her white flesh in the nude, so he calls upon God to let him leave the field safe and whole (lines 1425–30). Notably, though answering Hardré's accusation point, he is made neither to offer a general denial nor a word-for-word response, in the way that older accounts of early law might lead one to expect. The ensuing duel is a close-run contest; Ami, who has begun to fear that he was up against diabolical powers that he could never defeat, finally beheads the villain with his sword. Those who thought they knew what had really happened that night are astounded, though nobody cries foul or denies a result that all have seen.

What was the audience to conclude from this episode? The intended lesson was surely not that either having sex with the king's daughter or committing perjury by a trick was laudable or even licit in anything like normal circumstances. It may be permissible to conclude that men could on occasion work to make God's judgment come out right, and thus avoid the kind of decisions that made for the later maxim that "hard cases make bad law." Wicked men ought to lose their lawsuits. This thought may become relevant only where those involved actively sought God's mercy, and where their opponent placed himself so obviously beyond God's grace as Hardré had here. But the victory did not come without cost. It is surely not by chance that our heroic duo had much suffering to come before they were to live happily ever after. Such considerations draw me finally to consider more directly the role of God in real and fictional justice, along with the challenges of final proof.

God's judgment, oaths, and justice

Amile's escape is patently due to a judgment of God. His author appears never to doubt the routine operation of an active divine providence in everyday life. His characters, like most others in medieval French fiction, call upon God's aid at will. "Se Dex m'est en aie," they cry, "So help me God!," in order to summon God to support or (if he refused) punish them.[22] Our author expected his readers to rejoice in justice triumphant. The divine judge apparently chose to go by the *allegata*, even though these included a substitution trick that could not conceivably have escaped His omniscience. And if a divine judge is in some sense bound to follow the *allegata*, tempered only by His assessment of the moral worth of the parties, then surely human judges should follow suit. One purpose behind the display of divine omnipotence may have been to promote a less power-driven model of good law. But the devout approach God from below as petitioners; they do not expect to bind God, however cleverly they phrase their prayers, to be refused or granted. This leads to a second point. You phrased your petitions, written or oral, to the best of your rhetorical ability, showing your respect for your lord, by gestures such as bowing, kneeling, or even full prostration before him. Then you held your breath and awaited the response from on high.

This must be the context for the equivocal or ambiguous oaths that feature in several contemporary fictional works. Here lay a sensitive spot in the legal culture of the real world. Since people lie, and never more than in court, the men and women of the twelfth and thirteenth centuries would doubtless have been as attracted by polygraph lie detectors as many were in the last century. They stood committed, in principle at least, to approximate their own adjudications to the infallibility of a divine justice that always stood as a measure of human failure. Where, then, should they turn if not to God himself?

Oaths, the main means to persuade God to validate truth, were a major source of worry for all interested in justice. Some kind of recourse to oaths, often as asseverations of truth guaranteed by a higher power, is nearly universal. That oaths are found everywhere in medieval fiction surely reflects their importance in the general culture. They represent the strongest of disputative moves. This is a double-edged fact. The oath was too strong for many consciences. The Church was always afraid that people would take God's name in vain the way the Second Commandment told them not to (Ex. 20: 2–19; Deut. 5: 7–21). Moreover, people knew that they and others lied, and that we sometimes try to cover ourselves with ambiguous forms of words. Fictional authors could make a joke out of this. Readers of *Renart*, Branch 10, lines 140–50, 172–78, know in advance how to read Hersent's defense to the charge of adultery with Renard, when she protests that Reynard had done no more to her than he would to his mother, and that she has done no worse with her body than a nun.[23] Since oaths were patently superfluous for an omniscient God, orthodox doctrine was always in two minds on the topic. The simple word ought to suffice: "Let your yea be yea, and your nay be nay." Oaths should certainly not be used frivolously or too often (Mt. 5:37). Yet in this fallen world the imperfect needed help to raise the odds that sinful men and women would be truthful when this was crucial. So professors asked the ancient question: must one tell the whole truth? or was it enough not to lie?

In the end virtually all the theologians come down where we should expect in a twelfth century obsessed by motive and intention. Peter the Chanter (d. 1197) had taught his Paris theology students to be fully truthful for the health of their souls.[24] A concealed lie remained a lie, whatever the form of words. If made on oath it constituted perjury, a mortal sin.[25] These schools discussions include some quite persuasive *contra* arguments, supporting verbal understandings of truth, a position assisted by Gratian's inclusion in his dossier of an extract from Isidore, "Concerning one who swears by verbal trickery," which seems to aver that God receives oaths in the way that the human recipient understands them.[26] His point was, presumably, to warn the weak that God will judge oaths by comparing the truth, as He knew it, to the way a recipient was likely to understand the wording. Though later commentators were at pains to emphasize this correct understanding, there was scope here for one who so wished to suppress conscience and frame ambiguous oaths in an hour of need, perhaps on the ground that "right" was really theirs anyway.

The questions remained indisputably live into the thirteenth century, to an extent that indicates a continuing controversy outside as well as inside the schools and law courts. Even churchmen felt the lure of the accurate untruth on occasions when the morally justified were caught in the net of a tight rule or unfortunately formulated litigation issue. The canonist doctrine of *equitas*, inherited from Roman law, may sometimes have helped to relieve clerical consciences.[27] Canon law is, after all, unusual among legal systems in its privileging of the maximization of salvation above particular cases. The avoidance of *scandalum*, seen as the kind of publicity that harms simple souls in the mass, sometimes justified casuistry in ways not too distant from the ambiguous oath of literature.

The key perhaps lies in those undifferentiated notions of wrong discussed above, and in the way that a merciful God, all-knowing and concerned above all to maximize the number of saved souls, dealt with sin. God judges the whole person; he is less interested in specific allegations than individual salvation. All serious wrong harms him, but can (usually) be discharged after a full and wholehearted confession by proper penance. This makes the sinner a new person, and thus arguably immune from the earthly penalty for an offense committed by his previous person. After confession the former thief could therefore licitly swear innocence in some appropriate form of words and so evade the human consequences of his old self's evil act. This ingenious view of confession, that privileged divine justice over human, had some currency in the thirteenth century.[28] It spawned a line of vivid ordeal stories, in which guilty heretics, persistent fornicators, and adulteresses escaped conviction by a sincere confession followed by appropriate penance. It sometimes happened, however, that a temporary penitent later backslid and then found God's justice when, for example, a now several-days-cold hot iron scorched his hand. The message, that God will go to great lengths to give sinners the chance to repent but does not forget, was so fundamental that the withdrawal of Church support for the unilateral ordeals barely slowed the stream of retellings.

These two lines of argument go far to explain what fictional authors were doing when they introduced ambiguous (or equivocal) oaths into their narratives. I take Yseut's famous oath in Béroul's *Roman de Tristan* as my illustration.[29] The situation is that Yseut and Tristan have been committing adultery with great frequency but have contrived to keep Yseut's husband, King Marc, uncertain of their guilt. At length, Marc promotes the formal accusation of Yseut and has his court award that she purge her guilt with a public oath. He clearly hopes to resolve the situation for good. But he has underestimated Yseut's resourcefulness. She carefully arranges that on the day fixed for the oath Tristan, disguised as an ugly leper, will be at hand.

Béroul at first plays this for laughs. The chosen site resembles Ascot racecourse on a foul, rainy Gold Cup day. Yseut is dressed up for the occasion, yet must somehow cross a deep bog to reach the chapel without messing her outfit or destroying her resolve and morale. She permits the disguised Tristan to carry her across piggyback. She then shrugs off various attempts to word her oath to offer her own precisely weighed formulation:

> Qu'entre mes cuises n'entra home,
> Fors le ladre qui fist soi some,
> Qui me porta outre les guez,
> Et li rois Marc mes esposez.
> Ces deus ost de mon soirement,
> Ge n'en ost plus de tote gent.   (lines 4205–10)

[That no man entered between my thighs, apart from the leper who acted as beast of burden to carry me across the ford, and king Marc my husband. These two I exclude from my oath, but I do not exclude anyone else in all the world. (author's translation)]

After her successful path, all suspicions should have been at an end. Yseut seems at first glance to have escaped the charge with supernatural ease, and in doing so to have proved – to use Hatto's all too brilliant phrase from a different version of the tale – that verbal trickery could manipulate a God "as pliant as a windblown sleeve."[30] But for Béroul this conclusion is far from obvious. The couple return to their adulterous bed then die the tragic deaths that transform this entertaining and morally disreputable tale into one of Western culture's most enduring myths.

A contemporary audience might well read the outcome in the light of the theologians discussed above. Béroul set up Yseut's oath from early in his work. Yseut has planned her defense ahead of time, and is unfazed by the possibility of an ordeal (lines 3232–46). She lacks kin to help her secure a favorable proof award (lines 2353–54, 2362–65). In any case, the accusers are the *felons* and their hatred vitiates their case. God has already given the couple a second chance, after a full confession under the guidance of the hermit Ogrin (lines 1370–91). It no doubt helped that author and audience believed that the appearance of wrongful love was refuted by the love potion that caused their passion in the first place. Had they persisted in their new guiltless personas, all might have been well. After their further fall from grace, though, it is no wonder they die unhappily and alone.

In this reading, Béroul's poem ends tragically. It would then not support any hypothesis that the decades surrounding 1200 saw a general crisis of faith over the ordeal (or even of Truth itself), except possibly in the sensitive consciences of some clerical intellectuals. Nobody at this date, not even Gottfried, dared directly to deny an active providence. The prohibition of clerical participation in the hot iron and water ordeals enacted by the Fourth Lateran Council in 1215, as much human policy decision as theological pronouncement, purported to cover duels (*monomachia*) too. Yet men ignored this to continue adjudging and fighting duels; women continued to be impressed by them; and many authors resorted to them for set-piece thrills or plot resolution. There is no sign anywhere of skepticism over God's miraculous powers, still less of a new level of concern about truth. Literary duels never validate known false oaths and usually come to the "right" conclusion.

The ambiguous oath stands ultimately as a splendid witness to a tension underlying the whole discourse of dispute. The premise behind its proof of right and wrong is an inerrant God prepared to declare truth and make his judgments manifest in human courts. Yet many men prosecuted their feuds and disputes from motives of personal interest, with expectations quite as self-centered as any litigant today. They were equally disinclined to leave the results to chance or – worse still – the choices of clerics and court officials whom they could not control. So some bribed or relied on the influence of the great and powerful, others lied and perjured. Our authors knew this in more detail than we can ever hope to gain, and they knew their audiences knew it too.

Notes

1. For example, Gottfried, *Tristan*, trans. A. T. Hatto (Harmondsworth, 1960, rev. 1967), pp. 78–82.
2. Robert Grosseteste, *De Decem Mandatis*, eds. Richard C. Dales and Edward B. King (Oxford, 1987), 2.13–14 (p. 29); 8.1, 3, 6–7 (pp. 80–82).
3. For example, *Le Roman de la Violette ou de Gerbert de Nevers par Gerbert de Montreuil*, ed. Douglas Labaree Buffum, Société des anciens textes français (Paris, 1928), lines 551–56, 955, 969 etc.; Jean Renart, *Le roman de la rose ou de Guillaume de Dole*, ed. Félix Lecoy (Paris, 1963), line 3589.
4. *Brevia Placitata* (1951 for 1947), pp. 116, 127; *Novae Narrationes* (1963), B 11–3, C 11–3.
5. Paul Hyams, "The Proof of Villein Status in the Common Law," *English Historical Review* 89 (1974), 721–49, at 728.
6. *Brand, *Origins of the English Legal Profession* (1992), pp. 10–12.
7. *Hyams, *Rancor and Reconciliation* (2003), chs. 4–7.
8. *Brevia Placitata*, p. 16.
9. For example, *Curia Regis Rolls*, 8 John–10 John (1207–9) (1931), v. 197; 11 John–14 John (1210–12) (1932), vi. 118, 128.
10. *White, "The Problem of Treason" (2001), p. 107.
11. Bellomo, *The Common Legal Past of Europe: 1000–1800* (1995), offers a good survey, so long as readers understand that the *ius commune* (legal systems combining the best principles of Roman and canon law) is quite distinct from the English "Common Law."
12. *White, "Inheritances and Legal Arguments" (1987), p. 89.

13. Mike McNair, "Vicinage and the Antecedents of the Jury," *Law and History Review* 17 (1999), 537–90, at p. 546 n. 29; *Hyams, "Trial by Ordeal: The Key to Proof in the Early Common Law," in *On the Laws and Customs of England: Essays in Honor of Samuel E. Thorne* (1981), pp. 90–126.

14. John Hudson, "Court Cases and Legal Arguments in England, *c.* 1066–1166," *Transactions of the Royal Historical Society* 6th series, 10 (2000), 91–116, at 104.

15. *Brundage, *Medieval Canon Law* (1995), ch. 3.

16. John L. Comaroff and Simon Roberts, *Rules and Processes* (Chicago, 1981), ch. 3.

17. Peter Stein, *Regulae Legis: From Juristic Rules to Legal Maxims* (Edinburgh, 1966).

18. *English Lawsuits from William I to Richard I* (1990–91), i, no. 331.

19. *Ami et Amile*, ed. Peter F. Dembowski (Paris, 1969).

20. Margaret Clunies Ross, "Concubinage in Anglo-Saxon England," *Past and Present* 108 (1985), 3–34; Eleanor Searle, "Women and the Legitimization of Succession at the Norman Conquest," *Anglo-Norman Studies* 3 (1981), 159–70; *Bellamy, *Law of Treason*, (1970), ch. 4.

21. *Gratian, *Decretum* (1879–81), cited by *causa, questio, capitulum*.

22. Christiane Marchello-Nizia, "De l'art du parjure: Les 'serments ambigus' dans les premiers romans français," *Argumentation* 1 (1987), 399–405, outlines the case for this Augustinian reading. Grosseteste, *De Decem Mandatis*, 2.10–11 (pp. 26–28), rehearses the ghastly consequences of perjury.

23. *Le Roman de Renart*, eds. N. Fukumoto, N. Harano, and S. Suzuki (Paris, 2005).

24. Peter's *Verbum Abbreviatum*, c. 120 (PL, vol. 305, cols. 309C–11C), cited by John W. Baldwin, "The Crisis of the Ordeal," *Journal of Medieval and Renaissance Studies* 24 (1994), 328–53.

25. *Gratian, *Decretum* (1879–81), C. 22 q. 5 c. 12.

26. *Gratian, *Decretum* (1879–81), C. 22 q. 5 c. 9.

27. J. Rambaud, in G. Le Bras, Ch. Lefebvre, and J. Rambaud (eds.), *L'Âge classique, 1140–1378*, Histoire de droit et des institutions de l'Église en occident 7 (Paris, 1965), pp. 352–66, is a decent introduction to canonical equity.

28. Thomas of Chobham, *Summa Confessorum*, ed. Rev. F. Broomfield, *Analecta Medievalia Namurcensia* 25 (Louvain, 1968), pp. 529–30; Simon of Tournai, *Disputationes*, ed. Joseph Warichez, *Spicilegium Sacrum Lovaniense* 12 (1932), pp. 70–71; and Guido de Orchellis, *Tractatus de Sacramentis*, eds. D. and O. Van den Aynde (Louvain, 1953), p. 130, all rehearse this view before concluding against it.

29. *Tristan et Iseut*, ed. Daniel Lacroix and Philippe Walter (Paris, 1989).

30. Gottfried, *Tristan*, trans. Hatto, p. 248. Robert Bartlett, *Trial by Fire and Water: The Medieval Judicial Ordeal* (Oxford, 1986), pp. 18–19, cites this passage as evidence of skepticism about the judicial ordeals. But without any indication that it comes from Thomas' mostly lost source version, Gottfried's remark looks to be his brilliant own.

DAVID A. HINTON

3

Archaeology and post-Conquest England

Archaeology is usually described as "the study of the human past through material remains," and is dependent upon physical survival. For the Middle Ages, however, documentary evidence can also reveal how people interacted with their material culture: the environment and buildings in which they lived and moved and the things that they inherited, made, bought, stole, found or were given. "Inheritance" could be both family bequests and what survived from the past to help to shape the present: a medieval peasant, for instance, might unknowingly have worked within field banks that had been laid out in the Bronze Age. If he plowed over those banks to establish fields of a shape more suited to the new technology of open fields, or to create an assart for himself, his action would have been recorded only if subsequent disputes with his neighbors led to manorial court proceedings. Similarly, a Roman finger ring set with a gem might be found and returned to use, reinterpreted with Christian meaning, but would usually be documented only if it were subsequently stolen. Historians seek to go behind court records to consider what hedge destruction reveals about commoners' expressions of resistance, either to fellow peasants overreaching themselves or to overbearing landlords; or what thefts can reveal about the insecurity felt by their victims. In the same way, archaeologists are not content to observe a lynchet or a finger ring without passing on to question the meanings that they may have had for those who were constrained by or owned them, and how those meanings may have changed.

The search by medieval archaeologists for explanations of belief and behavior that were never made explicit in documents is a recent trend strongly influenced by social anthropology: applications of gender theory have been a notable example, with access analysis used to consider whether "deep space" for female occupants can be recognized in buildings, or whether humoral theory may have caused women to be more often buried on the north side of a church as a metaphor for the need to counter their warm and moist tendencies in life. Scientific applications are also much more in evidence: dendrochronology (tree-ring dating) to give absolute ages to standing buildings; geophysical prospection to reveal below-ground features; or strontium analysis of human and animal teeth and bones for evidence of foodstuffs eaten.

Food and nutrition

Food consumption is relatively well documented for the later medieval aristocracy, but not for the peasantry; for them, written records tell only of demesne workers' daily allowances, and of tithe and tax payments. Bread and pottage (a well-cooked homogeneous stew of grains and, perhaps, meat) were the staples. Although the archaeological record does not reveal the quantities of cereals grown, it can identify the species of grains found in carbonized or waterlogged deposits, or even surviving in thatched roofs. They were deliberately selected so as not to place too much reliance either on a single crop or on a high-yielding variety that was too prone to disease or rot; such risk avoidance strategies may have been favored alike by landlords wanting steady returns and peasants concerned to feed their families.

Because animal bones survive in greater quantities, the ratios as well as the types of stock reared can be discussed: sites vary, but most show that extreme specialization was avoided, as with grain. Analyses to examine the quality, diseases, and age of beasts at death lead to assessments of the balance between the value of stock alive and dead, and of that between demands for self-sufficiency, renders in kind, and cash rents. Most twelfth- and thirteenth-century animals were quite elderly when slaughtered. Only when surplus to rural needs did they enter an urban market which, although expanding, consisted mainly of people unable to afford much meat – and whose diet is even less documented than the peasants'. The growing population's primary need was for cereals, and the market was further restricted by the great lords' preference for demesne farming to feed their households. While arable intensity increased, cattle were more important alive to provide traction for plows and carts, for manure and for dairy products than as carcasses for meat and hides. Wool was England's main cash crop, so sheep, too, were usually slaughtered when past their prime for meat quality. Foraging pigs were tolerated less as land values rose.

The splitting of long bones for marrow extraction indicates use in pottages that stewed in the round-based cooking pots that were designed to sit for hours on open hearths. But economic rationality alone did not dictate consumption: the religious taboo on horse meat seems to have been observed even by the poor, except in extreme circumstances in the countryside, and green vegetables were perceived as animal fodder, though fruit was valued. Fowl provided some variety, as well as eggs, but wild birds were reserved for aristocratic tables, and the thrill of hawking; fresh fish from their ponds, squabs from their dovecotes, and venison from their hunting in forests and parks all gave the elite exclusivity.

Aristocratic demand for ostentatious foodstuffs and their elaborate preparation became even more marked after the Black Death, partly because better meals were available to higher-earning peasants and town dwellers. Changes in demand in the later fourteenth and fifteenth centuries are shown by a trend to slaughtering younger animals. Some bone evidence suggests that animals were larger and, therefore, better nourished, improving the meat. The choice of butchered cuts, and of fish, was wider. Pottery dripping trays show more meat being roasted, and sauce bottles suggest more effort in food preparation. The aristocracy reacted by adding carp and swans to their ponds, and foodstuffs to sumptuary legislation.

Food resources are also detectable in human skeletons: isotopes in bone collagen can now reveal who ate fish as an important part of their diet, with peasants at Wharram Percy, the rather remote village in north Yorkshire, not getting enough of it to impact on their bones, suggesting that they suffered vitamin deficiency from not having the wherewithal to buy in local markets. What are assumed to be lay benefactors of a Gilbertine priory in York, people rich enough to be buried at it, show similar isotopic results, however, unlike the canons there, who were eating more fish. The laity were less strict about the Church's fasting rules, the huge quantities of salt cod and herrings being shipped and carted around England notwithstanding, and presumably being viewed with some distaste.

In general, skeletons do not show signs of gross malnourishment; rather than frequent episodes of starvation, erratic access and supply shows in incidences of childhood rickets – but usually in adult skeletons, so many people survived. Infant and juvenile mortality was high, but not high enough to stem population growth. Males who reached 18 might reasonably expect to live to between 35 and 45, but females had a much higher likelihood of dying before they even reached their mid-30s, presumably because of the dangers of childbirth rather than greater susceptibility to disease, though women having less opportunity to buy food in a market could be a factor. Most people ate enough to grow to a good height – a man might expect to get to 1.71 m (5 ft 7 in), slightly more if better fed in a rich household or monastery, a woman to 1.58 m (5 ft 3 in).

Buildings and settlements

The excavation of Wharram Percy showed how below-ground archaeology can reveal the plans of buildings and the organization of their internal space, with evidence of room partitions, drains, and hearths. Interpretation of the uses that the space had can change: for instance, if drainage channels were found at one end of a building they would justify a claim that it was a longhouse, which had a central entrance way shared by humans living at one end and animals overwintering in the other. Dairies would also have needed outflows for excess liquids, however; only by chemical testing for concentrations of phosphate from animal urine having seeped into the ground can it be shown if stock had been sheltered. Furthermore, excavations on early medieval sites have not produced any definite examples; even the spaces that were interpreted as byres for cattle when tenth-/eleventh-century Mawgan Porth in Cornwall was excavated were more cautiously called either byres or working areas in the final report. The north Cornish coast is not an area where shelter from extreme winter cold would have been necessary; the "lower ends" do not have traces of stalls, and the entrances seem too narrow for animals to have been driven through.

Longhouses, therefore, may not have been introduced until the middle of the thirteenth century, as an adaptation of a rectangular house plan of "central hall + end-chambers" that by then was becoming standard for all but the highest and lowest in status. Nor were they built exclusively in the most extreme situations, on land not lived on until the pressures of the twelfth and thirteenth centuries, for they have been found in valleys as well as far up hillsides, but only in certain regions – at least not in the southeast from Hampshire to Lincolnshire, and perhaps not in the west Midlands either. The longhouse was easily explained when it was seen as something with a long tradition that was steadily abandoned in all but the most remote and conservative districts; if it was a new development taken up perhaps only quite late in the Middle Ages and only in certain regions, it implies greater willingness to embrace change than might have been expected of the peasantry. It also suggests lack of concern about dogma on humans being higher than the beasts, so that close contact and contagion of bestiality by association should have been avoided.

The full range of medieval peasant housing probably includes, at the bottom of the social scale, some cottars' shacks so flimsy as to be all but impossible to trace in excavations, though some may be represented by irregular lines of small post holes and stone cobble spreads, and indistinguishable except by size from what remains on a substantial peasant's toft like that at Westbury, excavated to very high standards before its incorporation within Milton Keynes, Buckinghamshire. Such limitations also mean that it will rarely, if ever, be possible to recognize phases when an outbuilding was temporarily adapted for the use of aged parents or younger siblings, but the scale of most houses strongly suggests a nuclear family, with impartible inheritance as the norm. Although the crofts in the plan of Wharram Percy vary in width, only a couple look as though they result from a large one being divided in half. Ditches, and in some areas moats, emphasized property divisions and households as self-contained and self-sustaining units, as did tenement boundaries in towns. Wharram looks like a highly regulated village, despite having two different owners and manors until 1254; whose choice does this organization represent – lords wishing for control or peasants wanting to maintain viability? The southeast of England paid more in taxation and had more dispersed settlements – but not always a richer or freer peasantry.

The Wharram Percy peasants usually had more than one building on their crofts: a house close to the street frontage and a fairly substantial barn behind. A rectangular structure at Seacourt, Berkshire, was identified in the early 1960s as a thirteenth-century barn, but has since been reinterpreted as the remains of a house; although its post holes were small, they may simply have been the framework for daub walls thick enough for comfortable insulation and for the weight of a thickly thatched roof. A one-roomed building that was interpreted as the house because it had traces of a hearth inside and had larger post holes may actually be a detached kitchen. The impression that some peasants in the thirteenth century could, despite population and other pressures, provide themselves with quite adequate accommodation is now reinforced by the evidence of standing timber-framed buildings from which dendrochronology dates have been obtained. Some small aisled halls in Essex shown to date from the first half of the thirteenth century are below manor-house level, at least two being identifiable as probably having belonged to virgators, substantial peasants farming 30 acres or so. Buildings at this economic level begin to survive because their timbers were on a low wall or a large stone "stylobate," preserving them from rotting in damp ground and making investment in solid timber and specialist carpentry worthwhile, though the primary motive may have been the perception that timber framing presented a better appearance to the world than walls of earth materials.

The most eye-catching timber construction, the "cruck," used the natural curves of a tree's stem and branches; a "full cruck" rose from ground level to the roof apex, where it was jointed to a partner. It was in use by the 1260s in rural houses. Slightly earlier dates have been obtained from some "base crucks" in manorial houses and barns, in which the curved timber rises only halfway up the roof slope, where it is joined to its partner by a horizontal collar beam. This allowed extra width in the space below, freeing it from internal aisle posts. Their dating allows the possibility that full crucks were derived from base crucks, but the sophistication of their carpentry suggests that the earliest survivals were not experimental, using a technique only recently introduced. On the other hand, one of their purposes is to span a wide space, and excavations show that earlier houses were by and large narrower than cruck buildings.

Emulation of base crucks would not explain why full crucks were used in the north, Midlands and west of the country, but never in the southeast south of the Humber, yet base crucks are known in all the counties around London and in Lincolnshire, though not in East Anglia. The distribution of full crucks conforms to no other division, political or cultural. Distribution maps of spoken dialects show no consonance with it, for instance. As with the longhouses, different regional practices can be observed in the thirteenth century, but that they are part of ancient traditions cannot be assumed.

Full crucks did not have a monopoly in the west, as box-frame buildings with regular pairs of straight posts occur there as well as in the east. The difference was not just in appearance, as different techniques had to be used to erect the two sorts of structure. Crucks and principal posts were both paired across the width of a building, and as they were prominent within it, any partitions were logically placed between them. Consequently, both suited the "hall + end-chambers" plan, and helped to standardize it. Their regularity articulated the internal space according to the length that a carpenter could allow between each pair, as well as dictating a room's width by the extent to which he could be allowed resources for an elaborate roof. From the outside, this could be "read" by someone who knew the code. In cruck buildings, a head height tie beam across the hall could be omitted by giving extra support to the collar with a pair of arched braces. As in the Essex small aisled halls, so with cruck houses it was important to provide a ground-floor space with an open hearth as the social center of the household. In the Anglo-Saxon period a ground-floor "hall" (Latin *aula*) had been the setting for many social interactions (like those portrayed in *Beowulf*), and for most people it remained an aspiration, though peasant usage of the *aula* is not well understood.

Two-storey buildings probably began to appear before the Norman Conquest, so the stone chamber blocks that were built in some twelfth-century castles and other aristocratic residences were not innovatory. Their upper rooms were heated by fireplaces and lit by two-light windows carved to match contemporary churches, so were clearly designed to impress, but whether as public "halls," or as "private" chambers augmented by a separate ground-floor hall elsewhere in the complex, has been debated. Ground-floor halls were the thirteenth-century preference, with two- or more storeyed chamber blocks adjoining the "high" end, and service rooms at the "lower," accessed by the cross-passage that formalized a ceremonial approach to the dais and high table. Such arrangements also lent themselves to courtyard plans. Despite royal and aristocratic lifestyles that meant sojourns in both England and France, continental practice did not simply transfer across the Channel: for instance, grand first-floor halls were built infrequently in the island, even after their fourteenth-century use at the top of society at Windsor and Kenilworth.

Rich urban merchants emulated but adapted the aristocratic lifestyle, building two-storey stone houses so that they could literally live over the shop, or warehouse, in the twelfth century, but in the thirteenth preferring a ground-floor hall and a courtyard. Most urban houses, however, had to be fitted into long, narrow burgage tenement strips, so that one standard pattern became a frontage with a shop and a chamber above, a hall behind, then perhaps another chamber block and behind that the back yard. Often, particularly in ports, these houses had semi-sunken stone-vaulted cellars below, usually separately leased and used for storage, more workshops or wine taverns. This two-tier living was locally adapted in Chester, where the Rows with shops both at ground- and first-floor levels may result from the difficulty of creating below-ground space in the underlying rock. In many towns, some frontages were divided into small units, with or without a room above for the occupants, with space behind for a merchant's courtyard.

Jettying, which allows an upper storey to become more prominent by extending its floor beams beyond the wall that supports them, seems to have been used in London by 1246, when it caused complaints about blocking streets; the earliest survival is late thirteenth century. Display seems to have been the main motive, since the jetties are nearly always on the most public fronts or sides of the building, though larger upper rooms must also have been an advantage in the most crowded zones. The beam ends may echo corbel rows supporting church parapets or machicolations on castles, but their function is so different that they had a different meaning for a substantial middle-income owner. The excessive jettying that required props to support the upper floors, creating covered walkways at ground level, is another example of local adaptation, as in Winchester and Totnes; at the former it is now known that several houses in The Pentice were not built in that way originally. Another distinctive urban development reflecting space pressures was the terraced row, with two- and three-storeyed examples for craftspeople surviving from the fourteenth century onwards; flimsily built units excavated in Winchester were probably single-storeyed for the poor.

Timber framing and its display were not confined to the peasantry and townspeople, but, as dressed and mortared stone was prohibitively expensive for most of them, carpentry may have given them a means of self-expression that led away from the emulation of the aristocracy implied by the small Essex halls of the early thirteenth century. At any rate, no manorial precedent has been claimed for the fourteenth-century "Wealden" house with two-storey ends, joined to an open hall but having the line of the jettied wall extended along it, so that it appears recessed; the most impressive used a crown post standing on a collar beam to span the hall. They were always assumed to be a rural development in the area where they are most common, Sussex and Kent, but in fact the earliest one dated is a house built in central Winchester just before the Black Death. This implies that "Wealdens" are an urban innovation taken up in the countryside, particularly those parts of it where big estates were fewest and manorial control was least, so that independent farmers could take advantage of economic opportunities and show off the results.

Wealden houses, which occur across a wider geographical area in towns than in the countryside, suggest that urban dwellers were more prepared to accept change and new ideas, and probably therefore that they would have been more dynamic as entrepreneurs. This becomes more marked toward the end of the Middle Ages, for it was urban dwellers who were the first to abandon the traditional open hall – tradition was not something that they needed to express unless they belonged to the richest merchant group with aspirations to join the nobility. First, in tall but narrow shops and houses, particularly in London, and subsequently in the fifteenth century in two-storey houses on tenements where space was not at such a premium, open halls became obsolete. The east of the country was the most open to such new ideas, being closer to the Continent.

The Black Death (1348–49 and repeatedly later, in lesser waves) and population decline affected settlements in various ways: new towns ceased to be created, those of the later thirteenth century having their growth stunted, spectacularly at New Winchelsea, Sussex, and many village markets were victims. Landlords invested in urban and rural houses and shops in order to maintain some sort of rental income, however. Inns provided a useful return on capital, offering hospitality to pilgrims still prepared to visit shrines to stave off the sickness, and to the many traveling merchants dealing in cloth, which brought prosperity to some production areas as well as to those who sold it. London became more of a focus for both government and capital, despite the huge mortality rate that saw new cemeteries being opened on its outskirts. Rural settlements were more visibly affected: a few were quickly abandoned, but most were like Wharram Percy or Tattenhoe, seeing some vacant crofts amalgamated, others reoccupied. Ridge and furrow atrophied in pasture fields shows the reduction in plowing for the benefit of stock rearing. The most likely sites to be abandoned were those that were the hardest from which to make a living; whether climate change had any significant effect is still open to question.

Defense, transport, and trade

Much current debate focuses on the functions of castles, such as the extent to which those of William the Conqueror were built to resist attack, or to act as launching pads for assaults, or to be impressive administrative and estate centers, making statements about the superiority of their owner as much as about his need to secure himself and his family against a rioting peasantry or siege by armies. The honor of the right to bear arms was also proclaimed by a military building – as it was by heraldry from the end of the twelfth century, increasingly displayed to show family, connections, and the network of the community, not only in castles but in churches and undefended houses too. Even in the fourteenth and fifteenth centuries, however, licenses to crenellate (a grant from the king or other designated major authority allowing fortified walls), formalized in the early thirteenth century, may not have been obtained merely for status reasons, as weak governments failed to control civil unrest and lawlessness.

Towns also sometimes sought a crenellation license, faced as they might be by the king's enemies, whether internal or external. Walled circuits often appeared on a town's seal, expressing its role as a royal defended place and as a self-contained social unit. The cost of their defenses caused many towns to fall into debt or to rely upon government relief, though that did not stop them from militarily unnecessary embellishments, particularly of their gates, to present a grand facade to the outside world and to display the coats of arms of their patrons for good political measure. Some appropriated stories of heroes and giants, so that London's mayoral seal of c. 1380 shows a gate with the figures of Gog and Magog, as well as the various saints and other religious figures whose blessing the city particularly claimed. Grimsby used the stories of Havelock the Dane and his foster-parents, Goldsborough and Grim, to give the town status. Other port seals showed ships, not only to display their maritime roles but also to proclaim their loyalty, as often they had to supply ships and galleys for royal service.

By the late Middle Ages, transports were not enough for the king's naval needs, and "great ships" like the *Grace Dieu* were built for Henry V. Bombards, cannons built from staves of iron rods held together by iron rings and using gunpowder, became more effective at battering walls and towers than catapults and other siege engines; although they were too cumbersome for most besiegers' purposes on land, a ship built to resist their recoil could be a floating battery. Urban gates and wall-towers had gun ports rather than arrow slits after the 1360s, at first for small-bore weapons, then cannons. Norwich and Southampton had "bastilles," effectively detached towers with greater height and strength. Royal need of guns and ships made taxation demands greater and was to force the creation of a state bureaucracy. Demand for iron made investment in the industry more viable, with the blast furnace being introduced at the end of the fifteenth century.

A license, to crenellate, or to have a deer park, was not an absolute legal requirement but was a key to exclusivity, especially for those without a long ancestral claim to a property; similar ideas were developed in thirteenth-century legislation about incomes and class, and in lay subsidies and their emphasis on disposable property, followed by fourteenth-century attempts at sumptuary laws on foodstuffs and costume that sought to enforce a sense of what was proper to each social rank. The marked increase in late medieval jewelry was not only because gold was more available, but also because elaborate settings for costly gems displayed their owners' access to resources that only the very wealthy could afford. Some were also overt demonstrations of loyalty to families and factions, part of the governmental breakdown which made a secure home an advantage. Sweet wines from Italy became sought after, and a few examples of Venetian glass and Spanish pottery show this Mediterranean contact in the late Middle Ages.

The impression made by the great ships that brought Italians to England is shown by the fifteenth-century drawing of a Genoese "carrack" scratched onto a piece of slate found recently in Southampton. The standard north European trade carrier of the later Middle Ages was the "cog," best known from a wreck raised at Bremen, capable of wallowing across the North Sea with tuns of Holland beer, brewed with hops for longer keeping and a new taste, returning with the cloth bales that became England's main export. London, Bristol, and other ports adapted their waterfronts, excavations showing how land was first reclaimed from a foreshore to enlarge a property fronting it, after which wharves and jetties provided deeper berthing for the bigger ships. Documents tell of cranes, and the staple ports had weigh-houses and halls where customs duties were paid. As well as the semi-sunken undercrofts, warehouses like the Town Cellars of c. 1300 at Poole and the Woolhouse of 1394 at

Southampton show the quantities of goods that needed to be stored on dry land.

Even before the cog was introduced, some vessels could carry over 60 tuns, so maritime shipping capacity became less and less a factor in restricting trade; with organization, large fleets could bring as much wine and salt as there was demand for. Was transport a deterrent to inland distribution? A thirteenth-century boat excavated at Magor Pill, Monmouthshire, was purpose-built to cope with the hazardous currents, cross-winds and mudflats of the River Severn. Iron ore with the boat was probably being carried from the deposits west of Cardiff to Newport or Bristol (though a Mendip source is a geological alternative, it is hard to see why ore from there should have crossed the Severn). Such vessels probably also brought smelted iron from the Forest of Dean to Gloucester blacksmiths and redistributed their products from it. The Magor Pill boat also had cereals in it, perhaps just by chance, but hinting at a grain trade. If goods like that could be carried on a river like the Severn, the technology was not a problem. In quieter waterways on the east side of the country, there was even less risk. Despite frequent complaints, weirs and mills were probably no more of a problem than seasonally fluctuating shallows and storms in uncanalized rivers.

Direct archaeological evidence for land transport is less informative: bridges were certainly built and maintained, stone ones surviving, a few wooden ones revealed by the bottoms of their piles. The effects of cart wheels on road surfaces remain uncertain, however. The extent to which road transport was restricted is best explored indirectly, through pottery, a low-cost item for which packhorses were probably a bit expensive. The ability of medieval potters to get their wares to market from predominantly rural kilns might depend therefore on a level track for carts, or safe waters for small boats. Perhaps a cargo for the Magor Pill boat was pottery made at Ham Green, near Bristol and the River Avon, as its products are frequently found in Cardiff. Recent recognition of large-scale production on the outskirts of Ely, Cambridgeshire, shows workshops able to get their products straight on to the Fenland waterways. Yet even in East Anglia, Grimston pottery had to make a 8-km (5-mile) road journey to Lynn, and although from there it could go round the coast, it must have been taken 48 km (30 miles) overland to Norwich, as much more has been found there than at the city's outport, Yarmouth. Pots made at Brill and Boarstall, Buckinghamshire, had to use land transport at least for most of their 15-km (9.3-mile) journey to the regional market at Oxford, where they competed with wares from the Forest of Braydon in Wiltshire that must also have come 50 km (31 miles) by land. Also from Wiltshire, pots from Minety must have been carted 8 km (4.9 miles) before they could be loaded on to boats to take them down the Thames, another 50 km as the crow flies but much more on the river. Pots were also coming up from the south, though the kiln sites are not known. None of these were worth shipping from Oxford down the Thames, however, as they are almost never found in Reading or London.

Pottery is the best type-model for a minor medieval industry. Although anyone with access to clay and firewood can make pots, such low-level "household production" was rarely if ever practiced; instead, urban and rural communities were served by specialist potters, operating individually in a "household industry" or "individual workshop," but who by working together to share the costs of collection of materials and distribution of products can be called "nucleated workshops." Many such groups were in or on the edges of forests or commons, tolerated where their digging would not ruin the best land, and close to wood or gorse for their fuel. Others were peasants firing kilns in their tofts in hamlets and villages, as in Brill or Lyveden, Northamptonshire, but still usually close to less restricted terrains than open fields and grazed meadows; at Lyveden, and probably elsewhere, individual tofts have evidence of discontinuous pot-making – knowledge remained in the community and could be revived when need arose. Iron-working was also practiced there, another individual enterprise heavily dependent on woods for charcoal, as well as on easily extracted ore deposits.

Not until the introduction of the blast furnace at the end of the fifteenth century did iron-making require large capital investment. In the same way, pot-making remained an individual enterprise, although kilns at Kingston-on-Thames, Surrey, might have been planned on a bigger scale in the middle of the thirteenth century, with an eye to supplying royal palaces as well as London. The white clay used there had to be carted to it, but it was well placed for taking the pots down the Thames to London, where it has been found in large quantities. The venture did not last, however, succumbing to competition from other parts of Surrey. The advantages of semi-marginal, rural pot-making locations generally outweighed the benefit of proximity to markets, and of superior skills developed from more intensive production; glazed wheel-making of high quality was well established in Stamford, Lincolnshire, but even there the craft died out in the thirteenth century.

A few urban or suburban kilns were started; those that had any duration probably also made tiles, taking advantage of the increasing demand for fireproof materials in larger towns, documented in London at the end of the twelfth century. In twelfth-century Canterbury, a kiln site was producing wares so similar to continental products as to suggest an immigrant potter, but the enterprise was soon abandoned, perhaps pressurized by high rents and complaints about the risk and smell of the firings, probably undercut by potters bringing their pots the 4.8 km (3 miles) from Tyler Hill. In the fifteenth century, however, there are signs of the increased specialization to come, as potters in Yorkshire and at Chilvers Coton, Warwickshire, learnt to take advantage of local coal seams for their fuel, though not yet venturing into firing larger kilns.

The range of pottery available in the late eleventh and first half of the twelfth centuries was limited, more so than before the Norman Conquest, and there was little glazed ware. The second half of the twelfth century saw a slow expansion in the supply of pots; even so, colorfully clay-painted and ornamented jugs were never more than around 10 percent of a potter's output. Clay pots had to face competition: from wood and leather at the lower end of the market, from glass and metal at the upper. Only for cooking the ubiquitous pottage did it have a significant advantage, and even then it is notable that peasants seem to have afforded a metal cauldron when they could. Pottery was a product of the earth, those who made it and fired it being dirty; in a society that rated cleanliness and distance from animals as signs of gentility over brutality, pottery and potters were perhaps to be avoided. Peasants turned away from making it when they could. The thickened and sometimes inturned rims of clay bowls suggest that, reluctant to put earth to their lips, people drank mostly from bowls made of wood, which rarely survive. They may, of course, have drunk directly from jugs, but the sheer size of the twelfth-century tripod pitchers suggests otherwise, not because they held too much to be an individual portion, but because they would have been too heavy to lift when full. Thirteenth-century jugs were less capacious as well as more gaily decorated, but they are still shapes from which liquid would be poured not drunk.

Small cylindrical beakers and lobed cups, forms difficult to make in wood and possibly more acceptable because the glaze disguised the clay below, began to appear in the thirteenth century, and perhaps became more common as wine drinking spread a little further down the social ranks, and perhaps also as ale was challenged by the stronger, hop-brewed beer; pouring jugs decreased in size, reflecting the new potency, and cisterns with bung holes at the base may show how the brew had to be allowed to settle so that it could be drawn off without the dregs. These changes were led by London, and some only slowly reached even East Anglia, despite its proximity to the Low Countries, the source of these changes. At the higher social level of guilds and merchants, pottery cups and beakers had to compete with pewter and copper alloy, and occasionally silver, if not much with glass. Even though metal cauldrons and frying pans challenged pottery in kitchens, the wider range of food and its preparation methods at least produced some new demand, such as dripping trays to catch the juice from roasting meat, and small measures for sauces. Wooden bowls may still have been preferred for serving individual portions, however, and the clay potters did not benefit from the growing use of flat dishes, as pewter was preferred.

Like glazed pots, brooches and decorated buckles are almost absent from the later eleventh century and first half of the twelfth century, despite an earlier upsurge in such trinkets. The Conqueror's taxation can be seen to have bitten deep into most people's ability to afford any superfluities. The second half of the twelfth century, and even more the thirteenth century, saw a return to the markets and fairs of small brooches and buckles, and of itinerants peddling them. Acquisition of petty luxuries was facilitated by increased coinage. The numbers of silver pennies found on excavations, or nowadays by metal detectorists, give a more representative idea of how much coin was in everyday use than do hoards, as their numbers are affected by the need to hide valuables in times of war and unrest. A turning point is the beginning of the thirteenth century, with single finds rising from an average of 5.1 for each year of King Henry II's reign (1154–89) to 12.1 in John's (1199–1216), peaking at 30.4 in Edward I's (1277–1307). Numbers then fall back, and in the first half of the fifteenth century are below the twelfth-century averages – the introduction of the 4d. silver groat and the half-groat would have had an effect on reducing numbers.

Spending and spirituality

Silver and base metals copied a growing aristocratic trend to the wearing of gold and gem-set ring-brooches. From the late eleventh century, belief in the spiritual powers of gems and other stones caused ecclesiastics to have them set in finger rings. For nuns, the eternal circle of a ring was symbolic of marriage to Christ. Wedding rings became usual for the laity as well, the large numbers of gold rings now being found by metal detector users show that better-off peasants could afford to buy them, not just richer townspeople. Inscriptions might be amatory promises of unending devotion, but even they can be seen as promises of eternal faithfulness such as Christ promised mankind. Many others are more overtly religious, though incantatory, with Mary often invoked, but also the supposed names of the Three Kings, and mishmashes of Hebrew and magic.

Objects could attest other forms of devotion. Visits to shrines in England and overseas, the more arduous the journey the better, were increasingly symbolized by the badges that people brought back with them, and which might be put to uses such as healing cattle, as well as simply worn to show where the pilgrim had worshiped. Bent coins, tokens of a vow to undertake a pilgrimage, are also found occasionally in locations such as post holes that suggest deliberative votive deposition. Surprisingly, they were rarely placed in graves, though a wooden staff symbolizing their journey seems to have been a way of showing a pilgrim. A papal *bulla* is more often found in a grave, and may mean that the person was buried with the indulgence that they had bought. Even small mirrors may exemplify the cross-over between the secular world and religious belief: to see oneself was an obvious advantage in a society that rated appearance so highly, yet was also a lure inviting vanity. Although to contemplate the body might aid contemplation of the soul, even this could lead to the demonic belief that to see the surface could lead to seeing the soul inside.

The Church was both a spiritual and physical presence, a society of institutions and of buildings, some open to all, some closed off but containing those who worked for mankind by their work of prayer. The various monastic orders were builders, owners, and investors, the heads of their houses were political players, and the changing requirements of their inmates reflected society as a whole. Abbots moving into separate lodgings, the subdividing of dormitories, or the constructing of gatehouses to serve as strong points for muniments as well as to impress the outsider that this was a City of God, all show fluidity of ideas. Conservatism can be seen in the reluctance to rent out demesne farms and to rely on the market for supplies; a major construction such as the woolhouse with its fulling provision at Fountains Abbey, Yorkshire, helped to make the monks self-sufficient in their clothing needs, though it could also provide a marketable surplus. More surprising is the discovery at another Cistercian house, Bordesley Abbey in Worcestershire, of a mill that had weaponry among its products, surely for either commerce or gifts to patrons, either way indicative of even the solitary orders' readiness to involve themselves in the secular world. Their difficulty in the fourteenth and fifteenth centuries of getting lay brothers to serve them is another sign of change. Indeed, it was difficult to get even clerics to stick to the old ways. The colleges of priests who served cathedrals sought to move away from communal living to enjoy the status of their own individual households.

A monastery, cathedral, or parish church was where all would lie until the Last Judgment, the clerics and the wealthy inside a building or in a more private outdoor space that most of the laity could not enter. Minor local variations of burial practices, such as lining a grave with stones, do not seem to have any deep significance or even regional consistency. Cemeteries served as a reminder of the end of the journey through life, where the individual passed from the human memory of their families into the anonymity of the family of the dead. Belief in the waiting-room for the next world, Purgatory, developed from the late twelfth century, and its effects can be seen in increased provision in churches for memorials and chantries where the dead could be prayed for. Care about burial became greater as belief in the body as a chamber for the soul at the Resurrection grew. Even in the extreme circumstances of the Black Death, when London's intra-mural graveyards could not cope with the number of dead and new ones were opened outside the gates, burial was in long trenches not individual graves, but the bodies were carefully placed, not merely thrown in, with heads to the west in the orthodox way, apart from a few that were probably shrouded so that the burial party could not tell which end was which. Only one mass burial pit has been found in London.

Many churches or chapels were placed to bless a market, to stand at a street junction, or at a gate, places where people had to choose a route and begin a journey, just as they had to choose a route through the journey of life. Even the layout of the main streets of a town might be seen as the arms of the Cross, like a church with transepts. Hospitals for lepers and others with visible afflictions were usually outside towns, to keep the physically stigmatized away from those who were in the image of God, but they were allowed in to beg for alms until it was realized, apparently after the Black Death, that disease could be infectious or contagious. Their houses were on approach roads so that they could serve as perpetual reminders of God's will, particularly near bridges so that the metaphor of their liminal place between two worlds became also a bridge between them. Indeed, they were specially selected by God to suffer in this world rather than in the next.

In most towns newly founded in the high Middle Ages, only chapels of ease were permitted so that established parish rights of baptism, marriage, and burial were not lost to holders of the tithes and dues. The custom developed that these advowson holders had responsibilities for the fabric of the chancel, which became a more separate space and gave the priest a more enhanced intercessory and mystical role with new liturgical requirements for elevation of the Host during Mass at an east end altar. Nevertheless, advowson holders might think it less necessary than did the parishioners to demonstrate their piety by building, and new chancels were sometimes even paid for by the laity to match their own provision of extended naves, new aisles, raised roofs, light-flooding windows, screens, floor tiles, images, and towers; demonstrations of their communal devotion.

Sentiment was not enough to prevent encroachments upon some urban cemeteries for profitable terraced housing, as in York's Goodramgate, or late medieval church amalgamations and demolitions. Guilds were also part of the changing fabric of a town with more than just a commercial role; their corporations mirrored the corporation of the clergy, and they had public roles as providers of alms, processions, and mystery plays as well as to create regulation of commerce and good fellowship among their members. Their halls might be opulent, but usually incorporated a chapel if not also a hospital in the later Middle Ages. The friars also had a visible presence in or on the edge of many towns after the beginning of the thirteenth century. They provided an alternative to parish church burial for the better-off, creating another physical expression of social division.

Lepers were not the only marginalized "other" in medieval England. The Flemings in the later fourteenth and fifteenth centuries were distinctive and often a focus for resentment and riots, but were recognizable by their speech more than by their appearance. More noticeable were the Jews, whose wealth in the twelfth century came to be increasingly resented, and complaints about the credit that they lent led to encouragement of beliefs in their anti-Christian behavior. Archaeologically, they are more identifiable in death than in life. The carefully tended "garden" that was their cemetery in York shows how visually distinct and separate they were; while they were useful to the king, they could look to protection from his castle, and many were buried close to one. Forced to wear badges in the thirteenth century, and with distinctive hats and perhaps faces, there was no hiding place for them, but those things are not revealed in what survives, and the richer Jews' stone houses are little different from those of the rich Christians among whom they lived; traces of synagogue use are rare, though two probable examples of a *mikveh*, a sunken ritual bath, in London's Jewry area, and on the outskirts of Bristol what is probably a *bet tohorah*, a well of pure water where bodies could be cleansed before burial in the adjacent cemetery, show how important their rituals were to them. That the *mikva'ot* both seem to be within private houses, and the *bet tohorah* well away from public gaze, shows how discreet the Jews found it prudent to be.

Conclusion

As in any society, medieval people expressed themselves through their buildings, their appearance, their behavior, and their modes of burial as well as in the writings of the elite literates among them. Archaeology is a path into their customs, mind-sets, beliefs, economic behavior, social ambitions, and choices. In the written record that people deliberately leave behind about themselves they do not tell of the things of which they were unaware; the physical record tells a different kind of truth.

Part Two

Cultural ideals and cultural conflicts

4

Social ideals and social disruption

Social cohesion

Communitas

Any traveler through the modern English countryside quickly gains an impression of the intense localism of communities formed long ago and of a long-lingering memory of lordly control over them. Techniques of agriculture that sustained these villages often required both a base-level ideal and a daily practice of communal cooperation. Yet these were scarcely (to borrow the words of a popular Monty Python film) anarcho-syndicalist communes; lordship exercised over villagers was another fact of life, accepted if perhaps not considered by all and in every aspect an ideal. Its reality remains embedded in a variety of colorful place names. Often some dominant family has stamped its name forever upon the land, or the lordship recorded is that of an abbey or episcopal see. Such evidence is a useful reminder of the distinctly local horizons to so much of medieval life in England as elsewhere in Europe.

Yet important as it is to remember the local or regional dimension throughout medieval Europe, it is likewise important to realize that the imprint of lordship was only the first of several matrices informing and enforcing a basic sense of community – a concept that need not be considered warm and cuddly. Two additional frameworks stretched their regulation over the landscape. These provide sound reasons for thinking that in the case of England an ideal of community operated not only at the level of villages but even at the level of the kingdom. By the time of the Norman Conquest, localities and regional communities

over much of the island had become a part of this larger community of
the kingdom. England took shape in relationship not only to the matrix
of local lordships, but to these two supra-local matrices. One was created
by a precocious monarchy, the other by a branch of the Church universal
that grew in tandem with the rising power of kingship. The process of
implanting these patterns had been far advanced by Anglo-Saxon kings,
monks, and bishops. After recovery from the invasion (and initial
Norman incomprehension of sophisticated Anglo-Saxon governing procedures) the process continued, imposing a matrix of institutional forms
that interlocked with the structures of local lordship. The realm was
divided into administrative and judicial districts called shires (which the
Normans would call counties), each watched over by a sheriff who held a
shire court; these shires were subdivided into smaller units usually
termed hundreds (sometimes wapentakes or even rapes), and these in
turn were composed of vills. Within each vill adult males were enrolled
into small sets known as tithing groups, responsible for keeping the local
peace. Often, though not universally, the vills coincided with local
"manorial" units of lordship. The governmental vill could also be a
manorial village. The growing towns might be hundreds in themselves.
But there was much diversity.

Authorities and governing structures, even when occasionally quar-
relsome, tend to rise together in a process of mutual reinforcement and
exchange of ideas. The institutional Church no less than the monarchy
gradually implanted its matrix on the landscape. By the eighth century
ecclesiastics had come to see England in terms of two provinces headed
by archbishops at Canterbury and York, with each province divided into
dioceses under bishops (with their own courts); the dioceses were made
up of parishes, with officials known as rural deans acting throughout
several parishes. Sometimes, though far from universally, the parish
coincided with a royal vill.

This triple layering of matrices of governance – manorial, royal, and
ecclesiastical – the product of years of messy and sometimes contentious
historical events, remained incomplete and it was not neat; often the
three layers did not simply coincide and quarrels over jurisdiction were
inevitable, but the possibilities for a larger *communitas regni*, a "community of the realm," were genuine. Some villages (or several, or a part of a
village shared among several lords) could be not only a lord's estate, but
also a royal vill and a parish with its priest (or his vicar as substitute).
A monarchy with capacity unusual for the time generally acted

cooperatively with a vigorous Church structure, both standing on a base of local units of lordship. The ideal of community, embedded for most folk in agricultural clusters under lordly domination, became building blocks of greater scope through the ambitious work of kings and elite clerics.

This idea of a larger community was powerful and could have succeeded only with support from all those whose political weight counted, a body of folk that grew larger over time as the social pyramid broadened with socio-economic as well as political change. In short, the idea of a community-wide realm did not simply flow top-down. Over time it may have reached, or grown from, surprisingly deep levels in the social pyramid. Striking evidence appears in an incident (noted long ago by the historian Helen Cam) recorded in a royal legal record. During the civil war troubling the late years of the reign of Henry III (1216–72), some villagers from a little place called Peatling, Leicestershire, assaulted a passing body of royalist troops, who, remarkably, brought them into court rather than destroying them or their homes. In defense of their action the accused villagers answered, as the court record states (translating their vernacular replies into legal Latin), that they had assaulted the troops "because they were against the good of the community of the realm and against the barons." Evidently, this group of villagers had got the most potent socio-political ideal of their age, that of *communitas regni*, and had absorbed the idea, pressed forward by critics of the current royal regime in this period of civil strife. A larger community exists in this view, and a body of barons can even take responsibility and leadership for it when they consider the king incompetent and troublesome. If this specific language had been lacking even among the elite who had forced Henry's father, King John (1189–1216), to agree to the Great Charter half a century earlier, even in this earlier movement of 1215 the idea of a lasting kingdom had finally dominated the opposition to John. It may have been touch and go getting hotheads to agree, but the rebels finally wanted to reform this community, not dismember it.

Such evidence from resistance movements thus joins that coming day by day in less contentious times when locals cooperated steadily in the operations of the king's government. The shire or county court met regularly under the direction of the sheriff appointed by the crown; circuits of justices from Westminster (known as justices on eyre) brought the crown's original jurisdiction out to localities to adjudicate a lengthening list of legal issues, at first limited to the major crimes known as felonies and (from the mid-thirteenth century) the many lesser yet troublesome quarrels termed trespasses. What has been concisely and aptly described as "self-government at the king's command" went forward as local juries were formed and assizes (legal proceedings dealing with issues defined by the crown) were held to settle both civil litigation and criminal charges. Ownership of property was in theory protected and those found guilty of crime were of a certainty hanged (their goods and chattels, however modest, forfeit to the crown ever anxious for revenue).

As the community of England was taking greater form and depth, social and economic forces were clearly at work in the background, generating new twists to the ideal and components of community. Scholars dispute the exact measure of population growth, but none doubt its direction and cumulative force. The creation and prosperity of a larger *communitas* were founded on a dramatic demographic expansion that took place over centuries and without at this stage exceeding the limits of food production. Towns had been growing in numbers and in individual size long before the Conquest. Their continued growth in the centuries that concern us produced local urban centers with significant degrees of both wealth and self-governance within the larger community of the realm. Significantly, this urban presence never became so powerful or independent-minded as to constitute a threat to the concept of a kingdom-wide community based on the governing matrices that we have noted. It was different in the Low Countries and northern Italy, where any ideal of a larger community proved impossible. In England the urban surge, while sufficient to draw upon and generate advantages such as increased trade and moveable wealth, remained too modest to contest a process of state-building. English towns of all sizes, even London (the only city to be compared with continental towns), were fitted into the institutional matrices guided by kings and the upper clergy. Many towns sought and received royal charters setting forth guarantees of their liberties with black ink on pale parchment, and all came to be incorporated within the royal and ecclesiastical governmental and judicial structures. Towns regularly paid taxes, sought and accepted justice from agents of the king and the Church, and supplied troops or ships for royal expeditions. Citizens of towns important enough to boast a cathedral and episcopal palace within their walls sometimes quarreled with their bishops, as towns controlled by abbeys quarreled with the abbots; but disputes rarely showed the ferocity of quarrels continental citizens prosecuted or lasted as long.

Pax, lex, ius et justitia

Beyond sheer force, what convinced most folk to cooperate in the processes of a larger community was an ideal for good medieval government that was simple to state and extremely difficult to achieve: they first of all wanted peace for their local communities and, in a more general way, the stabilizing peace of a larger *communitas* in the realm. This meant at base level not only defense against invasion, but also some tolerable level of internal security to make daily life tolerable. Yet more was involved. Good governing in the Middle Ages meant making and enforcing good law. It might fairly be said, then, that a foundational ideal of society was a concept of justice. Medieval Englishmen (in company with most of their fellows across Europe) would have accepted the definition of justice opening the great Roman law book of Justinian, which declares justice to be the constant and perpetual will to give every man his due. It is, of course (in addition to being non-modern in its gendered terms), a hierarchical view: not all men have the same rights due them; rights vary with status. Yet the idea of justice seems to have loomed large throughout the social hierarchy. It may well have been one of those basic notions that, as Bronislaw Geremek has emphasized, hold a society together and make social life tolerable. Medieval people could not hope for – most could scarcely conceive of – any genuine equality, but they clung determinedly to the idea that they should freely be allowed what was due them – either in highly specific and circumstantial terms (such as tenurial obligations and rights), or by their inclusion in one of the divinely intended groups or *ordines*, the "orders" constituting society (defined largely by status and occupation or profession). The "three orders" have achieved much prominence in modern analysis of medieval society – that is, groups of those who prayed, those who fought, and those who worked – but in the centuries we are examining, people who theorized about how society was put together usually came up with a great many "orders." Rather than the exact division and numbers, what seems important is this deeply held belief in sets of people intended by God for the functioning of human society. The humblest group, that of laborers, unsurprisingly had much in the way of obligations, little in the way of rights. The precise content of what was due and what violated the "liberties" of each order in society could, of course, change over time. Radical advances in what people in an order expected – or in the actual treatment experienced by members of the groups – were likely to be upsetting or even dangerous.

Lacking any polls or surveys, how do we know that these folk believed
in such ideals and especially nurtured a sense of justice? That they cared
about security will be obvious, but did they truly care about law and
justice as it could be managed by governing institutions? One strong
positive indication speaks at least to the layers at the top, the relatively
small but slowly increasing body of the privileged and those close to
them who could read (or had opportunity to listen to others reading):
they loved the story of their past told in Arthurian legends. The accounts
of the kings of Britain famously feature Arthur, but a quality that they
repeatedly praise in him they likewise attribute to all the good mythical
kings in the story: each keeps peace and gives or maintains good laws.
Geoffrey of Monmouth's widely read *History of the Kings of Britain* (*c.* 1138;
published in Latin and soon translated) sets the pattern picked up by
Wace (writing in socially broader Anglo-Norman French *c.* 1200) and by
Lawman (writing in the yet socially broader Middle English in the early
thirteenth century). Arthur and the other kings are all adept warriors,
able to cut down their enemies like reaping machines; but within the
realm, and in the realms they conquer, these ideal kings provide security
and good law: they give justice to all. They also, it should be noted,
stoutly protect churches and personally appoint good church leaders
(despite reformed Church doctrine which prohibited such lay investi-
ture). Geoffrey's readers (or hearers) learned that one predecessor of
Arthur, King Constantine, "maintained justice among his people, mod-
erated the rapacity of footpads, put an end to the oppressive behaviour of
local tyrants and did his utmost to foster peace everywhere."[1] Arthur
himself, Geoffrey says, "fostered justice and peace, the maintenance of
the laws and decent behaviour in all matters throughout his kingdom."[2]
Arthur spreads these blessings widely, for after conquering France he
"settled the realm peacefully and legally."[3] The appropriately named
writer Lawman pictures another mythical British king who recovered
order after a time of internal strife. He then

> sette þis lond; he sahtnesse wrohte.
> He sette stronge lawen; he was sturne þon dusien.
> He luuede þeo leoden; he his lawen heolden.
> Æuer-alcne godne mon; he aðelede mid gode.
> He hehte hælden griðe & frið; vppe leome & vppe lif.
>
> [settled the land, he worked for peacefulness.
> He established strong laws; he was stern with the foolish

But he loved those people whose lives were law-abiding;
Every single good man he honoured with property;
He enforced peace and truce upon pain of limb and life.]⁴

This equation of kingship with good law continues and even takes on new force later in the thirteenth century. The anonymous Middle English romance, *Havelock the Dane*, re-caps the theme near its opening:

It was a king bi are-dawes	[there was a king in olden times]
Þat in his time were gode lawes	[who in his time caused good laws]
He dede maken an ful wel holden ...	[to be made and fully kept...]
He louede God with al his micth,	[loved God all his might]
And Holi Kirke, and soth ant ricth ...	[Holy Church, and truth and right ...]
Wreieres and wrobberes made he falle,	[False accusers and tale-bearers he had destroyed]
And hated hem so man doth galle;	[hated them as one hates gall]
Vtlawes and theves made he bynde,	[Outlaws and thieves he had bound]
Alle þat he micthe fynde,	[All whom he could discover]
And heye hengen on galwe-tre –	[hanged them high on the gallows-tree –]
For hem ne yede gold ne fe!	[No ransom could buy them off]
Jn þat time a man þat bore	[In those days, a man who carried ...]
[*missing line*]	
Of red gold upon hijs bac	[pure gold on his back]
Jn a male with or blac	[In a white or black satchel]
Ne funde he non þat him misseyde	[He'd find no one who'd affront him]
Ne with iuele on hond leyde ...	[Nor maliciously lay a hand on him ...]
Þanne was Engelond at hayse	[Then ... at ease]
Michel was svich a king to preyse	[Greatly was such a king to be praised]
Þat held so Englond in grith!	[Who kept thus England in peace!]⁵

Such a king, the poet exults, was the very flower of regality: "Engelondes blome" (England's bloom; line 63).

We can add evidence of actions medieval people took to the witness of ideas they patronized and read or heard in imaginative literature. Simply stated, we can be sure that they believed in the king's crucial role in justice because in increasing numbers they brought their troubles into his courts. An investigator in the British Government archives could demonstrate this steady growth in court business visually by laying out comparable sets of court records side by side from intervals of say a generation. The result would resemble a staircase, with increasing royal jurisdiction recorded on increasingly hefty layers of parchment court records at each interval of time. The crown actively and regularly expanded the range of judicial cases it wanted justices to try (*ex officio* cases); but again the process is not simply top-down; suits flowed into royal courts because plaintiffs clearly wanted their cases heard there (*ad instanciam* cases). In fact, this combination – royal extension of its jurisdiction and an increasing press of business brought by anxious litigants – clogged the circuits of royal justices attempting to move through the counties and, finally, by the end of the thirteenth century killed this general eyre. Expectations had exceeded its capacity.

The peace-keeping and justice-giving role embedded in the Arthurian chroniclers even appears concisely in the technical language of royal law. Litigants who wanted to get their cases involving an opponent's trespass heard knew they must use key words: their enemies had come "by force and arms and against the Lord King's peace." This phrase may seem a tiny and archaic bit of legal vocabulary; yet it suggests broad attitudes about a larger community and the royal role in peace and justice.

If the royal judicial apparatus was reaching progressively deeper into the social pyramid to take on troubling social problems, the ecclesiastical courts dealt with other matters that often touched many lives. In fact, the border separating the two jurisdictions was a ragged and shifting frontier. Matters matrimonial and testamentary clearly belonged to ecclesiastical courts and generated a considerable volume of cases. Other issues, such as disputes over tithes and the naming of clerics to local livings, generated more contention with the king's judicial apparatus. The ecclesiastical interest in cases of illicit sexuality, investigated at a local level by archdeacons and their subordinates, will concern us in the section "Social contention and disruption" below. The volume of business and the wealth it generated apparently evoked an envious outcry from King Henry II that the archdeacons garnered an income greater than his own.[6]

Religion: clerical ideal, clerical caste, and lay piety and independence

We would, of course, completely underestimate the power and role of religion in forming and buttressing community were we to think only in terms of a governing agency. Much of what we can imagine sustained individuals and certainly much that sustained communal life was deeply rooted in ideas and practices that emerged from the theology and rituals of medieval Christianity. Influential churchmen had, in fact, been directing thought and effort toward infusing in lay folk a more thorough application and understanding of religious ideas and practices since the twelfth century. Theologians at Laon and later a circle of thoughtful churchmen in Paris led by Peter the Cantor (and including a number of English clerics) focused on a closer harmony between life in the world and basic religious principles. These efforts then flowed directly into the mainstream of English religious life through bishops' legislation implementing the statutes of the great Lateran council of the Church directed by Innocent III in Rome in 1215 (the same year that the Magna Carta reinforced communal ideas in another vein in England). With the expanding role of parish clergy in mind, scholars wrote many new handbooks to provide instruction on principles of the faith and especially encouraged the crucial process of dealing with sin – confessing sin and receiving absolution. Those who would not repent were reminded in vivid wall paintings and equally vivid sermons featuring *exempla* (pithy moral tales) that terrifying punishments awaited them – for an eternity in hell in the case of the utterly reprobate, and for the mass of the merely flawed, at least for a longer time than they wished to contemplate, in the cleansing fires of Purgatory. Adhering to the Ten Commandments, avoiding the deadly sins (and as many venial sins as possible), practicing charity – these goals were set before all the faithful. The obvious result should ideally be a reinforcement of social harmony.

But did this framework of ideas and rituals truly guide lay thought and behavior on all matters religious, in the process helping to generate social cohesion? We must ask the same question we posed about ideas of law and justice stemming from royal jurisdiction and action. It is a daunting task, best examined from the vantage point of the later Middle Ages; scholarly debate has focused on this period of the fourteenth and fifteenth centuries when the evidence is a little better and the looming Reformation adds urgency to the debate.

Social contention and disruption

No period of the history of medieval England can be imagined to have produced a harmonious social world of communities free from strife. A romantic lens always distorts our view of the past. The high Middle Ages (roughly the eleventh through late thirteenth centuries) were truly productive of organizing institutions and ideas; yet the age was far from idyllic and the cohesive ideals and forms we have examined could not exist free from competition, violence, and oppression. Many scholars think, however, that by the fourteenth and fifteenth centuries difficulties in maintaining social cohesion increased. The infamous Black Death bringing terrifying mortality will come to mind at once, and generations ago that was thought of as the single key to explaining all difficulties. At present, historians look to a wider range of forces and once again, the scope and difficulty of evidence causes debate over broad interpretation. Some question whether the difficulties encountered by governing agencies themselves actually increased, or if a sense of crisis stems rather from the great increase in our store of surviving evidence that records problems. Another debate focuses on the use of imaginative literature as evidence; some think of it as largely irrelevant, merely personal gripes or escapist fantasy; others insist that it provides a crucial window into how people thought and the values they attacked or maintained. There is, finally, the attempt to evaluate domestic consequences of warfare that had in the later Middle Ages taken on major dimensions. Was the Hundred Years' War between England and France and their allies (traditionally 1337–1453) a major factor influencing the "home front" of the kingdom? Did this concentration of energies and resources on war entail serious overextension of the king's government?

Community and upheavals political, social, demographic
England was, relatively speaking, a much-governed kingdom, yet it had been no stranger to internal warfare throughout the high Middle Ages. The Norman Conquest had brought devastation in its wake, and in the twelfth century King Stephen and the Empress Matilda had fought for the throne. In the mid-thirteenth century Henry III had to survive a civil war against determined forces led notably by Simon de Montfort. Yet the monarchy, or most assuredly the monarchs, encountered yet more trouble in the later Middle Ages. Only one English king out of nine was killed between 1066 and 1307 (and debate over how to

characterize this single royal death continues); but of the nine kings from 1307 to 1485 (counting, for symmetry, the young Edward V, one of the "princes in the Tower") no fewer than five kings were deposed and killed during recurrent quarrels over the succession. In a resolutely royalist and hierarchical age, foreigners loved to denounce the English as king killers.

Perhaps the most significant single event for understanding the difficulties of governance is the Great Rising of 1381 in which large bodies of rebels marched on London along both banks of the Thames, entered the city of London, and in several tense meetings confronted the boy king Richard II and his advisors with lists of demands. The crisis was severe and authorities at all levels were temporarily shaken as cracks seemed to threaten the very foundations of the royal *communitas*.

Yet the rising likewise – however surprisingly – provides striking testimony to the strength of the basic ideals we have already noted. It does not seem to have been a classic social revolt of the sort that had erupted in France a generation earlier (the Jacquerie of 1358), in which rural bands attacked and killed lords and their entire families in brutal fury. As revolts go, the Great Rising was almost orderly. Very few members of elite society were killed (a few local agents of the legal process); the Queen Mother and her attendants, encountered while they went on pilgrimage, were respectfully allowed to pass on their way; the rebels loyally posted home guards on the coast so that no French forces might descend during their march on London; they entered Canterbury Cathedral, but did not trouble the riches or the monks there and said they came only to look for the archbishop, Simon Sudbury, who was also, significantly, the royal treasurer (and they killed him later, dragging him from the Tower to be beheaded). Above all, in meetings with the king in person they apparently showed a touching faith in monarchy and in the king as fountain-head of justice; all their wrongs would be corrected by his acts. After the meeting at Mile End beyond London's walls many accepted royal assurances written out by court clerks, who no doubt scratched pen quickly on the sheets of parchment with many a nervous glance about. Famously, the remainder of the rebels accepted young King Richard's brave claim to be their leader, followed him about London, and dispersed. Of course, the promises were forgotten and the pardons were canceled; judicial inquests brought scores of men to the gallows. Most will concur that even limited rebel killings or official executions are deplorable; yet the modest scale of the mortality seems significant when set against the bloodbath in France where rebels killed lords and as noble vengeance ended the Jacquerie with even greater loss of life.

Since we cannot interview the bands from Essex and Kent marching on London, our knowledge of the exact ideals of most rebels remains murky. What chroniclers tell us they demanded in meetings with the king seems radical enough – abolition of serfdom, distribution of Church property to the parishes, standard rents, a single law for the entire realm, only one bishop for the realm. Some scholars find in these reported demands the very line of radical idealism animating the rebels. Others think horrified chroniclers projected their own fears and inflated their accounts to show how truly wicked the rebels were. Yet other scholars think rebel leaders, facing a royal administration that temporized and prevaricated (disingenuously granting each and every demand to defuse the crisis), had to outflank authorities by a move to the left, that is, to confront the government with demands so radical they could not be granted with fingers crossed behind the back. What does seem reasonable is that the rebels were sick to death of the taint and restrictions of villeinage, the unfree condition of many villagers, and that they were outraged over the judicial failures and increasing economic exactions of the king's government. The crown had not delivered on its promises to provide peace and order in the realm, though such assurances had been a centerpiece of government claims for centuries, stated in preambles to every statute read out in county courts. Royal agents had, however, tried fully to extract the heavy taxes needed for the king's war in France. Resistance to war taxation had, in fact, begun before the Great Rising itself: in what Edmund Fryde aptly termed the first act of rebellion, massive tax evasion wiped a third of the population of England from the assessment rolls recording those liable to pay.[7] Moreover, the apparatus of crown and parliament (which cannot be confused with a democratic assembly) had vigorously backed repressive labor legislation; they sought to keep wages at pre-plague levels, despite an actual fall in the number of laborers caused by the Black Death (well before the tax revolt with its apparent drop in population).

The resistance was genuine, but the evidence points overall not to an anarchic desire to destroy the governing frameworks, but rather to a radical movement of reform. Hope centered on the monarchy. With memories of childhood nursery rhymes in mind, we might term this the Chicken Little Syndrome: if the sky is falling, run tell the king. He'll make it all right. In other words, the rebels may have accepted much of the structure of the legal and administrative communities that shaped their lives, though they thought they could remove serfdom and oppressive taxation, and they seem to have believed that the king under their urging would purge his administration of "traitors" and produce an ordered countryside ruled by good laws and just men. The pattern seems worthy of note whether we consider it rational or a sadly misguided fantasy on the part of the rebels.

A crisis of law and justice?

Such an analysis of the rising of 1381 suggests that the king's justice was not seen to be working well in the late fourteenth century, a view that some scholars dispute. The debate is entangled with views of effects of the great war with France. One reason for problems in the administration of law and in public order could be the heavy concentration of the king and his administrators on pressing forward their efforts to conquer France. In one view (full disclosure: that of the author of this chapter), a medieval government with limited resources concentrated on war at the expense of law and order at home. In no small measure the argument turns on what to make of a large body of literary evidence. The best known case in point comes from the stories told of Robin Hood, for the moral of these tales is quite similar to what we argued was a theme of the rebels in 1381: in both the tales and the rising the king is revered and the problem is seen as corrupt and disloyal agents of the law, with the sheriff of Nottingham claiming top spot on the list of baddies in Robin Hood stories, but with fat and dishonest churchmen, such as the Abbot of St. Mary's York (or his cellerer), filling ample space beside him. Less popularly known today, but equally informative is the "Tale of Gamelyn." Here an evil older brother disinherits the virtuous but naive younger brother and is supported in the deed by local ecclesiastics; this evil brother then corrupts judicial process to get Gamelyn outlawed. In an orgy of violence that closes the poem, the hero sets all right and (like Robin Hood) finds his righteous violence – the only way to see justice done – approved by an understanding king. Such tales form the other side of the coin to romances like *Havelock the Dane* noted above as hearty endorsements of royal provision of good justice. Both literary types look to the crown for provision of just laws; but one type thinks that in hard times the crown needs some good local men to jump-start the system with violent self-help. Such works can be supported by a mass of shorter, more occasional verse often collectively called "the literature of satire and complaint,"[8] pieces that vigorously denounce the workings of judicial administration, both of Church and state. Those modern historians opposed to use of all such materials reduce all this literature to sour grapes and personal complaint. It is interesting, however, to note how frequently dissatisfaction with the workings of law courts resulted in assaults on justices themselves and overawing of courts by irate groups. One can debate whether these assaults are frequent enough to weigh significantly in the scales of interpretation; but their potent symbolism seems clear. When in 1304 Richard Cristien, the dean of Ospringe, an ecclesiastical official in the Province of Canterbury, was sent to the village of Sellinges, Kent, to cite those guilty of sexual offenses, outraged villagers assaulted him, forced him to sit backwards on his horse, holding the horse's tail, conducted him "with songs and dances" through the village and heaved him into "a filthy place." Since the backwards ride was used to punish those who were sexually impure, the villagers were likely objecting not to sexual correction so much as that correction exercised by one whom they considered impure himself. Readers of Chaucer's "Friar's Tale," in the *Canterbury Tales* (told as a satire on sexual correction by ecclesiastics), will find this case interesting. The clerics in the Chaucerian satire are greedily seeking profit by cases directed at an all-too-common human frailty, while sinning sexually themselves, or even entrapping sinners with women in their pay.[9]

We can look to critiques of the king's justices in the case of William Thorpe, who was (while a clerk of the court of King's Bench, though he later became Chief Justice of that court) knocked flat and treated contemptuously on his way to court in 1315. The specifics involve human urine and whether (as I once wrote) his enemies urinated on him or (as Richard Firth Green insists) they threw urine on him, the contempt registers and only the delivery mechanism is in question. When a contemporary justice, Thomas Setton, was publicly denounced by a woman named Lucy as a faithless traitor who should be hanged and drawn, he got damages from her. But shortly thereafter he was stabbed in the belly by a chaplain hired by enemies, and he died of the wounds. We might also consider incidents involving the more famous Justice William Shareshull, who was denounced by name in the Middle English poem *Wynner and Wastour*. More directly, he was abducted in 1329; his household was attacked by two prominent knights at York in 1333; his sessions in Wiltshire in 1336 were threatened with armed force (which may have hurried him off into another county); some of his properties were attacked in 1337, 1355, and 1358; his judicial sessions at Tredington were broken up by force in 1347; and a clerk and some laborers who said they wanted to assault him personally were brought to court in 1358. Most interesting was the incident at Ipswich involving Justice William Notton as well as Shareshull. The citizenry of this town, rich and poor alike, gathered once the justices had left; they feted some prisoners who had been convicted before the judges, honoring the convicted felons "as if God had come down from heaven." Then from the very steps of the hall where judicial pleas were held, the citizens summoned Shareshull and Notton to appear before them, under penalty. An irate crown saw that Ipswich lost its liberties, of course. Shareshull went on vigorously to the end, dying as a Franciscan novice.[10]

It could be argued that these incidents (and many more like them) are chance bits of evidence showing merely that good men active in the law make enemies. That defense weakens somewhat, however, when we note the problem of justices violating rules meant to regulate their behavior. Justice Thorpe was sentenced to be hanged and his considerable lands and goods (the latter deposited in eight monasteries) confiscated. His crime was accepting bribes and (like the crooked justice in the *Geste of Robin Hood*) illegally accepting retaining fees in direct violation of a royal ordinance which he had sworn to obey in the king's presence. These retaining fees in effect bought a justice. In the Robin Hood tale the good knight Sir Richard appeals on his knees for fair treatment, only to hear the retained justice spurn the plea, saying "I am holde with [bound to] the abbot ... Both with cloth and fee."[11] Thorpe, the historical judge, is pardoned by the king because of his good service, a result that no idealistic outlaw tale would have allowed. We might also consider the charge against a certain justice that he sold the laws of England as if they were cows. Examining the great mass of record evidence, John Maddicott (1978) found that retaining of justices by lords was widespread in the thirteenth and fourteenth centuries, and in another valuable study (1975) he dug out ready parallels between hated figures of authority (below the king) portrayed in the Robin Hood stories and historical figures active in law and administration.

It is worthy of note that so many of these justices rose from the ranks of what would soon be termed the gentry, that is, those just on the lower edge of elite social ranks. Men of this status took on a much greater role in royal justice in the last two medieval centuries, acting as judicial commissioners under varying titles and with varying powers, eventually becoming the famous justices of the peace. Some historians have seen this movement as a positive social broadening, almost an early step toward democracy. Others have seen these men as idealistic, heroic folk, bravely shouldering the burden of legal administration and motivated by an unalloyed belief in advancing the common good. My own view is that, sadly, the law has all too often sought the advantage of particular interest groups and that striving for the common good is regrettably not the prevailing motive in any society of which I have knowledge. It seems all too clear that we are often dealing (in the case of the gentry and the law) with rising members within a hierarchical society who thought of their own ascent ceaselessly and of the common good very little. This at least seems to be the picture that can be derived from the well-known Paston letters written by members of a Norfolk gentry family a century later. Fourteenth-century England seems from many points of view to be an honor society of the type that led the anthropologist Julian Pitt-Rivers to say so concisely, "the ultimate vindication of honour lies in physical violence." Did gentry interest in the law simply coincide with that of the crown in any age? The tireless scholar Bertha Putnam saw a conflict between a centralizing crown and local demands. Some recent scholars have denied this. We might ask about the record of county gents and the law before the demise of the circuits of justices, the general eyre; records show quarrels between franchise-holding gentry and the sheriff as royal representative. Why such quarrels? Did they arise out of differing views of common good or impartial justice? Were they generated from a sense among the gentry that they could (better than central government personnel) achieve such high and abstract goals? One might suggest instead the motives of power, profit, and prestige that always came with the exercise of justice in the Middle Ages (and many other ages).

No single line of evidence and argument may sway those unconvinced that the operation of the law was in difficulty during the later Middle Ages; they will continue to stress the positive side of law, the pure motives of its agents. The case advanced here, however, argues not that any single contrary line of evidence is convincing, but that the entire range of evidence points to dissatisfaction with the law and the likelihood of gentry distortion of the law for personal interests. The case rests on the investment of so much energy of royal administration in war, the rise in assaults on justices and overawing of their courts, the biting satire infusing a large body of literature (both high and low), the conviction of some justices for precisely those wrongs complaint literature charged against them, and the dissatisfaction turning into action in 1381. Taken altogether, this evidence suggests the possibility that all was not well and that many people were discouraged and some were outraged. Few can have given up on the ideal of a larger community organized and governed by king and churchmen with their apparatus of law; but many wanted it to work as officials had regularly promised that it would work.

A few radicals or the premature Reformation?

We have already encountered the problems of approaching large questions about social ideals and cohesion using the less than ideal evidence available. Our difficulties take on new dimensions altogether when we try to chart widespread religious ideas and their changes in the later Middle Ages. Scholars over the past several decades have investigated the vigor of continuing popular piety set against the coming of the Reformation. The task is daunting and has generated debate (sometimes at high temperatures) for decades. The evidence, thin on the ground and always hard to interpret, does not lead easily to generalizations; different sources sometimes simply seem contradictory.

All difficulties would dissolve at once if we could posit a population that either absorbed the teachings of the Church completely and obediently, even joyfully, and if these folk uniformly marched in step, only failing to live up to standards fully because of human frailty, not because of dissension; or if, on the other hand, we could imagine that lay folks were really at heart ever resistant and opposed to yet another authority with its rules, courts, and tithe collection, perhaps really, when they thought about it, opposed to basic Church teachings. What makes interpretation much more difficult, and so much more interesting, is that simplistic extremes cannot take into account all the evidence. We must wrap our minds around the characteristic medieval fusion of genuine lay piety with varying degrees of sturdy lay independence; we must recognize respect for the clerical *ordo* working alongside vitriolic verbal (and sometimes physical) anticlericalism. The proportions of the contrasting sets of ideas will likely show variations from one locality or region to another and will surely vary over time.

At the level of the parish, and using evidence mainly from the later Middle Ages (fourteenth and fifteenth centuries), the strong identity of local communities with their churches has been emphasized by Ian Duffy, Christopher Haigh, and other scholars. They stress evidence of active participation in scores of particular religious rites and festivals, along with membership in various guilds that conducted the comfortable routine of such activities. The feast of Corpus Christi, a highly popular feast day in the later Middle Ages, for example, celebrated the body of Christ not only in the theological sense of the Eucharist but also in the social sense – the local community as subset of the body of the faithful (though conflict sometimes erupted over issues of status in the ordering of local celebratory processions). The ideal of Corpus Christi could even represent the entire *communitas* of the kingdom as the overarching collectivity of the faithful, composed of all local communities. In this view, enthusiastic participation in all such activities by late medieval parishioners proves the success of the Church in winning devoted lay adherence. The break up of the Church in the sixteenth century is then read by these scholars as a top-down move imposed by the crown for political and (for Henry VIII) personal reasons, forcing change on a conservative laity that was, in fact, satisfied and resistant to the change. The opposing view, long dominant and clearly registered in studies by A. G. Dickens, Margaret Aston, and Anne Hudson, emphasizes longrange dissatisfaction with the existing Church leading to reform impulses that became radical when blocked by clerical authority that was unyielding and likely often venal or corrupt.[12]

These two lines of interpretation may well diverge so widely in part because investigators look closely at religion among different groups of lay folk. The degree of literacy in each group could be a crucial distinguishing feature here, dividing the population. A larger and more rural body tended to have less literacy, to be more dependent on the literacy of the clerics, more conservative, happier with current religious practices and beliefs. A distinctly smaller but significant (and growing) segment of society, likely to be urban and oriented to trade and craft occupations, had greater access to the Bible in English and to written arguments so often critical of current religious practices and beliefs.

The source for such critiques among the laity is well known. Open heresy cropped up in late medieval England that had virtually escaped the broader movement of heretical views that erupted on the twelfthcentury Continent. Modern studies by Anne Hudson and Margaret Aston have emphasized the importance of a group of thinkers centering on John Wyclif, an Oxford scholar whose increasingly radical ideas caused his ouster from the university and brought a formal condemnation by clerical authority. He was forced to retire to a country parish. Wyclif escaped the dread fate that awaited most heretics, largely because of the protection of King Richard's uncle, John of Gaunt, though his body was later exhumed and burnt. The views that he and his disciples espoused lived on, however, and informed beliefs of a group termed Lollards by contemporaries. Determining their numbers and estimating their significance form main lines of historical controversy. What remains more clear is that to consider the Lollards as a unified sect or the single carrier of all impulses to radical reform would be mistaken; the desire for reform seems to have been broader and the ideological content more varied in individuals.

Certainly, the actual course and outcome of these early attempts at radical reform proved significant. In the minds of many conservatives, the Great Rising of 1381 could be blamed on the unsettling effects of radical religious thinking. It was what you get when men like Wyclif are tolerated. By this point in the late fourteenth century medieval chroniclers had identified (and modern scholars have elaborately discussed) radically reformist ideas even among members of elite society. These are the famous "Lollard knights" linked to the court of Richard II (and some of them to Geoffrey Chaucer). Whether or not the Lollard knights formed anything like a group with consistent and common ideas, they suggest some flourishing of radical ideas close to the top of the social pyramid.

But if there was any possibility of an early reformation coming in England – a century and a quarter before Luther in Germany (as posited in a seminal work of Anne Hudson) – these hopes were wrecked by a radical mis-step in the early fifteenth century. Some would-be reformers had apparently pinned their hopes on working through parliament (inclined to be tempted by plans for disendowment of clerical wealth), but Sir John Oldcastle tried to move more swiftly. Apparently failing to convince his royal master, Henry V, he attempted a rising in 1414 that failed miserably and led to his own death. On a broader scale, his attempt led to the association of Lollard heresy with treason. This was a death knell for radical reform: Henry V stood as the orthodox sustainer of the community of the realm backed by the community of the Church. The two structures cooperated and their personnel often overlapped. A statute already passed in his father's reign (De heretico comburendo of 1401) had allowed the burning of heretics at the stake and prohibited unlicensed English language copies of the Bible. Clerical leaders such as William Courtney and Thomas Arundel, archbishops of Canterbury, who frequently held such key royal governmental posts as chancellor, had taken prominent roles in combating Lollardy and in prosecuting Oldcastle. Despite official action against it, Lollardy lasted and produced its tracts for many generations, but any realistic hopes for sweeping change had vanished. The two governing institutions that enforced community (on the foundation of that third matrix of many local communities) had closed ranks. How happy and contented the population of any village, town, or region were to live under this dual governance by the end of the Middle Ages remains a matter for continuing historical debate. A Tudor monarch would further fuse the communities of English Church and kingdom in a dramatic fashion, setting the stage for new controversies.

Notes

1. Geoffrey of Monmouth, *History of the Kings of Britain*, trans. Lewis Thorpe (1984), bk v.8, p. 132.

2. *History of the Kings of Britain*, bk vii.9, p. 124.

3. *History of the Kings of Britain*, p. 225.

4. Layamon, *Brut*, eds. G. L. Brook and R. F. Leslie, 2 vols. EETS 250–77 (Oxford, 1963, 1977), lines 1403–7; trans. Rosamund Allen (New York, 1992).

5. *Havelok*, ed. G. V. Smithers (Oxford, 1987), lines 27–61.

6. See Thomas Hahn and Richard Kaeuper, "Text and Context," *Studies in the Age of Chaucer* 5 (1983), 67–101, at 80–81.

7. E. B. Fryde, *The Great Rising of 1381* (1981), p. 11.

8. G. R. Owst, *Literature and Pulpit in Medieval England: A Neglected Chapter in the History of English Letters and of the English People* (Oxford, 1933, 1961), pp. 210–460.

9. See Hahn and Kaeuper, "Text and Context."

10. Richard W. Kaeuper, "Shareshull, Sir William (1289/90–1370)," *DNB*.

11. In *Robin Hood and Other Outlaw Ballads*, eds. Stephen Knight and Thomas Ohlgren (Kalamazoo, MI, 1996), lines 425–26.

12. See Margaret Aston, *Faith and Fire: Popular and Unpopular Religion, 1350–1600* (1993); A. G. Dickens, *The English Reformation* (1967); Eamon Duffy, *The Stripping of the Altars: Traditional Religion in England, c. 1400–c. 1580* (New Haven, CT, 1992); Christopher Haigh, *English Reformations: Religion, Politics, and Society under the Tudors* (New York, 1993); Anne Hudson, *The Premature Reformation: Wycliffite Texts and Lollard History* (Oxford, 1988); and Miri Rubin, *Corpus Christi: The Eucharist in Late Medieval Culture* (Cambridge, 1991).

5
———

"Celtic" visions of England

Defining "the Celts"

There was no medieval idea of contemporary celticity in the second half of the Middle Ages. Insofar as the word "Celts" might be used, it was in reference to Antiquity, prompted by Classical Latin authors. We must therefore understand that in proceeding under this banner we are imposing our sense of a linguistically defined overarching identity (deriving essentially from the work of Edward Lhuyd [Llwyd], d. 1709) on the cultural politics of an era innocent of that. Britons (Bretons, Cornish, and Welsh) and Gaels (of Irish, Manx, and Scottish sorts) were each aware of a common share of identity defined by heritage; Gaels shared mutually comprehensible language and social mores. But none could or did celebrate their celticity.

Englishness was a more immediate and tangible identity because the kingdom of the English had constituted a political focus since 927, and the Norman Conquest did not call that kingdom into question. Celticity and Englishness are false partners: *die Kelten* and *die Germanen* (the terms of nineteenth-century German scholars seeking the earliest cultures and "races" of Europe) are commensurate, but not useful in the present context. Bretons and Cornish and Irish and Welsh are such comparanda for the English at the beginning of our period, but many Bretons had received French culture and, although the Cornish language and culture endured, Cornwall was nonetheless but a county of England with no realistic hope of escape from the embrace of conquerors whether English or French in culture.

The origins of Scottishness are contested – and it is arguable that perceptions of Scottishness, thus defined, originated in Old Scandinavian usage early in the Viking Age. In Old English, *Scottas* were originally Gaels, as in Latin from the appearance of the word *Scot(t)i* in the late third century. Latin *Scotti* as "Scots" can perhaps be traced from the late tenth century, as also *Scotia*; leaving aside the continuing use of *Scotti* and *Scotia* for Irish and Ireland into the twelfth century, we cannot be certain just when these terms came together with a new political and cultural identity created during 889–900 in north-eastern Britain. Over the course of the later Middle Ages, of all the political focuses in Britain, Scotland, and Scottishness enjoyed the greatest – indeed, almost permanent – mutation. The cultural heritage of the kingdom of the Scots was the most complex of any Insular polity. Nonetheless, for political continuities, where identities were different over time, one might reflect on the campaign to Watling Street, during 939–43, of a Gaelic-Scandinavian army, and that in 1745 which brought a Highland Scottish army to Derby.

Mutual regard

How the English viewed "the Celts"
A useful starting point is Old English *w(e)alh*, plural *w(e)alas* (and adjective *welhisc*), a person of Celtic or Romance speech, a person fit to be a slave: speakers of West Germanic languages made this same distinction elsewhere, notably in what is now Belgium. In Anglo-Saxon England it was necessary to employ a *w(e)alhstod*, "interpreter," if one desired verbal communication. To what extent the early English found it necessary or useful for Britons (the local *W[e]alas*) and British (*welhisc*) identity to survive has long been a matter for debate.

When the kingdom of England was formed in 927 (and called *Saxonia* by a presumptively Frankish secretary in the new monarch's entourage), and for 140 years thereafter, the Anglo-Saxons expected to dominate all Britain – and probably Ireland too, in view of Viking Age politics. Already in the last quarter of the tenth century, the chronicler (and royal *ealdorman*) Æthelweard formulated the idea that what was once called Britain is now called England (*Britannia quae nunc Anglia dicitur*) – and thus originated millennium-long confusion of "English" and "British,"[1] "England" and "Britain"; this idea progressed strongly after the Norman Conquest and reached its apogee in the 1130s in Geoffrey of

Monmouth's epoch-making *History* of "the passage of dominion" (to which we shall return).²

What most Anglo-Normans resisted, however, was any suggestion that they had something in common with contemporary Britons other than some Normanized Bretons; indeed, Geoffrey himself made this very clear. In Wales, whether one's legal identity was Welsh or English was a matter of some consequence – as it had been in England itself and in border regions in the Anglo-Saxon period. This was, of course, something that was also known – as between Scandinavian settlers and native English – in late Anglo-Saxon England, and was of great consequence between "French" and English in the Anglo-Norman period.

There had long been an ecclesiastical element in English life that regarded Gaels as a potential or actual force for disorder. When the Angevin Plantagenet dynasty was inaugurated by King Henry II (1154–89), Ireland began to receive closer attention from the "English" government. Once established as lords of Ireland, Henry's successors found both the Irish natives and the culturally Anglo-French settler population troublesome in varying degrees. In sum, these neighbors, like the Welsh, were barbarians. The Scots, by contrast, occupied a more complex space in the worldview of the inhabitants of post-Conquest England. There was a savage element among them (articulated most clearly by twelfth-century northern English writers, such as Ailred of Rievaulx, and slightly later by the poet of *The Owl and the Nightingale*).³

How Britons viewed the English

When discussing the Insular Celts, one would be unwise ever to attempt a generalization of view, and this as true of Britons as of Gaels. For a substantial period after 1066, Welsh writers referred to the Normans as "French" (*Franci, Ffrainc*). On the other hand, those Bretons who were not Normanized viewed the Normans as just that: *Nor(d)manni*, "vikings."⁴ It may be that those who were Normanized shared Geoffrey of Monmouth's disdain for the Welsh. In some measure Anglo-Norman settlers in Wales went native, but this trend was by no means as pronounced as it was to become in Ireland. One strand of Welsh poetic convention remained vehemently anti-English, calling for the "Saxons" to be ejected from Britain. We can see the emergence over time of a less strident treatment of the English: in the fourteenth century the outstanding poet Dafydd ap Gwilym lost no opportunity to poke fun at English figures in Wales. As in any colonial context, the cross-currents of opinion were complex and numerous: they were already so in the twelfth century.

It is clear that King Arthur occupied a messianic space in British popular mythology, his return being directed at foreign oppression, which chiefly meant the English. Already at the beginning of the twelfth century we see Francophone observers commenting on this aspect of British culture. In the late Middle Ages, the Bretons too found themselves in military conflict with the English and no doubt saw new reason to hope for Arthur's promised role as deliverer from the Saxons.

From the end of the first generation of Norman military expansion into Wales in 1093 (when, according to one contemporary Anglo-Norman observer, "from that day kings ceased to bear rule in Wales," echoed by the more dire remark of a later Welsh chronicler, "then fell the kingdom of the Britons"), we have a passionate Latin lament by a Welsh writer, Rhygyfarch or (in Old Welsh) Ricemarch, for his conquered *patria*, Ceredigion.[5] This dispossessed member of an elite clerical family made the horrors of conquest very clear. That his relatives would, within a generation, recover much of their position is testimony to the shifting fortunes of conquest in Wales, a long process that might not have been anticipated in the fateful year of 1093.

The same decade gives us almost our last view of the Britons of the North, *Cumbras* in Old English, whose kingdom of Strathclyde – extending at its height from the Clyde valley southwards to the Cumberland–Westmorland border – had over the course of the tenth and eleventh centuries been pushed and pulled into an ever-closer relationship with the kingdom of Alba/Scotia. The kingdom of Strathclyde was dismembered by King William Rufus in 1092, with Carlisle and the River Solway made the northern markers of Anglo-Norman rule. But the eleventh-century Brittonic-speaking Strathclyders' voice has not carried into the modern world, and we can only guess at what their views might have been.

How Gaels viewed the English

The point already made about resisting generalization must be reiterated here. In this case there is a need to consider the Scottish dimension of gaelicity, for the interactions of Irish Gaels and Scottish Gaels with persons of English or Anglo-French culture varied a great deal.

Before 1166 there was no significant tradition of anti-Englishness among the Gaels of Ireland. Once the events of 1166–72 had unfolded, such an outlook would develop into a long-lasting tradition: in this, however, the "English" were assimilated to a historically flexible category of "Foreigners," *Gaill*, a conceptual space occupied by vikings from the 790s to the 1170s. It must be remembered that the first "English" king who came to Ireland and claimed rule there was Henry II, the first Angevin king of England, not English and only partly Norman. Again, as in Wales, the first references to these intrusive foreigners were as "French." Although in 1171–72 most of the more than 600 kings in Ireland accepted Henry II's lordship, either directly or through over-kings, in practice no medieval king of England did enough to achieve conquest. Much of the extension of English rule was left to private enterprise. Settlement certainly took place, extensively in some areas. Initially – and eternally, in principle – there was much mutual depiction as barbarians, outlooks caught already rather nicely in the writing of Giraldus Kambrensis (Gerald of Wales). At a practical level, however, local interaction led (in spite of governmentally dictated apartheid) to mutual assimilation: many settlers went comprehensively native, to the outrage of the government in London and its officials in Dublin. In the thirteenth century "degeneracy" became a significant issue and remained so until the full conquest of Ireland in the 1650s. This meant that a rift opened between settlers and government, a problem whose legacy could long be seen in Northern Ireland. Meanwhile, the Gaelic Irish remained typecast as savages.

In Scotland, on the other hand, the proximity of Francophone culture was a reality a century before the Irish had to deal with its politico-military dimension. It is clear that this presented an acute problem for the kings of *Scotia*, even though southern borders were often securely fixed, "the product of a series of compromises between northern rulers, who failed to extend their power as far south as they would have wished, and southern rulers who despite their greater wealth and potentially bigger armies lacked the resources to subjugate and permanently occupy the northern part of the island of Britain."[6] For these Scottish kings, Gaelic in their inherited culture, an additional complication was that "Lothian," the southeastern quadrant of their extended kingdom, was English (North Northumbrian) in speech. In the twelfth century the kings of Scots themselves embraced Francophone culture (initially because of their upbringing as hostage-princes at the Anglo-Norman court), and they famously began to import a new nobility both from continental *Francophonie* and from Anglo-Norman England. The English language, as "Scots," a native vernacular, spread west and north in Scotland from its heartland in Lothian and became a major cultural competitor with Gaelic. The notorious clash of "Highland" and "Lowland" values, Gaelic and Scots, was one result, again with mutual accusations of barbarousness.

Honorary Celts?

How Insular Scandinavians viewed their neighbors

A significant strand in the complex world of Insular ethnicities was the Scandinavian. Until the mid-1260s (and from at least the mid-1050s) the kingdom of Norway extended from the Arctic Circle to the Isle of Man. From 1153 the archbishop of Trondheim enjoyed a papally approved province that included all the "Norwegian" territories in what is now Scotland, as well as the Isle of Man. There had been a Scandinavian presence in the region since at least the 790s.

The Hebrides before the Viking Age were divided between Gaelic- and Pictish-speaking peoples. The line of division probably ran between the Inner Hebrides (Gaelic) and the Outer Hebrides (Pictish). With Argyll, the British mainland territory facing the Inner Hebrides, and a modest slice of northeastern Ireland, the latter islands comprised the early medieval Gaelic overkingdom of Dál Riata. The Inner Hebrides were settled, in varying density, by vikings whose descendants in the next generation were to be bilingual in Gaelic and Scandinavian. The same phenomenon can be observed in limited areas of Ireland associated with Scandinavian settlement. Initially, from the mid-ninth century, these bicultural products of the Viking Age were known in Gaelic as *Gall-Goídil*, "Foreigner-Gaels." That compound became, in the Gaelic fashion, a territorial name: thus, while originally it probably had a broad application around the western coast of Scotland, eventually it settled on the area of southwestern Scotland now known by the derivative Scots name Galloway (the counties of Wigtown and Kirkcudbright).

This bilingual culture was exported by vikings from the Hebrides (for which another Viking Age Gaelic name was *Inse Gall*, "The Islands of the Foreigners") in the earlier tenth century to Galloway, Cumbria (southern Strathclyde), Man, and (most remarkably) to western Normandy (the Cotentin peninsula in particular), where onomastic evidence has been the key to its identification. I have argued elsewhere that the Normans were heirs to a viking-view of the Gaels (of Ireland at least) that characterized them as uniquely lazy and libidinous.[7] We should no more generalize about Scandinavian or vikings' views than about those of Insular Celts (and for much the same reasons), but it is worth reminding ourselves that Scandinavians arrived in the Celtic-speaking world (as generally across Europe) as raiders, conquerors, and settlers, used to the advantages and self-confidence that accompanied successful aggression. There is some reason (including Old Norse literary works of the thirteenth century) to think that this attitude persisted as long as Scandinavian armies sought to enforce their leaders' will in Britain and Ireland – that is, to the mid-thirteenth century.

La Francophonie d'Angleterre

"English" and "French" vernaculars in the "Celtic" west and north

The oldest extant Scottish law-text, *Leges inter Brettos et Scottos* (this Latin title is for various reasons exceedingly difficult to translate convincingly and unambiguously) was written in French, probably early in the twelfth century. It contains English, Cumbric (Brittonic), and Gaelic technical terms. Here is a reminder of part of the ethnic and linguistic complexity of Scotland, culturally the most diverse of England's Insular neighbors.

It is essential to remember that French (and Flemish and Scandinavian) continued to be spoken, read, and written in the "English" colonies in the thirteenth century: linguistic and literary interaction with the local native languages and a translation literature were the result. For the Celtic-speaking countries, England was an important source of French culture from 1066 to the end of the Middle Ages. It was not the only one, however.

While the universities of Oxford and Cambridge attracted students from across Britain and Ireland, those in the Celtic-speaking countries, whether natives or colonists, who were able to seek a university education might (and did) take themselves to Paris or an increasing choice of regional French centers of higher learning. Scottish students – both before and after the fifteenth-century foundation of three domestic universities (St. Andrews in 1412, Glasgow in 1451, and Old Aberdeen in 1495) – studied in numerous French universities as well as at Leuven, Copenhagen (founded 1475), in western and northeastern Germany, at Cracow in southern Poland, in northern Italy, and in Rome.

French culture

Two recent British historians have seen the expansion of English power into the Celtic-speaking countries as aspects of much larger historical processes. Robert Bartlett has written of a process of colonization in which the successful peoples of Europe were engaged during the central Middle Ages. John Gillingham, in a long and continuing series of articles, now partially collected, has addressed many aspects of the question of civility and barbarity in the same period: the slave-owning societies of the Islands (and Scandinavia) were confronted by a Continental (and particularly French) outlook enjoying some different values that it regarded as more civil, more modern, more Christian.[8] Both English and "Celts" on the receiving end of the civilizing mission may have had reason to suspect hypocrisy. But the victors write the histories.

Within a century of 1066 the new elite, colonial though its origins were, was beginning to call itself English, and the "Celts" now had to associate this civilizing mission with the English. It would be possible to write Anglo-Celtic cultural relations in the later Middle Ages in terms of the spread of French culture and Celtic reactions to that. For the immediate purpose, two twelfth-century authors are of particular interest.

Geoffrey of Monmouth (Galfridus Monemutensis)

The Breton cleric, Geoffrey of Monmouth – presumably descended from a settler established in a post-Conquest Breton colony in southeastern Wales – passed his entire recorded career in the vicinity of Oxford. He died as bishop (1152–55) of Llanelwy/St. Asaph in northeastern Wales but almost certainly had been unable to visit or govern his see. This honorary Welshman made probably the largest single contribution to Anglo-Celtic cultural relations of any writer of the second half of the Middle Ages. If his Arthur inspired the young King Henry II, as has been argued, then that contribution was rapidly influential at the highest political levels. In the larger context of orally transmitted *matière de Bretagne* – the "matter of Britain" introducing persons, places, and events of British Britain – Geoffrey's work was highly influential too in European vernacular literature. His *History* had a major impact on Latin and vernacular historiography throughout Britain for the remainder of the Middle Ages. If (as scholars thought for much of the twentieth century) Geoffrey's *History* conveyed a message that the Normans were the heirs of the ancient Britons in their domination of the island of Britain, that was implicitly rejected by the "English" elite of the late twelfth century. It was only subsequently revived (before the Tudor period) in the context of specific Anglo-"Celtic" political interactions of the later Middle Ages.

We owe to Geoffrey three works, all in Latin: *The Prophecy of Merlin*, subsequently incorporated into his *History*, his *magnum opus* in eleven books, on the affairs of the Britons from their first peopling of the island of Britain until their loss of dominion in the 680s and the definitive capture of sovereignty by the English, with Æthelstan's creation of his English monarchy and claim to all Britain, in the 920s. Geoffrey's last work, a *Life of Merlin* in verse, returned him to his first literary subject but in a very different mode: this last enjoyed relatively little medieval circulation, unlike the other two, which were bestsellers.[9]

Geoffrey's vision was a British one, a lengthy and often glorious history of this eponymous people. It had the external form of a Latin history. It contained all the stuff of romance. Its politics have proved endlessly contentious, even after the decisive expositions by J. S. P. Tatlock, given final form in 1950. Geoffrey was one of relatively few medieval authors who had read Gildas' *admonitiuncula* – his "little warning," as with considerable understatement Gildas calls his "letter" on *The Ruin of Britain* (a non-authorial but apt title).[10] None who read this work escaped its message, that the Britons through their inherited addiction to sin were heading for destruction unless moral re-armament could be achieved. Those who came after, beginning with Bede, knew that the Britons had failed the test and that the English had destroyed their civilization and seized control of much of the island. Geoffrey's vision comprehended Gildas' in most of its elements. But the Britons' glorious (pre-)history set forth by Geoffrey was entirely novel. This was defended by a rampart of a characteristically twelfth-century sort, a vernacular source procured from Brittany by Geoffrey's colleague, Walter, archdeacon of Oxford, who alone owned it, and which Geoffrey faithfully rendered into Latin. This source was a phantom. The content was as mendacious as the authority. The *History* is full of outrageous historical jokes, developed in cheerful quasi-Goliardic irreverence by exploiting gaps in existing literature. Geoffrey closed his work by thumbing his nose at the leading Insular historians of his generation. He may even have arranged for one of them, Henry, archdeacon of Huntingdon, to encounter a copy of it at Le Bec in January 1139; a letter by Henry survives, expressing wonder at its narrative.[11]

Geoffrey catapulted British identity to the center of the British and Anglo-Norman historical, literary, ecclesiastical, and courtly stages as the Anglo-Norman world descended into a fifteen-year civil war. When a new stability was achieved through a treaty (1153) that established Henry Plantagenet as the royal heir, soon to succeed and long to rule (1154–89), the court became a famous literary center. One of King Stephen's last acts was to award Geoffrey an unattainable, perhaps even a joke, bishopric in Wales. But Geoffrey's *oeuvre* was already bestselling and his place in literary history assured. Thanks to him, the ancient Britons, King Arthur, Merlin, and much else achieved such celebrity: Geoffrey's game was won in England!

Geoffrey's *History* also contained many political messages for his contemporaries, not least about the evils of civil war – a Gildasian theme. His patron, Henry II's uncle, Robert, earl of Gloucester, deserves study in this context: through him, Geoffrey had access to a "legitimist" Anglo-Norman political culture that was strong in south Wales and southwestern England, and Robert's own court attracted a literary circle.

Geoffrey's vision of the English was, in British terms, clear-sighted and partly conventional. Where, in terms of Brittonic literary tradition, it was unconventional, was in his view of the Britons as politically and (once Christianized) even morally businesslike. Over time, the English had taken Gildas' message to heart: this was manifested in the kingdom of England and in their aspirations to rule all Britain, a project since brought significantly closer to fruition by Norman successes in relation to Wales and Scotland. But the Normans were now the ones who must pay heed to Gildas – or, instead, to Geoffrey of Monmouth.

Geoffrey's vision of the passage of dominion of Britain was contested in his own day, as was superbly demonstrated by R. William Leckie in 1981.[12] The power of Geoffrey's historiography was such that it became dominant in Wales, albeit with some of the adjustments necessary to render it less toxic to thirteenth-century Welsh sensibilities. Geoffrey was famously rude about Welsh degeneracy from ancient British standards, corrupted by association with the English; it was the Bretons who had retained the governing ideals of a glorious past. Welsh adaptations and translations went some way to neutralize this, as well as to adjust Geoffrey's characters and narratives to the conventions of Welsh literature. What is very striking is that the principal vernacular chronicle of medieval Welsh history begins in the 680s, when the Britons lost the rule of the island: the medieval title given to this work, which first extended to the effective loss of Welsh independence in 1282, was *Brenhinoedd y Saeson*, "The Kings of the English" – in other words, this was a historical account of the period in which the English were the rising power that finally extinguished British (viz., Welsh) independence. The author of this text, writing about 1300, had fully received Geoffrey's overarching historiographical message. Geoffrey's vision of the English included their definition and command of a final era of native British history.

Giraldus Kambrensis

We have already encountered "Gerald of Wales" (1146–1223). That name was but one of this remarkable chameleon's self-identifications. He was a churchman who found a cause. He became a writer who could not restrain his creative urge or his more turgid second and third thoughts. His was a mighty ego. And yet, apart from his own writings (which are voluminous, even though some works are lost), there is little trace of his life in external contemporary record.[13]

Giraldus emerged from a bicultural family of the highest rank in colonial Wales. His mother was the daughter of a Welsh princess who had become a mistress of Henry I, his father and grandfather were Norman barons. He was early destined for the Church and received the best Parisian university education. While he presented himself as a reformer, his family connections (one might unkindly speak of nepotism) delivered him office within the diocese of St. Davids. In him we find a classic subject for post-colonial analysis. He was self-reflexive, interrogating his different or competing identities and their implications, even laying out opposing blueprints of how Anglo-Norman and Welsh high politics should be played. He sought to sell "the west" as an exotic and interesting Other, much preferable to the fascination with "the east" (whose characteristics he portrayed as deeply unattractive) so widespread in an age of crusading.

Topographia Hibernica, "The Topography of Ireland," was his first and most masterly work (albeit progressively degraded in subsequent editions). While it has been reviled by Irish readers since at least the sixteenth century for its colonialist attitude, he showed much sympathy with the Irish while, nonetheless, finding them exotic, strange, and in many respects primitive. Through him we learn something of Irish perceptions of the invaders. His epigrammatic summations could be masterly: "Given only to leisure, and devoted only to laziness, they think that the greatest pleasure is not to work, and the greatest wealth is to enjoy liberty. This people is a barbarous people ... Their natural qualities are excellent. But almost everything acquired is deplorable." Giraldus' Norman-Welsh family was heavily involved in the first wave of conquest and settlement in Ireland, becoming major founding figures in the new colony. Insofar as their stake in Ireland depended in part on grants from an Irish overking in whose interest they had taken up arms, they could not afford wholeheartedly to call into question the rights of the native elite. At the same time there is no gainsaying the bloody and desperate ruthlessness of their campaigning in Ireland. Giraldus reported a conversation with the archbishop of Cashel, Tatheus (Muirges Ua hÉnna), in which Giraldus made the hostile observation that "no one had ever in that kingdom won the crown of martyrdom in defence of the church of God." Acknowledging what his rubric calls "a sly reply," Giraldus wrote: "the archbishop gave a reply which cleverly got home – although it did not rebut my point: 'It is true,' he said, 'that although our people are very barbarous, uncivilized, and savage, nevertheless they have always paid great honor and reverence to churchmen, and they have never put out their hands against the saints of God. But now a people has come to the kingdom which knows how, and is accustomed, to make martyrs. From now on, Ireland will have its martyrs, just as other countries.'"[14]

It may be argued that Giraldus provided the Francophone and Anglophone worlds (overlapping as they did) with the very prism through which they looked at the Gaels for the rest of the Middle Ages. Indeed, Protestant Britain maintained the colonialist vision of the Irish long thereafter. In the process, many of that shrewd but conflicted observer's perceptions have been rendered toxic. No medieval British writer can provoke a more vehement reaction in modern Ireland: he nevertheless deserves close study. It is part of the complexity of the colonial picture that some of his writing was translated into medieval Irish, but probably for the benefit of "degenerate" colonial families.

Civility and incivility

Civility: from Gerald of Wales to the Elizabethans
Modern scholars have detected civility – and the want of it – as a theme of Anglo-Celtic contacts in the later Middle Ages and the early Modern period. The "civility" of the English (as inheritors of French culture) and the "incivility" of the Britons and Gaels (the Scots – or at least their leaders – were rendered civil by effective politico-military action in the

late eleventh century) is an opposition less easy to perceive from the Celtic side. Many Britons and Gaels were in varying degrees "anglicized" by the presence of French-speakers in their midst, but, as I have already noted, many settlers became "degenerate" (as the Britons of Wales had done, in Geoffrey's *History*, through contact with the English!) by virtue of adopting the mores of their Celtic neighbors in the new colonies. Relatively little theorizing of this process was achieved until the Tudor age; but Giraldus Kambrensis may be held to have made a start in his self-analysis, writing which was a contribution both to anthropology and to autobiography – as well as a gift to modern post-colonial studies. However, core–periphery differences, old-fashioned prejudice against one's neighbors, and specific complaints – whether ecclesiastical, political, or social, but all deemed to be moral – contrived to catch the Welsh, Irish, and (eventually) Scottish Highlanders and (western) Islanders (both groups of whom were Gaelic-speakers in this period) in the prism of incivility.

Prophetic visions: politics and prophecy

The Insular Celtic literatures, both vernacular and Latin, are from an early date full of political prophecy. One significant slice of Brittonic prophecy was anti-English. On the other hand, Old English literature seems largely devoid of such prophecy (although the same cannot be said of pre-Conquest Anglo-Latin writing). The later medieval situation in England was very different from the earlier. The medium of transference (for this is what seems to have happened) was "The Prophecy of Merlin" at the center of Geoffrey's *History*. It is, therefore, somewhat ironic that *Prophetia Merlini* was based on non-Celtic sources. Nevertheless, Geoffrey's work seems to have encouraged pursuit of Welsh texts of that sort and to have validated the vigorous development of the form in English writing (whether in English, French, or Latin) in the later Middle Ages.

It is already apparent in tenth-century Welsh literature that one aspect of such prophecy was the expectation or hope of return of messianic figures, notably Arthur, a belief held by Britons of Brittany, Cornwall, and Wales. This was, for example, mocked by William of Malmesbury in 1125.[15] It was already a bone of contention between Bretons and French. The idea grew with the reception of Arthurian legend in the literary mainstream and may be held to have coalesced with the Grail legend, many of whose elements were Gaelic in origin.

Almost nothing survives of Breton (and Cornish) literature of the central Middle Ages, but we may be sure that it, with Welsh and probably Gaelic literature, had a profound impact on that of Francophone Europe during the twelfth century in particular, sometimes directly, sometimes by mediation. *La matière de Bretagne* put a new spotlight on the Britons. Perhaps the myth of return no longer seemed wholly absurd, but it was still politically dangerous. The name of Arthur was absorbed into the Plantagenet royal dynasty, though not entirely happily.

By the beginning of the thirteenth century, Welsh *littérateurs* in particular had learnt to respond with enthusiastic engagement, in reception of Geoffrey's *History* and of French-language Arthurian romance. Cross-cultural interaction of other related literary forms would follow, notably flyting. There is much reason to think that, in Wales at least, there was a market for foreign stimulus, particularly where that might be held to validate native literary themes and genres.

Documentation and justification

In the written forms of justification of rights, the traffic was almost wholly one way, from Anglo-French to Celtic, during this period. Celtic antiquity might be used, as at Glastonbury Abbey and (most spectacularly) in the creation of the bishopric of Llandaf, to justify a claim to jurisdiction or property or pilgrimage. It is worth noting, however, that in the case of Llandaf the stated provocation to action was the wreckage created by Anglo-Norman colonial lords in south Wales.

The work of Gildas or the prophetic utterances of Merlin might be quoted with serious political and historiographical intent. The lost Celtic source might (as most spectacularly by Geoffrey of Monmouth) be invoked in history or romance or (perhaps especially) hagiography.

For the Celts, however, the vision of England could only be a modernizing one, sometimes welcome, sometimes not, and as a source of invasion. Geoffrey of Monmouth treated modernity (as he treated almost everything) with ambiguity, but the twelfth-century Western embrace of novelty contained further implications for the "Celts." Their elite culture justified itself by constant appeal to ancient tradition. Their vision of the outside world, and especially of England, could thenceforth only be of a species of globalization, a process of relentless change driven from outside. The Anglo-French might also appeal to long-established rights and customs, but these would characteristically be cast in specific and professionalized documentary forms. Authentication was therefore of a different order. When that culture arrived in the Celtic world some misunderstanding and mutual incomprehension were inevitable, even where (as in Ireland) there had been some penetration by "European" documentary forms before invasion, domination, and settlement.

What all these cultures shared was the use of hagiographic narrative to justify their local saints and their churches' property and status. In Welsh saints' Lives in Latin, in versions of the eleventh and twelfth centuries, we meet local saints of Morgannwg and Tegeingl (in southeast and northeast Wales, respectively) as defenders of their lands and rights by spectacular miracles directed against Anglo-Saxons, Scandinavians, and French/Normans, as well as natives. It is doubtful that these stories were efficacious against Normans in the earlier years of conquest, but attitudes on both sides could change: while one Norman knight's wife was rendered infertile for sacrilege against the female martyr Gwenfrewy – "For it was right that [she] should thereafter be encompassed by mocking and derision, jeering and opprobrium" – the author of the closing chapter of the *Life of St. Illtud* could display his sympathy with *Angligenis et Normannigenis ciuibus* ("English-born and Norman-born citizens") rather than with the north Welsh.

Exoticism and the cult of saints

Norman invaders of England and the Celtic-speaking countries found the local saints unattractively exotic – the "uncouthness" of their names was much mentioned – and attempted either suppression of their cults or an *interpretatio franca* or both. However, attitudes soon changed, and native cults were embraced but thus transformed. There has been some study of the two-way spread of saints' cults in the Insular world in this period, but little evidence has been found for the adoption of post-Roman foreign saints in Gaeldom before the Friars reached Ireland in the mid-thirteenth century. Even so, the cults of native saints proved to be tenacious, although the literary evidence is thin, especially in the Brittonic world, until, and beyond, the later end of our period. Celtic saints were, however, adopted and mutated in England, and it is clear that (as in the pre-Conquest period) the results sometimes attracted pilgrims – both "Celts" and others.

Nevertheless, one aspect of the exotic incivility of Irish saints was remembered wherever Giraldus' *Topographia Hibernica* was read. Book II of the work closed with a chapter entitled, "That the saints of this country seem to be of a vindictive cast of mind." "This seemed to me a thing to be noticed, that, just as the men of this country are during this mortal life more prone to anger and revenge than any other people, so in eternal death the saints of this land who have been elevated by their merits are more vindictive than the saints of any other region."

Education

For inhabitants of the Celtic-speaking countries, access to a university education was to be had elsewhere in Christendom, whether in England (first at Oxford, but from the thirteenth century also at Cambridge), or in France or Italy – or, later, in the Low Countries, in Germany, Denmark, or Poland. Only in the fifteenth century did an Insular alternative open, at St. Andrews in Scotland in 1412 (and subsequently at Glasgow and Old Aberdeen). All this was in principle ecclesiastical education.

Another type of education for "Celts" might be had through child-hostageship in England (or in the varying Continental territories of the kings of England). This is first seen clearly (after the Norman Conquest) in relation to Scotland, when children of King Mael Colaim III (1058–93) – a troublesome serial invader of northern England – began to be taken from Scotland. This brought about nothing less than a cultural revolution in Scottish governance and elite self-perception, led by Scottish royals raised under the auspices of the Anglo-Norman court. Similar policies caused many Welsh royals to be brought up in England in the twelfth and thirteenth centuries, although we see more examples of (or represented as) imprisonment of rather older royals. Female members of Welsh royal dynasties could be treated as wards of the king of England and given suitable marriages. In time the same would be true of the Irish experience. Except during the Scottish Wars of Independence, however, there was a qualitative difference in Anglo-Scottish relations: while the kings of England always considered themselves to be the lords of the kings of Scotland, rulers in Wales and Ireland (neither of which countries had a monarchy) were clearly always much smaller fry and might be viewed as enjoying fewer rights. Certainly, in the early Modern period Irish royals educated in noble households in England were collectively a major transmitter of modern and "civilized" ideas to Ireland.

Law

All the Insular peoples had highly developed legal systems and thought by 1066. The various Insular Celtic legal cultures reflected societies that differed fundamentally from the West Germanic in two principal respects: Celtic societies either did not know or had only recently come to include nucleated settlement; and they did not for the most part know executive kingship. Anglo-Celtic interaction before 1066 had increasingly made the Welsh and Scots sensible of the power of English kings. When – after the involvement of Anglo-French kings in both those countries and in Ireland – the "Celts" had tasted a newer and perhaps more dangerous "English" power, both royal and baronial, they realized what savagery and mischief might come from those claiming to be more civilized. In this regard, we have already encountered the lament of Rhygyfarch ap Sulien for Ceredigion. Giraldus Kambrensis reported an Irish ecclesiastic's pointed comment on the same experience.

While Welsh and, in Ireland, Gaelic legal systems remained intact, they became those of oppressed subjects in conquered territories. Eventually, some natives would petition the king for grants of English law. In the territory of the king of Scots, English law had had a profound impact in the twelfth and thirteenth centuries, without a conquest ever taking place. In Wales we see the native law responding to the challenges of contemporary European jurisprudence; there is some reason to think that some similar developments occurred in Gaeldom, but the matter has barely been studied. The resulting paradox, a familiar colonial one, is that, just as English power could be seen as oppressive and arbitrary, England was also (with the universities and the papacy) a source of new legal ideas that provoked thought among native "Celtic" elites.

Concepts of authority

It follows that at the start of our period concepts of authority were very different in England and among the "Celts." This is not to say that divine authority was denied or that Holy Writ had a lesser status in either type of society. But expression of legal, or academic, or ecclesiastical, or royal authority could be couched in very different forms. The learned elites of Gaeldom, in particular, could express themselves in highly technical language in modes of thought that must have caused astonishment to colonial administrators. Authority came from very ancient right: "the backward look" is the phrase (it was Frank O'Connor's) often used to characterize it.

The particularist character of the Insular Celtic societies caused foreigners to be regarded both as one more complication in a particularist, Balkanesque political landscape or as a major threat to one's civilization, depending on one's particular angle of vision. The latter would lead to appeals to the papacy (and even other European powers) for succor. We find such appeals from Wales already in the twelfth century and from Ireland beginning in the thirteenth century. The Scottish Church and the Scottish monarchy both found reasons in the second half of the Middle Ages to appeal to Rome for protection from English embrace.

Narratives of "Anglo-Celtic" relations?

After Geoffrey of Monmouth, Ailred of Rievaulx, and Giraldus Kambrensis, only "national" narratives are found in the Insular zone, one might say. This would not be wholly accurate – and one must always be alert to the importance of local histories – but the statement points up a problem that does not seem to be resolved in historiography or in political or historical sociology until the Early Modern period. If the English were (by being a colonial power) so very important to the Insular Celts throughout the later Middle Ages, why do they not loom larger in "Celtic" historiography in the period? Is "the backward look" a sufficient explanation?

Is it the case that among the Britons the centuries since 700 were merely more of the same and that everything that needed to be said could be expressed in terms of the passage of dominion in the fifth to seventh centuries? In the second half of the eighth century (and without any obvious major territorial change) *Clawdd Offa*, "Offa's Dyke," became the effective cultural boundary, the eastern limit of Welsh law, which applied for the rest of the Middle Ages in spite of numerous political shifts. Wales' land boundary had, in other words, been defined forever by the English.

In Britain, every historical writer after the reception of Geoffrey of Monmouth might employ a sub-Galfridian discourse. Geoffrey had carried almost everyone with him in the essentials of his British narrative. Anglo-Scottish relations might easily be expressed in these terms, and from both sides, although the Scots added a dose of Gaelic national origin-legend to flavor the historiographic stew. For the late medieval Bretons, for whom the English became a troublesome enemy, the story (while Galfridian) was different again.

In Ireland the narrative was very different. As one of conquest, it was written in Latin and French by the invaders, and with some fanfare, but only at the beginning of the process. The detailed narrative record is to be found in annalistic chronicles, both native and colonial, concerned with specifics rather than the sweep of history. In Irish, traditional tales and pseudohistories were rewritten – and in them *Gaill* had their place, particularly in the stories of Fionn mac Cumhaill – throughout the later Middle Ages: it is arguable (but difficult to demonstrate) that these were intended to be read in relation to contemporary issues.

Geography, government, and identity

The problem of "British history," medieval and modern
For the sixteenth and seventeenth centuries, "The British History" was that bequeathed by Geoffrey of Monmouth and controverted by Polydore Vergil in the early sixteenth century. When, in 1799, the English historian Sharon Turner ventured to use medieval Welsh poetry in writing Anglo-Saxon history (almost certainly the first English scholar to do so), he was treated to a barrage of criticism by those who believed all "British" (and probably "Celtic") writing about history to be pseudohistorical. His response in 1803 was a brilliantly polemical monograph, which should remain required reading for all English historians and which demonstrated his mastery of the Welsh sources.[16]

Nevertheless, the English tradition of historiography remained determinedly contemptuous of Celtic sources until in the second half of the twentieth century a succession of scholars of "Celtic" ethnicity but with credibility among English historians – G. W. S. Barrow, R. R. Davies, and Brendan Bradshaw (and more recently Robert Bartlett) – forced "the British problem" into English historical debate. This has various dimensions: contemplation of medieval concepts of "Britain"; taking British history as a whole; problematizing Britain in relation to Ireland rather than the other way round; and, indeed, problematizing England as the central or sole player in medieval Insular culture (as Scott Waugh's chapter in this volume also notes).

The problem of a narrowly Anglocentric modern historiographical tradition was mirrored by an introverted traditionalism among writers on Welsh history who found it impossible to shed the Galfridian heritage and, indeed, to restrain themselves from adding new fantasies to it. While the writing of evidence-based history of ancient and medieval Celtic Britain began before 1900, it was only in the twentieth century that it started to dominate. Even so, the learned A. W. Wade-Evans (1875–1964) remained unrepentantly attached to a version of the medieval "British history," while some students of Welsh literature still seem reluctant to shake off related delusions. And Breton historiography is yet flirting (to put it no more strongly) with Galfridianism.

The legacy of Geoffrey of Monmouth, some 850 years after his death, remains astonishing. The creative genius that he manifested has complicated the understanding of British history, not least by seeming to provide something for all national players. Yet it was he who had the pan-British vision, even though its ultimate basis was ethnic. His work provided one foundation for the writing of the history of Britain in the later Middle Ages. (Although Ireland played its part in his great narrative, the Irish historiographic tradition never succumbed to Galfridianism.) But it would be a brave scholar who would say what Geoffrey's "Celtic(?) vision of England" might have been.

"Great Britain" and "The British Isles"

When Great Britain (viz., the island of Britain) was first so called is a matter of uncertainty – perhaps in the eleventh century in a forged document attributed to St. Dunstan (d. 988). In the twelfth century the longer-standing differentiation of "Greater Britain" (*Britannia Maior*) and "Lesser Britain" (*Britannia Minor*, viz. Brittany, a name of relatively recent application in English to Continental *Bretagne*, *Breizh*) became popular, and it was the former of these that was at length shortened to "Great Britain." This term was not, as is widely believed in the "Celtic" countries, a British (or, indeed, English) assertion of self-aggrandizement. It does reflect the important place that the concept of "Britain" had in British/Brittonic, Scottish, and English political thought from the Middle Ages: it was repeatedly transformed – in 1536, 1603, 1707, and 1801 – by the various unions with the "Celtic" countries.

"The British Isles," on the other hand, first appears as a descriptor in ancient Greek ethnography to mean the sum of Ireland, Britain, and their lesser islands; it is not impossible that it represented a wider ancient Celtic understanding of Britishness than is immediately apparent in later sources. For obvious reasons, "The British Isles" as a concept has been anathema to Irish nationalist opinion in modern times. As a result of failure of British educational tradition it is now unintelligible, in its received meaning, to British youth who take it to mean merely Britain and its minor islands, finding it incomprehensible that Ireland should be included.

These terms indicate how *imperium* and English (and ultimately British) power have become indelibly imprinted on the political consciousness of the Insular Celtic peoples. The visible origins of a notion of an English-dominated Britain lie in the mid-seventh century (and may be argued to have arisen from Gaelic inspiration); they grew further in the rhetoric of English monarchical government from the mid-tenth century. When the Normans became heirs to that government, they (and perhaps at first their churchmen, as also in the seventh century) rapidly came to think that they too deserved Insular *imperium*.

Nation, state, and big government

England was the first nation-state of the European Middle Ages, setting a trend that reached its apogee (and perhaps its downfall) in the period 1789–1945. Since the sixteenth century, historical writing has been conceived largely in terms of nation-states; failed nation-states and nations without states were increasingly written out of history. All of the Celtic-speaking countries come into this category. Only Ireland has succeeded in forcing its way into the club of nation-states, with nationalists in the others wishing to emulate its success (if without the same amount of grief). Scotland was an independent nation from its creation (at contested dates) to 1603, albeit with periods under English dominance: it is, nonetheless, in the terms stated above, a failed nation-state. The result of such history, in which the Celtic-speaking nations were subsumed into England (or Britain) or France, has been to encourage "Celtic" writers to attempt to cast their (ancient and) medieval histories in terms of successful nations with either monarchies or (on the German model) imperial overkingdoms. This should be a perfect subject for post-colonial analysis, but weaknesses of post-colonial theory and the perceived political power of the nation-state model have inhibited such development. This latter model is a highly relevant constraint on an effective analysis of the medieval "Celtic" cultures and an understanding of medieval "Celtic" visions of England and the English.[17]

Notes

1. *The Chronicle of Æthelweard*, ed. and trans. A. Campbell (Edinburgh, 1962).
2. Geoffrey of Monmouth, *The History of the Kings of Britain*, ed. Michael D. Reeve, trans. Neil Wright (Woodbridge, 2007).
3. Aelred of Rievaulx, "Relatio de Standardo," in *Chronicles of the Reigns of Stephen, Henry II and Richard I*, 3, ed. Richard Howlett, 179–99, Roll Series 82 (1886); trans. Marsha L. Dutton and Jane Patricia Freeland, *The Historical Works* (Kalamazoo, MI, 2005), pp. 245–70; *The Owl and the Nightingale*, ed. and trans. Neil Cartlidge (Exeter, 2001), lines 907–12.
4. I use the lower case spelling to indicate that this is a common noun not an ethnic term; see David Dumville, "Images of the Viking in Eleventh-century Latin Literature," in

Michael Herren, C. J. McDonough, and Ross G. Arthur (eds.), *Latin Culture in the Eleventh Century*, Publications of *The Journal of Medieval Latin* 5 (Turnhout, 2002), 1:250–63, at 250 n. 2, reprinted in his *Celtic Essays, 2001–2007*, 2 vols. (Aberdeen, 2007).

5. Michael Lapidge, "The Welsh–Latin Poetry of Sulien's Family," *Studia Celtica* 8/9 (1973–4), 68–106, at 88–93. For the Anglo-Norman and Welsh chroniclers ("John of Worcester" and the Brenhinaedd y Saeson, respectively), see *R. R. Davies, *First English Empire* (2000), pp. 4–8.

6. Geoffrey W. S. Barrow, "The Anglo-Scottish Border: Growth and Structure in the Middle Ages," in Wolfgang Haubrichs and Reinhard Schnider (eds.), *Grenzen und Grenzregionen*, Veröffentlichungen der Kommission für Saarländische Landesgeschichte und Volksforschung 22 (Saarbrücken, 1993), 197–211, at 197.

7. Dumville, "Images of the Viking."

8. See *Bartlett, *The Making of Europe* (1993), *Gillingham, *The English in the Twelfth Century* (2000).

9. As well as the Latin text and English translation by Reeve and Wright, see also the English only edition by Michael A. Faletra, *The History of the Kings of Britain: Geoffrey of Monmouth* (Peterborough, Ontario, 2008), which includes a translation of *The Life of Merlin* and other materials.

10. Gildas, *The Ruin of Britain and other Works*, ed. and trans. Michael Winterbottom (Chichester, 1978).

11. Partly translated in Faletra, *History*, pp. 287–88.

12. See *Leckie, *The Passage of Dominion* (1981).

13. See *Bartlett, *Gerald of Wales* (1982).

14. Giraldus Kambrensis [Gerald of Wales], *The History and Topography of Ireland*, trans. John O'Meara (1982), pp. 115–16.

15. William of Malmesbury, *Gesta Regum Anglorum: The History of the English Kings*, ed. and trans. R. A. B. Mynors, R. M. Thomson and M. Winterbottom, 2 vols. (Oxford, 1998–9), 1:520–21.

16. Sharon Turner, *A Vindication of the Genuineness of the Antient British poems of Aneurin, Taliesin, Llywarch Hen and Merdhin, with specimens of their poems* (1803), handily available on Google books.

17. I should like to express my gratitude to the Editor and to Dr. Clare Downham for their perceptive and helpfully encouraging readings of drafts of this chapter.

6
_____

The idea of sanctity and the uncanonized life of Margery Kempe

Although medievalists sometimes use the word "sanctity" as a synonym for "sainthood," people in the later Middle Ages rarely did. Rather, Middle English *saunctite*, like the Old French *saintete* and the still earlier Christian Latin *sanctitas*, tends to have a more general meaning, suggesting a state of blessedness or a righteous manner of living rather than canonized sainthood in a strict sense. In a story from the Middle English translation of the *Gesta Romanorum*, for instance, in which a young woman's supernatural ability to create a shirt from a tiny piece of cloth is moralized as the Incarnation, Mary's womb is described as having undergone "sanctificacion" (*sanctificatio*).[1] In this instance, the use of the word "sanctity" highlights Mary's body itself, as the vessel of creation and a site of blessedness, rather than drawing attention to her place in the roster of saints.

More common still was the sense of "sanctity" as lived righteousness. In *Piers the Ploghman's Crede* (*c.* 1390), one of the friars interviewed by the naive narrator describes "the pure Apostells life" that he and his brothers claim to imitate: they "suen hem in saunctite, and suffren well harde/ ... and in wo lybbeth/In penaunce and poverte, and precheth the puple,/By ensample of oure life."[2] Despite the poem's satirical nature, *saunctite*'s meaning here connotes a way of life in which actions accord with spiritual ideals. In these medieval works, sanctity is a lifestyle and not, in a narrow sense, sainthood.

Medieval religious culture resists description by means of precise and neatly subdivided categories that distinguish the canonized holy from all others. This is true even though the papal process of canonization had become, during the fourteenth-century Avignon papacy, highly regulated and elaborately judicial.[3] Saintliness was perceived as part of a much wider notion of "sanctity," itself best understood as having multiple dimensions, held together by the fundamental sense that the sanctified person both embodies and practices holiness. This dual quality of late medieval sanctity, as involving embodiment as well as practice, produces a tension between "blessedness" that comes from the outside, through the divine, and "righteousness" that is enacted, pursued, and perfected through one's life.

Margery Kempe's *Book*, written in the first half of the fifteenth century, was not widely known in its own period, but it may be explored as a key site for the elements of late medieval sanctity.[4] It is precisely because Margery Kempe fails to become a saint that we can see in her *Book* how the tension between recognition of blessedness coming from the divine alongside the human agent's pursuit of righteousness was represented.[5] The institutional apparatus of canonization, which demands that lives conform to certain patterns, did not exert its pressure in a totalizing way on the textualized life that we read: Margery's *Book* has generic affinities with saints' lives, but differs from them, most importantly, in the dynamic nature of the experiences represented. Not coincidentally, the *Book*, as its readers know, concludes with Margery's return to Lynn, her hometown, followed by a prayer – and not, as is the case in traditional virgin saints' lives, with post-mortem miracles, conversions, and beatification.

Blessedness

Modern readers, like a fair number of Margery Kempe's contemporaries represented in the *Book*, are sometimes irritated by the claims that the *Book* makes about Margery's intimate relationship with the divine. Traditional saints' lives do not affect readers in this way. When hostility is directed at the saint in such narratives, the textualized life makes it clear that those who are hostile are acting against God's plan. For example, in numerous virgin saints' lives, the suitors of the young, female saints are presented as violating a higher order when they try to impose their desires on the saint.[6] Further, the narratives are wholly sympathetic to the saint and her actions. In the life of Juliana from Jacob of Voragine's massively popular, late thirteenth-century Latin collection known as the *Golden Legend*, for instance, those trying to thwart Juliana are explicitly acting against God's will.[7] Her father, who orders her beaten because she will not marry the prefect unless the prefect converts to Christianity, and the prefect, who tortures and ultimately beheads her, are one-dimensional figures whose perspectives are never entertained by the text. In the generic universe of the saint's life, the saint's resistance and determination are unconflicted. She acts with resolution, and when those around her reject her, they do so because they do not count among those who follow the true path of righteousness.

In contrast, Margery Kempe's *Book* describes conflicts Margery experienced in a manner that allows readers to glimpse the difficulties inherent in discovering and living – as a person chosen by God – one's "blessedness." Recognition of blessedness is shown, in the *Book*, as opposition to life in the world. So, for example, like the virgin saints such as Juliana who reject their worldly suitors, Margery rejects the world's standards, ultimately giving up her fancy clothes and her businesses for a life of devotion. But in Margery's case, such rejection comes only after her involvement in the world has been described in some detail, thus drawing attention to the conflicted nature of her rejection. The *Book* emphasizes Margery's hopes for her business brewing beer, for example, and her disappointment and humiliation when the beer consistently goes flat and can not be sold. This draws the reader's attention to difficulty, and even lack of general sympathy, as part of the journey toward blessedness.

More importantly, the *Book* diverges from saints' lives in its insistence on showing that rejection of the world is an ideal that can be approximated but never fully achieved in this life. In the life of St. Christina, as in the life of Juliana, the break between saint and the world is decisive and complete. Christina, for example, was "taught by the Holy Spirit" not to sacrifice to her parents' idols. When her father reproaches her for failing to worship his gods, she denounces him, declaring that she is not his daughter. Calling him "man without honor, shameless man, abhominable," Christina distinguishes her spiritual path from her father's ungodly existence without any hesitation about her choice and with no spiritual uncertainty (*Golden Legend* [GL], vol. I, p. 386).

Margery Kempe, in contrast, is represented in her *Book* as continually struggling with her faith and her identity. The *Book* opens, in fact, with a moment of supreme, spiritual doubt that characterizes the difficulty of understanding one's own relationship to the divine. In this first chapter, Margery has just borne a child and experiences depression and severe mental breakdown because she can no longer believe in her own salvation. Although the chapter is sometimes described as concerned with postpartum depression, it might more accurately be described as an attempt to represent postpartum *despair*. The episode is about Margery's inability to confess a "secret" sin; weakened by pregnancy and a difficult labor, Margery believes that she will die and that she cannot be forgiven for the sin. When the priest is called to administer last rites, Margery is too ashamed to confess. Compounding her shame, the priest is "a lytyl to hastye" in his attempts to elicit a confession and rushes to correct her before she has finished talking.[8] Convinced that she cannot confess, she is certain that she will, therefore, be damned. The result is that she suffers from a mental breakdown.

Inducing feelings of shame about sin is a central goal of pastoral writing. It can be found, for example, in the well-known *Gesta Romanorum* and in Mirk's widely circulating pastoral guides from the 1390s.[9] Such texts include stories similar to the experience described in Margery Kempe's *Book*. Both the *Gesta* and Mirk's *Festial* present stories about a woman who cannot remove a bloodstain from her hand. In the *Gesta*, the woman has secretly murdered an innocent person because her own life is endangered; as a result, her hands become bloodied. In Mirk, the woman has blood on her hand as the result of a vision of Jesus in which, after He demands that she refrain from feeling ashamed of her sin and confess, He inserts her hand into His wounded side. Both accounts underscore the importance of confession: the hands of both the murderess in the *Gesta* and the ashamed woman in Mirk's anecdote are clean once they confess. In contrast, in Margery Kempe's *Book*, the narrative of the secret sin is used to reinforce the importance of conscious and willed faith in God. In the *Book*, Jesus appears to Margery after she has suffered from depression, including visions of demons that lead her to harm herself physically, and reminds her that He has not forsaken her and that she must not forsake Him. Her recovery is tied to her renewed faith in her worth in God's eyes and not to confession before a priest.

Throughout the *Book*, Margery has experiences of doubt similar to, if perhaps less spectacular than, her first episode of despair. She is frightened by potential violence, bad weather, and sickness, and although she learns over the course of the text to confront these fears, they are repeatedly shown to influence her feelings about her spiritual life and her ability to devote herself to God. In contrast to the confidence one finds in the saints' lives, the *Book* seems particularly concerned to draw attention to the difficulties involved in worshiping a God who, as the *Book* calls Him, is "hyd" (p. 194), that is, invisible to the human eye. This aspect of the divine is never removed from daily life, even for the specially chosen who at times, like Margery, have direct, visionary experiences of God and Jesus. For this reason, the *Book* emphasizes the importance of finding ways to feel secure in God's love in a manner that is absent from saints' lives' descriptions of sanctity.

Of particular importance for Margery in understanding her religious life is her bodily state. As the Virgin Mary was sanctified by having her body chosen by God as a vehicle required for human salvation, so physical experience and identity generally were tied to blessedness in the Middle Ages. The persistent attention to incorrupt bodies of saints long dead (like Cuthbert), to miraculous post-mortem healing of sores on the bodies of others (like Aetheldreda), and to the "odor of sanctity" wafting from saintly corpses indicates this directly.[10] For women especially, physicality was linked with sexuality. For virgin saints, chastity was a defining feature. Like Juliana and Christina, for example, St. Agnes knew even at the age of thirteen that to love God as her "spouse" meant that she would live as a virgin. When the prefect's son fell in love with her, she vehemently rejects him as an unworthy love in comparison with Christ, whose "love is chastity itself, his touch holiness, union with him, virginity" (GL, vol. I, p. 102). Margery Kempe, however, comes to desire a chaste life only after she has been married and borne children. The clear sense of destiny that guides the early medieval virgin saints is not part of Margery's religious narrative. Rather, she marries young and becomes pregnant "as kynde wolde" (p. 21) as the *Book* notes. Further, she continues to recognize her obligations to her human family even after she turns with greater devotion to her spiritual experiences. She cares for her husband in his old age and sickness, and she concerns herself with her son and his wife's welfare.

Margery's understanding of herself is defined by her bodily condition, and this definition is fraught with complications as the *Book* attempts to represent her life as sanctified. In particular, the clear hierarchy of virginity over married life is problematized: Jesus assures Margery that He loves wives as much as He loves virgins, while at the same time affirming the superiority of virginity (p. 59).[11] Margery struggles with this idea, initially responding as if her bodily experiences must exclude her from intimacy with God. Although Jesus promises her "the same grace that I behyte Seynt Kateryne, Seynt Margarete, Seynt Barbara, and Seynt Powle," he subtly qualifies this: "in so mech that what creatur in erth unto the day of dom aske the any bone [favor] and belevyth that God lovyth the, he schal have hys bone" (p. 61). She is "the same" as the famous virginal saints in that whatever her status of sexual purity, she can function like them after death as a mediatrix for those praying to her, and this should reassure her that she will "dawnsyn" [dance] with the virgins in heaven (p. 62).

The clarity found in accounts of saints' lives such as that of Agnes is clearly missing here, and this suggests that focusing solely on traditional, officially authorized exemplars of sanctity misses important aspects of ideas of holiness in the later Middle Ages – aspects that were, perhaps, present, even if undocumented, at every period of medieval culture. The Virgin Mary's "pure" body may have been one model of spiritual perfection, but that model had to be accommodated to the conditions of life governing human relations. Margery's *Book* shows its readers the difficulties of that accommodation. Lives and bodies exist in time and society, and, as the *Book* shows us, a sense of one's blessedness might come later in life and in the midst of its commitments, rather than full-born in childhood.[12]

Margery's struggles with her understanding of herself as a wife and mother are particularly striking to modern readers because they affirm our general sense that medieval religious culture was preoccupied with bodily chastity's spiritual consequences. There is no doubt that this was an important concern for Margery, as it had been for centuries of medieval culture, from the devilish torments and extreme remedies described in the founding textualized lives of ascetic saints such as Jerome's fourth-century narratives of Paul, Malchus, and Hilarion, to Peter Damian's eleventh-century treatise *De divina omnipotentia* struggling with the question of whether an omnipotent God could re-confer virginity in both body and soul, to the long tradition of obsession with this topic in the lives of nearly all women saints, including those mentioned. But perhaps even more important to Margery's presentation of the significance of human embodiment was how she associated spiritual certainty with emotion as experienced through the body. At the end of the first book, she observes that "drede" of her "felyngys" was the "grettest scorge" that she experienced on earth (p. 206). By "feelings," the text means visionary and especially prophetic insights that were associated with physical responses: Margery heard music, smelled scents, and experienced visions that she calls "toknes" (p. 93). These tokens, physical and "ghostly" [spiritual] experiences, provided Margery with the constant assurance that the virgin saints seemed not to need.[13]

Living a sanctified life

Overcoming doubt was understood as central to medieval religious life. In the discussion between Margery and the anchoress and visionary Julian of Norwich recorded in the *Book*, Julian reminds Margery, paraphrasing James 1:6–8, that the person who is "evyrmor dowtyng" [evermore doubting] disqualifies herself from receiving God's gifts (pp. 53–54). The reference to the New Testament verses from James brings together the dual aspects of the sanctified life with which the present discussion began. James is best known for his comments on the importance of "works": "For as the body without the spirit is dead, so faith without works is dead also" (James 2:26). For James, sanctity is revealed through action performed during life in the world. This concept is central to late medieval ideas about religion, as Margery Kempe's *Book* helps us see.[14]

Although St. Martin's cutting his cloak in two to give half to a beggar in winter was a staple of iconography and homily, traditional saints' lives are rarely focused on good works. There are obvious reasons for this, especially the common element in these narratives of martyrdom. But good works are important to a range of other kinds of writing in the later medieval period, including the alliterative poem *Piers Plowman* (c. 1375–85) and morality plays such as *Mankind* (c. 1465) and *Everyman* (c. 1500), as well as writing more clearly focused on spiritual development such as Hilton's *Mixed Life* (c. 1390) and even Chaucer's *Melibee* (c. 1390). Margery Kempe's *Book* exhibits concern with this aspect of medieval spirituality alongside its attention to its subject's understanding of her spiritual status as it was defined by the divine. Although critics often concentrate primarily on the "inner" experiences (the visions and emotions) represented in the *Book*, perhaps because they seem more unusual to us, the *Book* is equally, and rather untraditionally if we think of it as an attempt to record a holy life, concerned with the ways that sanctity has to be lived in particular economic, social, and political contexts.

The material world

Saints' lives often represent their subjects as part of an elite social class, and although personal financial considerations rarely contribute overtly to the saints' spiritual decisions, high social standing contributes to the contexts of these spiritual decisions. Agnes, for example, was in part protected from the prefect's son because of her "nobility," that is, socioeconomic status. Similarly, Christina grows up surrounded by gold and silver idols and is described as the daughter of parents of "the highest rank." When financial considerations enter into saintly decisions about life, they are usually described in relation to giving alms to the poor.

St. Anthony, for example, decides to follow the biblical injunction to sell his goods in order to give the proceeds to those in need (GL, vol. I, p. 93). Saints such as Lucy and Anastasia, similarly, are concerned with charity explicitly. These saints, unlike Margery Kempe, are represented as living in a world in which money and social standing do not hinder the sanctified person's spiritual life or induce anxiety in relation to her spiritual life – indeed, these establish a context in which choices for asceticism, humility, magnanimity, and poverty seem all the more wondrous.

Margery Kempe's *Book* draws attention to the economics of sanctity from a different perspective, removed from what might be called the "magnanimous" tradition of noble saints.[15] To be sure, although Margery was not from a social class comparable with that of Agnes or Christina, the *Book* does note that she was the daughter of the mayor of King's Lynn and observes that her financial situation was superior to her husband's – he asks her, for example, to pay off his debts when he agrees with her wishes to live chastely. Thus, Margery's financial status at least approximates that of the canonical saints. It is true, on the one hand, that she begins a number of businesses to make money. It is also true, on the other hand, that Margery had the luxury of pursuing her spiritual path with relative financial freedom. She continues, for example, to live as a lay woman outside the institutional Church, and she lives both off her own money and on money described throughout the *Book* as given to her by people sympathetic to her spiritual work. Yet despite what may look like a privileged attitude toward financial concerns on Margery's part, the *Book* also alerts its readers to the economic demands that the pursuit of a sanctified life places on believers. In contrast to traditional saints' lives, the *Book* includes observations about financial arrangements that affected believers and the religious institutions to which they belonged.

For example, when Margery decides to apply the same biblical injunction to her own life that St. Anthony followed, the *Book* emphasizes the difficulties inherent in financial decisions of this sort since they often involve people beyond the individual who decides to follow the life of poverty. When Margery is in Rome and understands that God wants her to give away all her money and possessions, she does so. Included among her possessions were goods belonging to Richard, the man with the broken back who traveled with her. When Richard discovered that she had given away his things he was "evyl plesyd" (p. 96). Rather than dismissing his complaints, Margery assures him that God will help her to pay him back: when we are back in England, she says, "ther schal I pay yow ryth wel and trewly be the grace of God, for I trust ryth wel that he bad me gevyn it awey for hys lofe wil help me to payn it ageyn" (p. 96).

So significant are the material consequences of Margery's decision that the *Book* traces her anxiety about it and demonstrates how her financial needs are met after she has no money of her own. In the chapter immediately following the one where Richard expresses his dissatisfaction, Margery is represented as "thynkyng and stodying wher sche schuld han hir levyng inasmech as sche had no sylvir" (p. 97). Jesus assures her that He will take care of her, asking not just his "friends" throughout the world to care for her, but even offering to have His mother beg in order to sustain Margery. Strangers in Rome take care of her, feeding her and giving her money after she tells them holy stories, and she is forced sometimes to beg on the street, until a visiting English priest gives her enough money to return home to England (p. 101). She meets Richard again two years later and repays him all his money from contributions by friends and strangers (p. 109).

The *Book*, like many other late medieval writings (such as *Piers Plowman* and *Mankind*), thus, shows an awareness of the power of money on all sides, but it also maintains that above this power is a divine ordering principle. At one point the *Book* describes a conflict between wealthy parishioners attempting to make two chapels equal in honor and authority to the parish church. Those who want this are "rygth strong and haddyn gret help of lordshyp, and also, the most of all, thei wer ryche men, worshepful marchawntys, and haddyn gold anow, whech may spede in every nede, and that is rewth [pity] that mede shuld spede [rather] than trewth" (pp. 67–68). Ultimately, despite assurances on the part of the bishop of Norwich, they do not get their way: they are unhappy with the terms offered and so the church "stod stylle in her worshep and hyr degré as sche had don two hundryd yer befor and mor" (p. 68). The *Book* makes the point that, despite the power of money, the "inspiracyon of owyr Lord" is more powerful. Unlike the earlier saints' lives that Margery so often has in mind, however, money is a visible force in the lives of all, including herself.

The *Book* teaches the same lesson found in St. Anthony's life: as Jesus tells Margery "stody thow for no good, for I schal ordeyn for the, but evyr stody thow to love me and kepe thi mende on me" (p. 109). The difference between the *Book*'s account and that found in saints' lives, however, is in the difficulties and anxieties that the sanctified person understands in relation to money. Margery's *Book* allows readers to see how the simplicity, or indeed absence, of financial concerns from hagiographic writing removes the sanctified person from the complexities of lived life. The *Book* reintroduces this complexity and need for negotiation, and thus demonstrates that spiritual life is, by necessity, entrenched in the material world.

Communities

In traditional narratives, saints tend to belong to a limited number of social networks. As a genre, the lives tend to identify female saints with two communities: their families (or households) and oppressed Christians. The life of the Roman St. Anastasia, for example, categorizes her first as the daughter of a noble, Christian woman and a pagan man, and second as a minister to imprisoned Christians. Only outlines of social interactions are provided in lives of traditional saints. Anastasia, the reader learns at the outset of the life, has been raised as a Christian in her mother's household. Her Christian ministry puts her at odds with the hostile, dominant community of non-Christians, including her husband, Publius. While we also learn that St. Chrysogonus had helped Anastasia's mother to teach Anastasia the Christian faith, this is as much as we learn about the mother's and daughter's spiritual community. In contrast, Margery is represented in her *Book* as enmeshed in numerous social and spiritual networks, and the text is concerned with illustrating how community shapes and responds to the individual living a sanctified life.

Like Anastasia, Margery is identified in terms of her home city, Bishop's Lynn (changed to King's Lynn after the Reformation) and her family affiliations (husband John; father former mayor of the city). In contrast to Anastasia, however, Margery's spiritual education is represented as coming through a wide variety of channels. No single authority, like Anastasia's Chrysogonus, influences her directly. Nor is her spiritual path shown to be unchanging. Rather, the *Book* shows Margery engaging with ideas that she has learned through regular attendance at church, by hearing books read and listening to sermons, from talking to her confessors and other spiritual advisors, and supernaturally through her revelations. The importance of these ideas and their place in various communities is fluid, and the *Book* emphasizes this fluidity as part of lived life.[16]

The emphasis on community vividly illustrates the complexity of sanctity. Different subgroups within communities, even those co-existing in time and space, possess different and sometimes conflicting ideas and

values. We can see this easily if we trace, for example, the *Book*'s representation of married life and sexual relations. Margery wishes she were a
virgin; her husband agrees to live chastely, but would not have made this
choice on his own; Jesus says he loves wives just as much as He loves
virgins; the secular world, represented at the beginning of the *Book*, values
childbirth and reproduction (and there is a biblical injunction to procre-
ate, as Margery knows). Members of different communities – earthly and
divine – feel differently about this, and readers can see how Margery
responds to these differences over the course of her life.

Her *Book* shows how the person pursuing a life of sanctity must make
choices, and it assumes readers who know that such choices are not made
in isolation. Saints such as Anastasia, Christina, Juliana, and Agnes live
in a world divided neatly between Christians and non-Christians. Their
decisions appear in the lives unmediated by social concerns and uncomplicated by ambiguous ideas. Margery, in contrast, inhabits a world in
which Christianity is presumed; except on pilgrimage, she encounters no
non-Christians. And yet despite this, along with the presumption of
Christian identity is an understanding of religious life as fragmented.
Sometimes, Margery acts in a manner reminiscent of the virgin saints.
Like them, for example, she challenges those who are hostile toward her
and people "merveylyd of hir cunnyng" (p. 134). She corrects those who
follow evil practices, like the lord's men who swear oaths and who, she
says, will end up damned if they do not mend their ways (pp. 134–35). But
often, Margery's responses to people and her interpretations of circumstances are presented as tentative rather than definitive. She is anxious
about the outcome of her actions and words and worries about her
relationships with other people.

This is particularly true when the *Book* describes Margery's prophetic
abilities, such as the passage in which Jesus instructs her to tell a woman
about the woman's dead husband (p. 56). In this instance, the widow is
displeased by Margery's message informing her that, first, her husband
is in Purgatory – that crucial place in late medieval culture for the
incompletely sanctified – and, second, that the woman herself will
ultimately be saved, but that it will likewise "be long er" she herself is
in heaven. The woman, refusing to believe that her husband is in
Purgatory (and perhaps that she is slated for that fate as well) tries to
get Margery's confessor to turn against Margery. The confessor refuses to
do so, and against this social pressure, his reassurance to Margery of her
value in God's eyes is crucial. The episode demonstrates how fraught

communal interaction is for the sanctified person, for her supporters, and even for those unwilling to accept that person's authority.

This focus on responses to distressing and disagreeable social interactions may be due to the fact that the *Book* is so closely concerned with the sanctified person's direct influence on people in her community. In traditional saints' lives, such influence is generally described in terms of opposition (the saint denounces her enemies, is tortured, and dies a martyr) and conversion (the saint's miraculous life and death inspire awe, conversion, and baptism). Thus, in the life of St. Cecelia, Cecelia first converts her husband, Valerian, and Valerian's brother, Tiburtius, then the narrative features further conversions: those of Maximus, who had the brothers executed, and Maximus' entire household as well as all of the executioners; those of 400 people who witness Cecelia's resistance to the prefect Almachius' demands to worship the pagan gods; and those who, the life implies, converted after Almachius' tortures left her miraculously alive for three days (GL, vol. II, pp. 318–23).

In Margery Kempe's *Book*, the sanctified person's influence is both more mundane and more pervasive. When Margery enters the lives of people, she is represented as changing the course of those lives in particular ways. For example, at one point she is praying in church and notices that the man praying behind her is very upset. She asks him why he is so distressed, and he tells her that his wife has just had a baby and is now "owt [of] hir mend" (p. 170). Margery goes to help the woman, who is immediately comforted by her presence. Margery prays for her daily and visits her at least once a day, even after the woman has been moved to a remote area of town in order to keep her crying from disturbing other people. Finally, the woman's mind is restored, and the *Book* attributes her recovery in part to Margery's ongoing care.

The *Book* suggests as well that communities can feel threatened by the presence of the sanctified person, an aspect smoothed over in traditional saints' lives. When Margery is brought before the archbishop of York for the second time, he observes that when he examined her the first time he found "no defawte in hir," yet despite this, he had given his servants money to take her out of the area "for qwietyng of the pepil" (p. 131). In the second encounter with the archbishop, Margery is accused of heresy and of lying about the pilgrimages on which she had gone. The archbishop dismisses these accusations, but holds Margery in prison because the duke of Bedford is angry with her and, he says, he does not want the duke to be angry with him (p. 132). Ultimately, she is freed, but in the course of her interrogation Margery is accused of having advised "Lady Graystoke" to leave her husband (p. 133). Margery denies having said this. Instead, at the time when she had spoken with the lady, she says, she had told her a tale about a woman who was damned because she did not love her enemies and another of a bailiff who was saved because he loved his enemies and forgave them (p. 133). The stories themselves point to the importance of lived and "active" life: salvation comes to the person who practices love. Equally important, in the context of community relations, is the accusation of encouraging women to leave their husbands. Margery, the *Book* reports, was understood as having great influence on the people around her. As the archbishop is quoted as having said in the *Book*, "I leve ther was nevyr [a] woman in Inglond so ferd [feared] wythal as sche is and hath ben" (p. 133).

Authorities

In traditional saints' lives such as those in the *Golden Legend*, the saint rejects the authority of the world in favor of power that she sees as transcendent. In the life of St. Euphemia, for example, the saint, a senator's daughter, demands that the judge Priscus acknowledge her noble birth and allow her to be martyred before "these nobodies, these common folk" (GL, vol. II, p. 139). Although this looks like at least partial acknowledgment of power in the world, Euphemia asserts her secular status only in order to hasten her transition to the "heavenly mysteries" on which she had contemplated. The conflict is between the pagan judge, who persecuted the Christians and put them to death, and Euphemia, who chooses martyrdom in exchange for life hereafter. The judge and his power are an obstacle to life after death, and although he persecutes Christians in the world, the emphasis in the saints' lives is, as a genre, on the future rather than on earthly existence.

Margery Kempe's *Book* shows far greater concern with life in this world than any of the lives in the *Golden Legend*. Because of this, the *Book* tends to explore conflicts between secular or religious authorities and Margery as negotiations.[17] For example, in the events leading up to her first interrogation by the archbishop of York, Margery was questioned by a group of clerics. Although she answered their questions with the proper, orthodox answers, she was nonetheless required to appear before the archbishop for further questioning. Released from prison because lay people vouched for her, she encountered one of the clerics who had spoken against her. He asked that she "be not displesyd" with him, and told her he felt he had to speak against her because the doctor of divinity, Master John Alcon, who served as judge "cryed so" that he "durst non otherwise don" (p. 123). The cleric, archbishop, and Margery are connected by intricate pressures and concerns. The cleric is torn between his allegiance to the group of authorities to which he belongs as at least a peripheral member and his respect for Margery's gifts. The archbishop is responsible to the people below him who have accused Margery. Finally, Margery is responsible to the institutional authority of the men who stand in judgment of her. The *Book* emphasizes the variability in their relations, in contrast to traditional saints' lives, demonstrating how fraught the sanctified person's existence can be in the face of worldly authority that is both necessary and fallible.

In traditional saints' lives, the need to negotiate with those in power is usually rejected. For saints such as Euphemia, the power of this world is cruel and perverted. The lives emphasize this perversity by drawing attention to physical torment. The judge Priscus, for example, places Euphemia on a breaking wheel, an instrument of torture that involved shattering the living victim's bones and whose spokes were filled with burning coals. The process is described in some detail in order to highlight the barbarity of the secular authorities. Although there are people in the textualized saints' lives who change, the change is almost always represented as a straightforward act of conversion. In Euphemia's life, one of her torturers is converted as he attempts to harm her, and the judge's chancellor becomes a Christian after he speaks with her following the tortures. Negotiation or compromise is impossible in this world, and no one would expect characters such as the judge Priscus to express conflicted sentiments in relation to his treatment of Euphemia.

In Margery's *Book*, in contrast, those who hurt Margery are fellow Christians, and Margery is shown to need the support of religious and secular authorities in order to influence those around her. Her *Book* shows the sanctified person seeking ways to accept and change her fellow believers, and not able, as in the lives from the *Golden Legend*, easily to dismiss her enemies, especially politically powerful ones, as deserving torment and eternal punishment. In Euphemia's life, Priscus is found dead "having chewed his own flesh" (GL, vol. II, p. 183). In Margery's *Book*, as suggested above, the cleric who stood against her in public is nevertheless shown respect.

This is not to say that Margery never opposed those in authority over her. The story of the White Friar, a famous preacher, who denounces Margery because she cries loudly and disrupts his sermons, is a case in point. Despite the fact that his sermons are spiritually inspiring, the *Book* makes it clear that his failure to recognize Margery's gifts is a serious failing. After a series of encounters with Margery in which he is shown resisting her sanctity out of pride (in his anger at her disruption of his sermons), the *Book* identifies his error. Not only does he try to insist that Margery deny that her abilities are spiritual gifts, but he goes to great lengths to bring the civic and religious authorities into the dispute. The situation becomes so threatening that her friends advise Margery to leave town. She does not, but, rather, continues despite the fact that, as her confessor says, "Ther is no mor agen yow but the mone and seven sterrys" (p. 151).

The lesson that Jesus teaches her in relation to the Friar concerns the world's opposition. She must persevere despite the Friar's persecution, and she must learn not to submit without question to the Church's authorities. Jesus tells her "it wer bettyr he [the Friar] wer nevyr born, for he despisith hys werkys in me" (p. 151). The phrase recalls the Gospel's words concerning Judas. In Mark 14:21 Jesus says "good were it for that man [the one who will betray him] if he had never been born." Although Margery's response, from our modern perspective, looks psychologically defensive, from a medieval one, the purpose behind the passage, or at least one of them, is to remind the reader that, despite a human desire for eternal salvation, some people, including people seemingly dedicated to the Church, will be damned. Just a few pages after Jesus tells her that the Friar will be "chastised scharply" and his name "schal ben throwyn down" and Margery's "schal ben reysed up" (p. 152), the *Book* reflects on those who are "worthy to be dampnyd" (p. 155).

Margery's rebellion against the Friar is not, of course, as active as those of the virgin saints. In the traditional martyr narratives, the saint denounces her enemies publicly and triumphs through her death. In Margery's case, that resistance must be ongoing and internalized. The sanctified person cannot "escape" into death but must, instead, perse- vere in this life. She needs to learn to respect authority, but also to listen when a higher authority instructs her to do something else. We can see this, finally, in her failure to consult with her confessor before she travels, at God's command, to the Continent. When she returns to England, she visits the Bridgettine Syon Abbey, a popular pilgrimage site, and talks with a hermit who tells her "yowr confessowr hath forsakyn yow for ye wentyn ovyr the see and wolde telle hym no word therof" (p. 229). Despite his words, the hermit helps her to get home and when she does, she goes to her confessor. The confessor "gaf hir ful scharp wordys, for sche was his obediencer" and chastises her because she had taken the journey without his knowledge (p. 230). But ultimately, things work out between Margery and her confessor. By placing herelf under his direction again, she regains his trust and "owr Lord halpe hir so that sche had as good love of hym [the confessor] and of other frendys aftyr as sche had beforn" (p. 230).

Conclusion: the past and the present

This chapter has been concerned with the ways in which Margery Kempe's *Book* can teach us about medieval sanctity in ways that traditional saints' lives cannot. Especially important for women, the *Book* shows us how the sanctified life was one of conflict, worry, and negotiation. Some scholars might argue that this is a difference in time, late antiquity versus the later Middle Ages, rather than in genre. But it seems more important to me to notice how the late medieval text lets us imagine the conflicted nature that the sanctified life surely always had, despite differences in historical periods. For women throughout the history of Christianity, the sanctified life has always been one at a remove from the Church's institutional authority. In this sense, Margery Kempe's *Book* lets us see, at least partially, how one woman may have negotiated this divide, and perhaps thus speaks for a long, vast, and undocumented range of medieval Christian culture.

Notes

1. *The Gesta Romanorum*, ed. J. H. Sidney, EETS ES 33 (1962), p. 172. The Latin reads "sanctificatum in utero matris sue" (ed. Herrtage Oesterley [Berlin, 1872], p. 375).
2. *Piers the Plowman's Crede*, ed. James Dean (Kalamazoo, MI, 1991), lines 104–5; 110–12.
3. On the canonization process see *Toynbee, *Saint Louis of Toulouse* (1929), esp. pp. 133–232.
4. On the *Book*'s early readers and history see *Lochrie, *Margery Kempe* (1991), pp. 203–35. See also Rebecca Schoff, *Reformations: Three Medieval Authors in Manuscript and Movable Type* (Turnhout, 2007), pp. 91–140.
5. *Waters, *Angels and Earthly Creatures* (2004), suggests reasons for this failure, pp. 120–23, 141–42.
6. See *Winstead, *Virgin Martyrs* (1997); *Wogan-Browne, *Saints' Lives and Women's Literary Culture* (2001); and *Sanok, *Her Life Historical* (2007).

7. *Jacobus de Voragine: The Golden Legend: Readings on the Saints*, trans. William Granger Ryan, 2 vols. (Princeton, 1993), vol. I, pp. 160–61. Further citations in the text are to this translation.

8. *The Book of Margery Kempe*, ed. Lynn Staley (Kalamazoo, MI, 1996), p. 22. Further citations in the text are to this edition.

9. *Mirk's Festial*, ed. Theodor Erbe, EETS ES 96 (1905), pp. 90–91. See further Rebecca Krug, "Margery Kempe," in Larry Scanlon (ed.), *The Cambridge Companion to Medieval English Literature* (Cambridge, 2009), pp. 217–28.

10. On "incorruption" of saintly bodies see *Bynum, *Resurrection of the Body* (1995), pp. 200–25.

11. On virginity and Margery Kempe see *Salih, *Versions of Virginity* (2001), pp. 166–241.

12. See *Kleinberg, *Prophets in Their Own Country* (1992), and *Weinstein and Bell, *Saints and Society* (1982).

13. The ability to interpret visionary episodes was discussed at length in the period. See *Voaden, *God's Words* (1999), and *Caciola, *Discerning Spirits* (2003).

14. James was important in this regard for "orthodox" as well as "heterodox" audiences. See Margaret E. Goldsmith, "Will's Pilgrimage in *Piers Plowman B*," in Myra Stokes and T. L. Burton (eds.), *Medieval Literature and Antiquities: Studies in Honour of Basil Cottile* (Woodbridge, 1987), pp. 119–32, and *Krug, *Reading Families* (2002), pp. 130–47.

15. *Murray, *Reason and Society* (1978), esp. pp. 355–62.

16. On the experimental nature of the practices described see *Newman, "What Did It Mean to Say 'I Saw'?" (2005), pp. 1–43.

17. See *Staley, *Margery Kempe's Dissenting Fictions* (1994), esp. ch. 1, and *Beckwith, *Christ's Body* (1993), pp. 94–102.

Part Three

Literacies, languages, and literatures

7

Visual texts in post-Conquest England

Seeing with medieval eyes is impossible for us. Yet we can try to use medieval descriptions of images – ekphrastic passages – as "medieval spectacles" to correct the distortions of our modern vision. A famous passage from the first version of Gerald of Wales' *Topographia Hibernica* (*Topography of Ireland*), finished early in 1188, describes with notable care the illuminations in a Gospel Book reputed to have been miraculously made nearly 500 years earlier, which Gerald says he saw on a visit to Kildare:

> Among all the miracles of Kildare nothing seems to me more
> miraculous than that wonderful book which they say was written at
> the dictation of an angel during the lifetime of the virgin [St. Brigit].
> This book contains the four gospels according to the concordance of
> St. Jerome, with almost as many drawings as pages, and all of them in
> marvellous colours. Here you can look upon the face of the divine
> majesty drawn in a miraculous way; here too upon the mystical
> representations of the Evangelists, now having six, now four, and now
> two, wings. Here you will see the eagle; there the calf. Here the face of
> a man; there that of a lion. And there are almost innumerable other
> drawings. If you look at them carelessly and casually and not too
> closely, you may judge them to be mere daubs rather than careful
> compositions. You will see nothing subtle where everything is subtle.
> But if you take the trouble to look very closely, and penetrate with
> your eyes to the secrets of the artistry, you will notice such intricacies,
> so delicate and subtle, so close together and well-knitted, so involved
> and bound together, and so fresh still in their colourings that you will
> not hesitate to declare that all these things must have been the result
> of the work, not of men, but of angels.[1]

Apparently Gerald's scrutiny of it was prolonged, for in an expanded version of the *Topographia Hibernica* written several years later Gerald says he admired the illuminations more and more, ever newly amazed the harder he scrutinized them. Although this is a case of Insular or Hiberno-Saxon art being viewed by post-Conquest eyes (those of a sophisticated clerical member of Henry II's court, one surely more used to the classicizing aesthetic of Romanesque art), there is no pejorative judgment here, except with respect to the casual viewer, who casts a superficial glance, perceives only a colorful splotch (*litura*) rather than a finely woven composition (*ligatura*), and passes on, missing the subtlety everywhere. Gerald, on the other hand, is a close "reader," who not only understands Christian iconography in order to identify the "mystic symbols" of the Evangelists, but takes a keen interest in details such as the number of wings each figure has, and in seemingly infinite variations achieved by differences of form and color. Not only does he marvel at the artistry involved, but he assumes that all aspects of the composition are meaningful, that they are worth looking at intently and puzzling over in order to penetrate the secret senses of the intricate designs.

Art historians have taken this ekphrasis to be a description of a manuscript such as the *Book of Kells* or the *Lindisfarne Gospels*,[2] where we see the Gospel text itself treated as a sort of interlace. Authorized by an account of its divine inspiration, a native, "vernacular" sort of figuration – stylized animal interlace designs that craftsmen had previously carved or formed with beaded wire on secular objects made of metal, wood, bone, or stone – was applied via drawing and painting to a new medium: the letters and pages of Gospel texts. Whatever the original reasons for such a transfiguration of the letters and the written text of the Gospels, the subtle depiction of Scripture as an intricate knotwork evokes in Gerald a hermeneutic desire to linger over the text and tease out senses not immediately apparent. A text made visible in such a finely woven, exquisitely intricate way seems to call for very close viewing and reading. The visual designs of the "Gospels of Kildare" function as an interpretive framework or gloss that directs the viewer's approach to, and understanding of, the verbal text of Scripture.

As a learned cleric, Gerald understood that this depiction of Scripture as an interlaced or woven fabric was a visual gloss evoking the original sense of Latin *textus* (past participle of *texere*, "to weave"), which meant something woven or, by extension, texture or tissue. The term was applied figuratively to language to mean a construction, combination, connection, or context and, in late Latin, specifically to a construction or combination of inscribed letters of the alphabet. In medieval usage, *textus* was a clerical term referring to the inscribed words or exact wording of an authoritative work, especially Holy Scripture. Gerald has no problem with – indeed, is highly approving of – a visual interpretation or gloss of Holy Scripture that turns it into a puzzling picture in which letters become figures as well as containing them, and the text of Scripture is shown to be an exquisitely complicated interwoven composition. Such a visual representation of the text of Scripture corresponds to exegetical (patristic and early medieval monastic) representations of it, in figurative language, as being full of "mystical knots of allegory" that need to be untied by explanation.[3]

Pictures as glosses of Scripture

For over two centuries following the Norman Conquest, there are few signs of resistance to visual glossing of religious texts in England, where there was already a well-established tradition of it. The need to make Latin texts understandable to native audiences had required verbal explanation, translation glosses for words and phrases, as well as more extensive glosses explaining literal and nonliteral senses of the text. In some Anglo-Saxon Latin manuscripts, verbal glosses and commentaries were supplemented or even replaced by pictorial representations (mostly line drawings with or without a color wash) on the same page as the text and whose primary purpose was to explain the text in terms its audience could more easily grasp, to bring it closer to home. The practice of pictorial glossing is found even in texts already made accessible by being translated into Anglo-Saxon, such as the "Caedmon" Genesis manuscript (Oxford, Bodleian Library, MS Junius II) from around the year 1000, which has an extensive pictorial gloss – or pictorial narrative – supplementing the translation, as does Ælfric's *Old English Hexateuch* (the first six books of the Old Testament) in a manuscript from the first half of the eleventh century (British Library, MS Cotton Claudius B IV).[4] For the most part, however, assiduous pictorial glossing accompanied authoritative Latin texts not vernacular translations of them, which were relatively few in any case (although more than on the Continent).

Pictorial compositions might function as interpretive glosses even though the text itself was not on the same page or in the same visual field, as when a series of biblical scenes was represented in painting on the walls of a church. We know from Bede's account that this was the case already in the late seventh century in the monastic churches Benedict

Biscop founded in Northumbria, first at Wearmouth, then at Jarrow, and equipped with panel paintings brought back from Rome for the purpose. In the church at Wearmouth, painted panels of the Virgin Mary and the twelve apostles were hung "from wall to wall" around or across a central arch, while on the south wall hung pictures of incidents in the Gospels and on the north depictions of Saint John's visions from the Apocalypse, so that "all who entered the church, even those who could not read," might have in mind "more firmly" the Incarnation and the terrors of the Last Judgment. At Jarrow, in both the monastery and the church, hung painted panels of an even more exegetical nature showing the concordance of the Old and New Testaments.[5]

Indeed, pictorial representations had been powerfully authorized as aids to understanding Scripture. In a commentary on the temple of Solomon written around 731, Bede argued in favor of the use of depictions of Holy Scripture in churches. As might be expected, he relied on the authority of Gregory the Great's letters chastising the bishop of Marseille for destroying such pictures as idols. In 599, Gregory had written that "a picture is displayed in churches on this account, in order that those who do not know letters may at least read by seeing on the walls what they are unable to read in books." In 600, in a second letter, he went on to associate those who "do not know letters" with clans of foreigners or pagan peoples whose native language was not Latin, suggesting that pictures were especially appropriate to far-flung missionary efforts among gentiles.[6] Writing in another context where Latin was not the native language and fluency in it rare, Bede waxed eloquent on the spiritual and affective efficaciousness of sacred pictures:

> Why should it not be allowable to recall to the memory of the faithful, by a painting, that exaltation of our Lord Saviour on the cross … and also his other miracles and healings … especially since their sight is wont also to produce a feeling of great compunction in the beholder, and since they open up, as it were, a living reading (*vivam lectionem*) of the Lord's story for those who cannot read? The Greek word for *pictura* is indeed living writing (*viva scriptura*) … and thus, as it were, to place a living writing before the eyes of all.[7]

By calling painted depictions of Scripture a "living reading," and "living writing," Bede may simply have been comparing the deadening labor of deciphering and understanding Latin to the livelier effects of viewing pictorial representations of human figures and actions. But coupled with "reading" or "writing," the word "living" also reverberates with New Testament notions, such as Paul's "living writing" (the Christian story inscribed in memory, "written ... not in tables of stone, but in the fleshly tables of the heart," 2 Corinthians 3:3) and Paul's promotion of spiritual over literal textual interpretation, the vivifying "spirit" of Scripture over its deadening "letter" (2 Corinthians 3:6: "*littera enim occidit Spiritus autem vivificat*"), by which the figurative or "spiritual" senses of the text transform an Old Testament literal sense no longer valid. Paul did not include pictures as the means for this, but Bede may have made this leap. And even if pictures did not interpret Scripture with Pauline typology by representing Old Testament scenes as prefigurations of New Testament ones (as those at Jarrow did), but merely represented scenes from Scripture in ways that brought these closer to the experience of the contemporary viewer, an element of "translation" and adaptation is involved that we may call visual glossing. What Bede seems to have meant by calling pictorial representations of Scripture a "living" reading or writing is that pictures translate and transfigure the Latin text, gloss it to make it understandable, and bring it by sensory means into the life of the viewer. A reading of the text provided by pictures is a "lively" one aimed at interesting and impressing the viewer, thus "writing" on his heart.

The Bayeux Tapestry as pictorial gloss

Few early Insular wall paintings or painted or embroidered hangings have survived the centuries, but for those that have we tend not to appreciate how often the pictures were intended as glosses of texts. This is especially true when the figures or actions of the pictorial compositions are given a central position in the visual field and are captioned or identified with Latin labels or short explanations, so that the pictures themselves are treated like texts in need of glossing. Such is the case with the first important testimony of post-Conquest Anglo-Norman pictorial art: the Bayeux Tapestry depicting the events leading to the Norman Conquest of England (1064–66), which was, from a medieval perspective, an important event in the scheme of Christian history. A Norman bishop, Odo of Bayeux, half-brother of William the Conquerer, earl of Kent from the Conquest until 1082, was most probably the patron who ordered and paid for the tapestry, which was hung for a few days each year in the nave of his cathedral in Bayeux as part of the festivities celebrating its saintly relics. However, the tapestry was probably designed and executed in England at St. Augustine's monastery in Canterbury, where there was a tradition, as at Christ Church monastery in Canterbury, of illuminating psalters, gospels, and saints' lives with pictorial narratives, as well as of using embroidery as a means of depiction, for example, on ecclesiastical vestments. The Norman abbot of St. Augustine's from 1072 to 1087 was one Scollandus (apparently of mixed background), formerly a scribe at the monastery of Mont St. Michel. The most likely date for the fabrication of the tapestry would be during the final stage of Odo's renovation of the cathedral of Bayeux, consecrated in 1077 in the presence of King William, the archbishop of Canterbury, and other great lords.[8]

The Bayeux Tapestry is a text in the etymological sense of the term; it is a long (almost 70-meter) band of linen cloth upon which figures are embroidered in color. The ground of the natural linen is not filled in with color, which makes it seem all the more like a parchment roll, or like the uncolored manuscript page that served as the ground for much Anglo-Saxon pictorial glossing. The tapestry band is not any broader (about 0.5 meter) than the height of the pages of many an early medieval illuminated manuscript created for liturgical use or display. The scenes on the tapestry are meant to be studied in chronological sequence from left to right, just as we read the Latin captions above the figures, for example, in a scene discussed below: "UBI HAROLD SACRAMENTUM FECIT WILLELMO DUCI" ("Where Harold swore a sacred oath to Duke William") (see Figure 7.1). Although the embroidered figures occupy the central space of the tapestry and the only verbal text in evidence glosses the figures (identifies them or their actions), the pictorial narrative of the Bayeux Tapestry must have been conceived as the explanatory gloss of an unseen text, for that is the implicit function of all pictorial narrative compositions at this period. No surviving Latin account is as partial to Odo and the relics of Bayeux as is the tapestry; thus, we had best consider the tapestry to be a tendentious visual gloss embroidering upon the sense of recent Norman chronicles, such as that of William of Jumièges (*Gesta normannorum ducum*, with an account of the Conquest added by 1070) or William of Poitiers (*Gesta Guillelmi*, probably written in the 1070s). The self-promoting Odo had the proper spin put on a written Latin account of the Norman Conquest by this gloss in pictures that could reach and persuade a wider public than a Latin text alone. And instead of commissioning this extensive visual gloss for the pages of a book beside the narrative text, Odo made it to be displayed on the

Figure 7.1 Detail from the Bayeux Tapestry – eleventh century. Harold swearing on the relics his oath of fidelity to Duke William. *Centre Guillaume-le-Conquérant*, Bayeux, Normandy. By special permission of the city of Bayeux.

walls of his church when it was full of viewers at the seasonal festival of the patron saints.

For a broad audience, the pictures performed the work of interpreting, offering a "living reading" of a written Latin chronicle account to cast light on and glorify the part played by Odo, bishop of Bayeux, and to emphasize the power of the saintly relics of Bayeux Cathedral upon which, in a central scene of the tapestry, Harold is shown swearing fidelity to William, taking the sacred oath that he would later break by assuming the English throne in opposition to William. In the scene preceding Harold's oath to William, they ride toward Bayeux, which is represented by a structure on a hill with a cupola, two towers, and spire labeled "BAGIAS," the last word of the caption preceding "UBI HAROLD ..." This strongly suggests what was not said in any surviving chronicle: Bayeux was the place where the oath was sworn, and the relics upon which Harold swore were those of the church there. During the swearing, William looks on composedly in the spread-kneed posture of majesty enthroned, while Harold stands spread-eagled between two reliquary shrines, one hand touching each. All gazes and gestures in the scene point the significance of Harold's action. Furthermore, the explanatory captions throughout the tapestry are in very simple Latin executed in a highly legible majuscule script. Viewers with only the most basic Latin knowledge would be able to spell out the captions and translate the gloss for those who could not read Latin at all. It seems likely that clerics would have provided guidance to the tapestry's interpretation during its yearly public display. Such an interpretive situation can be supposed as well for Latin-captioned pictorial narrative in the form of wall paintings, mosaics, and even stained-glass windows (sometimes so far out of reach as to be nearly out of sight). Just as a pupil would try to read a Latin text along with his teacher, the viewer would try to "read along" with the oral reading or lesson (*lectio*) explaining the pictures. Once initiated, the viewer could practice his "reading" of images on his own, perhaps discovering new details to be worked into the interpretation.

Close readers of the tapestry might well be impressed with the motivating role Odo plays in it, most clearly in the scene just before Harold falls in battle. Mounted and fully covered in chainmail, the bishop charges forward with an upraised staff in his right hand under the caption "HIC ODO EPISCOPUS BACULUM TENENS" ("Here is Bishop Odo holding a staff") (see Figure 7.2). For a more effective climax, this event, which happened earlier in the battle according to surviving chronicles, was moved to the end of the tapestry's narrative. By raising his staff, Odo "comforts the youths," because they believe William to be lost. In the action immediately following, William lifts both his visor and his staff to reveal himself and give the decisive impetus to the battle. The designers of the tapestry may have intended the clerical viewer to see more than a swordless and

Figure 7.2 Detail from the Bayeux Tapestry – eleventh century. Bishop Odo holding up his staff. *Centre Guillaume-le-Conquérant*, Bayeux, Normandy. By special permission of the city of Bayeux.

shieldless Odo heroically exhorting the Norman troops. With his upraised staff, emphasized by the caption, he may be understood as a providential figure analogous to Moses at the battle with the Amalekites, raising the rod of God to assure victory (Exodus 17:9–13). Indeed, Odo does even better than Moses in that he clearly needs no one to support his arm as he holds up the staff like a rod, and he does it in the thick of battle, rather than standing aside on a hill. And so does William, for the designer of the tapestry was not so bold as to give Odo the only upraised staff.

Without going as far as to read Odo and William as analogues of Moses, a viewer familiar with the Psalms might well associate their uplifted staves with God's rod (*virga*) for chastising and punishing sinners, here used to effect divine punishment upon the sacrilegious Harold and his followers. The Lord's chastising rod had been illustrated (although thinner and longer) in several scenes of a psalter that the designer of the Bayeux Tapestry must have known. Made in a monastery in Reims in the second quarter of the ninth century, from about the year 1000 the Utrecht Psalter[9] was owned by the monastery of Christ Church in Canterbury, where it was copied, but with the figures outlined in colored inks, in the early eleventh-century Harley Psalter (British Library, MS Harley 603). When he is holding neither the papal banner nor a scepter, William is shown with a staff similar to Odo's in two other scenes from the battle of Hastings. Surely we are not to imagine that a shieldless William chose to conquer by wielding a knotty club? Although there is no caption indicating that William held up a staff, that is what he, like Odo, is doing at the crucial turning point of the battle, and the hardness of William's staff is emphasized at this moment by two prominent knots (as opposed to one for Odo's). In Psalm 2:7–9, God gives "as an inheritance" to the psalmist (foreshadowing Christ) the "peoples to the ends of the earth" to be brought to obedience sternly, "broken with an iron rod" and "shattered like a clay pot." The Norman Conquest as depicted in the Bayeux Tapestry recollects this psalm, with much attention to the rod (or hard, knotty club) that chastises the unruly "inherited people" and, in the lower border, to lopped off heads and scattered naked bodies – shards of men whose "potter" was God.

Experiments in glossing the St. Albans Psalter

Extensive pictorial glosses, like extensive verbal ones, tend to become texts in themselves, replacing what they were intended to explain, especially when they are separated from the original text and placed in a new visual field or context. Indeed, the "distance" – both figurative and literal – between the letter of the text and its gloss was an object of constant adjustment and also, later in the Middle Ages, of contention. The manuscript containing the St. Albans Psalter, often considered to be the first major example of Anglo-Norman art in the Romanesque style, is an extensive experiment in pictorial glossing. Because there is now an excellent website devoted to color reproduction and explanation of all the images on all the pages of this manuscript codex,[10] it will serve to illustrate the different ways in which pictures were used to "translate" and interpret texts that appeared on the same page or later in the codex or in other manuscripts, and how these pictures were, in turn, identified or glossed by texts (Latin captions and longer commentaries). The St. Albans codex is particularly rich in layers of pictorial and verbal glossing, which served to adapt it to the needs and experiences of its intended users.

The various parts were executed in the first half of the twelfth century and compiled into one volume at the monastery of St. Albans, under the direction of Abbot Geoffrey of Gorham, for the use of Christina of Markyate. Until she took vows and became head of the priory of Markyate, she was a recluse first protected by a particular monk and then by the abbot himself. In the initial of Psalm 105 of the psalter, Christina is represented interceding with Christ on behalf of a group of monks, which may suggest that the gift of a psalter was a means of assuring the prayers of a prospective saint. The volume begins with a liturgical calendar illuminated with personified labors of the months and zodiac signs identified by written captions. The calendar, with its symbolic depictions of the natural world, is the outermost text in the manuscript, its "border." As a representation of cyclical time, the calendar is analogous to the border of the Bayeux Tapestry, which depicts stylized birds and beasts and scenes from the natural or everyday world – plowing, human mating, proverbial fables – and runs "around" the largely unidirectional representation of the march of divine history.

The liturgical calendar is followed by forty full-page, framed, richly painted scenes devoid of verbal glosses; these paintings illustrate key scenes of Scripture, beginning with two Old Testament scenes (the Fall and the Expulsion from Paradise), followed by a pictorial narrative of the Redemption that is unprecedented in the number of scenes it depicts from the life of Christ. Because King David's psalms were traditionally explained as foreshadowing and being about Christ, the long sequence of paintings of Christ's life serves as a sort of gloss on, and preparation for, understanding the psalter that follows. The picture cycle also interprets and harmonizes the texts of the four Gospels and the Book of Acts by selecting some episodes rather than others and weaving these into a single pictorial narrative of the life of Christ. Thus, it is a pictorial gloss on an absent text (as the Bayeux Tapestry is). There are needle holes in the parchment for affixing pieces of silk fabric, no longer extant, to cover the pictures. Like their gold frames, these cloth veils would break the narrative thrust of the pictures and suggest a contemplative, affective manner of viewing. Although the meditative techniques developed by St. Anselm of Canterbury and St. Bernard of Clairvaux in the late eleventh and early twelfth centuries involved elaborating and contemplating mental, not material, images, the visual gloss of Scripture provided by a painting might start the thought process for those who could not read Latin well.

The last pictures in the framed, full-page picture cycle all concern in one way or another recognizing Christ after his Resurrection. Four out of six of these give great importance to female witnesses: the three Marys at the empty tomb; Mary Magdalene informing the disciples of the Resurrection; doubting Thomas probing Christ's wound; St. Martin's vision of Christ clothed in the cloak Martin had shared with the beggar; the Ascension and Pentecost, both with the Virgin figured in the center, larger than the disciples. The scene from the fourth-century *Life of St. Martin of Tours* may have pleased Abbot Geoffrey, who was from Maine in France and had taught school in Le Mans, near Tours. (Local devotion to St. Martin may have sensitized Geoffrey to the symbolism of cloaks: he is reputed to have taken monastic vows after the cloaks that he had borrowed from the monastery of St. Albans to produce a saint's play got burnt.) However, the vision of St. Martin also serves to encourage spiritual recognition of Christ in the needy, upon Christ's own testimony (Matthew 25:35–40: "anything you did for one of my brothers here ... you did for me"). The depiction of St. Martin's vision demonstrates the truth of Christ's statement – clothing the beggar clothes Christ – and also gives a key to recognizing Christ through figurative interpretation, preparing a Christological understanding of the psalms and, closer to hand, a recognition of Christ in the life of Alexis.

The next pages of the manuscript use an image of King David, the dove of the Holy Spirit at his ear, playing a rebec (a minstrel's instrument), to introduce a versified Old French life of St. Alexis, who exemplifies a *beatus vir* (from Psalm 1, a "blessed" or saintly person). Indeed,

Alexis is identified as "Blessed Alexis, chosen youth" in a Latin caption above his head in the first of a sequence of three scenes of "continuous" narrative, where he is shown parting from his new bride, rejecting fleshly for spiritual marriage. In the first scene, within the marriage chamber behind the foregrounded marriage bed, Alexis is inspired by a dove to part with his bride, leaving her his ring and sword. The second interior scene is divided by arches into two spaces. The grieving bride is framed frontally in the central one, her long cord belt in full view. Under the second arch, Alexis heads for the open door, already turned in profile, looking and gesturing toward the ship that will take him away in the third scene. This pictorial gloss of the Alexis story brings out analogies with the prospectively saintly life of Christina of Markyate, who rejected her bridegroom to become a recluse (as Alexis did) and, after she had formed a strong emotional attachment to Abbot Geoffrey, was encouraged by him to take vows of chastity and become a nun (which she did in 1131).

The tinted drawings, with their bi- and tricolored captions exclaiming about Alexis' sanctity as well as his bride's chaste fidelity ("Oh blessed bride, ever bound to grief"), reinforce the gloss provided by the vernacular prologue to the poem, found only in this manuscript. The prologue appears just beneath the pictures, written in alternating red and blue lines, like the first two pages of the text of the following *Chanson de Saint Alexis*, thus creating a tapestry effect. Whatever personal meanings the pictorial glosses had for Christina or Abbot Geoffrey in particular, the unique vernacular prologue also provided an all-purpose gloss for nuns and monks, concerning the victorious struggle against the sins of the flesh (conventionally symbolized by woman). Here, however, both Alexis and his bride are meant to be victorious. Although the picture does not suggest as much in the parting scene, except perhaps by the detail of the bride's long cord belt, the verbal prologue under the picture emphasizes that Alexis, "out of the sovereign devotion of friendship, commends his young bride to the true living Bridegroom." The vernacular prologue explains that the story of the poem is a "supreme consolation and a spiritual remembrance for each of those who live purely in chastity and take dignified delight in heavenly joys and virginal marriage." They should be reminded by the story of their own renunciation of secular for spiritual marriage and encouraged to continue on this path.

On the leaf where the *Chanson de Saint Alexis* ends appears a Latin text with French translation of a passage from Gregory's letter to Bishop

Serenus of Marseille, previously discussed, but here presented as the reply of "Saint Gregory to Secundinus the Recluse, when he asked him the reason for paintings." (Christina of Markyate was, or had been, a recluse at the time this codex was given to her.) Perhaps the most telling thing about this adaptation of Pope Gregory's defense of pictures to teach those who cannot read letters is that the justification was felt to be necessary. The lost silk "curtains" over the pictures, which would have had to be lifted up to reveal them, may or may not suggest a worshipful attitude. From the needle holes in the parchment, it seems that fabric covered all the fully-painted pictures of the narrative of the Fall and Redemption, 72 out of 215 historiated initials (large initial letters with pictures inside) in the psalter and following prayers, and even two of the images accompanying the calendar (*Virgo* and *Scorpio*). Furthermore, the placement of the stitch marks for many initials meant that the silk tissue (perhaps woven with oriental figures) literally covered parts of the inscribed text along with its pictorial gloss. This does not necessarily indicate disrespect for the text (as opposed to the pictures), for there was a long tradition – most spectacularly displayed in Hiberno-Saxon Gospels – of using "carpet" pages (paintings of elaborately interwoven designs that resemble figured textiles) as cover pages for the written text. Such visually complex carpet pages played on the fundamental sense of *textus* as something woven and may have prepared the reader to consider the complexity of the following verbal text. In this light, the covering of a picture with a figured textile, as in the St. Albans codex, might even be understood as an incitation to consider the picture as "text," to "open" and try to "read" it.

On the one hand, the Gregorian reminder warns the users of this book not to worship (idolize) the splendid paintings in it, but to learn from the stories they tell: "It is one thing to worship a painting and another thing to learn what is to be worshipped through the story of the painting." On the other hand, the translated citation justifies, on didactic grounds, the bold use of such extensive and richly painted pictorial narrative (the Redemption cycle) without any accompanying text or verbal gloss, as well as the more modest use of tinted drawings: "For that which writing teaches to readers, painting teaches the same to the illiterate. For the illiterate see in it what they should follow. In it those who know no letters 'read.'" The stress on "following" in Gregory's Latin text and its French translation suggests not only adherence to the right beliefs, but also a more technical sense. Those who can read letters themselves can follow along with an oral reading by another person; those who cannot read letters can follow the pictures. That is why "la penture est pur leceun as genz" ("painting serves as a reading for lay folk"). There is no difference between Old French *leceun* and Latin *lectio*, for a *lectio* was not usually an uninterrupted reading of an authoritative text, but also an explanation of it, what we would call a lesson.

The pictorial narrative of Christ's life continues after the *Alexis* interlude with three full-page tinted drawings of Christ as pilgrim encountering his disciples at Emmaus and then ascending to heaven. As opposed to the earlier picture cycle, which is unaccompanied by any verbal gloss, the first of the Emmaus pages has, squeezed into the available space inside the frame, a sort of abbreviated Latin paraphrase of Luke 24:13–31, with the telling addition of a phrase – "Look at the sun" – that appears also in the Latin liturgical *Peregrinus* or pilgrim play (such liturgical drama might be considered another sort of "living reading" of Scripture). The function of the Emmaus scenes, coming after the picture cycle of Christ's life and the *Alexis* poem and before the psalter, is elucidated by the verbal gloss paraphrasing Luke, which explains what is going on between the pilgrims. Christ is explaining to his two disciples, who do not recognize him, that Old Testament history was bound to be fulfilled: "Beginning with Moses and the prophets he began to interpret that which was about himself in all the Scriptures." All three pilgrims look toward and point at the light of the sun, with Christ's staff serving as the most emphatic pointer and connector. They stay – so the verbal gloss says – for the last of the light. Is this not also the light that Christ provides through his elucidation of Scripture? The three Emmaus pictures powerfully legitimate and encourage the viewer's attempt to recognize Christ in the words of the following psalter. These pictures are about interpretation, about reading and seeing spiritually.

It is probably no coincidence that the Latin text squeezed into the frame above the pilgrims' heads is written in alternating colors (green, red, blue) that call attention to the text as image and turn the written gloss into a tissue of multicolored strands. There seems to have been a tradition of writing in multiple colors (and figures) to make the text more visible as a construction, to slow reading and suggest multiple senses. As we have seen earlier, the complicated textuality of Hiberno-Saxon Gospels such as the *Book of Kells* is emphasized by depicting the letters as being part of (and filled with) an intricate knotwork of different colored strands. Even in the Bayeux Tapestry, the black lettering of the

Latin captions suddenly turns to multicolored lettering from the scene of Odo's consecration of the meal prior to the battle of Hastings to the slaying of Harold. This alternation of colors from one letter to the next in the captions is not likely to be the embroiderers' whim. It could be a kind of highlighting meant to suggest to the viewer that the pictorial text of the battle below requires careful interpretation, that it represents more than appears at first sight.

In the St. Albans codex, the interweaving of different colors in the inscription of the gloss becomes more complex as the verbal exegesis itself becomes more complex. The final Emmaus scene, depicting Christ's disappearance by ascension, is reduced in size to make room for the colorful tapestry of this verbal gloss written in alternating lines of green, red, and blue, with no initial of any word in the same color as the body of the word. This extensive gloss is placed to the right, outside the picture frame, because it pertains to images on the following page, where the gloss continues, filling the space to the left of and under the uncolored drawing of two mounted knights fighting and the large painted B that opens the psalter ("*Beatus vir* ..."). Against the backdrop of this initial, a figure of King David holds both his harp and the open codex of his psalms while being inspired by the Holy Spirit, the huge dove poking its beak into his ear (see Figure 7.3). The symbolism of these pictorial figures is explained in a highly abbreviated Latin gloss, which serves as yet another exegetical preface to the psalter, pointing the way to its spiritual meanings. If we take this Latin gloss for a model of seeing and reading, the pictorial figures are to be closely scrutinized for whatever spiritual (figurative) meanings they may reveal; they are to be looked at and contemplated with both corporeal and intellectual eyes, "eyes of the heart."

The confrontation of the two mounted knights who have broken their lances and are fighting each other with swords is the starting point for an extended comparison between secular and spiritual warfare, addressed to the "leaders" of the "holy war in the church" who do battle with sin and the devil: "In our spirits we must set in order every art which these two warriors prepare in their bodies."[11] The glossator's tropological interpretation of the knightly figures is a lesson in spiritual athletism, in learning to fend off the devil: "we likewise, on the other hand with the eyes of the heart, must always keep watch with all virtue against our adversary who is constantly lying in wait to ambush us ... Let each be sure in heart, that unless he destroy his invisible adversary, he himself

Figure 7.3 St. Albans Psalter, Dombibliothek Hildesheim, HS God 1, p. 72 (property of the Basilika of St. Godehard, Hildesheim). Glosses upon glosses on the *Beatus vir* page opening the psalter. By gracious permission of the Dombibliothek Hildesheim.

shall be killed." The glossator moves from an individualizing moral interpretation of knightly battle to an anagogical one concerning the Apocalyptic battle between the forces of good and evil: "he who ... purifies himself constantly gains approval against the last day and the divine battle, which is foretold in the scriptures to come about between the holy church and the antichrist ..."

From the figures of the battling knights, the glossator turns to consider the figures foregrounded against the initial B. His way of describing them, as if justifying choices, suggests a role in designing these pictures: "It has seemed to me that the plan here is that the psalmist himself … should be drawn in the appearance of a king, and placed honourably in the middle of this B, and hold his harp in his right hand against his chest, and in his left hand have his own psalter, in which is written the blessed annunciation." The gloss goes on to explain the allegorical sense of the psalms (as prophetic "annunciation" of Christ), the "sound of the harp" (as "the voice of the holy church"), "his book" (the psalter as "the wisdom of prophecy and that divine prediction"). An additional verbal gloss elucidates the sense of this picture; in red, highly abbreviated Latin, the following appears on the pages of the psalter David holds open: "The blessed psalmist David, whom God has chosen, has gushed forth the annunciation of the Holy Spirit." Having led the reader/listener to a crescendo of apprehension ("By night and day the good and evil prepare themselves …"), the glossator abandons his apocalyptic warnings to offer the comfort and "sweetness" of the psalms as prophecy of Christ and revelation of the "way of salvation."

The initial B, with its interlaced terminals and foliate filling, serves as a backdrop for the figure of King David inspired, who is not contained within the letter but seems to float forward from it on his throne in an act of revelation. A similar effect of letters and figures seeming to come forward, because of their great magnification with respect to others on the page or because they overlap figures or frames "behind" them, can be experienced in Hiberno-Saxon Gospels, such as the *Chi Rho* page of the *Book of Kells*, or in later Anglo-Saxon illuminations, such as those done in the Winchester style (950–1100). It is as if the text had several "planes" as well as levels of interpretation, suggested by superpositions and differences in the size of different letters and figures within the field of the page. In the over 200 historiated initials of the St. Albans Psalter and the various prayers that follow it, items or figures overstepping or overreaching the frame of the letter to "approach" the reader or to gesture toward the written text appear very frequently. Indeed, the most striking visual effect of the psalter illuminations is the impression of enclosure and of surpassing it. The pictorial glosses of the text are placed within the frames of initial letters highlighted in gold, yet these pictures are more demonstratively linked to the text than all the other types of pictorial glossing in the codex. From within the letters, the human figures (the psalmist, Christ, naked souls, monks, nuns, priests) function as embodied connectors to bridge the gap between the written text and the viewer/reader.

The St. Albans Psalter presents the first extensive use of fully painted historiated initials in England. It marks a thorough revision of the technique of pictorial glossing used in the earlier Utrecht and Harley Psalters, where pictorial glosses were sketched in ink and set in an open, unframed landscape across the breadth of the bare parchment above or below the psalm texts. The designers of the Harley Psalter had already added colored ink shading to the sketches, probably to suggest spiritual senses beyond the literal. The designers of the St. Albans Psalter enlarged the palette of colors and entirely painted in the sketched underdrawing of its figurative initials. Whereas the "open" (and highly militaristic) depictions of earlier psalters reflected a Carolingian courtly milieu (the Utrecht Psalter was made in a Benedictine monastery under the direction of Ebbo, foster brother of Louis the Pious), the enclosure of human and divine figures within the space of the letter must have seemed more fitting for the affective devotion developed in the late eleventh and twelfth centuries in cloistered milieux. Psalters for monastic usage began by depicting initial letters themselves as human, plant, and animal figures before discovering the technique of using initial letters to contain such figures.

An explanatory gloss situated "inside" the letter might seem paradoxical in some respects. However, the St. Albans Psalter designer overcame this difficulty by representing the pictorial glosses as gestures of communication. Figures overreach and overlap the framing letter in both directions, toward the reader and toward the inscribed text on the page, connecting the two. Indeed, these pictorial glosses strive demonstratively to validate the inscribed word and the reading of it. The red Latin captions (*tituli*) identifying which part of the psalm is depicted are pointed to by the human figures in the initials or else written on an open psalm book held out to Christ and sometimes grasped and received by him – although not in the case of Psalm 52 ("The fool says in his heart, 'There is no God'"), where the fool sitting on the divine throne looks and holds his inscribed psalter away from Christ. The encouraging lesson of the initials for the beginning reader – and the psalter was the medieval beginner's book – is that the reading of the psalter brings one closer to Christ.

The focus of the depictions in the initials of the St. Albans Psalter is still largely on the literal sense of the psalms so that, as with the Utrecht

Psalter, figurative language is often materialized or translated literally into images. For example, in Psalm 2 the figurative expression, "Thou shalt rule them with an iron rod," is translated literally into a picture of a large Christ menacing with an iron rod rather like a baseball bat (shaped like Odo's staff in the Bayeux Tapestry) a group of smaller, obedient-looking foot soldiers armed with spears. However literal such "translation" of word into image may seem, the depiction is also exegetical in traditional patristic ways. It interprets the psalms allegorically as being about Christ by picturing Christ again and again as the chief actor and the object of the psalmist's petitions. It also interprets the psalms tropologically to offer a model of Christian behavior by picturing the close relationship of monks and nuns (as "psalmists") with Christ, who is shown listening, watching, instructing, blessing, teaching, extending a helping or saving hand.[12] Within the confined, tightly focused context of the initial letters, Christ is shown to be in constant, compassionate interaction with human figures. In general, the pictures of the St. Albans Psalter interpret the text of the psalms in a personally comforting way, especially in support of those choosing the conventual life of worship.

Pictorial glossing pushed to the limits in psalters for laymen

Just how far a pictorial gloss could go in adapting the sense of a text to the desires of its prospective readers can be judged by studying manuscripts, such as the Luttrell Psalter[13] or the newly discovered Macclesfield Psalter, which were made for lay owners, probably in secular ateliers, in the mid-fourteenth century. For example, in his psalter Sir Geoffrey Luttrell had a picture of himself made that took up over a third of the page. Splendidly armed astride his warhorse, he is being handed his helmet and escutcheon by female family members. Although Geoffrey's figure appears at the bottom of the page, which might suggest humility, it is also set off against the foil of a solid gold ground and enhanced by a frame, which the Luttrells or their equipment overreach or overstep in the direction of the viewer. Immediately above the frame is a Latin caption – "Lord Geoffrey Luttrell had me made" – written in exactly the same script as the text of the psalms. The nature and placement of this "portrait" flatter Geoffrey, for at the top of the following recto is the historiated initial glossing Psalm 109: "The Lord said to my lord, 'Sit to the right of me.'" In the initial, a crowned king holding a scepter (King David? Edward III?) sits on the right side of Christ/God holding the globe and conversing with him, while Geoffrey fully occupies the favored space on the right side of his lord and his lord's Lord.[14] Geoffrey's knightly readiness in this depiction may also flatteringly recall the verbal explanation of the jousting knights as "spiritual athletes" on the *Beatus* page of the St. Albans Psalter.

In addition to flattering lay owners, richly illuminated psalters and books of hours sought to add "spirit" to the Latin "letter" of the centrally inscribed psalms and prayers by means of surprising or provocative pictorial glosses in the margins, images whose relation to the text was riddling at best. Literal word illustration and the material, down-to-earth representation of figures of speech were sometimes taken to great lengths. Indeed, literalism could be exaggerated to the point of vulgarity through punning vernacular interpretations – "translated" into visual glosses – of single Latin words or syllables. In the ever-changing, unpredictable, fallen world of the margins of the Macclesfield Psalter, we find pictorial glosses of the text that reverse or twist its sense. For example, in the lower margin of folio 68r, directly below the Latin words of Psalm 45, verse 3, "so we will not be afraid" ("*propterea non timebimus*"), a startled man falls back in fright at confronting a giant flatfish with a thorn-like tail that flies at him through the air (see Figure 7.4). The whimsical gloss

Figure 7.4 Macclesfield Psalter, Cambridge Fitzwilliam Museum, MS 1-2005, fol. 68r, detail of page bottom. Man frightened by giant turbot. By permission of the Fitzwilliam Museum, Cambridge.

of the marginal image omits the "not" to translate only the word *timebimus*. The psalm text, continued on the verso, specifies what will not be feared: earthquakes ("*turbabitur terra*"). If we think of the surprising creature as a turbot (Old French *turbut*, from Old Swedish *törnbut*, compounded of the words for "thorn" and "flatfish"), the perverse vernacular pun that underlies this pictorial gloss comes into focus. The fellow is surprised and frightened by a *turbut terrae* – a "land turbot."

If the jousting knights of the St. Albans Psalter represent psalmody as spiritual combat, what should we make of the Macclesfield Psalter's clownish figures of combat, such as a man attacking a giant snail with a sword or a huge fly with a spear? If the soul striving toward God is represented as a nude man in the St. Albans Psalter, nudity in the Macclesfield Psalter is more often the condition of men lazing under the vine tendrils or engaged in exhibitionistic or voyeuristic activity, more often a sign of the flesh than of the spirit. Whereas the historiated initials of the St. Albans Psalter interpret the psalms in a personally comforting way, the pictorial glosses in the margins of prayer books for lay people, such as the Rutland, Luttrell, and Macclesfield psalters, take their distance from the letter, both literally and figuratively, and make of it what they please, offering a profusion of personal references and odd or surprising images whose connection to the text is puzzling. Indeed, we often wonder whether there could possibly be one. Perhaps such marginal images are, as often as not, temporary distractions from the text to pique the viewer/reader's flagging interest?

The striking pejoration of the sense of the verb *gloser* and its nominal forms *glose* and *glosing* in late fourteenth-century England, as demonstrated in the *Middle English Dictionary*, reflects growing distrust in verbal, but also visual, explanations of authoritative texts. Glossing had always involved interpreting and adapting a text to a particular audience, but this adaptation came to be perceived as a form of cover-up, an attractive lie for self-serving or flattering purposes, a disguise of the true (literal) sense of the authoritative text. To the mendicant preaching friar in Chaucer's *Summoner's Tale*, whom the narrator criticizes for serving the people with "trifles" and "fables" (line 1760), "Glosynge is a glorious thyng, certeyn,/For lettre sleeth, so as we clerkes seyn" (lines 1793–94). Because he judges Scripture to be too hard for his audience to understand ("it is hard to yow, as I suppose"), the begging friar does not follow the literal text but invents a gloss of his own about charitable giving where it "makes sense" to give (lines 1788–96).[15] What he teaches is his own self-serving interpretation, not Holy Writ.

A Middle English poem of complaint from around 1390 to the refrain of "Who says the Sooth [truth], he shall be shent [blamed]," charges that "the truth is kept hidden, while each man tries to be complex and ingenious" ("uche mon maketh touh and queynte"). The speaker adds, "To leave the text and take the gloss, they color and paint every word" ("To leve the tixt and take the glose,/Everi word thei coloure and peynte").[16] Although this criticism is probably aimed at preachers (and especially at preaching friars) who strive to make their explanations of Scripture more attractive or captivating through various rhetorical techniques "coloring and painting" their verbal glosses, the critique also nods in the direction of ingenious pictorial glossing of lay psalters and books of hours, which made the viewer/reader prefer the gloss to the text. With this denigration of glossing came an idealization of the "naked" text, one left in Latin or translated literally into the vernacular, a "plain" text inscribed on bare parchment, enrobed neither in allegorizing explanations nor in colorful painted images. The more "distant" from the letter or tendentious the gloss, the less tolerable to religious reformers. With the Reformation, the creative tension between visual or textual "gloss" and "text" would reach a crisis. We are lucky, indeed, that so few of the provocative marginal figures of the Macclesfield Psalter were rubbed out and that the manuscript has finally come back to light.

Notes

1. Gerald of Wales, *The First Version of the Topography of Ireland by Giraldus Cambrensis*, trans. John J. O'Meara (Dundalk, 1951), p. 67. For the Latin text see *Topographia Hibernica*, in *Giraldis Cambrensis Opera*, ed. J. F. Dimock (1867), 5:123–24. Translations are my own unless noted.

2. For photographic reproductions see J. J. G. Alexander, *Insular Manuscripts from the 6th to the 9th Century: Vol. 1* in *Alexander, Survey of Manuscripts Illuminated in the British Isles (1975–96). The seven volumes of this series, covering the years 600 to 1490, are a fundamental reference tool. A digital color reproduction that permits magnification of details of thirty-two pages from the *Lindisfarne Gospels* may be seen at: www.bl.uk/onlinegallery/ttp/ttpbooks.html.

3. Gregory the Great, *Moralia in Job*, 11.17.26, ed. Marcus Adriaen, CCSL 143A (1979), p. 601.

4. For reproductions from these manuscripts, see Elźbieta Temple, *Anglo-Saxon Manuscripts, 900–1066: Vol. 2*, *Alexander, Survey of Manuscripts*.

5. Bede, *Historia Abbatum* in C. Plummer (ed.), *Bedae Venerabilis opera historica 1* (Oxford, 1896), pp. 369–70, trans. D. H. Farmer, in *The Age of Bede* (1998), pp. 187–210; discussed by

Paul Meyvaert, "Bede and the Church Paintings at Wearmouth-Jarrow, " *Anglo-Saxon England* 8 (1979), 63–77.

6. This English translation, as well as the Latin text of Gregory's two letters (*CCSL* 140A), may be found in Celia M. Chazelle, "Pictures, Books, and the Illiterate: Pope Gregory I's Letters to Serenus of Marseilles," *Word and Image*, 6 (1990), 138–53, at 139–40.

7. *De Templo* 2, in *Opera Exegetica*, ed. D. Hurst, *CCSL* 119A (1969), pp. 212–13, cited and translated by Meyvaert, "Bede and the Church Paintings," p. 69.

8. On the development of this scholarly consensus as to the tapestry's origins, see *Gameson, *Study of the Bayeux Tapestry* (1997), especially pp. 157–211. For a digital color reproduction of the entire tapestry, which is displayed in Bayeux, see http://panograph. free.fr/BayeuxTapestry.html.

9. Digital reproductions of the entire Utrecht Psalter may be seen on the Utrecht University Library's website, http://psalter.library.uu.nl, where each pictorial detail is keyed to the word or phrase or passage of the psalm text it translates and interprets visually.

10. Jane Geddes and Margaret Jubb have created the University of Aberdeen's website exclusively for this manuscript (Hildesheim, Dombibliothek, MS St. Godehard 1) at: www.abdn.ac.uk/stalbanspsalter.

11. All English translations of this gloss are taken from the Aberdeen website, which also provides a transcription of the Latin text.

12. See *Haney, *The St. Albans Psalter* (2002), pp. 264–79.

13. See the digital color reproduction of thirty-two pages of the Luttrell Psalter (British Library, Additional MS 42130) at: www.bl.uk/onlinegallery/sacredtexts/ttpbooks.html. Thirty pages of the Macclesfield Psalter (Cambridge, Fitzwilliam Museum, MS 1–2005) may be seen at: www.fitzmuseum.cam.ac.uk/gallery/macclesfield/gallery.

14. Michael Camille, *Mirror in Parchment: The Luttrell Psalter and the Making of Medieval England* (Chicago, IL, 1998), p. 50.

15. See *The Riverside Chaucer*, 3rd edn., gen. ed. Larry D. Benson (Boston, MA, 1987), p. 130.

16. This poem from the Vernon manuscript (folio 407), which I have punctuated and spelled slightly differently, is part of the *Corpus of Middle English Prose and Verse* available at the *Medieval English Compendium* website, which also includes the *Middle English Dictionary*: http://quod.lib.umich.edu/m/mec.

8

Literacy, schooling, universities

Medieval literacies

Education and its delivery reflect the most salient aspirations of any culture. Teaching is the basic form of *traditio*, the "handing on" of values deemed culturally central. In its product, the educated person of whatever level of attainment, it has replicated not only those values useful socially but also provided the tools deemed necessary for perpetuation of that cultural system. This chapter will seek to examine some features of this process in England in the later medieval period, from about 1200 to the early sixteenth century.

Although there remains a common perception of massive illiteracy (generally exaggerated: it was perhaps higher in the early Modern period), medieval culture was considerably more "literary" than even the modern world of a half century ago. Everywhere in Europe, the centrality of literate behaviors to culture was insured by the conversion to Christianity, an event that occurred in Anglo-Saxon England from about 600. The centrality of the sacred text, the general propagation of its narrative and basic ideas, and the liturgical ceremonial that enacts its precepts all required books and the literate tools to use them. Such a mandate always provided an impulse for and one focus of English schooling.

However, long before the conversion of the Anglo-Saxons, it was well understood that any approach to the Christian text required educational tools inherited from the classical world. Although medieval society always respected holy *ydiotae* – unlearned people like the first community described in the Acts of the Apostles – the routine delivery of the Christian message would depend upon techniques of study developed in late antique Rome. Most influentially, St. Augustine of Hippo (d. 430), by training a professor of rhetoric, argued for the appropriation of the tools of classical literary commentary for Christian reading and teaching in his *De doctrina christiana*.[1] Following his example, inherited techniques of classical grammatical study were to provide the rudiments and methods of all European education, in England from the humblest parish school up to the subtlest training offered in this culture, the abstruse world inhabited by Oxford doctors of theology. Thus, as Langland says, "Grammer [was] þe ground of al" (B.15.372), the foundation of all knowledge.[2]

In the body of this chapter, I will examine aspects of this training, its methods, and its social utility. But one must understand that culturally mandated "school literacy" shrouds a great diversity of literate behavior and experience in the period. Much of the social practice of literacy remains quite antithetical to any modern notions of what constitutes "literate behavior," most particularly our sense that to be literate requires a command of multiple skills primarily ocular in nature.

Modern education mandates literacy of the eye and its guidance of the hand. It was far from thus in the Middle Ages. The commonplace pictures of grammar schools, for example, show students with both hands holding their books; moreover, they are seated on wooden "forms" (benches, whence "sixth form") and hold the books in their laps. They are not writing, were not necessarily taught to do so, and probably never sat a written examination. In cultural terms, reading was perceived as an intellectual activity, but writing probably only a handicraft. What grammar school images show reflects universal practice; in the Middle Ages vastly more people could read than write. Penmanship was professionalized as a guild trade, and only those with an interest in composition (which would include nearly anyone engaged in higher studies) really needed to produce words in script.

Further, we understand literacy as simply the command of certain skills practiced upon the mother tongue. Traditionally, in the Middle Ages *literatus* meant the command of no one's mother tongue, but of a learned language, Latin (see David Carlson, Chapter 9 below). And although a sense that literacy included more than an acquired foreign tongue grew steadily in the period, later medieval England was a polylingual culture. Moreover, grammar school, as we will see, clouded the question of appropriate literate competences considerably. As a result, in the later Middle Ages, the literacy of any individual might evoke a series of nonhomologous responses, depending on what language she or he was adept at and in what contexts (reading? oral comprehension? to what degree? writing?).

I have mentioned above the eye-centered ocular content of modern literacy, basically training for private silent reading and correspondence. Quite in opposition to such a premise, in the Middle Ages, literary culture often was strongly ear-centered, auditory, and performative. Early monastic tradition had perceived reading as a form of prayer; it was an action, expected to engage the whole body, and to be pursued, even in the absence of an audience, orally as a work of devotion. Some twelfth-century observers expressed surprise at great men who read silently to themselves. Similarly, as we will see in discussing schooling, the customary demonstration of academic competence, the equivalent of a modern written examination, was always improvisational and *viva voce*.

Moreover, people, whether literate in our sense or not, were accustomed (and expected) to engage with texts orally, through the ear. A well-known example appears in Chaucer's *Troilus*, when Pandarus finds Criseyde among a company of women hearing a romance of Thebes read aloud by one of their number (2.78–108, an experience replicated in the portrait of Chaucer himself reading to an assembled courtly company at the head of the most expensively produced copy of the poem).[3] Plainly, Chaucer here describes intelligent and "well-read" people, and they are capable of making literate critical judgments about a text orally communicated.

However, there are ample indications that "aural literacy" was considerably more widespread than simply among the literati, who might read if they chose. Chaucer's Wife of Bath, for example, seems to know her husband's Latin "book of wicked wives" only from translated excerpts he reads her; but she remembers them with great verbal exactitude (and in Middle English couplets, as at *Canterbury Tales* III.235–302 or 715–85), and no one would deny that she is capable of a detailed critical and analytical understanding of them. One could offer similar analyses of other late-medieval figures, for example, Margery Kempe or Lollard women. The latter, although often clearly incapable of eye-reading, could nonetheless memorize, perform, and recall selectively large portions of the English Bible; their reputation as "great reasoners in Scripture" implies that their recall included an ability to perform some impressive level of hermeneutic operations on their texts.

But these, perhaps liminal, examples scarcely exhaust the evidence for "aural literacy." It was everywhere apparent in medieval culture. As we will see, a capacity for literate performative skill, oral capacity assessed and judged on the spot through what the ear had heard and the brain absorbed, was built into formal instruction at every level. And a great deal of the most important literate business of medieval England was conducted and assessed performatively, for example, in such acts as pleading in local courts (in French) or delivering and hearing complex sermons (in English, Latin, French, or some combination of them).

Finally, as a number of examples above imply, literacy was inflected by gender issues. Although there exists murky evidence of opportunities for the schooling of women, grammar school was a male enclave. (Walter Ong once famously referred to its processes as "a male puberty rite.") But there is ample evidence for the careers of a number of highly educated women; as early as *c.* 1225, for example, the sisters of *Ancrene Riwle/Wisse* read books in all three of England's languages and were expected to copy out, as well as at least recognize the incipits in, their personal (Latin) liturgical books. Beyond the fairly clear outlines of schooling I will offer, ones certainly shared by that smallish group one may call "sophisticated men of affairs," the social group of greatest interest to historians and literary scholars, there existed a literate hinterland that exhibited exceptionally varied practices.

Grammar schooling

Formal education began with grammar school (or its cousin, song school, designed to train choristers). Such training was susceptible to a variety of delivery systems, all with their place in a full history of medieval education. Besides free-standing grammar schools, whose number increased exponentially during the period, such instruction was available in cathedral song or grammar schools, in monastic almonry schools, and from private tutors in the great houses of the kingdom. Yet whatever its institutional insertion, the intellectual and cultural focus of grammatical training, the emphasis of this discussion, was much the same everywhere.

While most schools seem to have been prepared to do the remedial work as necessary, children generally learned their letters at home, along with a rudimentary ability to form syllables and words. They may also have been exposed to a few basic texts; since salvation always remained the most fundamental goal of education, a typical "first text" was the most basic Christian prayer, the Pater Noster. Boys usually passed on to grammar school (or song school for choristers) when eight to ten years old; the course was expected to run for three to five years. However, at all levels of medieval education, dropout rates were vastly in excess of any modern expectations; well over half those who enrolled for an Oxford BA, for example, failed to get the degree. In the Middle Ages, education was always in play with a notion of cultural aspiration and service; how far one proceeded with a course was measured by the degree of advancement sought. At all levels, students were not enrolled for some formal certification, but for the learning process, as far as that enabled whatever vocational prospects were of interest.

Assuming children had built from letter to syllable to word, they would be prepared to begin their school training with the basics of Latin grammar. Their text had been composed by the mid-fourth-century Roman, Donatus, *Ars minor*, or some derivative version, customarily known as "The Accidence." This began, "How many parts of speech are there?," and it offered a complete conspectus of Latin grammatical forms and the terminations that express their relations. Preliminary reading exercises to instantiate this teaching were drawn, particularly for choristers, from basic texts of Christian devotion: prayers like the Pater Noster, the Psalter (repeated once a week in services, and thus absolutely integral to the liturgy), and staples of church music (hymns and sequences), which had their own teaching tools, for example, in England, Thomas Haume's *Troparium glossatum/Exposicio sequenciarum*. Chaucer's the "Prioress's Tale" depicts two young boys in the earlier stages of this training, the elder capable of recognizing and repeating words, but not of identifying them or construing them in accord with Donatus's principles. As he says, "I lerne song; I kan but smal grammeere" (*The Canterbury Tales* VII.536).

While Donatus – who had taught Jerome (d. 420), the translator of Hebrew Scripture into Europe's Bible, the Latin Vulgate – provided a comprehensive introduction to grammatical forms, he was not particularly helpful on Latin vocabulary. To remedy this gap, the young often received a few colloquies, model conversations, designed to inculcate basic vocabulary (a local Latin–Old English example known as Ælfric's *Colloquy*, though only the Latin portions were by him, was in circulation until 1200; a comparable successor tool was the *De nominibus utensilium* by the university scholar and Augustinian abbot, Alexander Nequam [d. 1217], which received Anglo-Norman glosses).⁴ Frequently geared to everyday domestic situations, such lexical training was designed to give students oral facility, since after the Norman Conquest English usage was discouraged, often violently so, in school. Children thus received what amounted to a fun "private code" language, one removed from everyday intercourse, which they were to speak to one another, as well as to their master.

But the guts of grammar-school training became progressively more challenging. For some notion of what be might be involved, we can turn to a fairly typical example of a schoolbook, Nottingham University Library, MS Mi(ddleton) LM 2. This sequence of separately produced pieces was joined, after several of them had been lost, at some point in the fifteenth century.⁵ The largest chunk of the volume (fols. 105–66) may well be one of the latest, copied in the mid-thirteenth century. However, it agrees in format with the remainder: the text a narrow column down the center of the page, written on alternate lines. This presentation allows the book to be glossed, to have explanatory notes entered to facilitate its use. Quite importantly, this portion of the book is pristine, with the presentation of only the bare texts.

This fragment contains the traditional set of texts taught in medieval grammar schools, "the six authors," all in verse, in the order that is conventional. As the example quoted in the Appendix below, and to which I will turn shortly, shows, these remained current – at this point in print – in the early Modern period.

The first of the six was the late classical collection of moral proverbs, *Disticha Catonis*; after its study, students advanced to the *Ecloga Theoduli*, a Carolingian poem debating the merits of the classics and Christianity. The program then returned to late antique writing with the fables of Avianus, a brief series of Æsopic stories, and the peculiarly chosen elegies of Maximianus, a lament of old age and lost love. The concluding two texts were late classical *epillia*: Statius' *Achilleis* (a youthful Achilles and his first love) and Claudian's *De raptu Proserpinae*.⁶

Knowledge of these texts was ubiquitous in the Middle Ages. In *Piers Plowman*, for example, Langland cites or alludes to them more frequently than any source except the Bible. "Cato" is quoted repeatedly, for example, B.12.22a; a Theodulus gloss underlies the discussion of Incarnation at B.1.153–58 (a discovery of Anne Middleton); "Auynet" (a French version of Avianus) is mentioned at B.12.259; "Walter of England" – a fable text that gradually replaced Avianus – is pillaged for the fable at B.Prol.146–208.⁷

Another common late curricular addition, Alain of Lille's (d. 1202) *Parabolae*, is used at B.18.408ab. Langland's persistent references to the exemplary Tobit (B.10.33) probably reflect another text added to the syllabus later, Matthew of Vendôme's *Tobias* (composed 1160s). Langland also cites the *Liber prouerbiorum* of Godfrey of Winchester (d. 1107), an obscure work that was not part of the curriculum but is consonant with his use of "Cato" and Alain. Similarly, Chaucer's "Merchant's Tale" provides a badly fractured version of Claudian's account of Pluto's abduction of Proserpine. Other vernacular poetry is similarly steeped. A late thirteenth-century manuscript presents an English paraphrase of the first elegy of Maximianus; near the end of the fifteenth century a glorious partial poetic translation into early Scots of "Walter of England" was made by a schoolteacher, Robert Henryson of Dunfermline.[8]

More important than the names of the texts is their status. All medieval education proceeded, at whatever level, from a narrowly delimited series of "set-texts," the basic authors or authorities. These were considered the most impressive examples of their respective kinds, with the further assumption that intelligent comprehension of them enabled passage to any other text (or to a wide variety, as we will see, of worldly occupations).

Other chunks of the Nottingham manuscript show the, at least partial, conversion to a different set of authors, in common use from *c.* 1200. The first and oldest portion of the volume (copied before 1230 or so) presents excerpts from a poem introducing the subject "grammar," Everard of Bethune's *Graecismus* (composed *c.* 1210); other booklets from slightly later in the century include the widely distributed similar poem by Alexander de Villa Dei, *Doctrinale* (composed *c.* 1200). And the manuscript provides a wealth of similar materials, including some widely used poems by English authors: a very late thirteenth-century fragment of the basic instruction in Christian doctrine, *Peniteas cito* by William de Montibus, chancellor of Lincoln Cathedral (d. 1213); and two widely disseminated poems designed to improve a student's vocabulary, the *Synonoma* and *Equivoca*, both by John of Garland (d. *c.* 1272). All these materials have heavy marginal and interlinear explanatory glosses, indicating they were used (the antique "six authors" of the manuscript, where the spaces for glosses remain unfilled, have not been). In one instance, another vocabulary poem by an Englishman, Serlo of Wilton's *De differentiis* (d. 1181), has, significantly as we will see, been equipped with Anglo-Norman glosses (two further ones added in Middle English).

What did boys learn from texts like these? The best way to find out is to examine tools produced to aid in teaching them. The Appendix to this chapter provides a sample, excerpts from the very lengthy first gloss from a commentary on the *Ecloga Theoduli*. Given the level of sophistication on display here, this is an explanatory tool devised to be used by masters, not students, to prepare for their classes. It follows an artificial rhetorical, not classroom teaching, model, but from it, one can intuit a logical program for teaching this text.

First of all, in a portion of this gloss I have not reproduced, the master should "divide" the text for his charges. He should explain that it has parts, each of which contributes to the total argument, yet should be examined in detail separately. He should then begin the grammatical analysis of the first relevant portion, here a distich, by giving a general summary of the sense (set off as section [1] in the Appendix).

Next comes perhaps the most important part of the exercise for beginners, "construing" or parsing the statement (section [3]). The master is to begin by eliminating the deliberately contrived (and thus difficult) word order of Latin verse by converting the statement into "natural" prose order. (Manuscripts for beginners often use dots to join grammatically related members, and dots, letters, or numbers so they can arrange the words themselves in order.) By this process, in company with a series of interjected explanations, the teacher clarifies the basic grammatical relations of the statement. Students may have thought similar terminations meant that words were grammatically related, but *terras* (accusative plural, the direct object) and *estas* (nominative singular, the subject) aren't parallel. *Ethiopum* (a third-declension noun) is glossed by the more overt second-declension form *populorum* and thus clearly identified as genitive plural (slow boys might have stumbled into thinking it was masculine accusative singular and the direct object); *aureus* "golden, gilded" here must be understood in a metaphorical sense. The glosses interjected in this procedure also indicate synonyms, either to introduce new lexical items or to jog student memories of past lessons.

More emphatic efforts at such vocabulary enrichment and in the finer points of understanding Latin occur in section [5] of the excerpt. *Torreo* is apparently a new verb, heretofore unseen by the students. It is presented with a full display of its principal parts (*torres* "you burn," a signal that for most forms it will follow *doceo* and those verbs like it the students have already learned in Donatus; then *torrui* "I have burned" and the unpredictable *tostus* "burnt") – and with an extensive list of synonyms.

Ethiops can mean either a male or female Ethiopian (*hic et hec*), but has no neuter form. Although it is a third-declension noun, its related adjectives all derive their forms from the larger first-/second-declension class that ends *-us -a -um* in the three genders.

In this account, the couplet also raises a number of finer grammatical points: the confusingly identical pasts of two verbs or the nominatives of two nouns, *cancer*. As the master says, these are *equivoca*, ambiguous forms, of the sort that John of Garland's poem addresses. In addition, there is considerable attention to etymology (often suppositious), patterns of word derivation. While these are surely excellent mnemonics, allowing students to group words of related origin, medieval fascination with the subject rested upon a belief that Latin "naturally" revealed the inevitable shape of experience, the deep patterns of creation.

Next, the master would outline the figures of speech (section [4] of the commentary in the Appendix below). One goal of all grammatical training was to inculcate attention to, and skill at, reproducing ornate language, eloquent self-expression. Always in the Middle Ages, stylistic sophistication was perceived as having suasive power (the point at which grammar and rhetoric begin to blur together). The master follows convention in emphasizing periphrastic figurative techniques. For example, in this account, "aureus axis solis" would have the same lexical force as "sol," since, as the parsing gloss indicates, the sun is understood to be brightest planet, thus rendering "aureus" logically redundant. Stylistically, of course, the two are miles apart, and elegance of composition is always associated with such "amplification." (In a similar vein, the poem is also the place where students, in subsequent glosses, first met the commonplaces of classical mythology that they would need to comprehend more sophisticated Latin poets, initially the two late epics included in the "six authors," but then Ovid, Virgil, and Horace.)

Finally, the master might address the hidden allegorical meaning of the passage (section [2]). Such a reading strategy was endemic to all medieval literary culture, as Chaucer's various references to the fruit and the chaff (notably at the end of "The Nun's Priest's Tale" or in "The Parson's Prologue") or Langland's walnut, with its bitter bark and sweet kernel (B.11.257–66), indicate. Such readings assume that texts should be spiritually efficacious, and explicating them at this level requires a developed eye for moral analogy.

As is fairly obvious, training in this fashion cultivates a good deal more than just a Latin literacy that probably exceeds that of modern graduates in Classics. Grammar masters insisted upon intensely analytical habits of mind, most particularly habits of a logical stripe that encouraged careful attention to principle and its application, and to similarity and difference. In his initial division, the master insists that parts of text are unlike one another in subject and purpose, and thus should be examined separately. Grammatical detail, however, frequently appears similar when it's not (*terras ... estas*) and must be properly categorized, the principles proper to each category developed appropriately. Allegory, however, pursues similarity, the analogous (parabolic) instance, even when it looks radically different. And simultaneously, a young man is expected to pay at least passing attention to expressiveness and grace.

The instantiated form of grammar school instruction built upon principles like this. At least initially, the classroom was run on inculcation by rote and by persistent drill. But the instruction I have outlined from the gloss would be given orally by the instructor as a lecture, a running commentary. Its goal was to indoctrinate in aural comprehension of reasonably complex (and abstract) Latin, and one classroom convention was to expunge English as much as possible.

Moreover, there is very strong evidence that, at least down to Chaucer's generation, in most prominent schools English never appeared and that explanations went on in Anglo-Norman French (which students would have been expected to pick up somewhere, perhaps from colleagues who might have been taught it at home). The main evidence is provided by the Chester chronicler Ranulph Higden, writing in the 1330s, who claims that all grammatical instruction proceeded in French, to the detriment of English; his translator, John Trevisa, writing in the 1380s, says that, since 1349, English had been introduced into classrooms, much to the detriment of students' French.[9]

While it is certainly hard to believe the universality of Higden's claim (although supported by Trevisa), there is ample grammar-book evidence for the prevalence of Anglo-Norman as a tool of classroom explanation. The earliest example occurs in British Library, MS Cotton Faustina A.x, French additions made at the end of the twelfth century; and French explanations appear, along with Latin ones, quite ubiquitously in thirteenth-century teaching books like the Nottingham manuscript.[10] Moreover, as late as the second quarter of the fourteenth century considerable emphasis was placed on French capacity (and English excluded) in situations of higher study. All three Oxford colleges founded at this time (Oriel, Exeter, and Queen's), as well as the general synod of the

English Augustinian canons, wrote into their governing statutes prohibitions on conversations not in Latin or French. And the Langland quotation with which I began offers a similar comment:

> Grammer, þe ground of al, bigileþ now children,
> For is noon of þise newe clerkes, whoso nymeþ hede,
> That kan versifie faire ne formaliche enditen,
> Ne nauȝt oon among an hundred þat an auctor kan construwe
> Ne rede a lettre in any langage but in Latin or Englissh.
>
> (B.15.372–76)

The poet, writing in the mid-1370s, laments the loss of full-scale Anglo-Norman literacy (along with the ability to parse, for which he uses the technical term of the *Ecloga* commentary, as well as diminished capacity at eloquent composition). All are for him equally signs of the loss of grammar itself.

While the master ran the grammar school show, the boys were not allowed to sit as quiescent puddings and were required to demonstrate their own skills at Latin orally. The exercise was known as "apposing" and was a *viva voce* examination, sometimes conducted as a *tête-à-tête* of student and master, sometimes (like a modern spelling exercise) formally before the class. The boys were to stand and deliver; given a French (later English) sentence, they were promptly to provide the accurate Latin equivalent. In schoolboy lore, "apposing" was a horrifying prospect with potentially severe results for the errant, a meeting with the schoolmaster's rod, his badge of office.

The surviving exercises for "apposition" are all from the fifteenth century, a point at which English had replaced French. But they are daunting indeed, and not simply in their content. One sentence, to be converted to Latin *ex tempore*, runs: "ȝyf Ion my felow were ybete as ofte as he doþ deseruy hit without dowte he wold become a gode chyld and an hesy wythyn a fewe days."[11] This sentence, leaving aside its threatening message, requires a passive subjunctive in one subordinate clause, but the indicative in the second subordinate clause (dependent on the first), and a present subjunctive (even though "wold" looks suspiciously past tense) in the main clause. Moreover, the impulse to render "hesy" as the common *facilis* (it should go in the nominative, not an object case), would merit rebuke, since the sense should require either *habilis* or *gracilis*. Pretty obviously, a boy had to display that he had learned grammatical Latin of considerable sophistication. But "apposing" also engrained prompt and accurate oral responsiveness, a logical approach to problems, and perhaps, for the intelligent, a modicum of verbal grace.

Training like this constituted the basic level of understood literate ability, at least until the mid-fourteenth century. It was what any intelligent person with a modicum of literary interest would know, in some way. And until the generation of Chaucer, that knowledge would likely have included operative trilingual skills.

University

If one chose to go on beyond grammar school, in England one had only two university options, Oxford and Cambridge. Students went up roughly at age 14–16 to enroll in the four-year course that led to a BA degree. This, the "arts course," was considered the *fons et origo* of all higher study, and the masters in the arts course functionally ran the university. Those academically stimulated might stay on for the three-year MA course, which (as a magistrate) conferred the right to teach university students anywhere in Europe. At its end, after a year plus as a regent master (a regular member of the teaching faculty), a small minority might pass on to one of the three professional schools, Medicine, Civil and Canon Law, or the queen of all, Theology. A doctorate in any of these subjects would require at least a further decade of study.

All higher instruction relied upon the same mechanism of "set texts" as did grammar school (with, as time passed, an increasing number of allowed options). University continued that insistence upon the intense knowledge of a limited set of eternal authorities, knowledge of which would prepare the student to tackle any analogous (and obviously lesser) text. Moreover, the institutional framework of university learning strikingly replicated that of the grammar school. In its form, it is completely foreign to any modern undergraduate experience outside Oxbridge, where it vestigially persists.

Before a student came up, his family or backers had to arrange residence, which, for the first two centuries of Oxford's existence, may simply have been in a rented room, and to arrange his tuition. These pre-arrangements cast up one difference from grammar school training, which increasingly was available free (and always very cheaply): university cost money – room rent, book costs, fees paid to one's various instructors, eventually a blow-out feast when one earned one's degree. Students needed substantial financial support and were thus frequently patronized. Langland's disappointed Wille laments the cessation of his studies with the death of his "fader and frendes" (C.5.35–43a); Chaucer's Clerk prays for the "freendes" who support him in his studies ("General Prologue," 299–302). While "friend" might cover any variety of blood-relations, as well as non-family members, it is clear that medieval higher education often represented a potential employer's investment in a young man of promise whose career he would later facilitate (and profit from).

When students came up, they did not register with the university (neither institution has any medieval records of its students). The student had arranged for tuition from an MA, a full teaching member of the faculty, and was entered on his roll of charges. This master was essentially responsible for the private tuition of the degree candidate, often in a small group with the rest of his charges. This behavior is the foundation of the modern Oxbridge tutorial, since, from the early fifteenth century, registration with a master was transformed into a requirement for residence in a university-approved lodging (a college or "private hall").

But even before that time, the relation was like that of pupil and tutor, and the instruction relatively informal. As far as we can tell (private tuition leaves no records), this academic work was most particularly centered in the university equivalent of grammar school "apposing." This included first "repetition," the student's oral demonstration that he had absorbed material transmitted by formal lectures; and most importantly, training for "disputation," formal public debate on academic questions, with an emphasis upon logical skills, as well as oratorical.

The university, or more precisely "the faculty of arts," offered more public forms of instruction, all of them in Latin. At the most basic level, there were "cursory lectures," taught by BAs (candidates for the MA); these provided only a literal reading or paraphrase of the set texts, designed to give students a basic and summary familiarity. They would have resembled sections [1] and [3] of grammar commentary discussed above. The more important "ordinary lectures," taught by MAs (regent masters, in their period before possible matriculation for a doctorate), presented full commentative addresses, embodying the more advanced steps noted in the grammar commentary. At their most advanced, they involved the lecturing master proposing *questiones*, difficult and arguable problems, raised by the text; this material fed the disputations heard by the student's own master. In addition, there were "extraordinary lectures" that offered instruction in optional texts.

Since lectures were required, and new material flooded student heads hard and fast, every working day of full term, all Oxford students were certainly writers, as well as readers. The more financially strapped among them may have made their own copies of the set texts, through dictation as it were, by copying out the version read aloud in cursory lectures. And all of them would certainly have taken some form of notes on what they heard; in some (mostly higher degree) courses, manuscripts composed of student lecture notes, called *reportationes*, still survive.

The faculty of arts also set the degree requirements. These are customarily couched, when recorded (much seems to have gone on at a quite informal level of faculty consultation, passed on to students orally by their masters), as hearing a specific set text in daily lectures for a certain number of specified weeks or terms. For the arts course, this constituted a broad-bore program, one that deepened grammar and rhetoric training from previous schooling by adding courses in the other five *artes liberales*.

The first three of these, grammar, rhetoric, and logic, formed the "trivium" (the triple way). For grammar, students read Priscian, *De constructionibus* ("Priscian minor"). These form the last two books of the *Institutiones grammaticae*, the most monumental treatment of the Latin language and its rules, from the mid-fifth century; students were to hear lectures on this text twice, perhaps thirty to forty ordinary lectures in total. In addition, they heard one set on another work of Donatus, *Barbarismus*. The remainder of Priscian's text, which overlaps training already received in grammar school (though vastly more sophisticated and syncretic in presentation), was offered as set of fifteen to twenty cursory lectures.

Since students could be expected to be pretty well equipped in grammar, training in rhetoric, the study specifically devoted to eloquent composition, was more extensive: in the 1431 Oxford statutes, it required a year's worth of ordinary lectures (forty-five to sixty in all) and included a range of options: a choice from among one of three foundational classical rhetorics (notably the *Ad Herennium* always ascribed to Cicero), or Ovid's *Metamorphoses*, or the works of Virgil. But both these studies were thoroughly dwarfed by requirements in the third segment of the "trivium," logic, always a two-year course of ordinary lectures, covering the full known Aristotelian canon and some Boethius. This was probably no accident, since Oxford's universal European fame rested primarily on the work of its logic masters in arts, secondarily for logically inflected science subjects.

These natural sciences formed the "quadrivium" (fourfold way). They included geometry (Euclid), arithmetic (Boethius), music (Boethius again), and astronomy (Ptolemy). A brief segment of the last course was devoted to computistical study, important in establishing the date of Easter and thus the order of the whole Christian year. This included as a text John of Holywood on the sphere (early thirteenth century), mentioned in the Theodulus commentary in the Appendix. After the arts course, the MA emphasized readings in "the three philosophies," natural, moral, and metaphysical, in the main set texts drawn from the Aristotelian corpus, and including *De anima* as a basic text of natural philosophy. Insofar as grammar appeared at this level, it was the modern "modistic" study, basically a theoretical description of Latin syntax, predicated on the "power" that forms grammatical relationship.[12]

A student's career reached its conclusion when his master gave his permission to proceed to his degree. He tendered this support when he felt the student had absorbed the required lecture materials and was prepared for public disputation. Such formal public argument before an audience (and before masters as judges) concluded the program and led to the degree.

The higher faculties preceded analogously. For example, for the D.Th., students attended lecture series in set texts, in this case on individual biblical books and on the Sentences of Peter Lombard, taken to be the basic introduction to issues in the field. At the same time, they participated in public dispute on specific theological *quaestiones*.

University faculties of law, however, remained anomalous. Enrolling in such a law course was actually restrictive and, in many respects, locally useless, for the law of England was common law, not that taught in university. The civil law course taught Roman Law, basically Justinian's *Digest* (an early sixth-century compilation, gathering pre-existing codes and commentaries); the ordinary lecture subject of canon law was *Extra* or the *Decretales* (decrees of popes and of recent general councils of the Church, gathered by St. Raymund de Penyaforte at the request of Pope Gregory IX and promulgated in 1234) and other "modern" collections. The foundational *Decretum* of Gratian (composed *c.* 1140) was in Oxford a topic of cursory lectures only. Although not central to English law, such men were extremely well placed for certain quite well-remunerated tasks: service in episcopal chanceries and the diplomatic corps, for example.

But England was governed by the common law, which, unlike the university faculty, was strenuously Francophonic. Anglo-Norman was the customary language of statute, as well as of pleading at the bar (where it remained in place until 1731), frequently of composing documents, and of the basic instructional texts (in the main, guides to the rules of civil procedure). Thus, pursuing the common law required an alternate school system. The universities, Oxford in particular, recognized its peculiar demands by what one might consider associated schools of paralegal studies. These specialized in teaching French and such ancillary skills as accounting and legal drafting, as well as another branch of medieval rhetoric, "curial writing" or *ars dictaminis*, the ability to compose artful (frequently cadenced prose) official correspondence.[13] Full education in the common law was provided (as it had been from the late twelfth century) only through practitioner instruction. This occurred first in the London courts and later through membership in one of the Inns of Court.

The social utility of educated literacy

The social impact of trained literacy in the Middle Ages was out of all proportion to the numbers of individuals involved. For example, Oxford was probably never larger than 1,600 enrolled students at any time in the period. But its products, far from all of them, of course, graduates, were integral to the life of the nation. And even non-Oxonian training could bring a great measure of worldly success and cultural impact.

The most ubiquitous literate presence in England reflected that basic motivation underlying the whole system of "Christian teaching" from Augustine on: the salvation of society. The Fourth Lateran Council of the Church (1215) insisted upon a program, Europe-wide in its scope, for better delivery of pastoral care, primarily through various forms of oral religious instruction. This demand produced a constantly voiced need for educated and thus inspirational spiritual leadership, dispersed throughout English society.

As a result, one form of patronage occurs ubiquitously in late medieval bishops' registers. Spiritual leaders eagerly permitted rectors to hire a vicar to serve their church so as to underwrite subdegree-length stays in Oxbridge. Given clerical salaries, such study must have been underwritten, either by the episcopal diocese or by the lay patron of the church involved. Thus, Thomas IV, Lord Berkeley, underwrote the stays of his local priest, John Trevisa, in Oxford, so that he might consult the Latin originals of sophisticated instructional materials that Berkeley wished translated.

But more usually, university short-termers were in orders, regular or secular, seeking arts course materials that would aid them in their teaching and preaching mission, and perhaps practice in hortatory and explanatory oral rhetoric. The university sponsored frequent public sermons, which would have provided available sophisticated models to take notes from – many of these survive as *reportationes*, too – and to emulate.[14]

In addition, arts, like grammar school, insisted on a capacity for seeing moral analogies in diverse materials. Coupled with the oral skills all study emphasized, a priest could improve his pulpit performance at sermon instruction. In the later Middle Ages, this field had its own rhetorical guides, *artes predicandi*, and myriad handbooks with materials useful for rhetorical amplification/dilation, mainly by the figure *parabola* (moralized analogies) deemed appropriate in this mode.[15]

But when Langland discusses clerics leaving their parishes, his views of the process are scarcely so benign. The poem's initial lament on the evils of modern times argues that typically clerics leave parishes to become transformed into something else, clerks, and especially royal clerks (B.Prol.83–96). The poet's disquiet addresses the most common and socially viable use of literacy in the later Middle Ages.

Although important, the parish was very far from the most usual and widespread social unit in medieval England. That was the "family." However, one needs to understand this term in its Latin sense *familia*, which refers, not simply to an extended biological unit but to a "household," "retinue," or "livery." Although diverse in exact implication, all these terms designate that group of persons who are necessary to support a paterfamilias and his kin. In the Middle Ages, the group gave their support most typically by facilitating the agricultural exploitation of property (but increasingly in the period, by commercial activity as well).

Such structures were ubiquitous in medieval England, beginning with the most important, the royal household, at the top, and extending, in less elaborated forms, throughout society down to, for example, individual merchants (supported by journeymen and apprentices) in their urban shops. Nor did all important "families" necessarily have biological centers; one great succession of "families" that constantly fostered and tapped university talent was composed of bishops.

Education prepared one for a culture of "service" within some larger enterprise. All large "families," of whatever sort, needed competent and educated "servants" – reeves, factors, bureaucrats of all sorts. And the flipside of such "service" was "patronage," starting with the funds that sustained students in Oxford. It is not accidental that all early Oxford colleges were founded and endowed by former royal bureaucrats; having profited from the royal "family," these men set out to reproduce their like and to sustain a tradition of local and national administration.

Education thus existed to create serviceable men, people who could function effectively within record-ridden bureaucracy. English government, as far back as centralized West Saxon institutions of the pre-Conquest period, emphasized written record and formal account. This investment in the "paper [or parchment] trail" had exponentially increased under the rule of Norman and Angevin kings.

One might consider the example of Chaucer, a consummate royal servant. While he may have had some (largely, it would appear, word-of-mouth) notoriety among his contemporaries as a pretty good poet, his livelihood and his courtly connections were otherwise predicated. He was an extremely competent administrator: a controller of Customs required to keep records in his autograph – and far and away the longest fourteenth-century holder of what seems to have been a graft-ridden position. He also served as master of the King's Works, a job that required management of large-scale building projects.

But to mention simply "the accounts" fails to exhaust what was at stake in a culture of "patronized service." All lords, indeed landholders of any stripe, had a considerable need for competent legal advice. At the highest levels, this extended to legal expertise in fields outside the common law. Episcopal dioceses had to follow the precepts of canon law in all their various operations, and, in their relations with the pope, might need expertise in the civil law followed on the Continent as well. Diplomatic enterprises, which necessarily dealt with continental powers, including the papacy, required civil law.

More broadly, schooling at every level had inculcated "transferable skills" useful in administrative situations. The grammatically literate had long practice at, and thus a developed capacity for, identifying appropriate general principles in a given situation and applying them constructively to specific circumstances. Following long years of oral training, they could also communicate their reasoning process effectively and assure compliance to or cooperation in it by others. Moreover, disputation would have given arts students skills transferable to situations requiring flexible negotiation (which equally implies the "frank exchange of views," those suasive oral skills inculcated throughout education). Finally, such persons were fully capable of the highest service, offering cooperative counsel to the paterfamilias on difficult matters affecting the entire corporate group.

This function was perhaps the solitary one where higher faculty doctors ever proved useful to society at large. No one ever tired of recalling the relationship of Alexander to Aristotle, whom Dante calls "[i]l maestro di color che sanno" ("the master of those who know") and who was the polymath foundation of all higher knowledge. Thus, John Wyclif was called into service as an "expert," although not very diplomatic, royal delegate in late 1370s; he was useful in a narrow arena, that is, the relationship of ecclesiastical endowments and royal rights. But his position was far from unique; Edward I, in addition to scouring monastic libraries for chronicle precedents, called in Oxford law dons as advisors during "The Great Cause" (the question of the lordship of Scotland) in the 1290s.

In certain ways, this scenario should not be unfamiliar. There are abundant modern analogies to such cultural behavior, although the multinational corporation may have replaced whatever notion of *familia* we have left. Oxbridge, for example, still believes that it creates literate, articulate, and analytical citizens. These are, like medieval literates, capable persons with "useful habits of mind," that is, engrained analytical behaviors well honed through protracted *ex tempore* training at identifying significant problems and conceptualizing methods of solving them. Such training, it is alleged, will prove applicable to any life situation; all that is needed is some variety of "conversion course," an introductory apprenticeship program that instructs in the particulars of the job in hand. Then, the trained mind will see how to get on with it, and will do so with calm and grace.

Appendix: excerpts from the opening gloss to the *Ecloga Theoduli*

This translates exemplary selections from *Liber Theoduli cum commento* (London: Wynkyn de Worde, 1509), sigs A iiv–A iiir (STC 23941, one of a half-dozen or so printed versions available in London, *c.* 1500–10). The gloss has been preceded by (a) a Type C academic prologue (see *Minnis,

Medieval Theory of Authorship [1984], pp. 19–25), (b) an explanation of the title *ecloga* and the use of dialogue form there, (c) a division of the text (the poem begins with a prologue in two parts, of which this couplet is the first), and (d) an introduction to the "higher senses" (the traditional medieval three senses of Scripture that build upon the literal text).

> *Ethiopum terras iam feruida torruit estas*
> *In Cancro solis dum voluitur aureus axis.*

> ("Now the hot summer burned the lands of the Ethiopians, whilst the golden axle of the sun is turned in Cancer.")

[1] Having put these things down at the head, it's appropriate to set to work on explicating the text. Thus, the poet says that Christ – disputation between truth and falsehood [the subject of the dialogue that forms the poem] first began with him – was the summer time in which the lands of the Ethiopians were burned. This occurred on account of excessive heat in the month of July, when the golden axle of the sun is said to be turned and moved in the heavenly sign Cancer.

[2] This is the strict meaning of the text, but in it one must see a mystical sense hiding under the shell, and it may be twofold. The first is [in part] that the heat and longing of sinners had made them black men like the Ethiopians … The second sense is that the troubling heat of this time of tribulations and persecutions had wounded and tormented the faithful …

[3] Construe the couplet: *Estas feruida* (i.e., hot) *torruit* (i.e., *torruerat* had burned) *iam terras* (i.e., the regions and the homeland) *Ethiopum* (i.e., of that people) *dum aureus axis* (i.e., splendid and bright like gold) *solis* (which is the brightest of the planets) *voluitur* (i.e., is moved) *in Cancro* (i.e., in this heavenly sign). Alternatively, *solis* may be construed with *Cancro*. And thus it's clear from the words what we should understand by summer and further what by the Ethiopians, what by the sun, and what by Cancer; therefore I won't repeat that while construing here.

[4] In this literal sense, you should understand that the author uses here a certain figure of speech that is called *cronographia* (which is to be understood as the description of time), just as poets frequently describe times, whence there's this verse, "*Cronographia* is used to describe a certain time" [from Alexander's *Doctrinale*, line 2578]. Also when *torruit* is explained as if it were *torruerat*, one time is used for another, and this is another figure of speech, which is called *antitosis* [the print reads *antithesis*], in accord with the verse, "More often I have heard of one time being used for another, etc." [*Doctrinale*, line 2601]. Also, according to some, when the text says "the golden axle of the

sun," it is "phrasal synecdoche" because there by the axle of the sun is
understood the sun itself. During the various months, the sun traverses
the signs and is moved in them, and exactly how the author
understands this may be seen in the tract on the sphere [by John of
Holywood]; to explain it all here would be frivolous and excessive and
an example of putting your sickle into someone else's harvest [an
elegant allusion to Deut. 23:25], for here I am performing only as a
historical and grammatical poet. Thus, in this text the part is put for the
whole, in accord with this verse, "If you take up the part for the whole or
vice versa, you will create 'synecdoche,' etc." [*Doctrinale*, lines 2517–18].

[5] Last of all, one should work a bit at the grammatical explanation of the
individual words in these first verses. Although in the subsequent
sections some terms may be explained, because it would be unduly
prolix, I will henceforth only touch upon the more difficult words. For
them, as well as for others, whoever may wish to see more extensive
information, let him look at Papias, Huguccio [of Pisa, whose widely
used dictionary is the *Magne derivaciones*], Brito, *Catholicon* [by Giovanni
Balbi of Genoa], the *Breviloquium* [a late fifteenth-century dictionary by
Johannes Reuchlin], and similar books.

Ethiopum: *hic et hec Ethiops*, a noun for a nation, is derived from
Ethiopia. Thus, Huguccio says "Ethiopes are so called from the son
of Ham [the print reads 'Cain,' but see Gen. 10:6] who was named
Chus ['Thus' in the print], from whom they take their origin. Chus
is understood to mean Ethiops in Hebrew." From it are derived the
adjectives *Ethiopius, -a, -um*, and *Ethiopicus, -ca, -cum*. Therefore
Ethiopia is understood to mean "shadows." *Terra*: is derived from the
verb *tero*, because it is ceaselessly trodden on [*teritur*], or (as *Catholicon*
says) from *torreo*, because it is burned with dryness. *Iam*: is an adverb of
time and has the compound forms *enam, iamiam*, and *iamque*, as
Everard of Bethune says. *Feruidus*: Priscian says that *feruo* [the
source of this adjective] and *feruo* have the same past tense, *ferui*.
Torreo: *-es, -rui, tostum*, means much the same as *urere, assare, siccare,*
cremare, or *vertere* or *voluere*. *Estas*: is derived from "heat" [*estus*] and is
the hot and dry part of the year, and there are four parts of the year,
according to the compustical verse "spring is devoted to Peter, etc."
The version in *Catholicon* goes, "Clement gives us winter, the
enthroned Peter spring." *Cancer*: is an equivocal term, as Everard says.
Here Cancer is taken as a zodiac sign, and thus Papias says, "The
fourth sign is called Cancer, because when the sun has passed into it,

it follows a retrograde/backward motion like a crab." *Catholicon* says, "Cancer is an animal, a sign, and a vicious infection. *Cancer, canceris* is a disease; *cancer, cancri* is a fish and a star."

Notes

1. A convenient translation is *On Christian Doctrine*, trans. D. W. Robertson, Jr. (Indianapolis, IN, 1958). Augustine's *Confessions*, the ultimate medieval statement of self-formation, is also thoroughly imbedded in the grammatical tradition, the author's journey to Christian internality figured as a modernized version of Aeneas' travails in Virgil's poem.

2. William Langland, *Piers Plowman: The B Version*, eds. George Kane and E. Talbot Donaldson, rev. edn. (Berkeley, 1988).

3. Corpus Christi College, MS 61, fol. 1v. A recent reproduction appears in Paul Binsky and Stella Panayotova (eds.), *The Cambridge Illuminations: Ten Centuries Of Book Production in the Medieval West* (2005), p. 275.

4. See Tony Hunt, *Teaching and Learning Latin in Thirteenth-Century England*, 3 vols. (Cambridge, 1991), 1:177–89, 2:63–122.

5. For a careful description, see William H. Stevenson, *Report on the Manuscripts of Lord Middleton Preserved at Wollaton Hall, Nottinghamshire* (1911), pp. 212–20.

6. Modern editions of the separate works are as follows: "Cato," *Disticha Catonis*, in *Minor Latin Poets II*, eds. and trans. J. Wight Duff and Arnold M. Duff (Cambridge, MA, 1982), pp. 585–639; Theodolus, *Ecloga: Il canto della verità e della menzogna*, ed. and trans. (in Italian) Francesco Mosetti Casaretto (Florence, 1997); Avianus, *Fables*, in *Minor Latin Poets II*, pp. 669–749; Maximianus, *The Elegies*, ed. Richard Webster (Princeton, NJ, 1900); Statius, *Achilleis*, in *Statius II*, ed. and trans. J. H. Mozley (Cambridge, MA, 1989), pp. 508–95; Claudian, *De raptu Proserpinae*, in *Claudian II*, ed. and trans. Maurice Platnauer (Cambridge, MA, 1963), pp. 293–377.

7. *The Fables of "Walter of England,"* ed. Aaron E. Wright (Toronto, 1997).

8. "Le Regret de Maximian" (title given in the manuscript, Oxford, Bodleian Library, MS Digby 86), in Carleton Brown (ed.), *English Lyrics of the XIIIth Century* (Oxford, 1932), pp. 92–100; Robert Henryson, *The Poems*, ed. Denton Fox (Oxford, 1981), pp. 3–110.

9. For the text, see Kenneth Sisam, *Fourteenth Century Verse and Prose* (Oxford, 1921), pp. 148–49.

10. See the fine image of the Faustina MS in R. M. Thomson, *Books and Learning in Twelfth-Century England: The Ending of "Alter Orbis"* (Walkern, 2006), p. 17. There you can see first Ælfric's bilingual Old English–Latin text (copied about 1075), and the later sequence of Latin marginal finding notes, as well as the French interlineation "pruz" (line 15), to explain "frugi homo uncystig mann." For an edition of the Anglo-Norman only (the book includes Old English corrections of *c.* 1100, here line 13, as well as added glosses in early Middle English), see Hunt, *Teaching and Learning Latin*, 1:101–11.

11. In Nicholas Orme, "A Grammatical Miscellany of 1427–1465 from Bristol and Wiltshire," *Traditio* 38 (1982), 301–26 (at p. 318, No. 28).

12. The set text was selected topics from Thomas of Erfurt (fl. *c.* 1300), *De modis significandi*. Although abstruse, this study appears in Langland's poem, for example, the discussions at C.3.333–406a, B.13.150–52.

13. See the texts in H. G. Richardson, "Letters of the Oxford *Dictatores*," *Formularies which Bear on the History of Oxford c. 1204–1420 II*, Oxford Historical Society 5 (1942), 329–450, principally works of Thomas Sansom.

14. Good examples appear in two surviving volumes copied by Bishop John Shippey of Rochester, an Oxford D.Th. who died 1360, and later donated to Oxford colleges for student use, now Merton College, MS 248; and New College, MS 92. For a *reportatio* of a famously controversial public sermon, see Simon N. Forde, "Nicholas Hereford's Ascension Day Sermon, 1382," *Mediaeval Studies* 51 (1989), 205–41.

15. For such texts, see T. M. Charland (ed.), *Artes Praedicandi: contribution à l'histoire de la rhétorique au moyen âge* (Paris, 1936). Charland's texts, which mainly explain how to manipulate the complex structure conventional in late-medieval sermons, are fairly useless without stores of amplificatory material to fill in that structure, provided in numerous "handbooks for priests." The grand English example, arranged as a careful (and subdivided) alphabetical index of topics, was composed by John Bromyard, a Dominican who died 1352, the *Summa praedicantium*. A more widely disseminated model book, designedly a one-volume production for purchase or copy by poor (Oxford) students, is the *Sermones Mawdeleyn* (1431), an annual cycle of fifty-eight sermons, providing rich selections of conventional amplificatory material; see Alan J. Fletcher, "*Magnus predicator et devotus*: A Profile of the Life, Work, and Influence of the Fifteenth-Century Oxford Preacher, John Felton," *Mediaeval Studies* 53 (1991), 125–75.

9

Anglo-Latin literature in the later Middle Ages

Anglo-Latin origins

Latin is a language of intimidation. This property is the reverse face of its more often remarked ecumenicism. Latin spread but did not attain the geographical diffusion of the Greek-language *oikoumenê* of Hellenistic antiquity, or the Arabic of the Islamic diaspora, or the Spanish of the early Modern period, or the English of modern industrial imperialism, nor did it gain comparable numbers of users. It spread but did not deepen as Latin after antiquity: restricted to use among thin layers of the European population, selected and self-selecting by education, matters of class, and gender. For almost all of those who have used it, even in antiquity, Latin has been an acquired, second language, more and less discontinuous with forms of everyday speech. As a second language, the high-cultural Latinity enabled something like transnational communication among persons otherwise cut off from one another by differences of natural language – what W. Martin Bloomer has described as its "liberating" function – but only among the few, only engaged in a restricted, specialized range of transactions: "Learning Latin removes (liberates) the individual from the familial and the local and the present, but it is an oppressive business."[1] Latin's influence, its historical importance or significance, is not so much a function of its diffusion or consequent intermittent facilitation of international communications, as it is a function of its exclusivity, in subordinate relation to the specific, transferable kinds of political-economic power, in the wake of which the language trailed.

From its origin (as far as can be detected) as one of a number of local languages current along the Italian peninsula – Faliscan, Volscian, the other Osco-Umbrian languages, Messapic, Venetic, Etruscan, and Greek – Latin spread and grew only in conjunction with the spread and growth of Roman political-economic hegemony. The stories the Romans told themselves about their own origins have this feature: the community succeeded by subordinating and incorporating others. Likewise, the stories they told themselves about the origins and development of Roman literature, in Latin, characterize it too as a tool of this same imperial dominance, or a by-product of it.

An imperialist imposition, associated with the exercise of power by force, corporal and spiritual, "it cannot be stated strongly enough that Latin is Latin."[2] Keith Sidwell's insistence on a point of linguistic pedagogy has a broader application: in contrast to the historical and contemporary alternatives in relation to which Latin takes on definition, the Latin literary tradition, like Latin the language, is distinctively one. From within the tradition, however, as it developed far from the imperial metropole and over centuries of post-colonial usage, it must also appear that Latin is not simple. Its unity, in its association with power and in contrast to the alternative languages, comprehends or subsumes a diversity of Latins within it that can, indeed, must be distinguished. Though one in its persistent association with authority, Latin has been fractured within from time to time: as the extralinguistic bases of authority have shifted, so have the language's particular applications.

In England in the high and late Middle Ages, Latin retained its unity as the voice of authority, even as authority shifted, from Church to the secular state, from the narrowest aristocratic basis to something broader under pressure of demographic change in the fourteenth century, and then from feudal to absolutist monarchy early in the sixteenth century. Concomitantly, Latin's forms of expression also shifted, attaining their greatest internal variety of kinds and breadth of uses and appeal *c.* 1400, until the early sixteenth century, when Latin largely ceased to function. A good part of the most consequential "English" literature had always in fact been Latin literature, Bede's *Historia ecclesiastica* (731) being the salient early post-imperial example. However, major literary work in Latin was not much done in England or elsewhere in Europe after Thomas More's *Utopia* (1516); and the other non-literary applications for which Latin had been used – monumental, proprietary, and ritual – either ceased or were taken over by English. The major figures are well known and widely discussed, and now there are surveys. What follows is particular analysis of a series of episodes, diachronically arranged, intending to illustrate the synchronic range of Latins in use in England at three late medieval points.

Glastonbury 1191

In 1191 the mortal remains of "King" Arthur were exhumed from the churchyard at Glastonbury Abbey in southwestern England:

> Huius autem corpus, quod quasi phantasticum in fine et tanquam per spiritus ad longinqua translatum, neque morti obnoxium fabule confinxerant, his nostris diebus apud Glastoniam inter lapideas pyramides duas, in coemiterio sacro quondam erectas, profundius in terra quercu concaua reconditum, et signatum miris indiciis et quasi miraculosis, est inuentum, et in ecclesiam cum honore translatum marmoreoque decenter tumulo commendatum. Vnde et crux plumbea lapide supposito, non superius vt nostris solet diebus, sed inferiori potius ex parte infixa, quam nos quoque vidimus, namque tractauimus litteras has insculptas et non eminentes et exstantes, sed magis interius ad lapidem versas, continebat: "Hic iacet sepultus inclitus rex Arthurus cum Wenneuereia vxor sua secunda in insula Auallonia." ... Ideoque tam profunde situm corpus, et quasi absconditum fuerat, ne a Saxonibus post necem ipsius insulam occupantibus, quos tanto opere viuens debellauerat et fere ex toto deleuerat, posset nullatenus inueniri; et ob hoc etiam littere, veritatis indices, cruci impresse interius ad lapidem verse fuerunt, vt et tunc temporis quod continebat occultarent, et quandoque tam pro locis et temporibus id proplarent.

> [Though common talk had it that, not subject to death, he became a phantom at his end, and was carried far away by spirits, in fact his very body itself was discovered, in these our own times, at Glastonbury, buried deep in the earth, between two stone standing-crosses, raised up long ago in the consecrated burial ground there, within a hollowed oak, marked with wonderful, indeed all but miraculous signs; and the body was then conveyed in honor into the church and commended fittingly to a marble tomb. A lead cross too was found, set into a stone, fixed not to its upper surface, as would be the custom now, but rather to its lower. We have ourselves seen this cross and have touched the letters graven into it, not faced upwards and outwards, but turned in, towards the stone, and they say: "Here lies buried the illustrious King Arthur with his second wife Guinevere on the Isle of Avalon." ... The body had been

buried as deep as it was as if to hide it, so that it would not be found by the Saxons who had occupied the island after Arthur's murder, whom Arthur had battled so laboriously while he lived and had almost completely wiped out. For this reason, the truth-telling letters engraved on the cross had been turned inwards, towards the stone, to conceal what they contained from that age, so too that they might reveal it later, at a different time and in different circumstance.][3]

The leaden cross discovered with the body survived into the seventeenth century (at least) when a careful antiquarian drawing of it was made for reproduction in William Camden's *Antiquitates Britanniae* (Figure 9.1).

Figure 9.1 Leaden cross at Glastonbury (from William Camden, *Antiquitates Britanniae* [1607], p. 166).

In addition to falsifying the contemporary transcription cited above, the engraving falsifies the whole episode: the letter-forms of the cross are not Arthurian period, nor could the historical Romano-British *dux bellorum* of *c.* 500 (as the *Historiae Brittonum* calls the figure we take to be the basis for the legend) yet have been a king at the time of his death, nor need he have been Christian. The letter-forms are also not twelfth century, however; so, if the cross is a forgery, it is a careful one. The letter-forms appear to mimic those of the earliest documents (tenth-century charters) held in Glastonbury Abbey at the time of the exhumation.

No matter the veracity of the cross's witness, the form itself of the inscription on it ("HIC IA | CET S | EPV | LTVS·INCL | ITVS·REX | ARTV | RIV | S·IN | INSV | LA·A | VALO | NI | A |." ["Here lies buried the famous King Arthur in the isle Avalon"]) encapsulates the basic epigraphic function belonging to Latin, taken over from the Roman invaders, still in the later medieval period in English history when the cross was invented. The *littere insculpte* here – "veritatis indices," the contemporary witness calls them – represent the basic utility of Latin: to be the voice of authority, even usurped for rendering falsehoods authoritative. Hardly ubiquitous, Latin took place only in such locations, where authority pronounced. Not only inscriptions, but likewise coins, governmental *acta*, ritual performances of official cult – things that in the nature of things have evanesced – left puddles (not a sea) of quotidian Latin, scattered about the verbal landscape, nonsensical in particular but articulate and clear on the matter of greatest moment. No matter that the words themselves were more or less meaningless (then as now) to all but the very few: Latin by itself stood for propagated authority by virtue of long-established historical experience. The authorities spoke Latin publicly; Latin bespoke authority: the occurrence of the language itself was *veritatis index*.

The epigraphic, monumentalizing function of Latin inhered also in the high-cultural literary performances where it was also used, albeit relatively more rarely and privately. The chief source of information about the Glastonbury exhumation is Gerald of Wales (1146–1226), quoted above, whose work might stand for the condition of the Anglo-Latin literature during the century and a half after the Norman Conquest of England (see also Chapter 5 above). The product of a racially mixed marriage, Gerald had a career in service of the Angevin Church and state (difficult to distinguish as those were because of this habitual sharing of personnel between the two kinds of institutions). Gerald wrote a great deal, including hagiographies, but was distinctively a chorographer. His widely copied works, the *Itinerarium* and *Descriptio Cambriae*, and the *Topographia Hibernica* and *Expugnatio Hibernica*, helped to define newly subject territories. His remarks on the Glastonbury exhumation show a sophisticated knowledge of the Arthurian matter that the exhumation itself already exploited. Gerald's presentation indicates that the Latin on the cross was part of a specific effort to enlist the language to bolster particular local ecclesiastical and political authorities. The abbey at Glastonbury needed money for building works; the king of the English needed, or was in the event able to use, an Arthurian dead body as part of a larger repressive response to indigenous British rejection of his impe- rial overlordship in Wales. Resistance was futile: the English king was more powerful, both materially and now symbolically too. By the exhu- mation, he seized (some) control of the same legend of Arthur's return that his opponents had been trying to use for their own ends.

In substantive perspective, this may have been the chief contribution of the Anglo-Latin literature of the post-Conquest period: the reformu- lation of the historiography of the British Isles in response to the territories' passage into the control of new rulership. In this sense, the chorographical rewritings of Gerald of Wales had a more influential counterpart in Geoffrey of Monmouth's *Historia regum Britanniae* (*c.* 1136–38). Geoffrey's work, too, is a forgery, akin to the Glastonbury lead cross. His prefatory assertion that the work was based on an aged British book – "quendam Britannici sermonis librum uetustissimum qui a Bruto primo rege Britonum usque ad Cadualadrum filium Caduallonis actus omnium continue et ex ordine perpulcris orationibus proponebat" ["a very old book in the British tongue, which set out in excellent style a continuous narrative of all their deeds, from the first king of the Britons, Brutus, down to Cadualadrus, son of Caduallo"][4] – is false. Though prompted by such earlier writings as he could have been familiar with – Gildas, Bede, the so-called Nennius – as well as by local traditions (oral, British) refracted indirectly elsewhere, too, the source (and the source of the writing's extensive influence) was Geoffrey's imagination.

The accomplishment of the *Historia regum Britanniae* is clear. Geoffrey's work "offered to its first, amazed readers a comprehensive and spectacular vision of the British past largely free of Christian assumptions," as Robert Hanning wrote: a reformulation of British history as secular, rather than religious, preoccupied not with proto- martyrs, missionaries, miracle workers, and conversions of the English, tendentiously demonstrating again and again (as Bede does) that the Christians' deity was and worked in the world; but instead a series of secular rulers and their secular doings, warrior-kings, their families, and their enemies near at hand and far.[5] The Arthurian matter in Geoffrey – particulars of it as well as the broad shape of his historical tale, retold interminably – must now seem to have pride of place, though it is also only an instance of the general historiographical achievement to which Geoffrey contributed: making local history secular. In this, Geoffrey's work had significant near-contemporary analogues, especially in the *Gesta regum anglorum* of William of Malmesbury (*c.* 1080–1143) and the *Historia anglorum* of Henry of Huntingdon (1084–1155). They, too, con- tributed secular histories of the peoples of the British Isles, which Geoffrey claimed to complete.

As radical in substance as the Galfridian (and cognate) reorientation of historiography was, toward secularism, the success of the same writ- ing relied also on a conservative rejection of change in its formal, linguistic properties. As did Gerald, William, Henry, and the others involved, broadly speaking, Geoffrey wrote Latin in conformity with norms of the Christian-imperial historiography – defined by Bede's work, as opposed to the Aldhelmian alternative, or the Romano-British of Gildas. Geoffrey's prefatory denigration of his own style is cast in terms that tend to belie the topos he invokes:

> tametsi infra alienos ortulos falerata uerba non collegerim, agresti tamen stilo propriisque calamis contentus codicem illum in Latinum sermonem transferre curaui; nam si ampullosis dictionibus paginam illinissem, taedium legentibus ingererem, dum magis in exponendis uerbis quam in historia intelligenda ipsos commorari oporteret.
> [Though I have never gathered showy words from the gardens of others, I undertook to translate the book into Latin in a rustic style, reliant on my own reed pipe; had I larded my pages with bombastic terms, I would tire my readers with the need to linger over understanding my words rather than following my narrative.][6]

Nonetheless, the various slightly inkish terms used here, in what remains the writer's profession of a commitment to stylistic plainness, do not much recur in Geoffrey's writing. Even contemporary criticism of Geoffrey's work recognized how his choice of Latin lent the work author- ity. For that *fabulator*, possessed of an *effrenata mentiendi libido* (untram- meled desire for lying), Latin had still done the job of cloaking Geoffrey's substance with an appearance of veracity: "per superductum Latini sermonis colorem honesto historie nomine palliauit" ("by embellishing it in the Latin tongue he cloaked all with the honorable title of history"), has the acerb William of Newburgh.[7] Lending authority, or making authoritative, is what Latin was for.

The same kind of substantive re-writing occurred contemporaneously in other genres of Latin literature, with the same relative simplification of style: the saint's life, for example, in verse or prose. Given the altered political conditions of the post-Conquest settlement, there had to be polemical contentual change in hagiography as in historiography or chorography; but the Latinate forms by which the altered authorities spoke remained the same here too, or were restored. Veneration of local Anglo-Saxon saints was necessarily troublous, one way or another, for the new ruling elites, secular and ecclesiastical. The new authorities were capable of exploiting the old cults as much as repressing them, however; more significant is that the chief development was more stylistic than substantive. English vernacular hagiography stopped, and hermeneuticism – the difficult glory of the Anglo-Saxon period insular Latinity – was eliminated or restricted, in favor of a reversion to the plainer *sermo humilis* of the Western Church ("the inverted snobbery of the Latin patristic tradition's rhetorically trained masters," in David Townsend's phrase).[8] Old cults turned to new uses, as historiography and chorography reformulated to fit the altered political situation; Latin persisted. That Latin was the appropriate literary-linguistic vehicle still for performance of authoritative accounts of secular and spiritual true histories did not yet alter until the fourteenth century, when the agent of change was inhuman: meteorological in the first instance, then bacterio-viral.

Westminster 1399

The official parliamentary instrument, "The Record and Process of the Renunciation and Deposition of Richard II" (r. 1377–99) by which the usurping King Henry IV (r. 1399–1413) was put on the throne, stands for what became of Latin in the post-plague period in England: its grotesque stylistic elaboration bespeaks contemporary authority's desperation to assert itself in altered socio-political circumstance. The high medieval growth left off, and by about 1300 the population of England may have already been in decline when serial demographic disaster occurred: the famine in 1317–18, less affecting the rich, followed by the series of not as discriminating plague visitations that came to England first in 1348–49.

By 1390, the population had been halved. The disproportionately reduced productive segment of the population in place by century's end was consequently empowered; their masters, in addition to prosecuting the usual though sharpened struggle against the productive elements, had also to struggle amongst themselves for control of what remained to take. King Richard II was put from the throne by his cousin in a fight over wealth, basically, in the characteristically illiquid forms of land ownership and derivative duties from landed production. The moment of the regal power's transfer from the one man to the other is documented in the "Record and Process."

Englisc had been used for a variety of official government documents before the Norman Conquest, including charters of ownership and the promulgation of laws; these charter functions – asserting proprietorship and enacting it – were largely taken over by French after the Conquest; by the early fourteenth century, when the English parliament began to take its familiar shape, the natural language in which to record its official *acta* was French; and French remained the language in which such proceedings were recorded for a long time to come. Except in late 1399, when, exceptionally, the parliamentary record breaks out in Latin. Evidently, the exceptional Latin was a sign of the occasion's singular historical importance; moreover, the Latin of the "Record and Process" has a particularly turgid elevation that is itself a sign of the occasion's historical significance. Here is a single sentence, in fact, though it comprises 318 words, the main verbs (in quadruplicate, characteristically) *deponendum pronunciamus, decernimus, et declaramus, et … deponimus*, coming after 240, *fere*-periodically:

> Nos Iohannes episcopus Assauensis, Iohannes abbas Glastoniensis,
> Thomas comes Gloucestrie, Thomas dominus de Berkeleye, Thomas
> de Erpyngham, et Thomas Gray, milites, ac Willelmus Thirnyng,
> iusticiarius, per pares et proceres regni Anglie spirituales et
> temporales, et eiusdem regni communitates omnes status eiusdem
> regni representantes, commissarii ad infra scripta specialiter deputati,
> pro tribunali sedentes; attentis periuriis multiplicibus ac crudelitate
> aliisque quampluribus criminibus dicti Ricardi, circa regimen suum
> in regnis et dominio supradictis pro tempore sui regiminis commissis
> et perpetratis, ac coram dictis statibus palam et publice propositis,
> exhibitis, et recitatis, que adeo fuerunt et sunt publica, notoria,
> manifesta, et famosa, quod nulla poterant aut possunt tergiuersacione
> celari; necnon confessione predicti Ricardi, recognoscentis et

reputantis, ac veraciter ex certa sciencia sua indicantis, se fuisse et esse
insufficientem penitus et inutilem ad regimen et gubernacionem
regnorum et dominii predictorum et pertinentium eorundem ac
propter sua demerita notoria non immerito deponendum, per ipsum
Ricardum prius emissa, ac de voluntate et mandato suis coram dictis
statibus publicata, eisque notificata et exposita in vulgari; prehabita
super hiis et omnibus in ipso negocio actitatis coram statibus
antedictis, et nobis deliberacione diligenti, vice, nomine, et auctoritate
nobis in hac parte commissa; ipsum Ricardum, exhabundanti et ad
cautelam, ad regimen et gubernacionem dictorum regnorum et
dominii, iuriumque et pertinentium eorundem, fuisse et esse
inutilem, inhabilem, insufficientem penitus, et indignum, ac propter
premissa et eorum pretexta, ab omni dignitate et honore regiis, si quid
dignitatis et honoris huiusmodi in eo remanserit, merito deponendum
pronunciamus, decernimus, et declaramus, et ipsum simili cautela
deponimus per nostram definitiuam sentenciam in hiis scriptis;
omnibus et singulis dominis archiepiscopis, episcopis, et prelatis,
ducibus, marchionibus, comitibus, baronibus, militibus, vassallis,
valuassoribus, ac ceteris hominibus dictorum regnorum et dominii, ac
aliorum locorum ad dicta regna et dominium spectancium subditis ac
ligeis suis quibuscumque, inhibentes expresse, ne quisquam ipsorum
de cetero prefato Ricardo, tanquam regi vel domino regnorum aut
dominii predictorum, pareat quomodolibet vel intendat.[9]

"We depose Richard" should do as a translation.[10] The point is the
document's irreducible verbosity, as if the sheer weight of words signi-
fied. Evidently, though Latin was still serving the same function of
voicing authority, in contrast to earlier documents discharging the
same charter function, the "Record and Process" had to try harder,
because authority itself was less secure and was shifting.

Authority's insecurity on the occasion also required broadcasting
news of the usurpation, relatively broadly, but by means of a range of
generic and verbal mediums (including English) that shows Latin too
shifting toward a more secular openness, toward secular popularity in
the same process. The range of Latins in evidence on the occasion was
broad. Copies of the "Record and Process" were circulated to monasteries, where, in some cases, the copies were used for the sort of historiography represented already herein by such a twelfth-century writer as
William of Malmesbury. The chief contemporary exponent of the still
vivid monastic tradition was the St. Albans Benedictine, Thomas
Walsingham (c. 1340–c. 1422) – a remarkable figure from any of a number

of perspectives, including his innovative classicizing contributions to English historiography, especially in the *Ypodigma Neustrie* – who both narrated the revolution and incorporated verbatim a copy of the "Record and Process" into his *Chronica maiora*. Nor was he the only regular historian to use the government account in this way.

More remarkable, however, because unprecedented, is the non-monastic historiographical use to which the same document was put: one of the civic chronicles of the city of London – phenomena of strictly fourteenth-century invention – has a verbatim copy of the "Record and Process" too, Walsingham-like, but rendered into metropolitan English, and confidently. Secular literature of this sort – what Anne Middleton termed "public poetry": writing on non-ecclesiastical, civic, and regnal affairs, secular-political in a narrow sense, by persons in secular occupation (though always still of clerical formation at least), for other persons similarly situated, like the English writer-bureaucrats Thomas Usk, Geoffrey Chaucer, and Thomas Hoccleve – was in Latin too by this time.[11] The contemporary pamphleteering has largely been lost, except as it is reflected in regular chronicle-keeping (Henry Knighton is said to have used over a hundred such sources), and except for the pamphlet of Thomas Favent (fl. *c.* 1388–1400), the *Historia sive Narracio de modo et forma Mirabilis Parliamenti apud Westmonasterium* (1388), surviving in something like original form. The London town clerk John Carpenter (d. *c.* 1441), who would later write a (Latin) program that John Lydgate and others would turn into civic spectacle in the 1430s, may already have been at work on the *Liber Albus*; and the secular memoirs (in Latin) of Adam Usk (*c.* 1350–1430) reflect his witness to and participation in the deposition of Richard II, which may have extended to something like drafting articles incorporated into the "Record and Process" itself.

The "Record and Process" appears to have been known to the poets, too: it was versified in the *Cronica tripertita* (1400) of John Gower (d. 1408). Best remembered now for his English-language *Confessio amantis* (*c.* 1390–93), though also as revealingly trilingual, Gower was the premier Latin poet of the post-plague period in England by any of a number of measures, though he was no clerk. Evidently, Gower was given (or obtained) a copy of the "Record and Process" and finished his Latin verse reworking and extension of it by February 1400, meanwhile also taking pay from the Lancastrian regime. It is hard to represent what Gower did on the occasion as a popularization – a thousand lines of disyllabically rhymed Leonine hexameters, from the grotesque prose of the "Record and Process" to the similarly labored floridity of the verse-style he chose. Nevertheless, Gower's Latin verse enarration represents another of the broadcastings of the Lancastrian version of events, and his stylistic choice was decorous, in that, like the authors of the "Record and Process," given the weightiness of the occasion, Gower chose the condign verse medium: Latin still, of course, also elevates.

Other Latin verse options were, and were to remain, available: "Goliardic" verse, for one: rhyming, short-lined stanzaic verse forms based on patterns of stress-accent rather than syllabic quantities, of twelfth-century continental development, persistently by clerks for clerks, were being composed and circulating in England at the time: on the mendicant troubles, for example, or on the Great Rebellion of 1381, one including this passage, enjoining greater state repression, justified by scriptural authority:[12]

> Ne fiat diis detractio,
> Aut principi rebellio,
>   Lex scripti dat Mossaici:
> Ex quo patet conclusio
> Quod maior non iudicio
>   Minoris debet subici.
> Nec ipsi tanquam iudici
> Parere neque vindici,
>   Pro quouis maleficio;
> Nam omnis lex sic in<fic>i
> Ac omnis rex sic deici
>   Seruorum potest odio.

> [The Mosaic texts proscribe both disrespect of the divine and rebellion against a king, whence comes plain the conclusion that no superior ought be subject to any inferior's condemnation. Nor should such submit to being judged or punished, for wrong-doing of any sort, since, by such means, all law would be corrupted and every king thrown down, for no more than the dislike of the servile.][13]

Nor is Gower's composition in Leonines even as ornate as the work of such thirteenth-century Anglo-Latin exponents of the high scholastic style as the clerics Henry of Avranches (d. 1262) or his adversary Michael of Cornwall (fl. 1243–55), still legendary for their prosodic complexities, whose fourteenth-century English followers, like the so-called "Anonymous of Calais," Gower could not match in ornamentation.

Accomplishments in the same style were inevitably indebted to widely-studied English teachers of it, chiefly Geoffrey of Vinsauf (fl. 1208–13). Gower might also have chosen the plainer, simpler (unrhymed) dactylic verse that he had developed earlier for his own *Vox clamantis* (*c.* 1381), which he wrote on a range of largely secular topics (estates satire, necessarily involving clerics, though only as implicated in broader secular social contexts; a *Fürstenspiegel* ["advice for princes"] and advice to the judiciary; the Great Rebellion; and so forth) for some largely secular readership. Other contemporary Anglo-Latin poets were developing the same plain-style, unrhymed dactylic verse, as for example, the other Lancastrian proponent who, covering the same series of events as the *Cronica tripertita*, accounted the revolution itself in these terms:

> Rex ad Hibernica regna ferocia vi properavit;
>   Appulit interea dux sua iura petens.
> Rex renuit regnum, dux rex fit, sicque coronam
>   Suscipit et regnum sceptra tenendo regit.

> [In force the king betook himself abroad, to Ireland (fierce country!);
> Meanwhile returned the duke, seeking but what was his by right.
> Richard renounced the realm, the duke became the king, and so,
> Putting on the crown, holding scepter, he now rules this realm.][14]

This is not the work of some highly trained clerical specialist showing what he could do with a technical flair meant to interest or impress only other such specialists, as Gower's *Cronica tripertita* might be characterized, where Gower had gone on at such ornate length, weighting all with sonic mannerism. Here is a passage from Gower's *Cronica* corresponding to the above, saying rather more though covering a good deal less. Style is the thing:

> TUNC PRIUS incepta sunt parliamenta recepta,
> De quibus abstractus Ricardi desinit actus.
> Ecce dies Martis, nec adest presencia partis.
> Non sedet in sede, quem culpa repellit ab ede.
> Denegat in scanno loca tunc fortuna tiranno,
> A visu gentis quem terruit accio mentis.
> R. non comparet; alibi sed dummodo staret,
> Causas assignat, et ad H. sua ceptra resignat.
> Substituit aliquos proceres tunc, iuris amicos,
> Ad quos confessus proprio fuit ore repressus.
> Hiis circumspectis aliisque sub ordine lectis,

R., qui deliquit, hunc curia tota reliquit.
Hunc deponebant, plenum quem labe sciebant,
Nec quis eum purgat, iterum ne forte resurgat.
Tunc decus Anglorum, sed et optimus ille bonorum,
H. fuit electus regno, magis est quia rectus.

[THEN PARLIAMENT was reconvened, before begun;
As Richard had withdrawn from it, his part was done.
On Tuesday Richard's party was not there in place
Enthroned; his presence was disbarred by his disgrace.
The tyrant's fortune kept him from his regnal throne;
His frenzied mind was terrified at being known.
R. wasn't there; he signs the terms by which he'll hand
The rule to H., provided he can elsewhere stand.
Some nobles, friends of law and right, he substitutes;
To these he speaks and from his mouth his case refutes.
With these and other statements read and scrutinized,
The whole court then the guilty Richard sets aside.
They then depose him, for they see his faults quite plain;
No one clears him from blame, lest he should rise again.
Then England's glory, H., the cream of all the cream,
Was chosen to be king; his virtue was supreme.][15]

In 1399, for Gower, as for others, Latin still had a weight of authority. Despite the accumulating secularization of writing, in part too its vernacularization, for matching momentous occasions, Latin was still proper, requisite even, the more elaborate the better in some applications. The cultural ecology of Latin usage in evidence at the moment of the Glastonbury exhumation of 1191 was altering, however. The range of possible Latins (like the range of possible literatures generally) broadened in the post-plague fourteenth century; also, even without exogenous influence, Latin's authority was already dissipating.

Flodden Field and France 1513

While King Henry VIII was campaigning in France in late summer 1513, with the "Holy League" arrayed against the French king, Louis XII, France's Scots allies invaded England, then suffered defeat at Flodden Field. Hardly epochal (outside of Scottish culture), still these events in France and the north of England concentrated English literary resources in an extraordinary way, again showing the realignments within uses of

Latin that had occurred by the early sixteenth century. A contemporary painting of the one Henrician battlefield triumph in France survives, with a *titulus* inscribed on it, from which Latin has all but disappeared, even its basic epigraphic function atrophied by this point: "The Bataile of | Spvrrs. Anno. | 1513."[16]

The first English Sallust translator, Alexander Barclay (*c*. 1484–1552), wrote two things, both in English verse, though one so influenced by Franco-Burgundian models as to be virtual French: "The Tower of Virtue and Honour"; while his public adversary John Skelton (*c*. 1460–1529) ("Wyse men love vertue, wylde people wantones," Barclay had written), himself a translator of M. Tullius Cicero and Diodorus Siculus, contributed four, in English or in Latin but not both, though Skelton was also responsible for a Goweresque trilingual suite of poems at about the same time.[17] Barclay was Benedictine, though he worked for the London printing industry, in particular repeatedly for the (occasional) royal printer Richard Pynson (*c*. 1449–1529), who first printed the other of Barclay's poems occasioned by the royal militarism: the "Gardeners Passetaunce." Skelton, too, was a priest, though not regular, and he too was involved with the printing industry: the second of his English Flodden poems, printed after mid-September 1513, superseded his first, printed only a few weeks before, it evidently having been rushed into print to exploit public interest, for the profit of its printer William Faques, sometime before a full report of the events had reached Skelton at London.

At the time of these 1513 performances, Skelton was styling himself *orator regius*. In fact, Henry VIII had at least one other official poet, whom he had inherited from his father, in effect, "the blind poet," as the records of payments to him regularly name him: Bernard André (*c*. 1450–1522), of Toulouse originally, though resident in England since about 1486. On the 1513 occasion, styling himself *poeta regius*, André contributed a Latin encomium of some 200 lines, in hexameters and elegiacs, rather than in one of the Greek-derived lyric meters that were his distinctive contribution to contemporary Anglo-Latin verse.

André had been the central figure of a *grex poetarum* about the court of Henry VII, other members of which were also still active in 1513: the Brescian Pietro Carmeliano (*c*. 1451–1527), in England since the early 1480s, contributed brief Latin verses, decoratively, for a news pamphlet-like printed publication put out by Pynson again, chiefly occupied with an anonymous (English) prose account of the Flodden victory. More or less official accounts such as this of English victories had been coming home from England's wars since the 1340s, in Latin and French, nominally authored by the king himself or some prince or other, though, of course, the writing itself was evidently scripted by clerical secretaries. This propagandistic function for dispatches continued into the sixteenth century. Some of the Henrician ones of 1513 survive, from France and from Flodden, and may have reached Skelton, André, and the others, who would have used them for writing some of the 1513 poetry. The dispatches were predominantly English by this time.

One of the jobs the earliest Tudor *grex poetarum* set itself for the reign of Henry VII was excluding others from royal patronage, particularly members of a younger generation, who, certainly by 1513, were expecting to profit more from their talents. Among the earliest performances of Thomas More (1478–1535) had been a suite of Latin poems welcoming the accession of Henry VIII in 1509; in 1513, More again contributed Latin verse in praise of the Tudors' military successes, as did also More's collaborator, the Dutch-born Desiderius Erasmus (*c.* 1467–1536), who was in penurious Cambridge residence at the time:

> Audivit olim censor ille Romanus:
> "Ludos iocosae quando noveras Florae,
> Cur in theatrum, Cato severe, venisti?
> An ideo tantum veneras ut exires?"
> At iure nunc imbellis audiat Gallus:
> "Ludum cruenti quando noveras Martis,
> Animos ferocis quando noveras Angli,
> Quid, quaeso, in aciem, timide Galle, prodisti,
> Ferro minaci splendidas agens turmas?
> An ideo tantum veneras, uti foede
> Fugiens sequenti terga verteres hosti,
> Ac si pedum certamen esset, haud dextrae?"
> Cato foeminas videre non potest, Gallus
> Viros. Cato mutare non potest vultum,
> Gallus nequit mutare pectus ignavum.

[That Roman censor was once told: "Since you knew what the games of jolly Flora are like, why, O strict Cato, did you come into the theater? Did you come for no other reason than to leave?" But now the cowardly Frenchman can rightly expect to hear: "Since you knew what the game of bloody Mars is like, since you knew the courage of the fierce Englishman, why, I ask you, O fearful Frenchman, did you come out to join battle, marshalling your splendid array of threatening troops and weapons? Did you come for no other reason than to take to your heels so basely and turn your back to the pursuing enemy, as if it were a contest for feet and not for the sword arm?" Cato cannot bear to look at the women; the Frenchman, at the men. Cato cannot change the expression on his face; the Frenchman cannot change his craven heart.][18]

Also, from the Erasmian correspondence, it can be gathered that their associate Andrea Ammonio (*c.* 1476–1517), a Lucchese who had been in England since 1506, wrote a proper epic on the events, though only half a dozen of its (unrhymed and otherwise classicizing) dactylic hexameters survive. Ammonio actually traveled to France in Henry VIII's suite, unlike Skelton or André, and acted afterwards as Henry's Latin secretary; he should be regarded as the occasion's official Latin poet. Ammonio also contributed Latin verse for publication in print with a Latin prose pamphlet justifying the contemporary English campaign in France that had provoked the trouble at Flodden, authored by a Henrician secretary of state named James Whitstones (d. 1512), printed (presumably for international consumption in some measure) again by Pynson.

Seven named poets, as well as the mostly anonymous *prosatores*, then also the various printers: sheer quantity is a distinctive feature of the literature of this occasion, not to be imputed to attrition of evidence from earlier periods. The amount of writing produced on the occasion bespeaks the degree of competition about it, and both bespeak a general commercialization of literary production. All the writers involved enjoyed periods of institutional support – in Church or state office, sometimes in education, private or public – but all also seem to have been more or less professional writers, interested in attracting patronage to themselves for their writing, be it personal or institutional, salaried or rated as piece-work. Printing may have been an agent of change in this respect: the new industry had interests in commercially generated profit that changed writing; eventually, it was to become the pre-eminent, then the exclusive institutional source of patronage for professionalized writers, displacing the Church, the state, and the individual rich person. Meanwhile, printing may also have been only a response to change: demographic recovery; growth of general production; accelerated trade; and so the notorious technological innovations of the European fifteenth century. Paper came first, which for the proliferation of writing was at least as important as printing itself, and, in fact, only made commercial sense once the cheaper alternative to the skins of domesticated animals was in place.

Despite the extent of this literary production of 1513, there is relatively little Latin. English outweighs it (and the French), even for such a function as official assertions of victory for general public consumption. The voice of authority sounds different too, in that what Latin remained is homogeneous. More literature, but less Latin; the lessened Latin, ossified, also only one kind. The regular churchly chroniclers so prominent in the literary records of earlier periods are all out. Contemporary narrative-historical accounts of the events survive only in the Latin *Anglica historia* of Polydore Vergil (*c.* 1470–1555), an Italian-trained critic of the Arthur legend, for example, whose work went into English as soon as it was finished (at about the same time that More was writing his *Richard III* simultaneously in both Latin and English), as well as in the civic-vernacular English history of Edward Hall (1497–1547). No more qualitative Latin verse, of the sort that was still possible late in the fourteenth century, occurs nor any Leonine quantitative verse of the sort that Gower had risen to, which both More and Erasmus were to ridicule.

What takes the place of the varied Latins in use late in the fourteenth century is a homogenized, non-rhyming verse, in one or the other of the Augustan dactylic meters, or (more rarely) in a Greek-derived lyric meter like the Erasmian choliambics quoted above, advertising its adherence to ancient canons of taste also by allusion, reference, and vocabulary. This style in Anglo-Latin poetry could become another hermeticism, to the degree that its ancient references became more and more recondite, sensible only to the most highly trained specialists: Erasmus' quotations of Martial in the piece cited above are a comparatively unsubtle example of the sort of ancient arcana these poets cultivated.

In pursuit of such antiquities, Latin verse disseevered itself from the relatively vivid varieties of public poetry in which it was still participating in 1399. The *Nachleben* of the grandest of the 1513 Latin epics on events are indicial: Ammonio's poem has disappeared altogether; André's survives in a single manuscript presentation copy for Henry VIII, unlikely to have been read at all. No one was much interested, except a handful of the poets' own *sodales*, like Erasmus, who were themselves engaged in propagating such writing. Better Latin, perhaps, if judged by Roman standards; less useful, though, because it was less broadly appealing.

The displacement of some of the mostly highly developed of the late medieval contributions to Latin by neo-classical styles of Latin verse composition, based directly on Augustan-imperial canons of taste, may appear to represent the birth of the modern. Resurrection of 1,500-year-old stylistic canons (however much we are still enthralled) hardly counts as a birth, it might be felt. Death rather is what occurs, the death of the medieval English traditions of Latin writing, certainly; with them perhaps also the death of Latin, when such uses of the language as remained, without the vital invention and variety that characterizes earlier uses, were only Roman-Augustan Latins re-animated.

Latin did not disappear from use in England, nor has it, but it did suffer a death at this point, in a strong sense, represented by the only Anglo-Latin writing ever to be thoroughly appropriated by properly "English" literary history, to become an honorary "English" work, though, of course, it is in Latin and had to be; also, the last strong work of the Anglo-Latin tradition, comparable in achievement to the earlier writings of Bede or Geoffrey of Monmouth: Thomas More's *Utopia* (1516). *Utopia* represents and enacts a death of the sort of authority itself with which Latin had been associated since its advent in Britain with the Romans. *Utopia* uses Latin's authoritativeness, but for its own ends, its "Latin ... reminding us not necessarily that the past is right and authoritative but that the present order of things is not written in stone";[19] and *Utopia* does so in order to undermine the possibility of any such authority and finally to undo it. More's every gesture in the work – the real though unreal American setting for the fictional commonwealth that is nevertheless a true commonwealth, for example; the decision, possibly Erasmus' rather than author-More's, to frame the description of the commonwealth in book two by the "Dialogue of Counsel" in book one; the dialogic form itself, among real and unreal interlocutors, the more real the less trustworthy, especially in the case of More himself; not to mention the framing parerga and correspondence framing the dialogic framework – all engender uncertainty, rendering authority incredible. By the time a reader reaches the notorious post-Peroration, where the narrator-character in dialogue called "Morus" dismisses the ideal commonwealth that author-More has created, but does so in terms that may yet praise it and blame the actually existing commonwealth, it has become impossible to credit any possibility of there being a stable, reliable authority:

Haec ubi Raphaël recensuit, quanquam haud pauca mihi
succurrebant, quae in eius populi moribus, legibusque perquam
absurde uidebantur instituta, non solum de belli gerendi ratione, &
rebus diuinis, ac religione, alijsque insuper eorum institutis, sed in
eo quoque ipso maxime, quod maximum totius institutionis
fundamentum est uita scilicet, uictuque communi, sine ullo
pecuniae commercio, qua una re funditus euertitur omnis
nobilitas, magnificentia, splendor, maiestas, uera ut publica est
opinio decora atque ornamenta Reipublicae tamen quoniam
defessum narrando sciebam, neque mihi satis exploratum erat,
possetne ferre, ut contra suam sententiam sentiretur, praesertim
quod recordabar, eo nomine quosdam ab illo reprehensos, quasi
uererentur, ne non satis putarentur sapere, nisi aliquid inuenirent,
in quo uellicare aliorum inuenta possent, idcirco & illorum
institutione, & ipsius oratione laudata, manu apprehendens intro
coenatum duco, praefatus tamen aliud nobis tempus, ijsdem de
rebus altius cogitandi, atque uberius cum eo conferendi fore, quod
utinam aliquando contingeret.

[When Raphael had finished his story, although many things came to
my mind which seemed very absurdly established in the customs and
laws of the people described, not only in their method of waging war,
their ceremonies and religion, as well as their other institutions, but
most of all in that matter which is the principal foundation of their
whole structure, namely, their common life and subsistence, without
any exchange of money, a feature that by itself utterly overthrows all
the nobility, magnificence, splendor, and majesty which are, in the
estimation of the common people, the true glories and ornaments of
the commonwealth, yet I knew that he was wearied with his tale and
was not quite certain that he could brook any opposition to his views,
particularly when I recalled his censure of others on account of their
fear that they might not appear to be wise enough, unless they found
some fault to criticize in other men's discoveries; therefore, praising
their way of life and his speech, taking him by the hand, I led him in to
supper, first saying, nevertheless, that there would be another chance
to think about these matters more deeply and to talk them over with
him more fully, if only this were some day possible.][20]

A convoluted sentence, indeed, turning itself against itself, repeatedly
duplicitous, making a point of its own duplicity: the authority of Latin
turns against authoritativeness. It is not that English was bound to
replace Latin, or did so; rather, the authority historically invested in

Latin ceased and could not be replaced by anything having like historical weight. It was not replaced. No stable, reliable authority, and so no more Latin for such an authority to pronounce: brave new world.

Notes

1. *Bloomer, "Marble Latin" (2005), p. 210.
2. Keith Sidwell, *Reading Medieval Latin* (Cambridge, 1995), p. ix.
3. Gerald of Wales, *De instructione principis*, ed. George F. Warner, in *Giraldi Cambrensis opera*, Rolls Series 21, pt. 8 (1891), pp. 127–28; all translations are mine unless noted. The reproduction of the engraving of the cross is from James P. Carley, *Glastonbury Abbey* (Woodbridge, 1988), p. 178.
4. Geoffrey of Monmouth, *The History of the Kings of Britain*, ed. Michael D. Reeve, trans. Neil Wright (Woodbridge, 2007), pp. 4–5.
5. *Hanning, *The Vision of History in Early Britain* (1966), p. 121.
6. Geoffrey of Monmouth, *The History of the Kings of Britain*, ed. Reeve, trans. Wright, pp. 4–5.
7. *William of Newburgh: The History of English Affairs Book I*, eds. and trans. P. G. Walsh and M. J. Kennedy (Warminster, 1988), pp. 34, 32, and 28.
8. *Townsend "Anglo-Latin Hagiography" (1991), p. 387.
9. London (Kew), National Archives: Public Record Office, C 65/62, m. 18; cf. *Parliament Rolls of Medieval England*, gen. ed. Chris Given-Wilson, CD-rom (Leicester, 2005), having embedded in it the pagination of *Rotuli parliamentorum: ut et petitiones, et placita in parliamento*, eds. John Strachey *et al.*, 8 vols. (1780–1832); the passage here is 3:422.
10. Chris Given-Wilson offers a more verbatim translation (*The Parliament Rolls of Medieval England*):

> We, John, bishop of St. Asaph, John, abbot of Glastonbury, Thomas earl of Gloucester, Thomas lord Berkeley, Thomas Erpingham, and Thomas Grey, knights, and William Thirning, justice, commissioners specially appointed to what is written below by the peers and nobles of the realm of England, spiritual and temporal, and the communities of the same realm, representing all the estates of the same realm sitting as a tribunal; having considered the multiple perjuries, and the cruelty, and the very many other crimes of the said Richard, committed and perpetrated during his rule in the aforesaid realms and dominion at the time of his rule, and before the aforesaid estates openly and publicly set out, displayed, and related, which were and are so public, notorious, manifest and well-known, that they could not and cannot be hidden by any evasion; and also the confession of the aforesaid Richard, acknowledging, and considering, and truly of his certain knowledge indicating that he was and is utterly incapable and useless for the rule and government of the aforesaid realms and dominion and their appurtenances, and because of his notorious faults, already acknowledged by Richard himself, and at his will and command made public before the said estates, and announced to them and explained in the vernacular, worthy to be deposed; after careful deliberation on these and all matters discussed relating to this business had been held before the aforesaid estates, and before us, by the commission, name, and authority given to us on this matter, we moreover as a further precaution

pronounce, decree, and declare Richard himself to have been and to be useless, incapable, utterly incompetent and unworthy, for the rule and government of the said realms and dominion, and of the laws and appurtenances of the same, and on account of the aforesaid, and by reason of them, deservedly to be deposed from every royal dignity and honour, if any of this dignity and honour should remain in him, and as a similar precaution we depose him by our definitive sentence in each and every one of these writings, expressly prohibiting any of the lord archbishops, bishops and prelates, dukes, marquises, earls, barons, knights, vassals and vavasours, and the other men of the said realms and dominion, and of other places pertaining to the said realms and dominion, or any of his subjects and lieges, from henceforth obeying or attending to the aforesaid Richard, as king or lord of the aforesaid realms or dominion.

11. Anne Middleton, "The Idea of Public Poetry in the Reign of Richard II," *Speculum* 53 (1978), 94–114.

12. An excellent guide to medieval Latin meters is included in *Rigg, *History of Anglo-Latin Literature* (1992), pp. 313–29.

13. "Presta Ihesu quod postulo," ll. 229–40, from London, British Library, Cotton Vespasian D.ix, fols. 164rb–va, though the poem was printed in Thomas Wright (ed.), *Political Poems and Songs Relating to English History Composed During the Period from the Accession of EDW. III. to that of RIC. III.*, Roll Series, vol. 14, pt. 1. (1859), pp. 231–49; my trans. 238 *infici* is conjectural; the manuscript reads *incii*, Wright *instrui*.

14. "The Metrical *Historia regum Angliae* Continuation," lines 259–62, in A. G. Rigg (ed.), *A Book of British Kings 1200 BC–1399 AD*, Toronto Medieval Latin Texts 26 (Toronto, 2000).

15. Macaulay, G. C. (ed.), *The Complete Works of John Gower*, 4 vols. (Oxford, 1899–1902), 4:337; trans. A. G. Rigg.

16. The painting, "The Battle of the Spurs, 16 August 1513 (*c.* 1513, Flemish School?)" in the (British) Royal Collection is reference number RCIN 406784.

17. *The Latin Writings of John Skelton*, ed. and trans. David Carlson, *Studies in Philology* 88(4) Texts and Studies (1991).

18. Erasmus, *Poems*, ed. Harry Vredeveld, trans. Clarence H. Miller, in *Collected Works of Erasmus: Vols. 85–86* (Toronto, 1993), No. 58, pp. 130–33.

19. *Bloomer, "Marble Latin," p. 223.

20. St. Thomas More, *Utopia*, eds. Edward Surtz and J. H. Hexter, in *Complete Works of St. Thomas More* (New Haven, CT, 1965), 4:244–45; their translation (helpfully divided into a series of sentences and a pair of paragraphs) has been adapted here to reflect more nearly the Latinate original.

10

The vernaculars of medieval England, 1170–1350

The Early English homiliary, Cambridge University Library (CUL) MS Ii.1.33, contains sermons and saints' lives and part of the Old English *Heptateuch* attributable to the prolific late tenth-century religious writer, Ælfric, abbot of Eynsham, whose corpus of work in English is the largest belonging to any single, known author before Chaucer. Datable to the later twelfth century, and with a provenance of Ely, this English manuscript represents, for many scholars of medieval literature, the last vestiges of the pre-Conquest Old English textual tradition. The extensive codex seems, at first glance perhaps, determinedly replicative, containing texts that virtually all belong in terms of composition to a period almost two centuries prior. The language of the homilies and hagiographies is predominantly late West Saxon, the standard dialect preferred by Ælfric and many English writers in the late tenth and eleventh centuries. Yet despite this old-world façade, a closer look inside the manuscript reveals a dynamic set of texts, linked by intensive editorial activity to the contemporary world of the late twelfth-century multilingual monastery, replete with evidence to illustrate the literary, religious, and intellectual milieu that facilitated the book's compilation.

Multiple interventions in English, Latin, and French to the prose texts in CUL Ii.1.33 show the detailed scrutiny to which the manuscript was subjected in its early years. The negotiation between the scribe–editor–readers and the texts takes the form of clarifications, expansions, annotations and *notae*, illustrating the research and reference use of the homilies and hagiographies. More than this, however, the reading of the English texts occasionally brings to the forefront of the scribe's mind other literary information that he (almost certainly a "he" in this particular volume) knows, information that demonstrates mastery of other

languages and an ability to reconcile knowledge between different linguistic codes. At folio 120r, for example, toward the end of a version of
Ælfric's sermon for the Memory of Saints from his late tenth-century
collection, the *Lives of Saints*, is a four-line set of Anglo-Norman proverbs,
a couple of which are taken from Guillaume de Berneville's *Vie de Saint
Gilles*. These proverbs are set apart from the English text on the page by
being written into the bottom margin by the manuscript's other main
scribe; their relationship to the English text is a fascinating demonstration of multilingual imbrication in the later twelfth century. This imbrication might be variously read as compromise, conciliation between
literary cultures or, indeed, given the distinctive separation of this quatrain, something more akin to confrontation, the main scribe seeing a
lack in the English text copied by his colleague, and feeling some obligation to expand upon this with the addition of a more contemporary,
potentially more erudite, Anglo-Norman excerpt:

> Li vilain dit en repruvier   · de jueune seint viel aversier
> Pur ceo dit li vilain verité   · Tels l'unt kin e t'en sevent gré
> Qu'entre l'aveir e le bricun · Ne sunt pas longes cumpaignun
> Li vilains dit la u il veolt   . Que oil ne veit a cuer ne duelt.[1]

The peasant says in a proverb: "From a young saint, an old devil."

> Through this the peasant speaks the truth (some receive it from you
> with gratitude) –
> Wealth and the fool soon part company.
> The peasant says whenever he desires: "What the eye can't see the heart
> can't grieve over."[2]

This quatrain with its internal rhyme begins with a paraph (the medieval
marker for a new section, which we have adopted as the paragraph mark)
noting the relevance of this text to the English homily it frames on folio
120r, though there is no corresponding mark within the text to specify its
referent. Its place in the lower margin draws the eye immediately to it,
ironically making this marginal comment upon the English text more
visually dominating than the text itself. Directly above the French, in the
English text, is the denunciation of pride, especially that derived from
wealth and status: "On hwam mæg se mann modigean þeah he wille · ne
mæg he on geþincðum forðan þe fela synd geþungenran · ne mæg he on
his æhtum forðan þe he his endedæg nat · ne on nanum þingum he ne
mæg modigean · gif he wis bið. Nu gehabbaþ gehyred hu þas halgan

mægnu oferswyþað þa leahtras þe deofol besæwð on us" ("In what way might a man pride himself, though he desire it? He may not by his rank, because many are more illustrious than him; nor can he by his possessions, because he doesn't know when his final day might be; nor in anything can he pride himself, if he is wise. Now you have heard how the holy virtues overcome the sins which the devil sows in us"). This reminder of the sins of the foolish and the prideful, and the metaphor of the devil as sower of sin (paralleling the conceit of the proverb being instigated by a peasant), seem to inspire in the Anglo-Norman scribe reminiscences of proverbs he knows from other texts – partly from the *Vie de Saint Gilles*, and partly from elsewhere, an inspiration that he clearly feels can be usefully passed on at this point as an additional set of exempla to the text of CUL Ii.1.33, and suggesting that this English written text was to be superseded by a French oral delivery.

While little of this might seem noteworthy, what is critically important here is the interplay between Anglo-Norman and English, a relationship which is at one and the same time both separate – through the visual gap between the marginal addition and the main text – and yet connected by the overarching themes of the persistent deceit of the devil, and the apparent derogation of worldly desires, implicit in the last two verse lines. The intertextual referencing to the *Vie de Saint Gilles* brings in a work that ostensibly belongs to a distinct linguistic culture, but this difference is mitigated by the shared genre of hagiography here (since the Anglo-Norman commentary reflects on Ælfric's text on the Memory of Saints) and the shared monastic contexts of production. And, notwithstanding the visual and formal separation of the English hagiography and the Anglo-Norman proverbial verse, there is an obvious easiness in the relationship between the two texts (and between the many other English and Latin or English and Anglo-Norman marginalia that this scribe also writes in CUL Ii.1.33). This evinces a multilingual effortlessness, which seems difficult for most of us to access today: a multilingual effortlessness marking a new era in literary production in the high Middle Ages and a major contrast to most of the decades of the twelfth century, where English and Anglo-Norman are rarely – if ever, in fact – found together in the same manuscript. This apparent ease of movement between languages by the end of the twelfth century is most notable, of course, only in the learned context of texts, like that quoted here, written in the monastic writing office or written elsewhere by professional scholars and scribes. Importantly, it is this ease of code-switching and the presence of multiple codes on the page that are the keys to understanding the complex, and still only partially understood, literary culture of England in the thirteenth and earlier fourteenth centuries.

The lack of self-consciousness in the varied language choices of the monastic scribe-editor-annotator of CUL Ii.1.33 shows that Latin, English, and Anglo-Norman were all, potentially, equally viable choices for writing in the two centuries after the Norman Conquest of 1066. The later Anglo-Saxon period, spanning four centuries from AD 700 to 1100, had been highly productive in literary and documentary terms, with many thousands of texts in Latin and in English composed within many hundreds of manuscripts. Despite incalculable losses of books and texts from this and the later medieval period, the surviving material ranges widely, from sermons and saints' lives to alliterative heroic and religious poetry; from pedagogical, liturgical, and medical texts to the *Anglo-Saxon Chronicle*, writs, letters, and law codes. Of particular importance to the generation of this intellectual and cultural phenomenon were the monasteries and monastic cathedrals of England, where many of these English and Latin writings were copied and collated into manuscripts; and where most of the 30,000 lines of vernacular poetry that survives was written into the four major collections, still extant.

For its part, the first literature in French emerged in England in the decades following the Norman Conquest, inspired, one might surmise, by the long tradition authorizing the prestige and status of writing texts in English. French was the language of the invading conquerors, those who divided the spoils and became the new aristocracy and senior clergy. It remained the language of the noble classes for the next three centuries, and was gradually established as the language of the secular law courts in England until the seventeenth century. Latin, the *lingua franca* of Christian Europe, remained the language of the Church and the ecclesiastical courts; to be officially literate (*literatus*) meant knowing and using Latin. For the twelfth century, most of the many thousands of texts composed and copied in England were produced in Latin, as they always had been, but far outstripping the numbers of works written in English and French. Indeed, the immediate post-Conquest period and the twelfth century saw a decline in the prestige of English as a language of official documents, but, especially after 1100, English was still employed as a language of teaching and preaching, and of disseminating general didactic and encyclopedic knowledge. Many manuscripts were manufactured at monastic cathedrals in this period, adapting works

from the late tenth and eleventh centuries (particularly those written by
Ælfric) for contemporary audiences and contemporary purposes. Some
new literary texts were written or translated into English, including
homilies, such as those known to us as the Trinity Homilies and the
Lambeth Homilies (Cambridge, Trinity College, MS B.14.52 and London,
Lambeth Palace, MS Lambeth 487), homiletic poems, like the *Orrmulum*
and *Poema Morale*, pedagogical texts, like extracts of the *Elucidarius* and
the *Dicts of Cato*, and saints' lives, including the lives of saints Nicholas,
Giles, and Neot.

While these texts exemplify the strength of the vernacular religious
tradition and its rootedness in the English monastic system, from the
twelfth century onwards (though not exclusively, since significant
exchange of ideas, texts, and literary forms had been disseminated
throughout Europe during earlier centuries) innovative forms of literary
composition were reaching England and the rest of Britain as a result of
its cultural proximity to continental Europe and the impact of the
Norman settlers. During the earlier twelfth century, Anglo-Norman
literary production had closely paralleled that of English precedents,
but the two appear never to have been in direct negotiation with one
another. The first text in Anglo-Norman seems to have been Benedeit's
Voyage of St. Brendan, composed around 1106 for Matilda, the first wife of
Henry I, and probably subsequently rededicated by Benedeit to Adeliza
of Louvain, Henry I's second wife. In the first half of the twelfth century,
this Anglo-Norman hagiography was followed by others of that genre,
including *La Vie de St. Alexis*, written for the anchoress, Christina of
Markyate; Wace's *Vie de Ste Marguerite*, and his *Vie de St. Nicolas*. It is
interesting to note that the twelfth century saw the composition of
these latter two saints' lives in new forms in both Anglo-Norman and
in English, but from completely different perspectives; together with the
production of the English *Hystoria Sancti Egidii* ("Narrative of St. Giles")
and the Anglo-Norman verse *Vie de Saint Gilles* by Guillaume de Berneville
in about 1170, mentioned above, it is apparent that both vernaculars
reflected and responded in similar ways to contemporary devotional
interests for multiple and varied readers who might have struggled
with Latin *Lives*, or who simply preferred to hear about their favorite
saints in their own languages. These early examples were, of course,
followed by many others as the twelfth century progressed, including,
in Anglo-Norman, the engaging *Vie de Saint Edmund* by Denis Piramus,
the *Vie d'Edouard le confesseur* by an anonymous nun of Barking, and the *Vie*

de Sainte Catherine by Clemence of Barking. Again, though, it is worth stressing that neither English nor Anglo-Norman textual materials appear together in twelfth-century manuscript compilations: they form separate discourses, possibly for quite different audiences, and emerging from distinct traditions. Current research suggests that English appears to have emanated almost entirely from the monastic institutions and monastic cathedrals of the pre-Conquest Benedictine Reform group: Worcester; Christ Church and St. Augustine's, Canterbury; Winchester; and Peterborough. These may have been produced for an in-house audience of non-Latinate audiences, or just as likely, for the pastoral use of parish priests affiliated to the institutions. The French texts during these decades, however, seem to have been written to order, many for female lay patrons, aristocratic in intended audience.[3]

In addition to saints' lives, the first half of the twelfth century saw a marked increase in the genre of historiography, initiated by major Latin works, such as William of Malmesbury's *Gesta regum Anglorum* and *Gesta pontificum*; Henry of Huntingdon's *Historia Anglorum*; Eadmer's *Historiae novorum*; and Geoffrey of Monmouth's *Historia regum Britanniae*. It is to the latter that literary history owes the widespread emergence of the Arthur myth, re-appropriated from his Celtic roots for the new beneficiaries of British legend, and most notably for the continental French in the later twelfth and thirteenth centuries (see also Chapters 1 and 5). All of these seminal works of historical writing had, and continue to have, a major impact on the ways in which this period of Britain's past is understood. One of the major impetuses for their creation was the desire to make sense of a new era for Britain, to refashion the Anglo-Saxon and Celtic legacies for the inheritors of the realm, and yet, as we shall see, rejected by the Anglo-Normans in favor of "Matter of England" romances.

Alongside these revisionary works were the final entries up to 1154 in the *Anglo-Saxon Chronicle*, the English account of history, which had been continuously maintained in a number of versions since the late ninth century. In French, too, historical writing was one of the first major genres to be composed, with Gaimar's *Estoire des Engleis* written before 1140 and based, in part, on the *Anglo-Saxon Chronicle*; and Wace's verse *Brut*, finished in 1155, based on Geoffrey of Monmouth's *Historia*. A fascinating figure, Wace wrote for the court of Henry II – one of the most dynamic and culturally significant royal courts of the entire medieval period. Wace added considerably to the legend of Monmouth, inventing the Round Table so that his Arthur would be seen to treat the knights of his extensive realm equitably and democratically, perhaps offering tentative advice for a real monarch. This Anglo-Norman version itself subsequently became one of the sources for the even longer English alliterative verse *Brut* of Laȝamon, composed in the west midlands in the thirteenth century and much more ambivalent about its treatment of the militaristic Arthur.

From the perspective of literary production in the twelfth century, Latin, French, and English were all used for major genres, such as historiography, hagiography, homilies, sapiential ("wisdom") writings, and pedagogic texts. There are major differences in the manner in which these texts were produced, with, for example, far more lay patronage of French and Latin textual production than is the case with English. Moreover, it is notable that many French texts were written by women, or explicitly dedicated to women; this was the case with Benedeit's *Voyage of St. Brendan* dedicated to Henry I's queen, and Gaimar's *Estoire des Engleis* written for Constance Fitzgilbert. However, despite these cultural distinctions in the form and function of these writings, there are – as shown thus far – notable similarities, worth investigating further for the light each genre in its specific linguistic medium throws on the other.

The span from the late twelfth century into the thirteenth century is difficult for any student of the period to apprehend holistically. In most scholarly chapters on Latin or any vernacular literature in this period, the three languages and their bodies of literature are discussed separately, or as fragmentary in themselves, or with an emphasis on one or another genre: hagiography or Romance, for example. It is this period, however, in distinction from the century following the Conquest, when manuscripts and their contents reflect a far greater sense of linguistic fluidity and permeability, a recognition in many cases of potential negotiation between languages and their literary traditions. This indicates the multilingualism of the literate classes, with English as a first language, spoken by the vast majority of the population, but also used for many types of written texts, and Anglo-Norman learned and used for new and older forms of literature, many of which significantly influenced the type of text subsequently translated or adapted into English. At the highest levels of education, Latinity awaited the scholar or serious cleric, and, from an official perspective, Latin and Anglo-Norman had formal documentary and textual functions to perform: administrative, religious, and governmental. But in every aspect of literary culture in this period, the transfer of texts into the various languages was no one-way linguistic street, with the good stuff written in Latin and then translated into Anglo-Norman for the well-to-do and into English for the ne'er-do-wells. The process is much more fluid and dynamic than that.

It can be illustrated by the famous *Guide for Anchoresses*, the *Ancrene Wisse*, composed in the first instance for three aristocratic women recluses *c.* 1225. This famous work was written initially in English by a religious advisor, who was possibly a Dominican, in north Herefordshire or south Shropshire, and it forms one of a significant group of English texts created for women by various authors; the other works being known as the Wooing Group and the Katherine Group. From the thirteenth to the fifteenth centuries, *Ancrene Wisse* (or *Ancrene Riwle*) was subsequently copied into many more manuscripts (seventeen survive in various forms); it was adapted for larger female audiences as well as for male religious readers; and, notably, it was translated into both Latin and French versions. All these texts bear witness to evolving themes and images in literature in this period. Among the most memorable are the extended metaphor of Christ as the knight-lover of the Anchoress in Book 7 of *Ancrene Wisse*, and the affective piety of the meditation on Christ in *On Ureisun of oure Louerde*, where the female contemplative imagines her relationship to Christ as that of faithful bride, speaking directly to him in the language of lovers: "Ihesu, min hali loue, min sikere swetnesse! Ihesu, min heorte, min sel, min saule hele! Ihesu swete Ihesu, mi leof, mi lif, mi leome, min halwi, min huniter: þu al þet ic hopie" ("Jesus, my holy love, my certain sweetness! Jesus, my heart, my joy, my soul's healing! Jesus, sweet Jesus, my love, my life, my light, my healing oil, my honey-drop: you are all that I hope for"). This intensely devotional text, inspiring religious women in their goal of salvation through a lifetime of total commitment to God, resonates with the language of physical love, of a personal and inspiring relationship between the *sponsa* (bride) and her heavenly bridegroom. It takes us from the exemplary text of the hagiographer and the didactic text of the homilist, toward a mystical, and virtually physical, experience shared by the contemplative and her God.

Indeed, among the most important developments in literature in the later twelfth and thirteenth centuries is the flourishing of Romance as a genre. This point, rather than 1066, seems to mark a genuine shift in the literary interests of patrons and audiences – one where the focus on Romance might be considered "new." With its emphasis on chivalric deeds, loyalty, love, and the reconciliation of the public and the private spheres through the individual's innate morality and exemplary cour-age, Romance suggests a demand for entertainment in which society could see its ideals reflected. For this audience of nobles – whether at the royal court or in their "provincial" manors – this fictional society both mirrors and creates the desire to present the formation of moral and social identity through intrinsic piety and the fulfillment of successive admirable deeds, and many Romances concern heroes temporarily exiled from their homeland during their adventures. This sense of the chivalric self undergoing a test of character might offer confirmation to the increasing desire to find a coherent identity – one of "new Englishness" for the Anglo-Normans a century and more after the Conquest. We might thus see 1170 as the turning point in English literary history, when Anglo-Norman and English vernaculars functioned in their par-ticular ways to cement the new era, whether the audience for the respec-tive texts was monolingual or bilingual, or in many cases even trilingual (competent in English, French, and Latin).

There is little doubt that the considerable body of extant medieval Romantic literature owes its great flourishing in late medieval England to the Anglo-Normans' enthusiasm for this genre – first in Anglo-Norman French, and subsequently, through its rapid adaptation and translation into English. Indeed, the great epic, the *Chanson de Roland*, survives in its earliest manuscript form in a manuscript of English origin, written *c.* 1170. From this period onward survive other notable examples of Romance, often composed by clerics; for example, Thomas d'Angleterre's *Tristan*, Hue de Rotelande's *Ipomedon* and *Protheslaus*; and the *Horn* of Mestre Thomas. This latter Anglo-Norman poem was sub-sequently transformed into the Middle English *King Horn* (*c.* 1225), a lengthy, but rapid, verse romance containing all the key elements that provided entertainment for aristocratic and baronial courts, both in major centers such as London and in the provinces. *Horn* and many other related poems belong to what has traditionally been referred to as Matter of England romance, taking as its central protagonist a legen-dary hero of the pre-Conquest age. In this case, the hero, Horn, is a prince and noble knight possibly meant to come from Surrey or somewhere southern (though he comes from Ireland in the Anglo-Norman version of Thomas: "Seignurs, or est Yrlande, lors fu Westir nomée," "Lords, it is Ireland now, then it was called Westir").[4] This poem raises themes evinced in numerous other Romances, involving the loss and regaining of kingdoms, the advocacy of innate nobility and strength through adversity, exile, and return, the acquisition of true love, and the stability of a dynastic succession based on justice and sincerity. At the poem's finale, the integration of a dynasty emerging from parents of different origins, and the revelation of the hero's true identity despite lengthy sequences of disadvantageous events, underscore the Anglo-Normans', or, by the thirteenth century, the English audience's, appreciation of stability through exemplary kingship, and particularly how the restoration of order is reflected within the depicted kingdom's more general social setting.

This example of a Romance privileging themes of adventure and resolution is illustrated by other thirteenth-century examples, written first in Anglo-Norman then often subsequently translated into Middle English (and sometimes again into early Modern English in the Renaissance). Among these are the *Roman de Waldef*, *Boeve de Haumtone* (*Sir Bevis of Hampton*), *Amis e Amillyoun* (*Amis and Amiloun*) and *Gui de Warewic* (*Guy of Warwick*). In many cases, major differences exist in the length of these respective English poems and their Anglo-Norman parallels, which are generally much longer, much more courtly, and given over to description and narration of noble pursuits. The English versions, when they are abbreviated, become terser in style, and thus faster moving in terms of the plot. In and of themselves, these structural and stylistic distinctions need not mean a great deal, but as a trend in the evolution of Anglo-Norman Romance and Middle English Romance, they indicate rather different performative contexts, and certainly, rather different audience expectations. One exception is the *Lai d'Haveloc*, which is just over 1,000 lines, and the English adaptation which may be based on the Norman *lai*, but is three times longer, with more characters and a more complex narrative. This Matter of England romance, deriving from an episode in Gaimar's twelfth-century chronicle, *Estoire des Engleis*, focuses on a protagonist of Danish extraction who becomes a great English hero, in a tale that raises the equally significant issue of just and dynamic monarchy at a time of political turmoil.

These Romances, so popular with the nobility or possibly, more particularly, the lower nobility, can be read alongside those also usually labeled as Matter of Britain Romance – but here focused either on Arthur, or, and principally, on his knights. From his literary genesis as a noble hero in Geoffrey of Monmouth's *Historia regum Britanniae*, Arthur was to become the central character in the later medieval period in England, in the work of Malory (in his fifteenth-century *Morte d'Arthur*), and the writer of the alliterative *Morte Arthure*, for example. Earlier, though, numerous romances, *lais* and lyrics chose one of Arthur's knights, or legendary knightly figures, on which to concentrate. The most famous writer of the *lai* is the later twelfth-century female author, Marie de France, whose twelve poems of varying length, based supposedly on Celtic sources, narrate the critical moment (an *aventure*) of various knights' relationships with their lovers. These Breton *lais* (short romances in octosyllabic couplets often meant to be set to music, with a major love interest, heroic deeds, and supernatural events), composed possibly for the court of Henry II, survive as a number of fragments, and in one full version in a thirteenth-century manuscript from, of all places, Reading Abbey.

Pausing a moment to look at this manuscript will allow us to see Marie's *lais* in one context, one historically specific moment, raising a number of questions that are central to this brief examination of Anglo-Norman and English literature in the thirteenth century. The manuscript, London, British Library, Harley 978 contains a large number of texts in the three languages current in England in the high Middle Ages – (in order of literary predominance) Latin, French, and English. Written by four or five scribes in the 1260s this manuscript seems – *prima facie* by its provenance of Reading Abbey, at least – to be aimed at a religious audience, one comprising Benedictine monks. This is a rather different audience, of course, from the courtly one, which represented the original intention of Marie in the composition of her *Lais* and also her *Fables, Ysopet* (based, she tells us, on English texts written by King Alfred, and dedicated to a Count William) and which many readers might still imagine for these texts.

Harley 978 includes musical, scientific, medical, romance, satirical, didactic, and prognosticatory material compiled from a variety of sources, and put together from booklets, some copied at Reading, others brought from elsewhere. Of particular note in the evolving world of medieval education and literacy (where we move from monastic schools and cathedral schools in the eleventh and earlier twelfth centuries to the emergence of universities in England and on the Continent), it seems that some of the texts might have been purchased from Oxford's burgeoning bookshops in Catte Street, catering for a diverse student audience among the scholars at the early university. Among the works contained in the codex are the following texts: Latin and French antiphons (responses sung in a church service); French *estampies* (poetic songs, derived from the repertoire of the northern French troubadours in the twelfth century, and accompanied by stringed instruments); the English song, *Sumer is icumen in*, complete with its music and a Latin religious song written immediately beneath it, set to the same music; medical works on herbs and plants; Marie de France's *Fables*; the debate between a body and the soul known as *Noctis sub silentio*; Latin Goliardic (satirical) poets, including extracts from the work of Walter Map, the twelfth-century Latin writer; the comic-satirical commentary, *La Besturné* ("The turned-back-to-front"), written by a clerical Anglo-Norman author named Richard, and datable to about 1262; the political work, the *Song of Lewes* (datable to 1264 and concerning Simon de Montfort and the baronial conflict against King Henry III); an Anglo-Norman treatise on falconry; and Marie de France's *Lais*.

The variety of texts here is not unusual among compilations produced in the medieval period. Earlier, extensive examples of large, apparently disparate volumes exist from the Anglo-Saxon period and the twelfth century, often attributable to one person as the owner or compiler. In the earlier period, those owners most often tend to be bishops or senior ecclesiastics, or, less certainly and less frequently, noblemen or women. An instance would be London, British Library, Cotton Tiberius MS A.iii, a large bilingual (Latin and English) compilation from Christ Church, Canterbury, in the mid-eleventh century, which contains saints' lives, prognostications, homilies, prayers, a charm, a lapidary, a monastic rule, and a text to examine a bishop before ordination. Recent work by scholars has shown that this manuscript, like many others from this early period, belonged to an individual ecclesiastic; in this case, possibly Archbishop Stigand. With these later examples of diverse compilations, it is often the case, too, that cohesion comes not from the texts included in the manuscript – sharing themes, or forms, or language – but from the particular requirements of principal, and subsequent, owners.

Harley 978 is an excellent case in point. In their eclecticism, its contents appear uncategorizable. Taylor calls this book a "personal miscellany" and cites another label given to it by an earlier scholar: a "monk's album or commonplace book."[5] The cogency, therefore, comes less from the texts included than from the preferences of an individual owner; here, Taylor's argument proposing the monk William of Winchester as the owner of Harley 978 seems convincing. This William, a learned Benedictine monk of Leominster and then Reading, and a former student at Oxford University, is an entertaining character, accused of "incontinence with Agnes of Avenbury, a nun at Lynggebrok, and with certain other women."[6] What can be gleaned about him provides engaging information for interpreting the manuscript he probably owned and left to Reading Abbey. Taylor surmises that "Harley 978, like other thirteenth-century manuals, served as a kind of courtesy book from which its owner could acquire social graces and useful knowledge … Harley 978 is a book that shows its owner how to do things"[7] – including, it seems, seducing women!

While knowing some contemporary evidence about the compilers and owners of medieval books brings us to a closer understanding of the specific reasons behind the inclusion of particular texts within a manuscript, more important is how this information permits us to comprehend the differences in the literary culture of this period compared with modern and contemporary expectations. In relation to Harley 978, for example, without knowing much about the owner of the manuscript, it would be possible to consider it a typical example of a multilingual, multigeneric, and multi-form book of the thirteenth century. That is to say, it combines French, Latin, and English texts of both religious and secular natures in the forms of poetry, prose, and music in an unself-conscious manner that defeats modern scholars' attempts to classify or categorize. Harley 978 is best known to modern scholars for two literary works: *Sumer is icumen in* and Marie de France's *Lais*; yet the first work belongs most appropriately to musicological study, not anthologies of early lyrics, and is written in English, the least significant of the languages in the manuscript. The second work, despite its obvious Romance affiliation, is situated in a codicological and institutional context suggesting a didactic, monastic use; as a work in French, it occupies a subordinate role anyway to the more prevalent Latin texts of the manuscripts. Not only are the texts now studied in disproportion to their appearance in the manuscript, but this book also illustrates how twenty-first-century generic boundaries are frequently inappropriate, misaligned with those of earlier literary periods, despite the pretensions of post-modernism and its scholarly practitioners to deny the validity of overarching uniformities and grand narratives.

These major investigative issues of language, genre, and cogency of theme or form emerge frequently in the discussion of the numerous extensive literary manuscripts of the thirteenth and earlier fourteenth centuries. Some of these books, for example, have until recently been labeled "Friars' Miscellanies," in the mistaken belief that they belonged principally to the orders of friars, who might have used them for their peripatetic cure of souls. Of these, four in particular deserve some discussion, each originating from the Worcester or Hereford dioceses between *c.* 1260 and *c.* 1280. Cambridge, Trinity College, MS B.14.39 and Oxford, Bodleian Library, MS Digby 86 both contain a multitude of texts written in English, French, and Latin; London, British Library, MS Cotton Caligula A.ix and Oxford, Jesus College MS 29 contain works composed in English and French. With few exceptions, scholars study each of these manuscripts in various states of dismemberment, their texts plucked for anthologies or analysis according to language, or genre, or form. Despite this unfortunate trend, which does not allow investigations into these works in their physical contexts, scholars seem most concerned to seek that which unites these collections: themes or visible coherences that create unity from ostensible disunity. It is unhelpful, then, that many of the texts – particularly those written in Latin, and many of those written in Anglo-Norman – are not available at all in modern editions or translations. As such, students and scholars can only partially access these manuscripts, which are simultaneously ordinary in their multilingual and multigeneric nature, and extraordinary in their fortunate survival.

There is, thus, a substantial amount of scholarship required on these manuscripts before any genuine understanding of their compilatory methods, their intended and actual audiences, and their reflection of and contribution to thirteenth-century literary cultures can be assessed with conviction. It is clear, however, that they represent literariness and literacies in ways that can most fruitfully be appreciated as very different to our own. The emphasis scholars place on the varying languages employed by these medieval manuscript compilers, for example, seems misleading from the manuscript evidence. In relation to Trinity B.14.39, for example, which contains 140 texts in Latin, English, and French, Scahill deduces that "The primacy of Latin in the hierarchy of languages, in addition to its quantitative predominance in the collection, suggests that in this milieu it was the preferred language for writing. English, I would argue, is present because it is the preferred language for oral delivery."[8] Whether or not English is preferred for oral delivery, it is preserved in writing, and, moreover, in a codicological format that does not discriminate visually or thematically between English, French, and Latin. This apparent ease of literary and scribal movement between languages is seen again in Digby 86, where English is the least present of the three languages.

Digby 86, datable between 1260 and 1280, and probably written in the region of south Worcestershire, was associated – possibly from its inception – with the Grimhill, Pendock, and Underhill families, local gentry who clearly attached great value to this manuscript (it was passed from Richard de Grimhill to his daughter, Amice, when she married Simon Underhill). It contains 101 texts derived from a variety of exemplars, over a short period of time, and put together in a manuscript compiled as a sequence of units. There is one main scribe – perhaps Richard de Grimhill, with whom this manuscript is often associated by scholars, and he seems to have obtained two quires written by another scribe (now folios 81–96), which may have served as his codicological exemplars for this extensive volume. What is particularly notable about this manuscript, then, both in its own right, but also in parallel with the other thirteenth-century collections of texts mentioned above, is the effortless contiguity of languages and of genres in this period; the fluidity of boundaries that seem so fixed to modern minds.

This is well exemplified by the work of the Digby 86 compiler-scribe-editor, who has collated material that clearly serves numerous functions from the liturgical (whether in the context of a pious individual or something like a manorial chapel) to the devotional to the comic to the scurrilous. The juxtaposition of these texts within this one volume unequivocally testifies to the permeability of the "literary," well beyond the bounds of what we usually think of Literature with all its *belle-lettrist* connotations. In the (now) opening quires of Digby 86, a sequence of French penitential and confessional works sits comfortably alongside the *Lettre d'Hippocrate*, itself contiguous with the exotic fantasy landscape portrayed in the fictional *Lettre de prestre Iohan*, with prayers, and with prognostications.

Texts potentially categorizable as fortune-telling or superstitious, such as charms, or days propitious for blood-letting, or how to interpret dreams are, for these medieval readers, as practical and necessary as the Gradual and Penitential Psalms, which, within folios, repeat the same Latin Psalm 129 quite unself-consciously. The exotic, seen in the *Letter of Prester John*, the various visionary texts, the dream narratives, and the beast fables, was potentially instructive and escapist. The first sets of texts salve the anxious mind and body; the second heals the soul; the third satisfies the curious. The Latin calendar helps to reassure the reader of important days of spiritual thanksgiving, and when those days are days for entertainment and relaxation, the multitude of romances, fabliaux, and lyrics contained in French, principally, but also English, fulfill that necessary part of life. If there seems something incongruent or odd to a modern reader in the immediate proximity of the Anglo-Norman sequence *Le blasme des fames* ("The reproach of women"), *Le Chastie-musart* ("The punished bawd"), and *La vie de un vallet amerous* ("The life of an amorous servant") with the Anglo-Norman *Des quatre files deu* ("The four daughters of God") and the English *Harrowing of Hell*, it certainly did not faze the Digby scribe. These textual connections – resonant with the Bahktinian carnivalesque so well documented in relation to later medieval works and images – dramatically usurp modern conceptualizations of thematic unity, or cogency of form, reminding us that our categories cannot be forced to apply to this earlier literature in all its manifestations.

Moreover, the usurpation of order is contained within some Digby texts that themselves refuse the containment of easy classification. The famous English lyric, "Stond wel moder under rode," here at folio 127r, given the French rubric *Chaucoun de noustre dame* ("A song of our lady") is elsewhere set to music, but nowadays is seldom printed or performed as song. It is pertinent to note that the vast majority of texts in Digby 86 and other manuscripts such as Jesus 29 have French rubrics, whether or not the main body of the item is French: was this because the texts were known by French titles, or was French the language of finding one's way around a large collection like this? Or was French the prestigious way of labeling a text? This lyric's dialogue between Christ and his mother, who stands at the foot of the cross, seems to demand vocal performance, as does the following verse homily, *Þe sawe of Seint Bede prest* at folios 127–30, which in Oxford, Jesus College 29 is known as *Sinners Beware*. The public performance potential of numerous other texts in Digby 86 might also explain their inclusion: the unique Anglo-Norman romance, *Le lai du corn* (folios 105–9v), an anti-feminist test of chastity, for example, or *Le Fablel del gelous* (the unique *Fabliau of the Jealous Man*, folios 109v–10r), or the amusing topsy-turvy *La bestournee* ("The Turning Upside-Down"), by an otherwise unknown "Richard," which is also included in Harley 978, the collection from Reading Abbey.

The textual links between Digby 86 and Harley 978 are evinced also in texts shared between Digby 86 and Oxford, Jesus College 29, and Digby 86 and London, British Library, MS Harley 2253, an extensive multilingual collection of the late thirteenth century and second quarter of the fourteenth century. In fact, most of the large manuscripts from the later thirteenth and fourteenth centuries have much in common by way of their extensive range of material, their bi- or trilingualism, and their apparent ease with the multigeneric nature of their contents. Moreover, as with Digby 86, it is the performative aspect of many of the texts that is striking, though perhaps not surprising given what we know of reading practices in this period, which often involved public readings to mixed groups in varied settings and in ways more complex that the simple delivery of a text by a single reader in a single language. In Harley 2253, something of this complexity is yielded by the very layout of the manuscript, as Susanna Fein and Carter Revard have recently demonstrated. This codex, well known for its inclusion of some of the most famous medieval lyrics, as well as the Romance, *King Horn*, again illustrates effectively the unself-conscious use of multiple languages both between texts, but also within texts – macaronically (shifting languages within a single work) – and if Carter Revard is correct, then the main scribe is a cleric who practiced as a legal scrivener and compiled much of the manuscript in the 1330s. Here, unmistakably in contrast to earlier manuscripts like CUL Ii.1.33 or Harley 978, is the major move away from a monastic setting: the professional, clerical scribe, compiling books from a variety of sources for delivery to audiences in contexts outside the monastic setting.

Harley 2253 is lauded for its secular lyrics, many of which survive uniquely in this manuscript. But the book is, like the others discussed earlier, as much about performance as contemplation and devotion; in a sense, these extensive medieval compilations are, potentially, all things to all people (or, at least, the elite literate of late medieval England and the auditory participants). This sense of a shared experience is explicitly apparent in a moving macaronic lyric, Marian in focus, "Mayden moder milde." This song effectively shows the comfortableness of moving between two languages and the clear expectation of a genuine understanding of both simultaneously. I present it as it appears on folio 83r of the manuscript, where the scribe-compiler writes it as a single long lyric of mixed-language verse lines, although it is usually edited to present a visually clear pattern of short verse lines separating the English and French into the abababab/cdcdcdcd rhyme scheme, further divided into eight-line stanzas:

Mayden moder milde, oiez cel oreysoun:	Maiden, mother mild, hear my prayer:
From shome þou me shilde me de ly mal feloun;	Shield me from shame and from the evil villain;
For love of þine childe, me menez de tresoun;	For love of your child, protect me from treachery.
Ich wes wod & wilde, ore su en prisoun.	I was mad and wild; now I am in prison.

Þou art feyr & fre e plein de
doucour
Of þe sprong þe ble, ly souerein
creatour.
Mayde, byseche Y þe vostre
seint socour.
Meoke & mylde be wiþ me, par
la sue amour.
Þo Iudas Iesum founde, donque
ly beysa;
He wes bete & bounde, que nus
tous fourma.
Wyde were is wounde, qe le
Gywz ly dona;
He þolede harde stounde, me
poi le greua.
On ston ase þou stode, pucele,
tot pensaunt,
Þou restest þe under rode, ton
fitz veites pendant;
Þou seye is sides of blode,
lalme de ly partaunt;
He ferede uch-an fode en mound
que fust viuaunt
Ys siden were sore, le sang de
ly cora;
Þat lond wes forlore, mes il
le rechata.
Vch bern þat wes ybore en enfern
descenda;
He þolede deþ þer-fore, en ciel
puis mounta.
Þo Pilat herde the tydyng, molt
fu joyous baroun;
He lette byfore him brynge
Iesu Nazaroun
He was ycrouned kynge pur
nostre redempcioun.
Who-se wol me synge avera
grant pardoun.

You are fair and noble and full of
sweetness.
Of you sprung the brightness, the
sovereign creator.
Maid, I beseech you your holy succor.

Be meek and mild with me, for your
love of him.
When Judas found Jesus, then he
kissed him.
He was beaten and bound, who
formed us all.
Wide were his wounds, which the
Jews gave him;
He suffered great pain, but little did
he grieve.
On stone as you stood, maiden, lost
in grief,
You rested under the rood, your son
you saw hanging;
You saw his bleeding sides, his soul
parting from him.
He scared every creature living in the
world.
His sides were sore, his blood flowed
from them;
That land was lost, but he
redeemed it.
Each child that was born descended
into hell;
He suffered death therefore,
then ascended to heaven.
When Pilate heard the news,
that lord was joyous;
He ordered Jesus of Nazareth
before him.
He was crowned king for our
redemption.
Whoever will sing me will receive
great pardon.

From the outset this is a penitential poem of profound contrasts. The opening phrase signifies one of Christianity's great paradoxes: the maternal nature of Mary as *theotokos* juxtaposed with her perpetual virginity. Contrast of perspective, enhanced by the balanced alternation of English and French structuring the rhyme throughout the prayerful meditation, is reflected in the movement from the individual's contemplation, beseeching Mary for mercy, to the universalizing invitation for all participants to share in this song and thus in absolution and redemption. The balance of antitheses operates at all levels of this lyric, as the speaker contrasts his or her sinful state, "Ich wes wod & wilde," with Mary's graceful beauty and nobility, "Þou art feyr & fre"; the love that Mary has for Christ and from which she will draw to save sinners ("Meoke & mylde be wiþ me, par la sue amour") is sharply defined against the kiss of betrayal, not love, given by Judas to Jesus in the next line. Again, in the final six lines the children of man descend into Hell and Christ ascends into heaven (eliding the usual Harrowing of Hell motif), assisting in the joyful denouement of the lyric. In a sense, the use of English and French here seems itself to be thoroughly inclusive, integral to the evangelizing nature of the text, explicitly calling on all hearers and readers to share in the message. And although the high level of literacy required to *read* this material was almost always the preserve of the elite in this period, nonetheless, this, and other texts like it, show that by the later thirteenth and fourteenth centuries, the two vernaculars were comfortably accommodating. This is in contrast to the scholarly myth of rivalry between French and English.

This shared experience with the careful balance of languages intratextually and intertextually, as well as throughout the extensive, eclectic manuscripts that characterize much of literary culture in the later thirteenth and earlier fourteenth centuries, is often interpreted as fundamentally distinct from the treatment and production of texts in the preceding century, from *c.* 1170 to 1270. However, the medieval period in its entirety yields far more when seen holistically, like the manuscripts and texts themselves, without our false categorizations of secular versus religious, French versus English, educated versus uneducated, written versus oral, central versus marginal. Our own hierarchies are in urgent need of reassessment if we are to understand a complex era of strategic literacy, generic fluidity, and linguistic competencies beyond our own experiences.

Notes

1. *Hunt, *Teaching and Learning Latin* (1991), 1:46. I retain manuscript punctuation here. Thanks to Mary Swan and Orietta Da Rold for many long conversations about this manuscript.

2. See *Traxel's thorough study of this manuscript, *Language Change* (2004), pp. 105–10. Traxel sees four scribes in the manuscript, I see two. Thanks to Lori Walters for checking my translation.

3. See *Short, "Language and Literature" (2003) and *Short, "Patrons and Polyglots" (1991).

4. Mildred K. Pope (ed.), *The Romance of Horn, by Thomas*, 2 vols., Anglo-Norman Text Society (Oxford, 1955), line 2184.

5. *Taylor, *Textual Situations* (2002), p. 93, citing A. J. Ellis.

6. Cited in *Taylor, *Textual Situations*, p. 111, from *The Register of Thomas de Cantilupe, Bishop of Hereford (AD 1275–1282)*.

7. *Taylor, *Textual Situations*, pp. 132–33.

8. *Scahill, "Trilingualism" (2003), p. 20. This seems a false dichotomy given the physical evidence.

English literary voices, 1350–1500

Medieval English vernacularity and "the desire of text to be made voice"

English culture *c.* 1300 might best be compared with Pushkin's Russia: the socially privileged, those who were literate, or at any rate with access to texts, spoke, wrote, and for the most part seem to have thought in their sociolect of French; the majority vernacular was the province of the peasantry and urban proletariat. Within two hundred years, following regime change and regicide, but without social convulsion on the Russian scale, the English language found itself promoted to the position formerly held by French, both as the language of secular state institutions and as a standard status language for literary composition. This is the change that all literary histories of medieval English culture would address.

The Russian parallel may be instructive. We need to reconceptualize, in more comparative and transhistorical ways, the relationship such accounts mostly assume between the vernacular and the national. Do writers see their choice of language as a sign of social identity, and, if so, broadly (nation) or more narrowly (kinship group, region, class)? Not only are vernacularities plural in both cultures (with minority vernaculars in both empires, such as Welsh or Ukrainian), but also in both cultures it is impossible to separate "vernacular" from "popular": Russian and English are associated primarily with the governed, French with the governors. So in Middle English, by the early fourteenth century, works use formulas that mark them as popular by destination, aimed at "lewed" folk (those who cannot read French or, if the subject is ecclesiastical, Latin). These quickly become tropes, and their truth value can never be assumed. They are a signal of translation, which is, of course, social and cultural as well as linguistic, as the "lewed" are given access to literate materials. That use creates a double-voiced discourse: the "I" that addresses its work to the "lewed" claims the authority of learning, and distinguishes itself from its audience; yet its use of a lower language sets it back in the position of the "lewed," guilty by association. The trope changes over more than a century, as the vernacular gains ground, and comes – ironically, in some cases (such as the guise of Chaucerian dullness) – to highlight the cultural inferiority of the trans- lator rather than that of the presumed audience. Worked into the very fabric of this new (aberrant, high) vernacularity is a complex and split *voice*, oscillating between the cultural conditions of textuality and those of secondary orality.

My use of "double-voiced discourse" already betrays the influence of M. M. Bakhtin, and it would be hard to find an account of the last generation that altogether fails to do so. Yet the use or misreading of Bakhtin has produced a narrative that betrays its theoretical model. This proposition can be repeated substituting for the name of Bakhtin those of Foucault and, to a lesser extent, of Deleuze and Guattari in *Toward a Minor Literature*, exploring why Kafka chooses to write in imperial German rather than demotic Czech: each has influenced modern accounts of medieval English culture, yet in ways that sometimes negate the impulse behind them. In Bakhtin's case, the paired binaries of his work have been scrambled, so that the dialogic has sometimes been opposed to the monoglot, which it is not; thus, if English poetry of the fifteenth century is less multilingual than that of the late fourteenth century (itself a moot point), it supposedly must be more monologic. This slip gives away the careful work of reading fifteenth-century liter- ature before it starts. It pairs uncomfortably with a formulaic reading of Foucault, already vulgarized by new historicism, claiming to produce a law of eternal recurrence in which containment necessarily follows sub- version. This again surrenders the fifteenth century without much of a struggle.

The notion of "minor literature" is a more useful tool for conceptu- alizing the relation between literature and government – such as we see in the profession of many named later Middle English writers, and in the still unfolding picture of textual production in the late fourteenth century. If it is salutary to recognize a "bureaucratic muse," we need all the more to allow for double-voiced discourse. It is not inevitably wise to insist that the bureaucracy produces or determines the literature, a logical enough step that leads to some notably reductive reading of Chaucerian voice. It also helps to look at the discursive context in which Deleuze and Guattari were writing, and at the theory with which they were in conversation – not least, Louis Marin's important *Utopics*. This might illuminate the ways in which fifteenth-century writers continue the project of making cultural room for secular fiction. Utopian discourse, writes Marin, is "not a discourse of the concept" but "a discourse of the figure": "a particular figurative mode of discourse," which "will always stay wrapped in fiction and fable-making." Marin's most disconcerting and plausible suggestion is to do with the political and therefore the textual function of utopic fiction: "Fiction is essential, for it allows ... a plural position of characteristics and differential signs within the same totality," its role not to harmonize opposites but to neutralize them by finding a kind of rhetorical zero-degree between contradictory terms "somewhere between yes and no, false and true."[1] Thus, figurative elaboration, as in much fifteenth- and later fourteenth-century prosody, is of a piece with the number of distancing devices often classified as irony, the most important of which is free indirect discourse, voices readers see as discordant but are unable to source; and both are reflexes of fiction-making. It is a culturally pleasing paradox: bureaucracy has a stake in the production of fiction – in the conditions, in fact, that enable Chaucer, Langland, or Hoccleve to play with persona and voice.

In medieval usage, voice, *vox*, has twin, somewhat paradoxical, meanings: as quotation, the trace of an authority cited if not always endorsed; and, notwithstanding, as independent human utterance. The usage binds together senses modern theory has wanted to draw apart – textuality and orality, presence and absence. The most useful source here remains the notion of voice and vocality described in the work of Paul Zumthor. Zumthor's output on the subject was prodigious, working and reworking the interdependence of three crucial concepts in his view of literature, especially the poetic: *mouvance*, the instability of texts in a memorial and manuscript culture; intertextuality, the ways in which texts partly compose and partly differentiate themselves from contemporaries and precursors; and the need, even in the works of a literate culture, to consider voice as well as text, though "the desire for live voice lives in all poetry, but it is in exile in writing." The vocality of a literate culture is subject to text, what Zumthor calls a secondary orality. What matters for such a culture is not so much the texts it produces as those on which it subsists, those cultural base texts that experience a fragmentary, transformative, and discontinuous performance in vocality. "In voice," says Zumthor, "speech is uttered as recall." Following Zumthor, this chapter will focus at start and end on specific conversations and the sometimes irregular spaces in which they occur: the first in a tomb, between the living and the dead; the second in the anchorhold of a church, a tomb for the living, between two female religious, one of them a solitary and the other much in the world. The central sections of the chapter will consider all that is culturally at stake in what Zumthor calls, in a luminous phrase on which he made many variations, "the desire of text to be made voice."[2]

New work: a dialogue in a tomb

Literary culture re-imagines temporalities, asserting relationships with the dead, the living, and the unborn. It is both made and found, new work and recovery, seeking to discover its antecedents and to change them. Like the writers we study, scholars and readers desire to know the past, in order to discharge our obligation to it and to reclaim it. Every narrative of historical culture is in that sense a modernism, an imposition on the past in which its traces are shaped into a new story. In the case of English literary production in the late fourteenth and fifteenth centuries, important recent discoveries have re-energized the field. We will continue to learn more, for example, about how vernacular literature was written and copied in London, about connections between court and city, and about the role of government scribes and administrators. Yet it remains hard not to falsify the past by claiming that we know it. Readers want just that: to know the past as we know a person, and, impossibly, to hear its voice. The processes of culture are fraught with discontinuities and paradox: part building, part archaeology, part séance.

These terms are prompted by the lapidary alliterative poem *St. Erkenwald*, which stages a multiple play of temporalities. Though unrhymed alliterative poetry of the late fourteenth century often has affiliations with the west of England, this is a London poem. The zest with which it describes building work in St. Paul's:

mony a mery mason was made ther to wyrke
harde stones for to hewe with eggit toles
many grubber in grete the grounde for to seche
that the fundement on fyrst shuld the fote halde[3]

is evocative of the Ricardian urban project of the 1380s. Yet the poem's architectural "new work" belongs to a much earlier period, that of the Anglo-Saxon Bishop Erkenwald, who nonetheless serves as the readers' proxy and contemporary for much of the poem. Erkenwald's own time is literally built on foundations of cultural difference. The poem's lengthy opening deals with the reconsecration and renaming of pagan temples as Christian churches, a past to which Erkenwald's moment is linked by his rebuilding. It is the point beyond which history yields place to prehistory, to the presumption of civilizations of which nothing is known. Prehistory irrupts into the poem when the builders discover the tomb of a noble pagan buried beneath the lowest crypt. The corpse is miraculously uncorrupted, and richly arrayed, but they can neither identify it nor read the runic inscriptions they find: "the bordure enbelicit with bry3t golde lettres/bot roynyshe were the resones that ther on row stoden" (lines 51–52). Erkenwald, away from the city on an episcopal visit, is sent for and hurriedly returns. His meeting with the forgotten past is quietly miraculous: the corpse wakes up, and they talk (it is unclear in what language). The corpse tells its story. He was a just pagan judge, buried with all honor to mark his love of justice. Yet as a pagan, though righteous, he remains in Hell – overlooked, as he explains, by Jesus at the Harrowing. Erkenwald prays for his soul, and weeps; a tear falls on the body, which at once crumbles to dust and is gone.

It is a haunting fable. Scholarship has worked to anchor it in various external contexts to do with contemporary politics, ecclesiastical or theological or textual, such as a possible argument with Langland's treatment of the righteous heathen in *Piers Plowman*. Instead of Trajan's simply bursting out of Hell, the pagan judge here requires Erkenwald's intercession. Erkenwald's weeping is sometimes seen as figuring the sacrament of baptism, but in fact no name is ever conferred on the judge. This is a poem not about name but about voice. In another work, the theological scandal would be overwhelming: how could Jesus ever neglect a soul deserving salvation? There is undoubtedly cultural pressure behind the motif, coming from the strong contemporary interest in universal salvation. But the poem's detail springs from the judge's own words, is not contradicted or corroborated, and largely serves the almost intolerable pathos of his speech. The miracle is that a previously unimaginable history may appear in person, and speak to the living. The moment of meeting is transient as voice itself. It fulfills Walter Benjamin's dictum, except that it does not so much flash as sound: "The past can be seized only as an image when it flashes up at the instant when it can be recognized and is never seen again."[4]

We might follow Benjamin, too, in recognizing this poem as a fable about the genesis of narrative, in which the poet through Erkenwald and his men plays the role of storyteller "located at the juncture where the traveler returns to those who never left."[5] It is a poem about cultural memory, though cultural memory here is in large part rhetorical invention, written for an age that is not afraid to fake its history, as in Geoffrey of Monmouth, or its legitimacy, as in many an institution's founding charter. Benjamin writes of such memory, and here again he could be writing of *St. Erkenwald* and its culture: "Language shows clearly that memory is not an instrument for exploring the past but its theater. It is the medium of past experience as the ground is the medium in which dead cities lie interred."[6] It is on the dead cities that we build new work. Building is a metaphor for rhetorical invention from classical times, and is given new life by Geoffrey de Vinsauf in his *New Poetry*. The image is used by all major fourteenth-century English poets who know London, and must have made for an almost literal interplay between literary invention, the built environment, and other material artifacts.

Yet the *Erkenwald* fable is more disturbing than this. For in producing the new work – Erkenwald's building, the poet's text – the human remainder, once uncovered, is emptied of its substance. The bishop's compassionate tear has the effect not of baptism but of exorcism. Reinventing the past is a sure route to its permanent loss, made all the more poignant by the unexpected contact; either that, or it can be invented only on the premise that it is already lost. If there is not quite Benjamin's "flash" in the poem, there is an insistent and material gleam. The language describing the remains of the dead judge is opulent:

> so was the glode within gay al with golde payntyde
> and a blisfulle body opon the bothum lyggide
> araide on a riche wise in rialle wedes
> al with glisnande golde his gowne was hemmyd
> with mony a precious perle picchit theron
> and a gurdille of golde bigripide his mydelle. (75–80)

This is no charnel-house but a thrilling pagan treasury – like the dragon's hoard in *Beowulf* – so that at the poem's end we feel for the first time the bleak austerity of new dust. The poem deliberately casts its encounter between temporalities as the discovery of buried treasure. Erkenwald will strip the tomb of its substance; what will linger is nothing material, and it has only an exemplary function.

One might say, punning on the ecclesiastical term, that Erkenwald's role is to translate the corpse – but in a way that leaves no trace of the original. The poem constructs itself as a tradition for London and St. Paul's, for hagiography, and for its own activity of constructing legendary traditions – that is, for its own role in something equally constructed or imaginary that could be called a "literary tradition." None of it has much reliably historical foundation, even though the desire to make one is the poem's agenda. This may sound like a truism: literature, after all, is imaginative work. But, first, the culture's notions of imagination and intellection at play are different from ours; second, its boundary between the imaginary and the fake is not where we might respectably put it; and, third, English vernacular literature comes into self-awareness in the fourteenth century as an orphan, both worrying about its legitimacy and fantasizing an elevated genealogy. James Simpson, in his influential volume of the *Oxford History of English Literature,* emphasizes that the Reformation accounts for discontinuity in sixteenth-century literary culture; on a purely literary comparison, there would be much temperamental and generic affinity to link the mid-sixteenth century with late fourteenth- and fifteenth-century vernacular culture.[7] But the real discontinuity is between the first generation, in the late fourteenth century, and its successors in the fifteenth century. The sixteenth-century writers have a significant vernacular literary tradition to draw on (however much to modern eyes they seem to misunderstand Langland, misread Chaucer, and so on). By contrast, the generation of Chaucer, Langland, and the *Erkenwald* poet had reason to feel themselves lacking in such grounding, at least in English, and so cultivated a more active sense of innovation and experiment, "new work."

Translating tradition

It is hard to foreground the unknown, yet that must often be the task of the literary historian of medieval England. An overarching narrative of literature written in Middle English before about 1325 is just not possible. As Elaine Treharne shows (Chapter 10 above), there is more of a history to write when we see English texts in a continuum and dialogue with Latin and, especially, French and Anglo-Norman. Recent study of the vernacular has broadened into a recognition of vernacularities; the European vernaculars flow from the eleventh century onwards out of each other and Latin, like lava streams. "Middle English," from the melting pot of an actively multilingual culture, can plausibly be seen as an emergent creole. Yet bi- and trilingualism have radically different social identities: as high literate culture, the product of a Francophone master class; and as oral hybrid, through which English or Welsh speakers gain some purchase on the other languages around them. The story we tell is that translation of Latin or French texts into English begins as the gift of the first group to the second, "lewed men" lacking facility in those languages. Texts proclaim just this, well into the fifteenth century – and well beyond any point at which such claims can be seen as historically plausible. All we know about language acquisition, especially in multilingual contexts, runs against such orderly differentiation: illiterate people can gain a limited proficiency in the languages they hear, as lay men and women did with ecclesiastical Latin; and the literate enjoy the languages they study, and cannot help translating them or mixing them with and into the vernacular. Every use of English, every site and region of textual production is different and demands its own history. But there are circumstances in which the claim to write for a "lewed" audience is a construction, often a rhetorical fiction, and "lewednesse" becomes a byword for translation.

Translation needs to be understood in the broadest sense, not just as the carrying over of texts in whole or part from one language to another (often with a major degree of adaptation), but also as the carrying over of literary activity itself, often quite unpredictably. The adolescent Geoffrey Chaucer likely started his career by writing *chansons* and *rondeaux* in Anglo-Norman. He appears to have begun composing as a poet in English by imitating and adapting the French *dits amoureux*, in order to shadow French courtly poetry in the English vernacular. As for Italian, he probably commenced his study of it as a child at the London docks, helping his vintner father negotiate with Italian merchants. Government service provided him further opportunities, as a diplomat and as a long-serving Controller of the Customs: translation is a form of luxury import, and was Chaucer's business. But his activity, though more literal than most, cannot be seen in isolation: it is part of a much wider push to produce an English equivalent of the book cultures of other languages and places, both of modernity (France, and in Chaucer's case Italy) and of the past (Latin classics).

There seems to have been an efflorescence of all forms of English writing from the mid-fourteenth century, a surge that responds to the rapidly changing social status of the English language itself – in law, in government, and in parliament, though not yet in the universities. The production of new unrhymed alliterative poetry, largely, but not exclusively, grounded in Latin prose sources, is another key aspect of that flowering, not opposed to Chaucer's or Gower's but complementary to them. The project to translate the Bible, based in Queen's College Oxford, is at this stage simply another aspect, and its proscription in the early fifteenth century not only skews the subsequent direction of literary production, but helps to maintain the hegemony of poetry over prose well into the second half of the century. The Bible project is unusual, however, being fittingly and scrupulously concerned with fidelity to its (Latin) source, the Vulgate. Beyond it late fourteenth-century poets make vernacular play in free and imaginative biblical adaptation and paraphrase (*Patience*, *Pearl*, much of *Piers Plowman*) – all of which should be seen as the work of a translating culture.

Such activity entails some extraordinary reshaping of time and space: in Langland's case, for example, having his dreamer attend the Crucifixion; in Chaucer's case, bringing together Augustan Rome and medieval England in *The Book of the Duchess*, where the dreamer walks in the woods while Augustus Caesar hunts, or placing more than a thousand years of literary tradition as statues in the one long hall of Fame's palace. This creates what Foucault calls a heterotopia, a space in which impossible simultaneities are represented. *The House of Fame* figures urban space as the place of new cultural work. It insists on the peripatetic nature of our experience of urban space, and represents that space itself as radically mobile, the whirling wicker world of Rumor beyond the courtly palace of Fame. The only place apparently offering stasis, though hardly fixity, is built on ice, and when he is asked what he wants there the dreamer replies, in that ringing phrase, "I wot myself how best I stand" (*House of Fame*, line 1878), and immediately walks on. The space of high European cultural tradition is a place to perambulate on the way out to the ambivalent but dynamic marketplace next door. As on the road from London to Canterbury, the city is a space to walk in, away from, and towards – movements that stand for, are, and enable, cultural exchange.

And the moment of modern theory enters that exchange when Michel de Certeau quietly equates walking with writing, and presents it in terms of pedestrian speech acts and rhetoric, with its turns (tours) and detours. In modern theory and in Chaucer's poetry alike, the city also fulfills an ambivalent function as a site of authority: ambivalent, because of the potential (as in *St. Erkenwald*) for movement away as well as movement toward. In the literature there is less of the architect's sense of a predictable teleology than the archaeologist's mood of not knowing what may be found. Yet the city is a site of growing power, and literary innovation is one of its building projects.

As with other European literary vernaculars, the highest genre remains dream vision: the tradition is itself subject to translation. In *The Poetics of Space* Gaston Bachelard concludes that consciousness of recurrent significant space is shaped by the "intimate immensity" of dreams; and de Certeau, weighing up walking and writing, decides that language is not necessarily the dominant term, for both are forms of dreaming. The textual space of a dream poem emblematizes the potential of vernacular poetry. Chaucer bases the population of birds in his poem on the list that Alanus de Insulis in *De Planctu Naturae* imagines as an adornment to the robe of Nature – in the Latin, her *textus*. Out of the textual flatness Chaucer has made space by imagining volume, the volume of vernacular utterance. When the dreamer enters the garden, this noise of birds is spatially oppressive:

> so huge a noyse gan they make
> That erthe, and eyr, and tre, and every lake
> So ful was that unethe was there space
> For me to stonde, so ful was al the place. (312–15)

Space here is sound; the Latin text is converted into three dimensions, and vocality is the vernacular difference, at one with secondary orality (the Latin text made voice). This sort of spatial play projects the drama of vernacular invention onto the most productive hesitation of Chaucer's career and culture, between writing and speech.

Reading successors

There is much cultural continuity into the fifteenth century: translation remains the main business, attended to in successive generations by, for example, Lydgate and Caxton, though with Caxton helping effect the switch to prose. The ambiance of writers remains steadfastly multilingual, even though daily London life furnished fewer opportunities than in Chaucer's time for speaking French or Anglo-Norman. While Lydgate and Caxton work their way dutifully through a single source, Hoccleve continues the play of combining multiple sources that characterized the previous generation of Langland, Gower, and Chaucer. Even the way his successors treat Chaucer – respectful of the man and steeped in the texts, yet unafraid to remodel their dead author – is eminently Chaucerian. The work of innovation proceeds at the level of prosody and the fast-track enrichment of English literary vocabulary, sometimes to the point of exuberance.

Why then does modern criticism tend to stress the differences between the first generation and its successors? Overarching narratives again play their part: the desire to tell or retell a story about Arundel's Constitutions of 1409 as an unprecedented moment of instant repression, or (older stories) about the "triumph of English," in which the narrative requires that multilingualism give way to monolingualism. Both these stories are somewhat influenced, as I have suggested, by careless adaptation of a Foucauldian prescription via new historicism: literary freedom is seen as a form of cultural subversion that must inevitably give rise to its own containment. Some critics have realized, however, that literary freedom may actively seek or require the comforts of mild containment, not least that of a regular salary. Government service and literary production in this period are partners, not enemies. Modernist periods last only for so long. Belated successors are postmodern whether they know it or not. The literary activity I have been describing is surely an early modernism. I leave it to Early Modernists to explain why it is not also a Renaissance, maybe the only one England had – occurring, like European ones, in the fourteenth century, and in which the fifteenth century played the unenviable but productive role of successors.

Such a renaissance would be grounded in the vernacular rather than a scholarly humanism. Yet even in England one might see the successors' role as that of codifying, organizing, and extending the new. This is a self-aware professionalization of culture, and for all the differences much depends, in England as in Italy, on the role of secretaries. Many of the more prolific English poets from Chaucer onwards were employed in government or royal service (for instance, Hoccleve in the Privy Seal, George Ashby as Clerk of the Signet, Stephen Hawes as Groom of the

Chamber, Skelton as royal tutor) or in comparable positions in a great household (such as Trevisa and Walton at Berkeley Castle, or Stephen Scrope and William Worcester by Sir John Fastolf). The prevalence of such secretaries was noted in contemporary writing, and conventionally regretted by the writers themselves, as in *The Book of Noblesse*. They are presumably in office to do partly this, not as propagandists, or as advisors, or as in-house critics, but as generators of cultural capital for the fifteenth-century rudiments of a citation index. A good deal of their literary production is shaped, or at least colored, by writers' daily work. Nostalgia for peace in fifteenth-century writing, for example, is more than just a literary topos. A kind of pragmatic pursuit of peace is partly an inheritance from Chaucer, some of whose work may be read as subtle propaganda for the foreign policy of Richard II. Hoccleve in *The Regement of Princes* follows both this and Gower's "In Praise of Peace," in arguing against war with France and blaming internal disunity on ambition and greed. For Hoccleve, "where pees is, Crist is ther" (*The Regement of Princes*, 5025–26). In the anonymous *Court of Sapience*, war is represented as "divisioun," the devil's undoing of Christian unity, and Lydgate calls it "mortal outrage" (*Fall of Princes*, 4.221). Of the seven English kings from Richard II to Henry VII five met violent deaths. It is not too hard to see the commendation of peace in so much English writing of the fifteenth century as the bureaucrat's desire for quiet, stability, and continuity in the face of so much upheaval. It is also an aspect of European humanism, and fulfills Boccaccio's prescription: poets should be peacemakers, and the power of poetry should permeate the conduct of the state. Lydgate, a monk brought by his literary activity into the world of secular power, translates these words in the *Fall of Princes*, and takes the many opportunities that work presents to emphasize their moral to his patron, the notoriously belligerent Duke Humphrey of Gloucester. Keats would have found this to be poetry with a palpable design upon us, by writers whose interests in government and in literary production are inextricable, and who produce a hybrid poetic grammar of public life.

The result looks remarkably like a fifteenth-century version of a "public sphere," as defined by Jürgen Habermas, a bloc whose interests are religion, virtue, good policy, civil government, and good manners set out in "an implacable model of discourse," in which we find "a cohesive body of moral thought, a collective sensibility," and in which cultural, political, and social preoccupations are intimate.[8] Given what we do not know about the currency and circulation of many texts, it would not do to press this suggestion too far, especially since Habermas has resisted application of it to periods other than the eighteenth century. Yet it does seem to provide an insight into a great deal of fifteenth-century writing, and into the feeling of moral and group commitment that it exudes. It was a small world, after all, in which social power and cultural value were mediated, often among the same groups of people; a world – but at the same time a small circle – of multiple alliances in which there was easy movement between court and country, metropolis and provinces, kinship groups and households, courtiers and clerks and gentry. Like eighteenth-century Augustan England, it was a classicizing age, in which mixed genres were nevertheless prevalent. In the mixed genres of fifteenth-century writing, the boundaries between discourses were located not in literary genres at all but in ethical choices, educational curricula, questions of manners and good conduct, government, kingship, law and business.

None of this is to imply that fifteenth-century writers find a public role easy or without tensions. Malory and George Ashby write as prisoners; Ashby, an old Lancastrian retainer in defeat, shapes an ad hoc poetic identity from allusions to Hoccleve's breakdown as easily as to Boethius' imprisonment; both are at once intertextual and experiential. Hoccleve writes extraordinarily and at length of his return to work at the Privy Seal after a major mental breakdown. Skelton often sounds on the point of having one, elevating his various insecurities into his poetic subject. By devising in *Speak Parrot* a kind of private, late hermeneutics, idiosyncratic but coded like a cryptic crossword that challenges his readers to decode audacious political complaint, Skelton parodies the development in fifteenth-century poetry of a shared poetic code for discussing matters of state. The major antecedent here is not Chaucer or Langland but Gower, who works in all three literary languages and has a separate identity in each, and whose poetry in all three languages nonetheless uniquely registers the pressure of his times. Gower is in many respects a violent and bipolar writer, and proffers his work as a mirror of his age: a response to the uprising of 1381, to the minority of Richard II and to the Lords Appellant, to the overthrow and death of Richard, and to the Lancastrians' repudiation of civil liberties. In Gower the idea of the "rule of law" is a work in progress, a fraught act of translation from different languages – a polymorphous problematic of authority and rebellion.

The nature of vernacular literary culture, after all, is an intricate negotiation between respect for authority and rebellion against it.

The vernacular writer, who compiles an assemblage of found texts with new purposes for a new audience, does not entirely align with that authority: he is not an *auctor* but a *lector*, "a slave or servant who read aloud to his master." The definition is Tom Docherty's, who notes that in the model of lector and audience, "the person dictating or rehearsing the text (nowadays considered as the position of 'author') is in the place of slave or servant and reader, with no personal authority, and no ability to inaugurate or initiate the text or its lecture."[9] This usefully describes the primary model of authorship in a culture of vocality, which splits political and discursive authority and estranges both from authoriality. Central to this is the role of readers reading, a narrator and audience caught up in a common and complex hermeneutic. Authority within and on behalf of such writing is shared between the book, the audience, and the reader of the moment, and it belongs potentially to all possible readers.

What this entails can be illustrated by the famous Pardon scene in the various versions of *Piers Plowman*. The pilgrims meet Piers and work his half-acre, after which Piers receives a Pardon on their behalf from his master, Truth. The Pardon sent from Truth is not in the usual form of a pardon, and appears to be metamorphic in the text itself: its conditions are described for several hundred lines, yet when the Pardon is seen, "al in two lynes it lay, and not a leef more" – these lines being the Latin of the Athanasian Creed, based on Matthew 25 ("Those who do well will go into everlasting life/And those who do ill into everlasting fire"). The unpredictable confusion of voices here is made all the stronger by unmarked and unsourced voicing within the narration, for instance, citing conflicting authorities. Is this meant to be the dreamer's voice, or does it belong to the document itself? In the A and B texts, the Pardon is ultimately torn by Piers "for pure tene." Is this a cancellation or a confirmation of the two lines? In the C text, it remains untorn. Is the meaning the same here, or different? In all three versions there first follows an unquiet argument between the Latin-citing layman Piers and a priest, who looks at the document and "can no pardoun fynde." How can readers be sure who is right? How does the sequence speak to contemporary and subsequent lay challenges to clerical authority, notoriously by Wycliffites? The noise of the dispute breaks into the writer's dream – in which, as dreamer, he is looking over the shoulder of the priest at the document itself. He then as narrator complicates the interplay of voices and authorities further by debating the truth of dreams before he launches the next part of the work by extrapolating the Pardon's key verb ("do well") as noun ("Dowel") and sets out on a frantic search for it along a multiple chain of interlocutors.

Is this simply the correct next move in the genre of personification allegory, or a hermeneutic error on the dreamer-writer's part? Again, an act of reading is highlighted, at the very time that the dreamer uses his paraphrase of the dream to reach the conclusion that we should eschew the activity that the episode presupposes, interpretation: "I have no savour in songewarie." He continues the movement of the entire passus by opposing his own conclusion with biblical authorities (Daniel, Joseph). This repeats the dialectic of authority between Piers and the priest, and revives the equivocating voice(s) of the initial Pardon sequence. The repetition enhances the ongoing dilemma, for there are no grounds, at the end of Passus VII as throughout, that allow us to ignore disjunctions of authorities highlighted within the text in order to assign an unequivocal authority. These are not just local difficulties of authority, a patch of tricky ground: they constitute a Fault, and we read *Piers Plowman* as if in mid-earthquake. They arise, I think, from the impossibility of a type of authority, an explicit belief in individual inspiration. It is lacking in *Piers Plowman* because the one necessary textual authority to license and make manifest such a claim is also lacking: vernacular scriptures. Reading practices precede the text that might authorize them. This sequence represents what is possible in the rebellion against institutional mediation without having an English book to substitute for it (as Milton and Spenser needed the Geneva Bible). For Langland, the English poem, even as it is being written, is placed in the position of trying to be that Book, of making an astonishingly acrobatic but by no means consistent or consistently successful attempt to authorize itself, to construct one sort of ad hoc authority as it subverts others. As in the next example, voice comes close to being the subject of such work rather than merely its mode.

New work: a dialogue in an anchorhold

The Book of Margery Kempe presents a long and unusually full account of the one conversation between Margery Kempe herself and Julian of Norwich, here called only "the anchoress." In modern eyes these are two of the most important writers of Middle English prose. This is the first account in English of a meeting between two major authors, and one might expect it to be more famous. Neither woman, however, was widely known as a writer in her lifetime or had any expectation of being a literary figure. Both represent themselves as technically illiterate, dictating their work to scribes who double as confessors – it is as if the feminine weakness stands apologetically for the mother tongue itself. The extraordinary meeting has a more general bearing on our understanding of how voice registers and makes the vernacular difference:

> And then she was commanded by our Lord to go to an anchoress in the same city who was called Dame Julian. And so she did, and told her about the grace, that God had put into her soul, of compunction, contrition, sweetness and devotion, compassion with holy meditation and high contemplation, and very many holy speeches and converse that our Lord spoke to her soul, and also many wonderful revelations, which she described to the anchoress to find out if there were any deception in them, for the anchoress was expert in such things and could give good advice.
>
> The anchoress, hearing the marvelous goodness of our Lord, highly thanked God with all her heart for his visitation, advising this creature to be obedient to the will of our Lord and fulfill with all her might whatever he put into her soul, if it were not against the worship of God and the profit of her fellow Christians. For if it were, then it were not the influence of a good spirit, but rather of an evil spirit. "The Holy Ghost never urges a thing against charity, and if he did, he would be contrary to his own self, for he is all charity. Also he moves a soul to all chasteness . . .
>
> Any creature that has these tokens may steadfastly believe that the Holy Ghost dwells in his soul. and much more, when God visits a creature with tears of contrition, devotion or compassion, he may and ought to believe that the Holy Ghost is in his soul. St. Paul says that the Holy Ghost asks for us with mourning and weeping unspeakable; that is to say, he causes us to ask and pray with mourning and weeping so plentifully that the tears may not be numbered . . .
>
> . . . I pray God grant you perseverance. Set all your trust in God and do not fear the talk of the world, for the more contempt, shame and reproof that you have in this world, the more is your merit in the sight of God . . ."
>
> Great was the holy conversation that the anchoress and this creature had through talking of the love of our Lord Jesus Christ for the many days that they were together.[10]

The two voices of this account are distinctive. Margery Kempe speaks first and apparently at some length, but what she has to say is presented simply, sequentially and in summary. Julian's response begins carefully, but turns into an eloquent vindication of Margery's tears, and a moving call to suffering and endurance. Theirs are textually mediated voices, and the account, like the entire book, is not secure historical witness. If it is not transparently a piece of history, does it deviate in the approved way that saints' lives deviate or in the perverse way that other fictions do? Did Margery Kempe ever really meet Julian of Norwich, and, if so, did they talk along anything like the lines here outlined? We have to deal, perforce, at the level of the text's own representation of a conversation attributed to historical figures, one that takes care to individualize their voices. Julian of Norwich sounds like Julian of Norwich elsewhere: the voice is so consistent with her writings that, if the words do not belong to this historical context, they must be based on clever pastiche (mainly of Julian's ninth vision) or other of her utterances. This is a very full representation of a conversation, and – unlike others in *The Book of Margery Kempe*, in which she is subject to various forms of examination – stress falls on the relatively equal play of the participants and the mutual ease and pleasure with which they converse.

Many scholarly accounts nevertheless emphasize the difference between them, not only of age and religious status but of spiritual temperament. They note how established in the Church and well regarded Julian was, while Margery was always anomalous and suspect. So the two speakers here are often characterized by means of dichotomy: quiet/loud, calm/disturbed, confident/hysterical, orthodox/heterodox. Those who insist on a "serene" Julian in opposition to a "hysterical" Margery must be reading a different Julian of Norwich from the one I read, which begins with a woman actively wishing on herself a life-threatening illness. As a result of her very extremity she speaks with Jesus; but she also suffers terrible despair, depression, and doubts as she hears devils murmur and chatter around her bed.

Margery and Julian have much in common. Both are in a more or less anomalous relation to ecclesiastical hierarchy. Though Julian is in a cell, she may well be irregular: Margery Kempe is introduced in the 1521 print of her sayings by the phrase used of Julian here, "an ankres." Both may well be lay: there's no compelling evidence that Julian entered any order. Both are associated with the cultural transmission of ideas associated with St. Bridget and the Brigittines, the "recluse society" of Norwich, and both form part of the strong cultural attachment in Norfolk to St. Bridget and the abbey of Syon. The attachment links to another, to

Carthusians in Shene and, especially, Mount Grace: the sole manuscript of *The Book of Margery Kempe* was preserved, used and obviously valued in Mount Grace, and it's in Shene that James Greenhalgh writes the manuscript of Julian's Short Text, British Library, MS Additional 37790. Few manuscripts survive of Julian; like Margery Kempe, her work seems to have been best known in charterhouses and classified for adepts only, like other advanced works of vernacular spirituality such as *The Cloud of Unknowing*. Neither of them produces a posthumous cult in pre-Reformation England – a fact held against Margery but not against Julian. Margery Kempe and Julian of Norwich both center on conversations with Jesus, who initiates the process and who offers to suffer more for her if that would help; both concentrate on mercy and grace rather than hell or punishment. They also share the devotion to Christ's body and wounds that finds lyric intensity in Rolle and narrative definition in Bonaventura's life of Christ; and they both have visionary recourse to the stock of visual images in churches of the area, especially (in Julian's case) the roodscreens.

In Julian Margery finds her most accessible model for opening her book with a serious illness, in Margery's case the complications of childbirth, an illness which leads in both cases to depression and, yet more strikingly, inhibits confession: Margery's confessor famously cuts off her speech at a critical moment, while Julian professes herself so assailed by doubt of her visions that she is unable to seek absolution. There are also formal relations. Julian's Long Text presents her as "a symple creature," and furnishes a handy precedent for Margery Kempe's description of herself throughout as "this creature." Both make a great point of their dissatisfaction with the first version of their memoirs. Margery details her first scribe's shortcomings, and Julian speaks of a first version, jotted down in May 1373, so far from ideal that it required lengthy revision and amplification in a second version. Though critics used to insist on "radical differences" between the two, but it is clear that Margery Kempe claims Julian of Norwich as a model, both generically and in person. Julian is her closest precursor in conversation with Christ, "holy dalliance," and that is the very loaded phrase in which Kempe chooses to celebrate their conversation – as the two East Anglian women to whom Jesus intimately speaks talk, and talk, and talk, "be comownying in þe life of owyr Lord Jhesu Crist many days þat þei were togedyr."

For Julian is there being "expert in such thyngys" precisely to endorse the "ful many holy spechys and dalyawns þat owyn Lord spak to hir sowle" – she is there to validate a voiced relationship. Julian thanks Margery for coming and advises total obedience to God's will, the sole condition being that it accords with charity. That proviso is not a reservation about Margery but a looking back to Julian's own doubts in the dark night of her soul. The crucial corollary is that Julian further endorses Margery's resolve to live in chastity – a resolution readers have already seen enacted in her negotiations with her husband but which this advice, as a flashback, antedates. Julian gives unreserved support to Margery's tears in a way that would have pleased Margery's early Carthusian readers, who calmly noted in her swoons and outlines the behaviour of their own colleagues. Julian counsels "patyens" and "perseuerawns," and makes the climactic distinction of the passage between God's language, "holy dalyawns," and "þe language of þe world" which offers only "despyte, schame, and repref." Two women's voices join against the world, and speak up for voice.

In the (I would say artfully) disordered sequence of *The Book of Margery Kempe*, Julian's endorsement follows what chronologically it precedes, Margery's interview with Archbishop Arundel. Her interview with the promoter of the 1409 Constitutions should be like a bookseller's meeting with Savonarola; but her text has him finding no "defawte" in her "wepyng" or "the maner of dalyawns that owyr Lord dalyid to hyr soule" (36). She has her conversation with the censor, "tyl sterrys apparyd in the fyrmament." When Margery Kempe meets Arundel, then, she opens herself to the possibility of literate inquisition; but what meets Arundel is vocality, a discourse of religious conversation shared by Margery Kempe and Julian of Norwich and, as we find later, already authorized by Julian. Inquisition is a less congenial genre providing people with a chance to talk about their religious beliefs. Sometimes through the stereotyped formulae of that genre, which hardly offers the lack of constraint shared by Julian and Margery, the archive gives a glimpse of what people thought. Famously, Arundel got as good as he gave from William Thorpe in 1407; and Bishop Alnwick's inquisitions of 1428–31 in Norwich furnish just a few moments when Alnwick's notary, John of Exeter, departs from his normal language of record, Latin, to record English phrases used by the Lollard speakers. In each case the English phrase contains a pun that cannot be captured in Latin, and defeats translation: for example, "every Fryday is a fre day." The vernacular speaker has found a mode that defies authorized literacy.[11] Other Lollard interrogations, though full of Lollards' own code and formulae as well as the interrogators', give similar glimpses. In that of Hawise Mone, the shoemaker's wife of Loddon, confession takes flight in a well-presented eloquence that may be Mone's own, first in the development of the standard Wycliffite view of clergy ("these singemesses that be cleped prestes ben no prestes, but thay be lecherous and couetouse men, and fals deceyuours of the puple") and, second, in a briefer *ad lib* supporting the negative view of pilgrimages, "for all pilgrimage goyng serwyth of nothyng but oonly to yeve prestes good þat be to riche, and to make gay tapsters and proude ostelers."[12] Mone's home was the center for those East Anglian Lollards who followed the teaching of William White and, after his execution, his wife Joan. Mone never had a public teaching role, and would probably have been counted as illiterate. Yet to catch traces of her voice in this way is to realize that this is an odd form of illiteracy, full of quotations from texts Mone may never have read and redolent of a community's conversations to which we have otherwise lost access. A form of agency has been assumed by secondary orality; aural memory is empowered as kind of unseen text. This agency and empowerment grow out of vernacular composition and its address to and from the "lewed." They, rather than ideological affiliation, form the connection between the openly heretical Mone and the determinedly orthodox Kempe. They form the bedrock of vocality.

In the conversation between Julian of Norwich and Margery Kempe voice is a value, the value exalted by the conversation itself. Julian's conversation with Margery Kempe sets up a rhetoric of the holy at odds with the dominant pastoral rhetoric of the day, that of confession and penitential examination. Pastoral discourse is tireless in its complaints about the difficulty of controlling the tongue, and routinely misogynist move in gendering the errant tongue as female. The only antidote is verbal restraint, with the aim of controlling the tongue, which one text calls the "universitye of wikkidnesse."[13] The whole discourse is challenged by two women who show their holiness by talking for days. Julian's distinction between God's language and "the language of þe world" overtly adapts pastoral distinctions about the uses of language to their advantage. What makes the difference for Julian is incarnation, Word indwelling word beyond the power of pastoral rhetoric to police; but it remains the case that to authors of pastoral rhetoric such a claim would seem at best naive and unprofessional, at worst deceptive and dangerous.

Julian, of course, is licensing Margery's chthonic outbursts as much as their sweet discourse. Nevertheless, her own writings give to Jesus an easy, conversational intimacy that itself transgresses the norms of pastoral rhetoric. When Julian amplifies one remark, "See how I have loved you," into a succession of sentences said "to make us glad and cheerful," she helps establish a pattern of divine near-garrulity that will be augmented in *The Book of Margery Kempe*. Pastoral rhetoric is a near-hegemonic discourse of the fifteenth century, one which determines a good deal of social policy in Church and state: Arundel's Constitutions are pastoral rhetoric raised to the state of exception. For Julian and Margery, however, pastoral rhetoric takes its place precisely as a source of opposition within "the language of the world." Julian's conversation with Margery Kempe records a religious faith in vocality. I have tried to explore it as a rarely visible form of cultural literacy: the desire of text to become voice, and its more distant corollary, the aspiration of voice to be made text again. It has consequences of its own for culture, as literature talks its way into being.

Indeed, the polarities in modern accounts of English culture – high and low, religious and secular, canonical and marginal – begin in the double movement revealed here. Culture is a deliberate act of building, and over this long period we observe its making, extending, and reshaping. Yet its material is language, both the literature of poets and the words of people who speak or, for us (but not to us), once spoke; and I have suggested that we think more about vocality than textuality, or indeed vernacularity, in framing their relation. The building takes in much that it cannot know. Voice is its underground, by which it is both upheld and, as by a stream, eroded.

Notes

1. Louis Marin, *Utopics: Spatial Play*, trans. Robert A. Vollrath (Atlantic Highlands, NJ, 1984), pp. 8, 54.
2. I have relied on my own translations from Paul Zumthor's French and on recollections of my conversations with him: Paul Zumthor, *Introduction a la poésie orale* (Paris, 1983), pp. 159–60 ("Toute poésie aspire a se faire voix"), trans. Kathy Murphy-Judy, *Oral Poetry: An Introduction* (Minneapolis, 1990); "Pour une poétique de la voix," *Poétique* 40 (1979), 514–24 at 519.
3. *St. Erkenwald*, ed. Morse (1975), lines 39–42.
4. Benjamin, "Theses on the Philosophy of History," in *Illuminations*, ed. Hannah Arendt, trans. Harry Zohn (New York, 1978), p. 255, quoted in Michael Taussig, *Walter Benjamin's Grave* (Chicago, IL, 2006), p. 28.

5. Taussig, *Walter Benjamin's Grave*, p. 42, summarizing Benjamin's "The Storyteller," *Illuminations*, pp. 83–109.

6. Benjamin, "A Berlin Chronicle," in *Reflections: Essays, Aphorisms, Autobiographical Writings*, ed. Peter Demetz, trans. Edmund Jephcott (New York, 1978), p. 25.

7. James Simpson, *Reform and Cultural Revolution: The Oxford English Literary History, Vol. 2: 1350–1547* (Oxford, 2002).

8. David Lawton, "Dullness and the Fifteenth Century," *English Literary History* 54 (1987), 761–99 at 792.

9. Thomas Docherty, *On Modern Authority* (Brighton, 1987), p. 18.

10. *The Book of Margery Kempe* (1985) trans. Windeatt; Middle English text (2004), ed. *Windeatt.

11. The material is presented in Steven Justice, "Inquisition, Speech and Writing: A Case from Late Medieval Norwich," *Representations* 48 (1994), 1–29.

12. "Confession of Hawisia Moone of Loddon" (1430), in *Selections from English Wycliffite Writings*, ed. Hudson (1978), pp. 34–37.

13. *A Fourteenth Century Biblical Version*, ed. Anna C. Paues (Cambridge, 1904), translation of James 3:6.

Part Four

_____

Legacies and re-creations

12

Literary reformations of the Middle Ages

When Elizabeth I died in 1603, a number of preachers and commentators noted how the Scottish rule of the whole of Britain had been prophesied long before, by a man named Thomas Rhymer or Thomas of Erceldoune. It so happens that despite the Tudor ban on the publication of prophecies, this one has survived, since it was rushed into print soon after Elizabeth's death, probably in London though it was provided with a false Edinburgh imprint to be on the safe side. The text as it appears here is one item in a small book entitled *The Whole Prophecie of Scotland*, and the relevant lines, a question-and-answer between the narrator and Thomas, run as follows:

> "Who shal rule the Ile of Bretaine
> From the North to the South sey?"   [sea
> "A French wife shal beare the Son,
> Shall rule all Bretaine to the sey,
> that of the Bruces blood shall come
> As neere as the nint degree."
> I franed fast what was his name,   [asked
> Where that he came from what countrie?
> "In Erslingtoun, I dwelle at hame,
> Thomas Rymour men calles me."[1]

Thomas himself seems to have had a real historical existence, in the late thirteenth century, but one thing that is certain is that this part of the prophecies ascribed to him was written much later. Unusually for a true prophecy, it was nonetheless written before the event – the most reliable being those invented retrospectively. This particular prediction seems to have been altogether too convenient, in its insistence on the predestined outcome of the succession question, for anyone to have pointed out that it was not quite as accurate as it looked, since it was a generation out: James I and VI was of the tenth generation from Robert the Bruce, not the ninth. The prophecy was presumably, in fact, composed shortly before the birth of a child in 1542 to Mary of Guise, the French wife of James V – a child who turned out to be a daughter, Mary Queen of Scots (who herself became a "French wife" by marrying the Dauphin). The primary function of prophecies is rarely in fact to predict the future: they are set in the past in order to make what has happened since seem both inevitable and ordained. An earlier version of Thomas' prophecies current in the 1520s had "foretold" the Tudor descent from the blood of the Trojan Brutus in place of the Stuart descent from the blood of the Scottish Bruce, and its detail is correct down to the location of Henry Tudor's landing at Milford Haven;[2] but this degree of accuracy shows it to be the more usual kind of political prophecy, the kind that authorizes the present by grounding it in a past prophetic vision invented for the current occasion. This 1520s version indeed makes that act of retrospection explicit, as Thomas instructs his interlocutor to

> set thy fote on myne,
> And ouer my Shulder loke thyn Iie   [eye
> The fairest sight I shall shewe the syne   [then
> That euer saw man in thy countre. (13–16)

Only by looking backwards is it possible to see forwards; only by stepping back into the past can one see where the present has come from.

Thomas of Erceldoune had a double existence, as a figure from the historical records and as a continuing legend. He lived in the much-warred-over border areas between Scotland and England, and some time around 1300 he produced – or was believed to have produced – a set of nonsense prophecies about when the wars between the two countries would end. Perhaps within decades, certainly by the early fifteenth century, he was made the middleman for a much more extensive, and indeed infinitely extensible and regularly extended, set of prophecies supposedly given him by an elf queen, in whose realm he had passed many years after sexually assaulting her in the local Eildon Hills. In the version rewritten in the 1520s, the fairy queen becomes the Virgin Mary, and she stays such in most of the later texts, the Reformation notwithstanding. The preachers of 1603 seem to have seen no difficulties in accepting such an intermediary for the prophecy of the Stuarts. The elf queen did nonetheless survive, in the ballad *Thomas Rhymer* (which cuts the prophecies, to concentrate solely on the sexual encounter and the sojourn in "ane other contree," here specified as Elfland), and in what looks like a random reappearance of the fifteenth-century text printed in 1652, at the height of the Cromwellian Commonwealth, in a collection entitled *Sundry Strange Prophecies of Merlin, Bede, Becket* – names that assume the importance of looking backwards in order to look forwards. There is reason to believe that Spenser had Thomas' elf queen in mind in casting the unseen heroine of his national epic as a fairy queen, a figure who embodies the entire destiny of England, past, present, and future. Elf queens, Spenser's Gloriana among them, most often belong in romance; and the location of the source of prophecy backwards in time in order to see the here and now of its new generation of readers finds a close parallel in ancestral romance, stories that offer legendary narratives of the founding of a dynasty. Ariosto introduces Merlin into the *Orlando Furioso* (1516–32) to give a long prophecy of the future of the house of Este, a future that brings history forwards as far as the patrons of the poem; and Spenser gives a comparable series of prophecies of the future of Britain down to the Tudors, some of those also ascribed to Merlin, in the *Faerie Queene* (1590–96).[3] Virgil had incorporated a prophecy of Rome into the *Aeneid* (I.279, VI.756–892), but what Ariosto and Spenser are doing derives much more directly from medieval patterns of romance. Both writers invent a mythologized past in which the key event is a union between hero and heroine that gives rise to the dynasty they celebrate. Spenser promises such a union twice over, indeed, once for the mythopoeic Arthur of his own text with that fairy embodiment of Elizabeth, and once in the characters of Arthegall and Britomart, whose "fruitfull Ofspring" are promised to restore "the feeble Britons" (III.xxiii; necessary since the "historical" Arthur died childless). Prophecy requires a past to be written from, ancestral romance requires a past to bring the present about, and the *Faerie Queene* draws prophecy and romance together. Both genres take for granted, and inscribe in their texts, a sense of the Middle Ages as a continuing dynamic and creative force.

History itself functions in many of the same ways as prophecy: it brings about the present in ways that can retrospectively seem both inevitable and providential. History, for the Elizabethans, both in its factual and its pseudo-factual forms, was a product of the Middle Ages. Both the late medieval history of the Wars of the Roses that immediately preceded the Tudor age (and which was therefore as close to the great Elizabethan writers as Victorian history is to us), and the early history of Britain invented in the twelfth century by Geoffrey of Monmouth, offered them a teleological view of history of which the final divinely driven aim was the glorious accession of the house of Tudor. Geoffrey's account of the founding of Britain by the descendants of the Trojan diaspora and of the imperial career of King Arthur was still widely accepted as true, and was repeated as such in Holinshed's great *Chronicles*. Brutus' line had been preserved in the British heritage in Wales, and the Tudors accordingly claimed to be more centrally in the line of both Brutus and Arthur than were either the Yorkists (despite the incorporation into their ancestry of the line of the Welsh princes) or the main line of the Lancastrians. Edward Hall's *Union of the Noble and Illustre Families of Lancaster and York* concentrated on the Wars of the Roses that had eventuated in the Tudor accession, and Holinshed, too, despite covering the whole history of Britain in his vast *Chronicles*, devoted a large amount of space to the same period; Samuel Daniel wrote an eight-book epic on the subject, and prose, verse, and drama all quarried it for material. Providence, what is foreseen by God, could easily overlap with more literal prophecy, what is foreseen by humankind: hence, the easy absorption into *Henry VI* Part 3 of Henry VI's prophecy of kingship for the young earl of Richmond, Henry Tudor, or Richmond's own prophetic prayer for the happiness of England under himself and his heirs that closes *Richard III*.[4] The belief that the present could learn from the past, that the lessons of history repeated themselves, also carried an element of prophecy about it, though often a more ominous one: hence, Elizabeth's famous, "I am Richard II, know ye not that?" when the keeper of the state records discussed with her his epitome of records from the kingdom's past.[5]

In a culture self-consciously trying to remodel itself on humanist principles, English history was furthermore a good topic for epic: hence, Michael Drayton's Virgilian choice of title for the thoroughly medieval content of his *Mortimeriados* (1596), on the barons' wars under Edward II. There was a huge appetite for retold history, reflected, for instance, in the bestseller, *Mirror for Magistrates*, on which more below. The English Middle Ages offered a hoard of good stories, romantic and sentimental as well as political and moral: hence, the laments written for Henry II's mistress Rosamund and Edward IV's Jane Shore. The more catchy or nationalistic of such episodes made the transfer to the streets in the form of broadside ballads. The average subject of Elizabeth I knew far more about the country's history over the previous few centuries than the average subject of Elizabeth II does now. If much of it was (like most modern historical films or television series) unscholarly or ideologically slanted, a new group of antiquarians also set to work to recover the past on its own terms.

Just as the present is the consequence of the political events of the past, so its culture is created and shaped by the culture from which it emerges. The point is so obvious it ought not to need saying, were it not that the cultural and literary historiography of the early Modern period has so consistently emphasized the opposite that it is easy to overlook the simple fact of continuity. The subjects of the Tudor and Stuart monarchs knew, even without their familiarity with prophecies and teleological readings of history to remind them, that their experience was predicated and grounded on what had happened in the centuries we have come to know as the Middle Ages. It was evident from the moment they looked around them. London, it is true, was increasing rapidly in population and new building was proceeding apace both inside its walls, in buildings such as the Royal Exchange, and outside, most impressively in the form of the great mansions such as Essex House that were being built along the Strand toward Westminster; but the city itself had not varied from its long-established street plan, enclosed by medieval walls pierced by their original gates – Aldgate, Moorgate, Bishopsgate – and linked to the south of the river by its medieval bridge. The city was still dominated by the huge bulk of Old St. Paul's, one of the largest churches in Europe and an unchanging testament to the piety and the civic pride of its founders and benefactors through all the changes in religious practice; though without those changes, more finance might have been devoted to rebuilding the 400-foot spire that had soared above the city until it was burnt in 1561. In the cathedral precincts, where once there had been scriveners' stalls, there were now printers' outlets, but various of the most popular items for sale were ones that had been around in manuscript form for a couple of centuries before they were put into print: romances such as *Guy of Warwick*, *Bevis of Hampton*, and *Sir Eglamour*. With more money, you could buy a handsome folio edition of the complete works of the "ancient and learned English poet" Geoffrey Chaucer. Perhaps the biggest visual change was inside St, Paul's, where in late Tudor England, as in all the churches of the realm, the long-familiar religious paintings and stained glass and statues had been painted over or smashed; but there is plenty of evidence that people had not forgotten. There was change all around, and it might well have been the most noticeable thing to the Elizabethans as it is to us, since alteration is so much easier to see than continuity; but most of what was there had been there for a long time. A visitor time-traveling from the fourteenth century to Elizabethan London would scarcely have had to readjust his bearings, whereas a visitor from the eighteenth century would have been utterly bewildered. It was the Great Fire of 1666 that obliterated the medieval city, leaving only a few traces for Hitler's bombers to destroy, and one great edifice, William the Conqueror's great Tower, to stand in for all that has been lost.

If the physical traces of England's medieval capital have largely disappeared, many of the institutions created in the Middle Ages have survived and flourished. The period's genius for such things has, indeed, had the paradoxical effect of making their achievements almost invisible, since they are rarely thought of as medieval in origin at all. Representative democracy in the form of Parliament was invented in the thirteenth century, and although its form has changed dramatically over the centuries, not least with the universalizing of the suffrage and the emergence of political parties, all modern democracies owe their existence to that originary moment. Universities (and therefore by extension books designed for an academic readership, including this one) were likewise a medieval invention. The whole English legal system too was founded in the Middle Ages: not just the jury system and the Inns of Court, but the dual streams of common law and statute law, themselves given a new accessibility in the early seventeenth century by the work of Sir Edward Coke (who also helped to ground the resistance to Charles I's claims of royal prerogative in medieval precedent, not least Magna Carta). Even the rejection of Roman Catholicism at the Reformation, and with it the belief in a single Christendom (an idea already long battered but by no means defunct in the century before Luther) and the authority of the pope, was less significant than what remained. Although it lost much of its power, within England the Church as an institution remained remarkably constant through all the cataclysmic upheavals of the Reformation and the Civil War, with many of its priests remaining in post from one theological regime change to the next. Its theology may have gone through various stages of controversy until it settled into a contested but broad Anglicanism, but the Church of England continued the Church of Rome's representation in every parish in every town and village by its parsons and its medieval buildings. Castles apart, those buildings were still the tallest, most visible, and longest-lasting structures in the landscape of England. They remain so for the villages, and even the cities were dominated by their cathedrals until the development of the skyscraper. The churches furthermore continued to provide the social and religious focus of community life, a consistency of spiritual instruction and support compared with which reformist movements were always, except for those two decades of the 1640s and 1650s, fringe events, and an organizational system that maintained its hierarchy of parishes and dioceses and archdioceses even while it combined civil with religious administration. The Parliamentarians did at last manage to abolish the episcopacy, so succeeding in doing what the Calvinists had been trying to do for a long time, but the bishops returned with Charles II, and have been around ever since. Even in theology there was less change than one might imagine – or rather, the more radical manifestations of Calvinism were increasingly contested, largely by some of those same bishops, over the decades following the Elizabethan Church Settlement; and although the Calvinists won out under Cromwell, the accepted norm within the Anglican Church managed to preserve elements familiar from its Catholic predecessor. The shift in emphasis from the Incarnation, including transubstantiation and corporeal forms of worship such as creeping to the Cross at Easter, to the Word, with its stress on the reading of the Bible in English and on preaching, was a genuine one, but its victory was not total. One of the most famous Anglican divines, Lancelot Andrewes (1555–1626), who was educated in the fiercely Reformist atmosphere of Cambridge, increasingly urged both a theology and liturgical practices that incorporated elements from the old religion. He was distressed not least by the lack of ceremony, by Protestantism's refusal to acknowledge the body and the senses alongside the Word; and when he campaigned for the return of the practice of kneeling for prayer and for the administration of the sacrament, it was with a thoroughly medieval analogy drawn from the Bestiary version of natural history: that God has not made a human being incapable of kneeling, with "knees like an Elephant, that cannot bend."[6]

That quotation is interesting not merely because it indicates how forcefully the old habits of a worship that was corporeal as well as textual insisted on surviving, but because of the deep habits of analogical and symbolic thought that it represents. Such habits had been inculcated over centuries, and were too deeply embedded to disappear the moment the English Bible was made available in the churches. Andrewes presumably believed that the Bestiary was right about the physiology of elephants, in ways that later scientific observation would discount, but more important is the ease with which he moves from the elephant to God, and the assumption that his audience will have no difficulty in following him. Thinking by analogy and metaphor still came naturally to the minds of people in the early Modern era: hence, both the richness of Shakespeare's language, and the ease with which he could take his audiences with him. Andrewes takes it for granted that the natural world can reveal things of God: that Creation is, in effect, the book of God. The concept summed up in Alan of Lille's famous thirteenth-century formulation, that every created thing serves as a book or a picture, a mirror of God –

> Omnis mundi creatura
> Quasi liber et pictura
> Nobis est in speculum[7]

– was still deeply familiar a century after the Reformation. It is explicit, for instance, in Henry Vaughan's "The Tempest," printed in 1650, where he urges that humankind

> would hear
> The world read to him! all the vast expense
> In the Creation shed, and slaved to sense,
> Makes up but lectures for his eye, and ear.

And what those lectures give him is an account of the cosmos as it was traditionally understood, the "discarded image" in C. S. Lewis' phrase, in which each element seeks its own level, its own home, in a material and spiritual hierarchy in which earth, water, air, and fire exist in layers from the lowest and most material to the most life-giving and spiritual. The apple by this account falls to the earth but floats in water, not because of mathematical issues of gravity or mass, but because of the divinely implanted natural attraction of its constituent elements to their parents:

> *Plants* in the *root* with earth do most comply,
> Their *leaves* with water, and humidity,
> The *flowers* to air draw near, and subtlety,
> And *seeds* a kindred fire have with the sky.

Only man "sleeps at the ladder's foot," willfully obstructing the air and fire of his immortal part from rising up toward their natural home.[8]

Vaughan and Andrewes look equally odd to an age accustomed to scientific methods of thought; and to match that new methodology, we have been trained in a more literal interpretation of language and the universe, the factual discourse promoted by the Royal Society and the age of reason. Perceiving an equation between the anatomy of elephants and proper behavior in church does not represent how, as moderns, we think. Andrewes' analogy may perhaps have been surprising even at the time, but that furthered its main aim of being memorable – memorable in the most direct sense drawn from works on the art of memory, that advised making a bizarre mental picture associated with the thing to be remembered in order to impress it most unforgettably on the mind; and that meant that it fell within recognized conceptual and analogical frameworks twice over, as part of the Book of God and as part of a mnemonic system. Those sideways leaps between categories are characteristic of what we think of as metaphysical imagery, and such imagery is indeed in many ways the apex of medieval patterns of thought. Augustine had set out the theory of how words mean something beyond themselves – of how moving from the idea of a lamb to the Lamb of God is simply one more step in the process of symbolic representation that takes you from the sound of the spoken word "lamb" or the black squiggles representing the sounds on paper to the woolly creature in the field.[9] Two millennia of Christian thought have made that particular image so familiar that it no longer seems strange, despite its superficial similarity to such representations of divinity as the Hindu elephant god Ganesh. Such images, moreover, do not need to be commonplace. Even in the Middle Ages, Christ could be not only a lamb but an earthworm; and Herbert's image of the crucified Christ as a viol or a lute belongs squarely in the same tradition:

> His stretched sinews taught all strings what key
> Is best to celebrate this most high day.[10]

In conceits such as this, Augustinian language theory, scholastic analysis and Counter-Reformation meditational practices merge.

If the intellectual tradition of Herbert, Andrewes, and Vaughan, university-trained men who, like many medieval clerks, spent their lives in the Church, continued to ground itself in medieval models, so too did more popular traditions of narrative and storytelling. At the same time that Vaughan was writing the poems that made up his *Silex Scintillans* collection, someone (we have no idea who, though he was probably male, Royalist, and from the northwest of England) was assembling a collection of his own, of popular romances and ballads along with a few Cavalier lyrics, in a manuscript now named after the antiquarian who rescued it from being used as firelighter, Bishop Percy. The Percy Folio Manuscript (more technically London, British Library, Add. MS 27879) bears witness to the continuing life of medieval metrical romance two or three centuries after its heyday. Some of the romances copied into it shortly before 1650 had originally been composed, or put into English from Anglo-Norman, in the fourteenth century, including *The Birth of Merlin*, *Guy of Warwick*, *Sir Degarré*, *Sir Launfal*, and *Sir Eglamour*. All of these are known to have been printed by early Tudor publishers, and the Percy texts may well derive from those printed versions; but another of its fourteenth-century romances, *Lybius Desconus*, is otherwise known only from medieval manuscripts. A further group of texts that can be reliably dated to the fifteenth century – a metrical version of *Sir Gawain and the Green Knight* entitled simply *The Grene Knight*, a king-in-disguise story entitled *John de Reeve*, and the spooky *Eger and Grime* – make their first recorded appearance here. *Eger* made the transition to street literature and was widely known in the later seventeenth and eighteenth centuries, but the others would be lost altogether if it were not for the Percy Folio.

The survival of these romances is of more than purely antiquarian interest. It points to the deep attraction of romance narratives, with their perennially gripping motifs of quests and testing, love and adventure, the supernatural and the uncanny. Further evidence of the popularity of such stories is provided by their adaptation in the seventeenth century into abbreviated chapbook form. Two such romances out of the many that survived in new incarnations deserve special mention. One is *Guy of Warwick*, which carried a certain cultural cachet since it claimed to tell the story of an English Saxon hero who was the ancestor of all the later earls of Warwick. It made a bid for the higher status of Spenserian-style romance epic twice in the seventeenth century, once in a version by a commercially unsuccessful poet named John Lane, whose enormously long version was never published, and again by Samuel Rowlands, who knew his market very well indeed: so well, that his version was given several makeovers to keep up with changing fashions, into heroic couplets after the Restoration, and then into prose as a quasi-novel – though the prose adaptation was so close that the lines and rhymes are often reconstructible. In this form, it remained in print, with scarcely a break in its history, until the 1920s, some decades after late Victorian scholarship had "rediscovered" Rowlands' original.[11] The second romance is one of comparable age and antiquity, *Bevis of Hamptoun*. It does not figure in the Percy Folio (not, at least, in the portion that survived the firelight-ing), perhaps because it was still available in print in its original Middle English couplet form, with updated spelling. Like *Guy*, it was widely known – probably, indeed, universally known, in the sense that the whole population of England had access to it either directly, by reading it in one of its many cheap editions, or, for the illiterate, by hearing it read. It is quoted by Poor Tom in *King Lear*, as a text that would plausibly be as familiar to an earl's son as to the lunatic outcast he is pretending to be; it was one of Spenser's inspirations for the *Faerie Queene*, most closely for the Redcross Knight's dragon fight. It is also the single most influ-ential text after the Bible behind John Bunyan's *Pilgrim's Progress*, first published in 1678. Bunyan's genius was to tap into the continuing popularity of these texts, and even more into the deep imaginative appeal held by their stories, and to convert them into a form that became one of the bestsellers of all time. He gave the giants and dragons and combats of his sources the thoroughly medieval treatment of religious allegory, and cast it in the equally medieval form of a dream vision: both of them forms that evidently gave his readers no problems. And 150 years after pilgrimage had been abolished as papist superstition, it caused no anxiety among the godly that a spiritual journey should be represented as a pilgrimage. Metaphor was still an automatic way of thinking, and dragons had lost none of their appeal.

The romances, whether in their original form or in chapbook adapta-tions, carried something of the timelessness of fairytales about them: probably no Shakespearean playgoer demurred at the idea of a lunatic from pre-Roman Britain quoting *Bevis*. The literature of the high culture of the Middle Ages presented more complex issues of survival and reception. Chaucer, Gower, and Lydgate were all printed within a few years of the introduction of the press to England, but their later histories diverged. Gower was probably the least well known of the three, though Ben Jonson thought him a model of English grammar, and, more famously, he was given the accolade of Shakespeare's closest adaptation of a source in his entire works: *Pericles* not only follows the plot of the romance of Apollonius of Tyre with exceptional faithfulness, but also introduces Gower himself onto the stage as its choric storyteller, and initially allows him to speak in the tetrameter couplets of his *Confessio amantis*. The play is fairly certainly a collaboration, and it has often received less than generous critical comment; but there is no reason to think that Shakespeare was not wholeheartedly involved in the project.

He seems, indeed, to have had Gower's story in his mind ever since his early *Comedy of Errors*, in which he gives a soundly humanist comedy based on Plautus a frame drawn direct from the *Confessio*, including the relocation of the action to Ephesus and the verbal detail of the lost wife's becoming an "abbess."

Lydgate enjoyed a much fuller afterlife than Gower, though the literary movement he inspired rapidly dissociated itself from his name. If tragedy is, as has been claimed, the modern world's substitute for religion as to where to seek the meaning of life, then Lydgate can claim a significant part in the process. Many of his works were printed and reprinted in the first half of the sixteenth century, though in view of the fact that he was best known under the soubriquet of "the monk of Bury," it is not surprising that most of them ceased independent publication after the death of the last Tudor Catholic monarch, Queen Mary. His only poems still to be in print into the next century were those that were mis-ascribed to Chaucer and appeared under his name. His best-known work also had a Chaucerian grounding, though it was one that it rapidly left behind: the "Monk's Tale" offered a series of "tragedies" (Chaucer defines the word with care, since he effectively introduced the term into English, as the fall of a great man from prosperity to misery through the instability of Fortune) loosely modeled on Boccaccio's *De casibus virorum illustrium*, the "falls of great men." Lydgate, the real-life monk who in the prologue to his *Siege and Destruction of Thebes* had cast himself as an extra Canterbury pilgrim, took up the challenge to offer a monk's tale that would outdo them all. His vast *Fall of Princes*, translated from a French version of Boccaccio's text, consisted of a series of accounts of those who had fallen from Fortune's wheel, spoken by the ghosts of the victims themselves. A reprint planned for 1554 was apparently censored, and in its place a small group of English poets led by William Baldwin set about writing a new series on the same model, the "great men" now being drawn from English history from the mid-fourteenth century, when Boccaccio finished his work, to the advent of the Tudors. As *The Mirror for Magistrates*, the work became a smash hit, and went through a series of enhanced editions that added in further tragedies from other areas of English and early British history. Although these tragedies took the form of narrative rather than drama, the fact that they were spoken in the first person, with generous amounts of lament, moralizing, and descriptions of the ghost's gory wounds, made the transition to theater an easy one. It has been estimated that over thirty Elizabethan tragedies were inspired wholly or largely by the *Mirror*, among them those of Shakespeare's "history" plays that were initially designated tragedies: *The True Tragedy of Richard Duke of York* (*Henry VI Part 3*), *The Tragedy of Richard III*, and *The Tragedy of Richard II*. Later *Mirror* characters to figure in his plays include Cordelia – Cordelia rather than Lear, since, according to Geoffrey of Monmouth and all later historians and poets, she restored her father to his throne, so that he himself did not end as one of Fortune's victims. It was Lydgate, in summary, who established the model for most Elizabethan tragedy as concerning the overthrow of the "hasty climber" or the tyrant, and who gave it its strongly political slant in contrast to the more legendary or mythological subjects of Greek and Latin drama. Roger Mortimer, himself an item in one of the *Mirror*'s supplements, sums up the tenor of this kind of tragedy in Marlowe's *Edward II* in ways that would be typical if it were not for the Marlovian refusal to draw the obvious moral:

> Base fortune, now I see, that in thy wheele
> There is a point, to which when men aspire,
> They tumble hedlong downe: that point I touchte,
> And seeing there was no place to mount up higher,
> Why should I greeve at my declining fall?[12]

Shakespeare tended to be more orthodox in the dying speeches of his overreachers: Warwick the Kingmaker, the duke of York and, a couple of decades later, Cardinal Wolsey, all offer more familiar moralizations of their careers of ambition. Macbeth's raw ambition and tyranny cast him as a tragic hero in the *Mirror* mould; and Lear, whose fall is compared with a great wheel rolling down a hill, invokes it all the more strongly for Shakespeare's changing of the story. All this may seem to be getting a very long way from Lydgate; but it is basic to Elizabethan tragedy that it was far more deeply rooted in the tradition of political downfall than in the ancient legends used by Seneca or the (much less familiar) Greek tragedians, or indeed in Aristotle's *Poetics*: a work that was still very little known in England in the sixteenth century, and which was valued by those who did know it almost entirely for its rules about stagecraft and generic purity, the infamous "unities" so deeply alien to medieval and most Elizabethan drama.

Chaucer was the one poet of the three who continued to be extensively read after 1600. He was by far the most respected of the Middle English poets, and, indeed, became an iconic figure in the "writing of England" in both poetic and ecclesiastical terms. The first edition of his complete works, in 1532, called it just that: *Works* – the English equivalent of the Latin *opera*, the term normally reserved for the most authoritative Classical authors. Further editions followed every few years, each optimistically adding more works that might or (more often) might not be genuine, until the great edition of 1598, revised in 1602, included a Life of the poet, a portrait, and a genealogy in the form of a family tree draped around the portrait setting out his close relationship (by marriage) to the houses of both Lancaster and Tudor. It was a striking visual way of inscribing him in the center of national history. Further evidence of that centrality appears in the way that both Catholics and Protestants sought to appropriate him to their cause after the Reformation, though it was the Protestants who decisively declared possession of him, just as their cause won out over Catholicism. The wishful ascription to him of a few Wycliffite works helped to cast him not only as the father of English poetry but as a forefather of the Anglican Church. Foremost among these was the *Plowman's Tale*, probably a Lollard anti-episcopal poem of the early fifteenth century that was later provided with a frame that associated it with the Plowman of the *Canterbury Tales*, so supplying a tale for one of the pilgrims who had never been given one. It is on grounds such as these, along with his genuine anticlerical satire, that John Foxe enlists him among the earlier English forerunners of the true church in his *Ecclesiastical History*, better known as the *Book of Martyrs*.

Throughout the sixteenth and early seventeenth centuries, however, it was as a poetic master that Chaucer was most admired and imitated. Recent criticism on the early Modern era has tended to ignore or dismiss his influence, but the evidence to the contrary is clear, in terms of both informed praise and imitation. Skelton paid homage; Wyatt imitated him; Ascham called him "the English Homer"; Sidney marveled at his skill in a "misty" age; the academic Gabriel Harvey thought him a poet "above all other"; Robert Greene cast him as effectively the patron saint of English poetry; Spenser replaced Virgil with Chaucer as the master-poet, claimed that his spirit lived on in him, and based the pivotal visionary meeting of Arthur and Gloriana in his national epic *The Faerie Queene* on Chaucer's own "Sir Thopas."[13] New stories were written on the model of the *Canterbury Tales*, individual tales were recast as broadside ballads, there were two attempts to finish the incomplete "Squire's Tale," and his works were mined for dramatic plots from the mid-sixteenth century to the early seventeenth century; the favorite was the "Knight's Tale," with three known dramatizations and one free adaptation, *A Midsummer Night's Dream*, plus a later Restoration version that added a second woman to provide a happy ending for both the heroes. Shakespeare, indeed, drew on Chaucer as often as he did on Plutarch, with three plays and the rhyme royal *Rape of Lucrece* all showing his influence to varying degrees. Chaucer could provide him with creative inspiration, as in the *Dream*, with its basic materials of a newly married Duke Theseus and of two lovers pursuing the same woman in a wood outside Athens, all under the eyes of a set of unperceived supernatural beings who combine the divine scenario of the Knight's gods with the squabbling fairies of the Merchant; even its *Pyramus and Thisbe* has Chaucer's "Tale of Sir Thopas" as its only precedent for virtuoso awfulness. *Troilus and Cressida* offers a very different kind of homage: it implicitly associates Chaucer with Homer and Virgil as one of the great authorities for the story of Troy, but it presents a bitterly un-illusioned reading of both Classical heroism and idealizing love. Its immediate source material comes, in fact, very little from the Classics: the part of the plot that involves the lovers is drawn from Chaucer, and the part that concerns the war is predominantly taken from a fifteenth-century version of the story of Troy mediated by Caxton – a version that was indeed the best-known and most widely read source for Trojan history into the eighteenth century.[14] The play that offers the closest adaptation of Chaucer, the Shakespeare–Fletcher collaboration of *The Two Noble Kinsmen*, is much more faithful to its original, but that too foregrounds the human and metaphysical problems that Chaucer had built into the "Knight's Tale." It also incorporates one of the strongest eulogies to England's master-poet into its Prologue, where Chaucer is described as a poet both noble and learned, such as

> never went
> More famous yet twixt Po and silver Trent,   (Prologue 13–14)

a formulation that sweeps in every poet from Petrarch to the poets of the English Midlands, Spenser and Shakespeare himself among them. The homage expressed a still living tradition, with further Chaucerian adaptations by Fletcher and Field following. Milton, too, was an admirer, inscribing Chaucer in *Il Penseroso* as a storyteller he would gladly call up from the dead.

In view of the hunger of early modern playwrights for plots to fuel the constant demand for new plays, the use of medieval sources is scarcely surprising – and not just Gower and Chaucer and (indirectly) Lydgate, but also various early romances, *Guy of Warwick* and *The Birth of Merlin* and

The Twelve Peers of France, and so on. More surprising is how influential medieval drama was on early Modern stagecraft. The emphasis in both contemporary and modern commentary on generic divisions and on the influence of Seneca, plus the very obvious break with the past in the shift from a primarily religious to an almost entirely secular drama, have tended to blur the strong continuities. For most of the first two decades of Elizabeth's reign, the dominant form of theater, and the form still seen by the largest number of spectators, was the mystery cycles: plays that actively refused generic restrictions, whose very point was to mix kings and peasants, and which employed black humor to counterpoint the most moving action, the Passion and Crucifixion. "Tragedy" and "comedy" were late arrivals in the terminology of English, not least in their dramatic senses, and they were assimilated only gradually and awkwardly into the theatrical lexicon in the course of Elizabeth's reign; what had been written before that, and what continued to be written, were simply "plays." English plays, moreover, in marked contrast to their Greek and Latin counterparts, acted their action. Violence and death happened in front of the spectators' eyes, not offstage to be reported by messenger. The stage could represent any time, any place; there was no limitation to the amount of time represented, or the number of characters on stage at once; no bar to the existence in the same play of a prince and a gravedigger, or the presence of the highest social ranks in a comedy. Comedies, indeed, were more likely to model themselves on romances, with their happy endings, than on the corrective satire of humanist prescription. For all its dependence on Plutarch, a play such as *Antony and Cleopatra* makes the most of medieval models of dramaturgy; so does *Tamburlaine*, despite Marlowe's humanist ambitions, and, even more explicitly, *Dr. Faustus*, with its morality pattern of the soul pulled between its good angel and the devil, with damnation as the greatest tragic fall of them all. *Pericles* makes the connection between this free-ranging stagecraft and its medieval origins explicit, as it presents its hero's years of voyaging across the Mediterranean in ways that explicitly acknowledge the impossibility of any kind of realistic representation, demanding the audience's imaginative complicity in staging the unstageable. The text of the play may be an editor's nightmare, but as every production shows, it is one of Shakespeare's greatest *coups de théâtre*.

It was not until the mid-seventeenth century that the big changes came. The single great iconic moment was the execution of Charles I, with its sweeping away of the whole system of government that had held sway for most of a millennium. His death was intended to remove any idea that the monarch was appointed by God, that he was answerable only to God, and was next below Him in the hierarchy of sovereignty – a doctrine that itself overrode the long-established principle, confirmed in the traditional coronation oath, that the king ruled under the law. Yet what was put in the place of the monarchy was rule by that thoroughly medieval invention of parliament: scarcely in the form in which it had been envisioned by the thirteenth-century barons who forced its creation, but nonetheless still with the idea of representation of the population at its core. And rule by parliament itself lasted only a short while, initially because the assembly refused to do Cromwell's bidding, then, after his death, because the only viable form of government imaginable turned out to be the restoration of the monarchy. Charles II did not try to claim any divinely endorsed political absolutism, but he, like every British monarch from Edgar in 973 to the present day, was anointed on the breast at his coronation with consecrated oil that marked him out as holding a unique position under God. If the political system reverted in outline to its medieval pattern, however, other areas of life – science, the visible form of London itself – had equally iconic moments that changed the scene for good. The founding of the Royal Society in 1660 was one of these, with its agenda of seeking out facts about the natural world in a way entirely separate from either theology or from the affective and metaphorical language in which they had previously been described. And in 1666, the city of Chaucer and Shakespeare burned. The theaters had been closed in 1642, and although Restoration London acquired two private theaters, both socially and theatrically they were radically different from what had been offered by the public playhouses, and drama did not begin to recover anything resembling its medieval freedom of conception and staging until very recently. By the end of the century, Dryden had to rediscover Chaucer for a readership that knew little about him beyond the name; and although the chapbook romances still delighted the young and the less educated, high culture had to wait for Warton and Hurd and the Romantics to affirm the need for the imagination as well as the reason to be fed, and to offer the medieval romances as nourishment. The Middle Ages, in other words, had ceased to fuel the fires of the present moment: they had become antiquarian, to be rediscovered rather than lived.

Notes

1. "The Prophecie of Thomas Rymour," lines 239–48, in *Murray (ed.), *Romances and Prophecies* (1875), pp. 48–51.

2. "The Prophisies of Rymour, Beid and Marlyng," lines 143–46, in *Murray (ed.), *Romances and Prophecies*, pp. 52–61.

3. Ludovico Ariosto, *Orlando Furioso*, ed. Lanfranco Caretti, 2nd edn. (Turin, 1992), III.9–20; Spenser, *The Faerie Queene*, ed. Hamilton (2000), III.iii.25–49.

4. *Henry VI Part 3*, IV.vi.68–76, *Richard III*, V.v.29–41, ed. *Evans, *Riverside Shakespeare* (1997).

5. *The Progresses and Public Processions of Queen Elizabeth*, ed. *Nichols (1823), 3:552–53; the original document no longer survives.

6. *The Pattern of Catechistical Doctrine*, Second Comandement, ch. 7, in *Lancelot Andrewes*, ed. McCullough (2005) p. 27.

7. *Raby (ed.), *The Oxford Book of Medieval Latin Verse* (1959), pp. 369–70, lines 1–3.

8. *Henry Vaughan*, ed. Rudrum (1976), pp. 220–21, lines 17–20, 33–36, 39.

9. See especially Augustine, *De Doctrina Christiana*, ed. and trans. R. P. H. Green (Oxford, 1995).

10. "Easter," in *George Herbert, *Works*, ed. Hutchinson (1941), pp. 41–42, lines 11–12.

11. Cooper, "Guy as Early Modern Hero," in *Field and Wiggins (eds.), *Guy of Warwick* (2007), pp. 185–99.

12. *Edward II*, V.vi.59–63, in *Complete Works of Christopher Marlowe*, ed. Bowers (1981).

13. For these and other comments, see *Brewer (ed.), *Chaucer: The Critical Heritage* (1978).

14. *The Recuyell of the Historyes of Troye*, editions from 1475 to 1533; *The auncient historie of the destruction of Troy*, licensed in 1591, surviving editions from 1596 to 1738.

13

Re-creating the Middle Ages

The re-creation, re-envisioning, and reinterpretation of the Middle Ages, or medievalism, may be more than the imitation of artistic style, often implying a desire for the authentic or imagined values and way of life of the medieval era. Both conservatives anxious to preserve traditional values and those seeking radical change have invoked the Middle Ages in support of their social ideals. From the nation's beginnings, medievalism has also proved a powerful influence on cultural conceptions in the United States of America. The idea of the Middle Ages has served as an inspiration both to high culture and to popular culture in a variety of artistic media and social forms.

English medievalism is largely a phenomenon of the nineteenth and twentieth centuries – the word "medievalism" was only coined in the mid-nineteenth century – but it has some significant precursors in earlier times. For example, when Sir Thomas Malory remarks in the *Morte d'Arthur* that he cannot tell what Launcelot and Gwenyver might have been doing in private because "love that tyme was nat as love ys nowadays," he is making a conscious distinction between his own time and that of the Arthurian stories.[1] Even a fifteenth-century text, then, may have a medievalist consciousness of a difference between "then" and "now" that allows for points of comparison between the two time periods and real or imagined ways of life. Similarly, William Caxton, in his preface to his edition of Malory's works, argues first for the historicity of King Arthur, then uses this claim of historic truth to point a moral example: his goal is "that noble men may see and learne the noble actes of chyvalrye, the jentyl and virtuous dedes that some knughtes used in tho dayes, by whyche they came to honour, and how they that were vicious were punysshed and ofte put to shame and rebuke . . . "[2] The

Arthurian stories set examples of positive behavior and also recall a time when wickedness was duly punished.

Malory's and Caxton's yearning for a time of uncomplicated morality, bold action, and human and divine justice anticipates the medievalism of later generations. The irony is, of course, that many of the English medievalists saw the fifteenth century as the time of the "true" Middle Ages that they wished to recreate. As we have seen in earlier chapters, post-Reformation England's relationship with the Middle Ages was conflicted. Renaissance thinkers held up for emulation the classical traditions of Greece and Rome, while tending to associate the Middle Ages with primitivism, superstition, and the domination of the Roman Catholic Church, which English writers increasingly claimed was anti-English. Yet while some viewed the Reformation as a dramatic disjunction from a corrupt past, others chose to emphasize English tradition and borrowed freely from the Middle Ages for both artistic and political ends. A key example is Edmund Spenser's *Faerie Queene* (1590–96), where the knightly quest of characters such as the Red-Crosse Knight and Britomart allegorically represents Protestant Christian ideals, while the court of Prince Arthur reinforces the Tudor monarchs' claim of descent from King Arthur.[3]

Until the later eighteenth century, however, the majority position was that England had progressed beyond the Middle Ages from a time of superstition to an age of reason, and the medieval period was seldom a subject of major study. Even antiquarians, who professed an interest in all objects pertaining to the past, tended to show more interest in classical remains than indigenous English work. During the Victorian Medieval Revival, medievalism still functioned as a counter-voice to the widespread opinion that British society was progressing toward a state of higher civilization, yet it had a powerful effect on the arts and values during the nineteenth century, and that influence has continued in a wide variety of forms to the present day.

The beginnings of the Medieval Revival came with a renewed interest in medieval style. Horace Walpole published the first "Gothic" romance, *The Castle of Otranto*, in 1764; the book purported to be a translation, but it initiated a genre of mysterious stories usually set against a background of medieval remains. Walpole built his own house, Strawberry Hill, in the "Pointed" or "Gothic" style of ornamentation inspired by medieval ecclesiastical architecture and ornament; books such as Batty Langley's *Gothic Architecture, Improved by Rules and Proportions* (1742) provided patterns for the construction of modern Gothic buildings. Meanwhile, a few devotees of the past began to suggest that the Middle Ages might provide not just a source for design but also a pattern for values. In Richard Hurd's *Letters on Chivalry and Romance* (1762), Hurd presents knightly conduct as a positive value, even if much of his sense of what the Middle Ages were like is derived from sources such as Spenser's *Faerie Queene*.

By the turn of the nineteenth century, most Western European nations, including Britain, began to take a pride in their national pasts. Even in France, where the French Revolution had claimed to be a rejection of history, antiquarianism took a solid hold. The term "romantic" moved from having a pejorative meaning – as fantastic as the romances of the knights of King Arthur or Charlemagne – to describing a desirable feeling prompted by a sense of the natural or primitive. Song collectors began to show an interest in the oral tradition of ballads and folk songs, resulting in such collections as Thomas Percy's *Reliques of Ancient English* Poetry (1765) and Sir Walter Scott's *Minstrelsy of the Scottish Border* (1801–3); even though in many cases the ballads collected may have been composed much later than the Middle Ages, these collections indicate a new respect for national tradition and for medieval themes and language. Joseph Ritson, for example, collected and edited ballads about Robin Hood in an attempt to establish the authentic tradition. Collections such as Thomas Moore's *Irish Melodies* and Felicia Hemans' *Welsh Melodies* featured declaredly new poems set to traditional (although not medieval) tunes, many of which recalled Ireland's and Wales' medieval independence. The poets of what is now called the English Romantic movement frequently adopted traditional ballad forms and wrote poems with medieval settings, including S. T. Coleridge's "Christabel" (composed about 1798 and published in 1816) and John Keats' "Eve of St. Agnes" (1819).

Major social changes in Britain helped spur this search for tradition and national identity. Although Britain did not undergo a political revolution like France, the Industrial Revolution contributed to social upheaval. A smaller proportion of the population earned a living by farming, while the numbers who worked in manufacturing and commerce grew. During the early years of the nineteenth century, factories with steam-powered machinery began to mass-produce a wide range of manufactured goods for both domestic consumption and for export. Ports such as Liverpool and manufacturing centers such as Manchester and Birmingham experienced massive population growth. As a smaller percentage of Britons lived in rural communities where everyone knew each other, a more idealized view of the Middle Ages emerged, evoking a time when the community was centered around the village church and where rich and poor lived in co-existence, sharing an agricultural economy in a feudal relationship.

Some radical writers tried to reclaim the Middle Ages as a means of expressing their dissatisfaction with the current state of British society. At a time when civil rights such as *habeas corpus* were under attack, populist publications asserted that England needed to reclaim the principles of Magna Carta. In his early radical years, Robert Southey wrote a drama called *Wat Tyler*, which praises the fourteenth-century Peasants' Revolt as a kind of English precursor of the French Revolution; Southey was embarrassed when his enemies published the play about twenty years later.

The greatest contributor to a sense of the medieval during the British Romantic period, however, was Sir Walter Scott. Scott first gained public attention as an editor and a poet; his major long poems, *The Lay of the Last Minstrel*, *Marmion*, and *The Lady of the Lake*, are set in the sixteenth century, but allude frequently to times of chivalry and knightly honor. The poems were also well known in America, the anti-slavery campaigner Frederick Douglass choosing to name himself after a character in *The Lady of the Lake*. Scott probably gained inspiration for the form of the historical romance when he edited the antiquarian Joseph Strutt's unfinished story *Queenhoo-Hall*, which describes in detail (and very often at the expense of plot) many ancient English sports and pastimes.

Scott published *Ivanhoe*, his first novel set in England and also the first actually set in medieval times, in 1819. *Ivanhoe* had a major influence on the ways that the nineteenth-century Britain viewed the Middle Ages. First, the story draws on the seventeenth-century notion of the "Norman Yoke," which, as Christopher Hill has shown, claims that the English Saxons had a constitutional system of government until the Norman Conquest of 1066, when it was replaced by a strictly hereditary and often oppressive monarchy.[4] Scott imagines the social division between Saxons and Normans prevailing into the time of the Crusades; for example, Scott fixes the legendary figure of Robin Hood in the Crusader era of Richard I and gives him a Saxon identity, in contradiction to Joseph Ritson's claim that Robin Hood was a nobleman with the Norman name Robert Fitz-Ooth. Second, Scott makes the tournament and knightly conduct a central part of his vision of the Middle Ages. He continues to make use of the English Protestant notion that the Roman Catholic Church is devious and untrustworthy, but relegates this to his depiction of minor characters, rather than making it central to his vision of England's medieval past. The story ends with a union between Saxons and Normans, and the creation of an English identity. In later years, *Ivanhoe* was seen as an instructive book for young people, although not everyone saw its chivalric values as positive, Mark Twain going so far as to blame Scott (in *Life on the Mississippi* [1883], ch. 46) for the attitudes that led to the American Civil War when he asserted that without the "Sir Walter disease" the Southern character "would be wholly modern, in place of modern and medieval mixed, and the South would be fully a generation further advanced than it is." Although the Knights Templar are villainous in *Ivanhoe*, Scott's novel was one of the sources of inspiration for the Klu Klux Klan, who depicted their campaign for the supremacy of the Anglo-Saxon race as a crusade. A number of Scott's subsequent novels have medieval settings, including *The Talisman* (1825), a novel set in the time of Richard I's Crusade and remarkable for its sympathetic portrayal of the Muslim leader, Saladin. Scott also wrote an essay on chivalry for the *Encyclopaedia Britannica* that was used extensively as a reference source about knightly conduct.

Scott suggests that the Saxons, Normans, and Jews of *Ivanhoe* each have specific cultural practices and characteristics. Racial identity took on a new importance when Victoria succeeded her uncle William IV to become queen in 1837. Her court advisors, many of whom were of German origin themselves, made her initially unpopular marriage to Prince Albert of Saxe-Coburg seem more palatable to the British public by stressing the common Saxon ancestry of the English and inhabitants of the German states. As Reginald Horsman has shown, this notion of an Anglo-Saxon character that survived the Norman Conquest was also influential on the American idea of "manifest destiny," so that "by 1850, the emphasis was on the American Anglo-Saxons as a separate, innately superior people who [were] destined to bring good government, commercial prosperity, and Christianity to the American continents and the world."[5] In later years, Victoria and Albert owned a statue by William Theed portraying them as Anglo-Saxons. Pageantry surrounding government had always had a quasi-medieval element – for example, numerous suits of armor owned by monarchs from Tudor and Stuart times survive in the Tower of London – but Queen Victoria's court stressed this connection with history in new ways.

Another inspiration for the revival of medieval ideals was Kenelm Henry Digby's *The Broad Stone of Honour*. The book went through a number of revisions after its initial publication in 1822, as it evolved into an idealization of knightly conduct that suggested that England's best hope was for young aristocrats to take on the medieval values of their ancestors and become leaders. Digby's central exemplars are Crusaders, and the book suggests that the modern-day aristocracy should wage a crusade against poverty, ignorance, and social upheaval. Digby's work therefore modeled the kind of paternalistic medievalism that became common during the Victorian period.[6]

The best-remembered example of the early Victorian enthusiasm for aristocratic medieval ideals is the Eglinton Tournament of 1839. The earl of Eglinton and his friends spent a long time planning the event, modeling the rituals of the tournament closely on those described by Scott in the Tournament of Ashby-de-la-Zouche in *Ivanhoe* (interestingly, in twenty years, *Ivanhoe* had become a source-book for medieval authenticity). The plan was for full-scale jousting and a precise re-enactment of an authentic medieval tournament, with hundreds of costumed participants. Mark Girouard has described the preparations and outcome of the tournament in detail in *The Return to Camelot: Chivalry and the English Gentleman*.[7] On the actual day of the tournament at Eglinton Castle, thunder, lightning, and torrential rain turned the tournament field into a sea of mud. The knights' horses could not keep their footing and the jousting had to be abandoned.

As Mark Girouard points out, the jousting was carried out successfully a few days later when the weather improved. By that time, however, the tournament had become a laughing-stock, especially in publications generally unsympathetic to aristocratic pretensions. The Eglinton Tournament was still being mocked when *Punch* started publication in 1841, even though a number of its early illustrators, such as John Doyle, were fairly sympathetic toward medievalism. The Ullathorne Sports episode in Anthony Trollope's 1857 novel, *Barchester Towers*, where the Thorne family tries to stage traditional medieval feats of strength, similarly makes gentle fun of the aristocratic notions that attempted to revive ancient pastimes.

The Eglinton Tournament did not, though, mark an end to re-creating the Middle Ages, although it may have temporarily turned attention from the imitation of style to the adoption of the supposed social values of the Middle Ages. *The Broad Stone of Honour* was also an inspiration to the "Young England" movement of Lord John Manners and other young aristocrats who sincerely believed that re-creating the Middle Ages would be England's salvation. The future Tory Prime Minister Benjamin Disraeli associated with this group, and reflected some of these notions in his novels *Coningsby* (1844), *Sybil, or the Two Nations* (1845), and *Tancred* (1847). In *Sybil*, Disraeli responds to the social conditions of the Industrial Revolution by contrasting the "two nations" of the rich and the poor. Disraeli's trilogy assumes that racial inheritance influences character, and in *Sybil*, the true aristocrats (as opposed to those who pay for invented family trees) are of Norman descent and equipped through blood to rule; the working people, with their manly strength and commitment to fairness and truth, are the descendants of the Saxons. (Disraeli, himself of Jewish descent, had written *Alroy*, a novel depicting twelfth-century Judaism, early in his career, and suggests in his crusader-themed novel *Tancred* that being Jewish may be best of all.) In Disraeli's envisioning of British society, the "Norman Yoke" should not be oppressive, but rather a source of order and justice: Disraeli, in fact, sees benevolence in feudalism, as represented by Sybil's care for the poor.

Thomas Carlyle took a slightly different approach in *Past and Present* (1843). Claiming inspiration from the depiction of medieval society in the *Chronicle of Jocelin de Brackelonde* in the Camden Society publication, the book seeks to address the "Condition-of-England" question; this phrase is found in *Ivanhoe*, but Carlyle made it his own. *Past and Present* focuses less on charity toward the grateful poor as in the Young England envisaging than on a picture of strong leadership in the person of Abbot Sampson. Carlyle suggests that the medieval monk embodies the heroic characteristics of leadership that present-day industrial capitalism lacks.

It is significant that the claimed inspiration for *Past and Present* is a publication by the Camden Society, because the number of societies recovering and reprinting medieval texts was beginning to grow, and the Camden Society was one of the foremost of these. Antiquarian editing and publishing dated back to figures such as Thomas Hearne in the early eighteenth century, but it received a new impetus from the "bibliomania" of the Napoleonic era, when early printed editions and manuscripts commanded huge prices. The first antiquarian publishing club was the Roxburghe Club, founded in 1812 in memory of the bibliophile John Ker, duke of Roxburghe, who died in 1804. Although the bibliophiles had tended not to distinguish between classical texts and medieval works, the Roxburghe Club, which had a highly selective membership of twenty-five, often printed English works, such as the first publication of the medieval romance *Havelok the Dane* (1828). The Camden Society, founded in 1838 and named in honor of the Elizabethan antiquary William Camden, was one of many less exclusive publishing clubs that followed.

The medieval past emerged as a legitimate field of study as scholars produced histories focusing on the Middle Ages, rather than merely presenting the Middle Ages as a phase in English progress toward a better future. Sharon Turner's *History of the Anglo-Saxons* and subsequent history of the later Middle Ages is an early example of a text that does not quite abandon the Enlightenment notion of continued human progress, yet is sympathetic toward the achievements of earlier times. Early Victorian antiquarians such as Thomas Wright, one of the first historians actually to use the term "medieval," were even more inclined to admire medieval society. Wright's many publications included the printing of a text of the *Canterbury Tales* and the Chester Mystery Plays, and a number of studies of medieval life and culture such as *A History of Domestic Manners and Sentiments in England during the Middle Ages* (1862). A number of British scholars followed the example of the Brothers Grimm in the German states in attempting to recover and categorize traditional stories. In the 1840s, the term "folklore" was coined, giving further legitimacy to the study of oral traditions and popular culture. The fact that many early folklorists were inclined to attribute later traditions to the Middle Ages demonstrates the extent to which they had been re-integrated into public consciousness as a period with a distinctive culture, rather than a place-marker between the Roman period and the Renaissance.

Another dominant voice in the Victorian re-creation of the Middle Ages was Alfred, Lord Tennyson. One of Tennyson's earliest poems, "The Lady of Shalott," is a narrative of a woman cursed to experience the outside world of King Arthur's Camelot only through a reflection. The sight of Sir Lancelot tempts her to look directly through the window of her tower, bringing the curse upon her. There is no such story in Arthurian legend, although Tennyson may have partly recalled the story of Elaine, the Fair Maid of Astolat, from Malory. Around the same time as the earliest versions of "The Lady of Shalott," Tennyson produced a blank-verse version of Malory's *Morte d'Arthur*. At the time of composition, Tennyson probably associated the death of King Arthur with the sudden death of his best friend Arthur Henry Hallam in 1833, particularly since Sir Bedivere laments, "now the whole Round Table is dissolved,/Which was an image of the mighty world,/And I, the last, go forth companionless . . ." Yet he was later to re-use this versification in other forms. He published it as "The Epic" in 1842 with a framing narrative connecting it with Christmas and the coming of Christ (the last line is "And the new sun rose bringing the new year"). It found a final place as the end of Tennyson's twelve-book epic *Idylls of the King*. Tennyson published his first four Idylls, each centered around a woman in the Arthurian story, in 1859; his source material was both Malory and Lady Charlotte Guest's translations from the *Mabinogion* and other Welsh Arthurian stories (1838–49), but Tennyson and his illustrators give the Arthurian stories the trappings of the post-Conquest Middle Ages. Tennyson revises Malory, who tends to sympathize with Lancelot, so that King Arthur is the moral center of the poem (Mordred, for example, is not Arthur's son born of an incestuous relationship with his sister, but his nephew). The fall of the Round Table is thus attributed to Guinevere's moral weakness; in retirement at Almesbury, she reflects, "It was my duty to have loved the highest."[8] The final structure of the *Idylls* emphasizes the cycle of the year, and also the decline in royal power; the Epilogue "To the Queen," makes a connection between King Arthur and the current state of royalty, and asks Victoria to "accept this old imperfect tale,/New-old, and shadowing Sense at war with Soul,/ Ideal manhood closed in real man" (lines 36–38). Tennyson thus stresses the allegorical element of his use of the Middle Ages, even though the relationship between story and allegorical meaning varied substantially over the course of his poetic career,

At the same time, architecture and the decorative arts found inspiration in the Middle Ages. When the medieval Palace of Westminster, the home of Parliament, burned down in 1834, the competition to find a design for a replacement building was limited to applications in the Gothic or Elizabethan style, a departure from only a few years earlier, when Sir John Soane, himself an avid antiquarian, had proposed a neo-classical Houses of Parliament. The choice emphasized that English legal practices were not imitations of Greek and Roman governmental practices, but rather derived from the common law of the Middle Ages; English law represented tradition, not imposed innovation.

The Palace of Westminster project helped bring to prominence a number of figures at the center of the Victorian Medieval Revival. The winning design was by Charles Barry, who was assisted in drawing the plans by Augustus Welby Northmore Pugin.[9] Pugin had been designing furniture in the Gothic style since he was a teenager, and had already assisted Barry in the interior design for a number of Gothic-inspired projects. As the new House of Commons and House of Lords took shape over the next fifteen years, the building became a triumphant statement of England's legal inheritance from the medieval period. Stained glass and murals depicted key moments in English history, while the style imitated the medieval palace or cathedral.

About the time of his initial collaboration with Charles Barry, Pugin had become a Roman Catholic; in 1836 he published *Contrasts; or, a parallel between the noble edifices of the fourteenth and fifteenth centuries, and similar buildings of the present day; shewing the present decay of taste*. The engravings contrast the beauty of medieval architecture and the compassion of medieval society with the utilitarian styles and social attitudes of the 1830s. For example, "Contrasted residences for the poor" shows a medieval monastery dispensing Christian charity, contrasted with a workhouse built in the style of Jeremy Bentham's *Panopticon* where the bodies of the poor are sent for dissection. Although there do not seem in actuality to have been workhouses built in the panopticon style where a central tower would ensure that inmates were always under observation, the references are to the Anatomy Act and the Poor Law Amendment Act of 1833–34, which the poor viewed as imposing punishments on poverty. Pugin's decision to become a Roman Catholic (interestingly, Kenelm Henry Digby had made the same choice) is hence both aesthetic and idealistic.

Since the Reformation, the English had tended to regard the Roman Catholic Church as a potential threat to the realm, the Anglican position being that loyalty to the pope was contrary to loyalty to the English crown. Catholics had been able to vote on the same terms as Protestants only since 1828. As we have seen, the Reformation was seen as a critical moment that simultaneously rejected Catholicism and the values of the Middle Ages. The Oxford Movement of the 1830s sought to purify the English Church through the revival of ritual and tradition. Under the leadership of John Henry Newman, John Keble, Edward Bouverie Pusey, and others, the group published *Tracts for the Times*, some of which celebrated the lives of medieval English saints. The series caused a national scandal in 1841, when Tract XC, authored by Newman, argued that the Thirty-Nine Articles of the Church of England were not incompatible with Roman Catholic doctrine. Newman was, hence, claiming that the English Reformation was not the major shift in thinking that Protestant historians had asserted, but rather that the English had underestimated the connection with the Church traditions of the Middle Ages.

The decorative and architectural art of the Victorian Medieval Revival was often commissioned for Christian purposes. Many churches were built in the Gothic style, and even in the Great Exhibition of 1851, which had the express purpose of demonstrating the current state of the decorative arts, the items in the Mediaeval Court tended to be religious in purpose, including fonts, lecterns, shrines, ceremonial vessels, and candlesticks. Around the time of the Reformation, Protestants vandalized or destroyed ancient shrines and statues in English churches (the Victorians often attributed the destruction to the Cromwellian army of the English Civil War period, but, in fact, most of the iconoclasm was much earlier). The revival of the highly ornate, reverential medieval style for church decoration and accoutrements was thus an earnest attempt to restore both Roman Catholic and Anglican churches to their medieval state.

The Medieval Revival also had some influence on church music. Two well-known re-creations of the Middle Ages are the song "Good King Wenceslas," an entirely invented episode in the life of the medieval saint that concludes with the Victorian moral, "Ye who now will bless the poor/ Shall yourselves find blessing"; and "O, come, O come, Emmanuel," in which translated medieval words are set to a medieval plainsong-style melody. Both were the work of the Anglican clergyman John Mason Neale, who translated many medieval texts to be used as hymns.

For devotees of the medieval such as Pugin, an interest in medieval style seems to have led to the reclaiming of medieval belief. John Ruskin, a major Victorian apologist for the medieval period, agreed with Pugin as to the "decay of taste," but was more interested in the social structures represented by the medieval style than in specific religious practices. When Ruskin pointed out that European culture was dominated by a "trinity of ages," namely, the classical, medieval, and modern periods, he seemed to be repeating the tradition narrative of history. For Ruskin, though, the medieval period was not merely a gap between the two ages of knowledge and reason, but a potential model for industrial society. Ruskin's primary example of the aesthetic and social strength of the Middle Ages is the Gothic cathedral. In *The Stones of Venice* (1851–53), he laments the current "division of labour" of the modern industrial system, as well as the privileging of order and regularity. The Gothic cathedral, planned by anonymous architects and constructed for the glory of God, allows scope for the individual craftsman to exercise "an imagination as wild and wayward as the northern sea; creatures of ungainly shape and rigid limb, but full of wolfish life; fierce as the winds that beat, and changeful as the clouds that shade them."[10] Ruskin presents this "savageness" as a virtue, and urges his readers, "Never encourage the manufacture of any article not absolutely necessary, in the production of which *Invention* has no share."[11]

One of Ruskin's goals in developing a theory of medievalist creativity was to justify the work of the Pre-Raphaelite Brotherhood. The Pre-Raphaelites, whose founding members included Dante Gabriel Rossetti, William Holman Hunt, and John Everett Millais, joined together in 1848, when most of the members were still in their early twenties, to protest against the current state of the visual arts. They claimed to draw their inspiration from Italian painting before Raphael, and some early works, such as Rossetti's painting of the Annunciation, are in the tradition of medieval devotional art, sometimes combining text with illustration in the style of medieval manuscripts. Rossetti in particular used the works of Dante as a source, as in *Beata Beatrix* and *The Blessed Damozel*, and even changed his middle name "Dante" to his first, to stress his connection with the medieval poet. Yet the Pre-Raphaelites also found inspiration in English literature, including the works of Shakespeare, Keats, and Tennyson, which provided a literary means of approaching the Middle Ages. Tennyson's "Lady of Shalott" inspired some 200 Victorian artworks, ranging from a drawing by Rossetti's future wife Elizabeth Siddal to a large-scale allegorical painting by Holman Hunt, which Hunt explained as meaning that the Lady, representative of the artist, should have remained in her enclosed state. A favorite contemporary novel among the Pre-Raphaelite circle was *The Heir of Redclyffe*, by the Tractarian author Charlotte Mary Yonge. In the novel, a young heir to an aristocratic property, Sir Guy Morville (a descendant of one of the knights who killed Thomas Becket) demonstrates Christian charity and dies in an act of self-sacrifice. The story was also popular among soldiers in the Crimean War era, who perhaps found in its praise of chivalric virtues (a recurring theme in Yonge's later novels) an idealization of the soldierly profession.

The young William Morris and Edward Burne-Jones seem to have read *The Heir of Redclyffe* as college students; they were also familiar with the work of the Pre-Raphaelite circle and Ruskin. By 1858, they were fully members of the Pre-Raphaelite circle; Morris worked with Rossetti and Burne-Jones to produce never-completed frescoes for the Oxford Union, and also published poetry, including *The Defence of Guenevere and Other Poems*. The title poem finally allows Guinevere to speak in her own voice and delay her execution as an adulteress long enough for Lancelot to save her. Other poems, such as "The Haystack in the Flood," depart from the sense of the Middle Ages as a time of decorum and charity by depicting realistic violence. Morris' only surviving oil portrait is of Jane Burden, one of the Pre-Raphaelite models, as an adulterous medieval queen, either Guinevere or Iseult. (Ironically, in 1859, Morris married Jane, who later had a much-publicized liaison with D. G. Rossetti.)

Edward Burne-Jones went on to have a successful career as an artist by specializing in paintings of a decorous Middle Ages. For instance, his illustrations for Morris' edition of Chaucer depict only the courtly stories, and not the bawdy ones. Whereas most Pre-Raphaelite paintings narrate a story, Burne-Jones' figures create a mood of tranquility and culture in keeping with late nineteenth-century aestheticism. Morris, too, showed these characteristics in his designs for fabric, wallpaper, furniture, and printing. Yet Morris' politics represent a different kind of social criticism from the desire for order of many of his contemporaries, being more closely aligned with the populist medieval tradition. While many social commentators saw the Middle Ages as a time when the rich cared for the poor, some continued to believe that they represented a time of greater equality. Early in the nineteenth century, William Cobbett had praised the rural economy of the Middle Ages, while the Chartists of the 1830s and 1840s sought democracy and social equality through the tradition of Magna Carta, arguing that all Britons ought to be granted written constitutional rights. Morris' ideas were declaredly aligned with socialism. In *A Dream of John Ball* (1888), focusing on the priest who participated in Wat Tyler's revolt; and in *News from Nowhere* (1891), he used the medieval form of the dream vision to suggest both a socialist medieval past and a medievalist future where everything was in common ownership. Morris was also instrumental in encouraging the study of Norse literature in Britain through a number of translations and romances.

By the end of the nineteenth century, the medieval period was a legitimate field of study for scholars of literature, history, and languages. Early nineteenth-century histories of the Middle Ages such as those by

Henry Hallam, Robert Southey, William Cobbett, John Lingard, and others were declaredly partisan, aiming either to show society's progress beyond the Middle Ages to a higher state of civilization; or to reclaim a continuity with England's medieval heritage, and especially the benefits derived from the Roman Catholic Church structure. The model of "scientific history" emerging in the later half of the century stressed the use of archival support. While histories such as E. A. Freeman's massive *History of the Norman Conquest* were really just as partisan as earlier efforts, they included extensive quotation from medieval sources in an attempt to support their claims. The amateur editing of such series of the Camden Society publications was supplemented by the more scholarly standards of series such as the Early English Texts Society, founded by F. J. Furnivall in 1864. (Furnivall also participated in the founding of the Chaucer Society, the Ballad Society, and other literary clubs.) The American scholar F. J. Child was the chief editor for a collated collection of English and Scottish popular ballads; unlike early editors such as Percy and Scott, who sometimes could not resist the temptation to improve upon old ballads, Child aimed for authenticity. Other scholars worked to recover folk traditions such as mummers' plays. Some of these folk traditions are reflected in the novels of Thomas Hardy, who drew upon the customs of southwestern England in novels such as *Under the Greenwood Tree* (1872) and *The Return of the Native* (1878). In *Tess of the D'Urbervilles* (1891), Tess Durbeyfield's discovery that she is descended from the historic family of D'Urberville proves her undoing when she is preyed upon by the current, although less authentic, bearer of the D'Urberville name.

English folk music was the inspiration for a new wave of British composers in the early years of the twentieth century. While England does not have composers to match the grand-scale medievalism of Wagner and Verdi, the most successful English composer of the later nineteenth and early twentieth century, Sir Edward Elgar, wrote numerous pieces inspired by the Middle Ages. These include the King Arthur Suite; *King Olaf*, based on Henry Wadsworth Longfellow's "Saga of King Olaf" from *Tales of a Wayside Inn*, itself structured in homage to Chaucer's *Canterbury Tales*; and *The Dream of Gerontius*, based on a poem by Newman. Benjamin Britten was later to use medieval texts in works such as *Noyes Fludde* (inspired by the mystery play) and *A Ceremony of Carols*.

The idyllic past captured in the folk revival of the turn of the twentieth century was snatched away by the horrors of the First World

War. Early recruiting propaganda presented the war as an idealistic quest to end wars, and the volunteer army as chivalric heroes, but the carnage of trench warfare was so far removed from the vision of the Middle Ages that the Modernist period tends to reflect the Middle Ages as something desirable but unattainable, losing the sense of continuity with the past that the Victorians had fostered. Modernist writers, nevertheless, frequently referenced medieval works: for example, the epigraph to T. S. Eliot's *The Waste Land* is drawn from Dante, and David Jones makes extensive use of medieval themes in *In Parenthesis* (1937); the central figure is named John Ball, while Jones also references the *Mabinogion* and Malory. In Virginia Woolf's most experimental novel *The Waves* (1931), the death in India of Percival, who is seen as a hero by his friends, obliquely unites the human loss of the First World War with the sense that medieval chivalry is no longer possible.

Yet if the medieval dream of a just, ordered world did not work in the twentieth century, the Middle Ages could be re-created in other forms. From the beginning of the industry, film-makers noted the cinematic possibilities of the Middle Ages.[12] Film could capture knights in armor in a way that was simply not possible on the stage. Cecil B. de Mille made an epic of *The Crusades*, based very loosely on Richard I and the Third Crusade, in 1935. Michael Curtiz's 1938 movie *The Adventures of Robin Hood* presented the Middle Ages as a time of good-hearted adventure, where the evil are vanquished and a source of humor, and the good are merry and successful. The film, starring Errol Flynn, exploits the possibilities of medieval combat with sword-fighting and archery. The figure of Robin Hood, rebelling against unjust authority and promoting a kind of social equality through the redistribution of wealth, seems to have been particularly appealing to American audiences, and there have been many subsequent adaptations of the story, both for cinema and television.

In retrospect, many medieval-themed films provide a commentary on their own times. Laurence Olivier's *Henry V* (1945) adapts Shakespeare's play, but depicts medieval warfare in detail as a patriotic tribute to England's struggles in the Second World War. Richard Thorpe's *Ivanhoe* (1952), which unlike most Hollywood realizations of the Middle Ages was actually filmed in England, retells Scott's novel but focuses on the Jewish aspects of the story as an indirect assertion of the new state of Israel's right to exist.

Romanticized as many of these film depictions of the Middle Ages are, their goal is the representation of universal human aspirations and emotions in a setting that captures the authentic feel of past times. In a more systematic way, scholars of the Middle Ages study documents and archaeological remains to try to understand what past times were actually like. Twentieth-century scholars thus followed the lead of later nineteenth-century scholars in setting the goal of understanding the real Middle Ages. Scientific methods such as carbon-dating and DNA analysis can be used to supplement written documents and learn more about everyday life in England in the past. Medieval studies is a recognized field of scholarship that now encompasses not only history and literature, but also sociology and anthropology. Most medieval scholars have claimed to be using evidence to create as close a picture of the actual Middle Ages as possible, and distinguished their work from medievalism, the study of later attitudes toward the Middle Ages represented by such journals as *Studies in Medievalism*, founded by Leslie Workman. In recent years, however, more scholars have come to believe that even our understanding of the Middle Ages as one period with identifiable characteristics is at least partly shaped by the attitudes of post-Reformation thinkers, and particularly the nineteenth and twentieth centuries. They retain the goal of understanding the "real Middle Ages," but realize that emphases and interpretations are often affected by the scholar's own cultural concerns.

On the other hand, the twentieth century also saw the growth of medievalist fantasy. Drawing on elements in medieval romance, such as magical transformation, and supernatural creatures, such as dragons, fantasy retains from chivalric medievalism the possibility of doing mighty deeds, but places these actions in a world where the laws of nature do not necessarily apply. The Middle Ages, hence, becomes a space where both artist and audience (or writer and reader) can exercise imagination.

The masters of British fantasy literature of the twentieth century, J. R. R. Tolkien, and his close friend, C. S. Lewis, share a scholarly background in medieval studies and the creation of fantasy worlds that display the marvelous but nevertheless provide a space for working through Christian, or at least humane, values. Both served in the First World War and took up academic posts at Oxford University in the 1920s, by which time Tolkien had already published a scholarly edition of Sir Gawain and the Green Knight. Lewis' lasting claim to critical fame is *The Allegory of Love* (1936), which theorized the concept of courtly love to an extent now disputed by modern scholars. In 1937, Tolkien introduced readers to his vision of a medieval fantasy world that nevertheless reflected the spirit of Judeo-Christian morality in *The Hobbit*. Lewis' *Narnia* series, beginning with *The Lion, the Witch, and the Wardrobe* in 1950, created a Christian allegory for child readers through the magical medieval society of Narnia, where English children could be warrior-rulers. Tolkien continued his vision of Middle Earth in *The Lord of the Rings* trilogy of 1955–56. Whereas Lewis' imaginary world seems influenced by the high Middle Ages with occasional Norse overtones, Tolkien's seems more in the tradition of Germanic philology and works such as the *Nibelungenlied*.

It is hard to determine the exact indebtedness of popular culture's medieval fantasy to Tolkien, but sword-and-sorcery art, texts and role-playing games have much in common with the quest form of *The Lord of the Rings*, as do the use of maps and a variety of sentient beings (for example, halflings, orcs, dwarves, elves, and so on). Another early influence was Lord Dunsany, author of such fairytales as *The King of Elfland's Daughter* (1924). The term "sword and sorcery" emerged in the early 1960s as a means of defining the fantasy subgenre produced by such writers as the American Robert E. Howard, who created Conan the Barbarian and Kull the Conqueror in the 1930s. The fantasy adventures, where mighty swordsmen battle the power of wizards and magic, take character elements from Norse mythology. Howard most likely believed in the theory of the dominance of the northern European, or Aryan, race that had influenced earlier medievalists such as Wagner and that was to take on disturbing ramifications in the Second World War era.

Fantasy adventure makes little claim to historical authenticity and often mixes fifteenth-century armor with Viking-style warfare; even its conception of wizardry is not really a medieval one, but probably more derived from the witch panics of the early seventeenth century. Fantasy's central appeal may be that in a time when real warfare is capable of destruction on a massive level, medieval combat continues the human (or superhuman) face of conflict, and that the strong, resourceful, and virtuous prevail over the treacherous and cunning, usually in the format of the one-on-one duel. Magic also provides a means of escape from predicaments, and there can be little doubt that part of the attraction of these games is that they empower the players.

Fantasy adventures were well adapted to the graphic novel and comic strip form; Hal Foster's *Prince Valiant*, which began in 1937, being a long-running example of a loosely Arthurian tale that draws realistic design elements from the later Middle Ages. The *Marvel* comic's character Thor (devised by Stan Lee, who also created Batman, the "Dark Knight") is imbued with the power of the Norse god through possession of his hammer and is seemingly able to come and go between the human realm and the gods' kingdom of Asgard. Among role-playing board games, where players choose their own characters and embark on epic adventures, *Dungeons and Dragons*, developed by the Americans Gary Gygax and Dave Arnesan and first marketed in 1974, is the best known. Medieval spells are also a part of trading-card games such as *Magic* that emerged in the 1980s. Role-playing games took on a new life in the video game age, with titles such as *World of Warcraft*, which now claims seven million on-line players, showing its indebtedness to Tolkien. Even video games designed for younger players, as is Nintendo's "Zelda" series, create medieval fantasy worlds where players take on the role of sword-swinging hero. Although the "Zelda" series was devised by a Japanese company, elf-like people in a setting more reminiscent of the European Middle Ages combat a variety of threats to their peace. A significant element of medieval fantasy, then, is its tendency to generalize the Middle Ages through the use of recognizably medieval artifacts and tropes without regard to specific historical nations and cultures.

The sword-and-sorcery fantasy novel, like the role-play medieval game, is predominantly an American invention, as is the Society for Creative Anachronism (SCA), "dedicated to researching and re-creating the arts and skills of pre-17th-century Europe."[13] The Society is set up in "kingdoms" ruled by monarchical hierarchies, somewhat ironic since the United States did not have a Middle Ages or a monarchy; there is a non-North American "kingdom" in the SCA, the "Drachenwald." Medieval motifs have proved appealing to the fans of heavy-metal rock music, with its loose indebtedness to magical fantasy and its use of Gothic lettering and embellishments; and to the Goth subculture, a form of rebellion against Judeo-Christian values. Contrary to the nineteenth-century ideal of a medieval world in which each person knew his or her place, medievalism may be a form of individualism and resistance to the dominant culture.

A declaredly English offshoot of this interest in role-playing is J. K. Rowling's "Harry Potter" series of novels, which have proved far too popular to be considered as countercultural. As in C. S. Lewis' "Narnia" series, English children are empowered in a magical parallel world, although, in the case of Harry Potter, this world is not entered through a portal but secretly co-exists with the human world. The children gifted with magical ability receive an education at Hogwarts School of Witchcraft and Wizardry, a mysterious medieval castle that serves as a boarding-school. The books in the series are structured after the English school year, and climax in an epic battle where Harry Potter must use his courage, wits, and magical ability in the kind of problem-solving seen in role-playing games.

In recent years, Tolkien's *Lord of the Rings* trilogy and the "Harry Potter" series have been made into very successful films. The film medium is able to exploit the visual aspects of the Middle Ages, such as costume and weaponry, ironically making fantasy appear almost realistic. Whereas the *Lord of the Rings* films, directed by Peter Jackson, were filmed in New Zealand, the "Harry Potter" series uses English locations in a way that tends to re-emphasize a feature recurrent in English medievalism, class structure. Just as Disraeli's *Sybil* describes the two nations, "The Rich and the Poor," the Harry Potter books divide the world between the wizards and the "Muggles," or regular humans.

The "Harry Potter" phenomenon thus has something in common with perhaps the most prevalent means of re-creating the Middle Ages in England today, the heritage industry. Tourism to medieval sites is by no means a new phenomenon; for example, the ruins of Tintern Abbey conformed with the Romantics' ideal of a picturesque spot, while the Tower of London, which even housed a menagerie, was a tourist desti-nation almost as soon as it stopped being a prison. A number of sites associated with medieval history now claim to re-create the experience of being in the Middle Ages; for example, the *Canterbury Tales* visitor attraction, subtitled "Medieval Misadventures," at Canterbury tries to recapture the "sight, sound and smell of fourteenth-century England" as it re-tells Chaucer's stories and re-creates the shrine of St. Thomas Becket.[14] The Jorvik Viking Centre at York, constructed on the site of an archaeological dig, is similarly "participatory" in its depiction of a ninth-century Viking settlement. Cities such as York have tried to revive medieval mystery plays, and many English communities have troupes of Morris dancers. A number of English castles have presented jousting, usually with considerably more success than the Eglinton Tournament. Medieval World, the organization that has run the Camelot Theme Park in Lancashire, where the slogan is "A Wizard Day Out," for the past twenty years, began offering jousting at Warwick Castle in 2006.[15]

If some of these examples seem to trivialize the concept of the Middle Ages, at the very least they show the continued fascination with re-creating the medieval past. Whether with the goal of understanding the historic past, giving scope to imagining a world bolder or better than the present, or recapturing the aesthetics of a bygone time, each generation reworks motifs and themes from the Middle Ages to serve specific cultural purposes.

Notes

1. Thomas Malory, *Works*, ed. E. Vinaver, 2nd edn. (1971), p. 676.
2. In *Works*, ed. Vinaver, p. xv.
3. On Hurd's indebtedness to Spenser see Kristine Louise Haugen, "Chivalry and Romance in the Eighteenth Century: Richard Hurd and the Disenchantment of *The Faerie Queene*," in Clare A. Simmons (ed.), *Medievalism and the Quest for the "Real" Middle Ages* (2001), pp. 45–60.
4. Christopher Hill, "The Norman Yoke," in *Puritanism and Revolution: Studies in Interpretation of the Seventeenth Century* (1958), pp. 50–122.
5. Reginald Horsman, *Race and Manifest Destiny: The Origins of American Racial Anglo-Saxonism* (Cambridge, MA, 1981), pp. 2–3.
6. *Chandler, *A Dream of Order* (1970), remains the most comprehensive overview of this phenomenon.
7. Mark Girouard, *The Return to Camelot: Chivalry and the English Gentleman* (New Haven, CT, 1981), especially pp. 88–110.
8. Jerome H. Buckley (ed.), *Poems of Tennyson* (Boston, MA, 1958), p. 458, line 652.
9. See Paul Atterbury and Clive Wainwright (eds.), *Pugin, A Gothic Passion* (New Haven, CT, 1994), particularly pp. 106, 219–25.
10. John Ruskin, *Selected Writings*, ed. Dinah Birch (Oxford, 2004), p. 37.
11. Ruskin, *Selected Writings*, p. 44.
12. For an expansive list of films invoking the European Middle Ages, see *Harty, *The Reel Middle Ages* (1999).
13. www.sca.org.
14. www.canterburytales.org.uk.
15. www.medievalworld.co.uk.

Guides to further reading

Introduction: medieval English culture and its companions

On "culture"

Burke, Peter, *What is Cultural History?*, 2nd edn. (2008).
Kuper, Adam, *Culture: The Anthropologists' Account* (Cambridge, MA, 1999) (a critique of all the anthropological uses of the term "culture" as positing a false image of an objective and fixed entity and as produced for various ulterior purposes).
Malinowski, Bronislaw, "The Problem of Meaning in Primitive Languages," Supplement to C. Ogden and I. Richards, *The Meaning of Meaning* (1923), pp. 146–52 (seminal presentation of language as defined solely by function).
Argonauts of the Western Pacific: An Account of Native Enterprise and Adventure in the Archipelagoes of Melanesian New Guinea ([1922]; reprinted New York, 1961) (classic account of symbolic economic and prestige-oriented system of exchange).

On literature in culture (see also Chapter 11)

Regionalism and its relation to literary study

Barrett, Robert W., Jr., *Against All England: Regional Identity and Cheshire Writing, 1195–1656* (Notre Dame, IN, 2009).
Hanna, Ralph, "Yorkshire Writers," *Proceedings of the British Academy* 121 (2003), 91–109.
London Literature, 1300–1380 (Cambridge, 2005).
Riddy, Felicity (ed.), *Regionalism in Late Medieval Manuscripts and Texts: Essays Celebrating the Publication of a Linguistic Atlas of Late Mediaeval English* (Cambridge, 1991).

Nationalism in history and literature

Cooney, Helen, *Nation, Court and Culture: New Essays on Fifteenth-century English Poetry* (Dublin, 2001).
Forde, Simon, Lesley Johnson, and Alan V. Murray (eds.), *Concepts of National Identity in the Middle Ages*, Leeds Texts and Monographs, 14 (Leeds, 1995).

Lavezzo, Kathy (ed.), *Imagining a Medieval English Nation* (Minneapolis, MN, 2004).

Smyth, Alfred P. (ed.), *Medieval Europeans: Studies in Ethnic Identity and National Perspectives in Medieval Europe* (1998).

Turville-Petre, Thorlac, *England the Nation: Language, Literature, and National Identity, 1290–1340* (Oxford, 1996).

Social visions, social implications, and visions of history and culture in medieval literature

Fyler, John M., *Language and the Declining World in Chaucer, Dante, and Jean de Meun* (Cambridge, 2007).

Galloway, Andrew, "Gower's Quarrel with Chaucer, and the Origins of Bourgeois Didacticism in Fourteenth-Century London Poetry," in Annette Harder, Alasdair A. Macdonald, and Gerrit J. Reinink (eds.), *Calliope's Classroom: Studies in Didactic Poetry from Antiquity to the Renaissance* (Leuven, 2007), pp. 245–68.

Patterson, Lee, *Chaucer and the Subject of History* (Madison, WI, 1991).

Staley, Lynn, *Languages of Power in the Age of Richard II* (Philadelphia, PA, 2005).

Strohm, Paul, *Social Chaucer* (Cambridge, MA, 1994).

On medieval philosophy (see also Chapters 2 and 8)

Kenny, Anthony, *Medieval Philosophy, New History of Western Philosophy: Vol. 2* (Oxford, 2007).

Kretzman, Norman, Anthony Kenny, and Jan Pinborg, *The Cambridge History of Later Medieval Philosophy* (Cambridge, 1982).

On economic history (see also Chapter 3)

Postan, M. M., *The Medieval Economy and Society, The Pelican Economic History of Britain: Vol. 1* (Harmondsworth, [1972], 1984).

On the history of women in medieval England

Dinshaw, Carolyn and David Wallace (eds.), *Cambridge Companion to Medieval Women's Writing* (Cambridge, 2003).

Goldberg, P. J. P. (trans. and ed.), *Women in England, c. 1275–1525* (Manchester, 1995).

Women, Work, and Life Cycle in a Medieval Economy: Women in York and Yorkshire c. 1300–1520 (Oxford, 1992).

On Jews in medieval England and elsewhere (see also Chapter 3)

Cluse, Christoph (ed.), *The Jews of Europe in the Middle Ages (Tenth to Fifteenth Centuries)* (Turnhout, 2004).

Delaney, Sheila (ed.), *Chaucer and the Jews: Sources, Contexts, Meanings* (New York, 2002).

Mundill, Robin R., *England's Jewish Solution: Experiment and Expulsion, 1262–1290* (Cambridge, 1998).

Rubin, Miri, *Gentile Tales: The Narrative Assault on Late Medieval Jews* (Philadelphia, PA, 1999).

On lordship

Bean, J. M. W., *From Lord to Patron: Lordship in Late Medieval England* (Philadelphia, PA, 1989).

Faith, Rosamund, *The English Peasantry and the Growth of Lordship* (Leicester, 1999).

Hicks, Michael, *Bastard Feudalism* (1995).

Maitland, F. W., *The Constitutional History of England* (Cambridge, [1908], reprinted 1974), pp. 141–64 (still valuable and extraordinarily clear summary, though disputed).

Reynolds, Susan, *Fiefs and Vassals: The Medieval Evidence Reinterpreted* (Oxford, 1994) (major challenge to the reifying and anachronistic use of "feudalism" as a concept).

Waugh, Scott, "Tenure to Contract: Lordship and Clientage in Thirteenth-Century England," *English Historical Review* 101 (1986), 811–39.

A wide range of further "companions" to medieval English history and literature is available; especially notable are these:

Brown, Peter, *A Companion to Chaucer* (Oxford, 2000) (wide-ranging reassessment of the many contexts and issues focused on Chaucer).

A Companion to Medieval English Literature and Culture, c. 1350–1500 (Oxford, 2007) (extensive range of topics, contexts, genres, and demonstrations of "readings" of particular works and authors).

Donoghue, Daniel, *Old English Literature: A Short Introduction* (Oxford, 2004) (tidy and judicious survey of literature before the Conquest).

Godden, Malcolm and Michael Lapidge (eds.), *The Cambridge Companion to Old English Literature* (Cambridge, 1991) (wide-ranging survey of important genres and contexts for pre-Conquest literature and pre-Conquest culture).

Rigby, S. H., *A Companion to Britain in the Later Middle Ages* (Oxford, 2003) (extensive range of reassessments of historical topics and their scholarly traditions).

Saul, Nigel, *A Companion to Medieval England, 1066–1485*, 2nd edn. (Stroud, 2005) (authoritative brief treatments of a selected range of historical facts and topics).

Scanlon, Larry, *The Cambridge Companion to Medieval English Literature, 1100–1500* (Cambridge, 2009) (chapters on key contexts, genres, and authors).

Chapter 1: From court to nation

Political surveys

Frame, Robin, *The Political Development of the British Isles 1100–1400* (Oxford, 1990).

Matthew, Donald, *Britain and the Continent 1000–1300: The Impact of the Norman Conquest* (2005).

Ormrod, W. M., *Political Life in Medieval England, 1300–1450* (Basingstoke, 1995).

Prestwich, Michael, *English Politics in the Thirteenth Century* (Basingstoke, 1990).

Historical surveys

Bartlett, Robert, *England under the Norman and Angevin Kings 1075–1225* (Oxford, 2000).

Carpenter, David, *The Struggle for Mastery: Britain 1066–1284* (2003).

Harriss, Gerald, *Shaping the Nation England 1360–1461* (Oxford, 2005).

Prestwich, Michael, *Plantagenet England 1225–1360* (Oxford, 2005).

Biographies

Bates, David, *William the Conqueror* (1989).

Crouch, D., "William Marshal: Court, Career and Chivalry in the Angevin Empire," *DNB*.

Goodman, Anthony, *John of Gaunt: The Exercise of Princely Power in Fourteenth-Century Europe* (1992).

Maddicott, J. R., *Simon de Montfort* (Cambridge, 1994).

Prestwich, Michael, *Edward I* (Berkeley, 1988).

Saul, Nigel, *Richard II* (New Haven, CT, 1997).

Warren, W. L., *Henry II* (New Haven, CT, 1973).

War and finance

Curry, A., *The Hundred Years' War* (Basingstoke, 1993).

Harriss, G. L., *King, Parliament and Public Finance in Medieval England to 1369* (Oxford, 1975).

Vale, Malcolm, *The Origins of the Hundred Years' War: The Angevin Legacy 1250–1340* (Oxford, 1996).

Law, government, and parliament (see also Chapters 2 and 4)

Brown, A. L., *The Governance of Late Medieval England 1272–1461* (Stanford, CA, 1989).

Davies, R. G. and J. H. Denton (eds.), *The English Parliament in the Middle Ages* (Manchester, 1981).

Holt, J. C., *Magna Carta*, 2nd edn. (Cambridge, 1992).

Musson, Anthony and W. M. Ormrod, *The Evolution of English Justice: Law, Politics and Society in the Fourteenth Century* (Basingstoke, 1999).

Warren, W. L., *The Governance of Norman and Angevin England 1086–1272* (Stanford, CA, 1987).

Lordship and nobility

Coss, Peter, *The Origins of the English Gentry* (Cambridge, 2003).

Crouch, David, *The Image of Aristocracy in Britain 1000–1300* (1992).

Given-Wilson, Chris, *The Royal Household and the King's Affinity: Service, Politics and Finance in England 1360–1413* (New Haven, CT, 1986).

The English Nobility in the Late Middle Ages (1987).

McFarlane, K. B., *The Nobility of Later Medieval England* (Oxford, 1973).

Chapter 2: The legal revolution and the discourse of dispute in the twelfth century

Some basic introductions to legal history and its principles

Bellomo, Manlio, *The Common Legal Past of Europe: 1000–1800*, trans. Lydia G. Cochrane (Washington, DC, 1995).

Brundage, James A., *Medieval Canon Law* (1995).

Hart, H. L. A., *The Concept of Law* (Oxford, 1961).

Hudson, John, *The Formation of the English Common Law* (1996).
Peters, Edward, *Torture* (Philadelphia, PA, 1996).

More specialized studies

Bellamy, J. G., *The Law of Treason in England in the Later Middle Ages* (Cambridge, 1970).
Brand, Paul, *The Origins of the English Legal Profession* (Cambridge, MA, 1992).
Hyams, Paul, "Trial by Ordeal: The Key to Proof in the Early Common Law," in M. Arnold, T. A. Green, S. Scully, and S. D. White (eds.), *On the Laws and Customs of England: Essays in Honor of Samuel E. Thorne* (Chapel Hill, NC, 1981), pp. 90–126.
"The Common Law and the French Connection," *Anglo-Norman Studies* 4 (1982), 77–92, 196–202.
"The Charter as Source in the Early Common Law," *Journal of Legal History* 12(3) (1991), 173–89.
"What Did Edwardian Villagers Understand by Law?", in Zvi Razi and Richard Smith (eds.), *Medieval Society and the Manor Court* (Oxford, 1996), pp. 69–102.
"Rogues and Respectable Folk in Common Law and the *Ius Commune*: Due Process versus the Maintenance of Order in European Law," in Peter Coss (ed.), *The Moral World of the Law* (Cambridge, 1999), pp. 62–90.
Rancor and Reconciliation in Medieval England (Ithaca, NY, 2003).
Nemo-Pekelman, Capucine, "Scandale et vertue dans la doctrine canonique médiévale (XIIeme–XIIIeme siècles)," *Révue historique de droit français et étranger* 85 (2007), 491–504 (rare treatment of a topic crucial for canon law).

Important works of Stephen D. White

White, Stephen, "Inheritances and Legal Arguments in Western France, 1050–1150," *Traditio* 43 (1987), 55–103.
"Imaginary Justice: The End of the Ordeal and the Survival of the Duel," *Medieval Perspectives* 13 (1998), 32–55.
"The Problem of Treason: The Trial of Daire le Roux," in Pauline Stafford *et al.* (eds.), *Law, Laity and Solidarities: Essays in Honour of Susan Reynolds* (New York, 2001), pp. 95–115.
Feuding and Peacemaking in Eleventh-Century France (Aldershot, 2005).
"Alternative Constructions of Treason in the Angevin Political World: *Traïson* in the *History of William Marshall*," *e-Spania* 4 (2007), http://e-spania.revues.org/document2233.html.

Some important legal texts

Beaumanoir, Philippe de, *Coutumes de Beauvaisis*, 2 vols., ed. Am. Salmon (Paris, 1899, reprinted 1970), trans. F. R. P. Akehurst (Philadelphia, PA, 1992).
Brevia Placitata, eds. G. J. Turner and T. F. T. Plucknett, Selden Society 66 (1951 for 1947).
English Lawsuits from William I to Richard I, ed. R. C. van Caenegem, Selden Society 97–98 (1990–1).
Glanvill, ed. Derek Hall (Oxford, 1993).

Gratian, *Decretum*, in *Corpus Iuris Canonici*, ed. E. Friedburg (Leipzig, 1879–81); quaestio 5 treats oaths.

Novae Narrationes, eds. E. Shanks and S. F. C. Milsom, Selden Society 80 (1963).

"Très ancien coutumier de Normandie," in *Coutumiers de Normandie: Tome I*, ed. Ernest-Joseph Tardif (Rouen, 1881).

Yearbooks of 12 Edward II, 1319, ed. J. P. Collas, Selden Society 82 (1964) (contains a notable study of Old French accusation words used in England).

Chapter 3: Archaeology and post-Conquest England

Comprehensive outlines of the physical evidence about medieval England are: J. Steane, *The Archaeology of Medieval England and Wales* (1985) and H. Clarke, *The Archaeology of Medieval England* (1984), which take a thematic approach; and C. Platt, *Medieval England* (1978) and D. A. Hinton, *Archaeology, Economy and Society* (1990), which are written chronologically.

Books on individual topics are much more numerous; of the most recent work, C. M. Woolgar, D. Serjeantson, and T. Waldron, *Food in Medieval England* (Oxford, 2006), summarizes work on animal bones, crops, and other aspects of nutrition and consumption considered in the first section of this chapter. Excellent overviews of buildings are: J. Grenville, *Medieval Housing* (1997), A. Quiney, *Town Houses of Medieval Britain* (2003), and A. Emery, *Greater Medieval Houses of England and Wales*, 3 vols. (Cambridge, 1996–2006); major articles are by S. Pearson in K. Giles and C. Dyer (eds.), *Town and Country in the Middle Ages*, Society for Medieval Archaeology Monograph 22 (2005), M. Gardiner in *Medieval Archaeology* 44 (2000), and D. F. Stenning and N. W. Alcock in *Vernacular Architecture* 34 (2003) and 37 (2006), respectively. Settlement studies have been led by the Wharram Percy excavations, now with ten published volumes of results, and summarized by M. Beresford and J. G. Hurst, *Wharram Percy: Deserted Medieval Village* (1990). The Tattenhoe excavation was published by R. Ivens, P. Busby, and N. Shepherd in 1995, Mawgan Porth by R. Taylor for R. Bruce-Mitford in 1997. An especially useful recent area survey is by R. Jones and M. Page in *Medieval Archaeology* 47 (2003).

Development pressures in the last fifty years have meant that excavations have taken place in very many towns, though with a bias toward the larger ones. Canterbury, Southampton, and London led the way because of bomb damage in the 1940s, with King's Lynn, directed by H. Clarke, and Winchester, directed by M. Biddle, setting examples of planned programs in the 1960s that were followed by Oxford, York, London, and Norwich, and then by Northampton, Hereford, Bristol, Exeter, and a host of others. Synopses have included J. Schofield and A. Vince, *Medieval Towns* (1994), D. Palliser (ed.), *The Cambridge Urban History of Britain: Vol. 1: 600–1500* (Cambridge, 2000), P. Waller (ed.), *The English Urban Landscape* (Oxford, 2000), and K. D. Lilley, *Urban Life in the Middle Ages, 1000–1450* (Basingstoke, 2002). Important articles include those by T. B. James and E. Roberts in *Medieval Archaeology* 44 (2000), N. W. Alcock in *Medieval Archaeology* 45 (2001), D. Dymond, *Antiquaries Journal* 78 (1998), D. Martin in D. Rudling (ed.), *The Archaeology of Sussex to A.D. 2000* (King's Lynn, 2002), R. H. Leech, *Vernacular Architecture* 31 (2000), and G. G. Astill in T. Aston (ed.), *Social Relations and Ideas* (1983).

The main protagonists in the debates about castles are C. Coulson, M. W. Thompson, M. H. Johnson, O. Creighton, R. Higham, A. Lowerre, and R. Liddiard, all of whom have published books in the last decade, as has A. Wheatley on literary approaches. A fiery article by C. Platt in *Medieval Archaeology* 51 (2007) will inspire further discussion. Individual studies with wider implications include R. C. Turner on Chepstow in *Antiquaries Journal* 84 (2000), and M. Fradley on Caernarfon in *Medieval Archaeology* 50 (2006). Fighting at sea is dealt with by S. Rose, *Medieval Naval Warfare 1000–1500* (2002), and sea transport by G. Hutchinson, *Medieval Ships and Shipping* (1994). For the Magor Pill boat, see the report by N. Nayling published in the Council for British Archaeology Research Report series, No. 115 (1998), and for other examples of inland water transport see J. Blair (ed.), *Waterways and Canal-Building in Medieval England* (Oxford, 2007).

Archaeologists' love for broken bits of pot results in many studies of individual types and production sites. Examples of the latter include P. Spoerry on Ely (2008), M. Leah on Grimston (1994), P. Miller and R. A. Stephenson on Kingston-upon-Thames (1999), J. A. Cotter on Canterbury (1997), and P. Mayes and K. Scott on Chilvers Coton (1984). The marketing of pottery in Oxford and London has been studied by M. Mellor in *Oxoniensia* 59 (1994) and by A. G. Vince in *Medieval Archaeology* 29 (1985). The nature of the potters' craft is considered by D. Peacock, *Pottery in the Roman World* (1982); his classifications have also been used recently by R. W. Unger, *Beer in the Middle Ages* (Philadelphia, PA, 2004). A general study is M. R. McCarthy and C. M. Brooks, *Medieval Pottery in Britain A.D. 900–1600* (Leicester, 1988). For all forms of artifact, see D. A. Hinton, *Gold and Gilt, Pots and Pins* (Oxford, 2005), and for metalwork and coins the Portable Antiquities Scheme website, www.finds.org.uk.

Religions and the physical traces that they leave are another major focus for all archaeologists; those studying the Christian period have always studied churches and monasteries, but new approaches to their meanings are shown by C. P. Graves, *The Form and Fabric of Belief*, British Archaeological Reports British Series 311 (Oxford, 2000). Burial has become of increasing interest as well, partly for the study of skeletal remains, but also for the various practices revealed: work includes essays in S. Bassett (ed.), *Death in Towns* (Leicester, 1992) and R. Gilchrist and B. Sloane, *Requiem* (2005). Articles by G. Coppack, *Medieval Archaeology* 30 (1986), on Fountains, G. Astill *et al.*, *Archaeological Journal* 161 (2004), on Bordesley, D. Stocker, *Vernacular Architecture* 36 (2005), on the Vicars Choral, and by J. Bond in G. Keevil *et al.* (eds.), *Monastic Archaeology* (Oxford, 2001), on aspects of estate management are especially useful. K. Giles, *An Archaeology of Social Identity*, British Archaeological Reports British Series 315 (Oxford, 2000), is a new approach to the guilds; P. Skinner (ed.), *Jews in Medieval Britain* (Woodbridge, 2003), and J. Hillaby and R. Sermon, in *Transactions of the Bristol and Gloucestershire Archaeological Society* 122 (2004), consider one "other" group; see C. Rawcliffe, in *Anglo-Norman Studies* 23 (2001), for another, lepers, and C. M. Barron and N. Saul (eds.), *England and the Low Countries in the Late Middle Ages* (Stroud, 1998), for a third, Flemings.

Chapter 4: Social ideals and social disruption

Cam, Helen, *The Hundred and the Hundred Rolls: An Outline of Local Government in Medieval England* (1963).
Campbell, James, *The Anglo-Saxon State* (2003).
Faith, Rosamond, *The English Peasantry and the Growth of Lordship* (1997).
Fryde, E. B and Natalie Fryde, "Peasant Rebellion and Peasant Discontents," in Edward Miller (ed.), *Agrarian History of England and Wales: Vol. III* (Cambridge, 1991), pp. 744–819.

Keen, Maurice, *England in the Later Middle Ages* (1973).

Pollard, A. F., revised Richard W. Kaeuper, "Notton, William (*d.* in or after 1365)," *DNB*.

Maddicott, John R., *The English Peasantry and the Demands of the Crown 1294–1341*, Past and Present Society, Supplement 1 (1975).

Law and Lordship: Royal Justices as Retainers in Thirteenth- and Fourteenth-Century England, Past and Present Society, Supplement 4 (1978).

Miller, Edward and J. Hatcher, *Medieval England: Rural Society and Economic Change, 1086–1348* (1978).

Medieval England: Towns, Commerce and Crafts, 1086–1348 (1995).

Musson, A. J., *Medieval Law in Context* (Manchester, 2001).

Chapter 5: "Celtic" visions of England

Barrow, G. W. S., *The Anglo-Norman Era in Scottish History* (Oxford, 1980).

Scotland and its Neighbours in the Middle Ages (1992).

Bartlett, Robert, *Gerald of Wales, 1146–1223* (Oxford, 1982).

The Making of Europe: Conquest, Colonization, and Cultural Change, 950–1350 (Princeton, NJ, 1993).

Bradshaw, Brendan and J. S. Morrill (eds.), *The British Problem, c. 1534–1707: State Formation in the Atlantic Archipelago* (New York, 1996).

Davies, R. R., *The First English Empire: Power and Identities in the British Isles 1093–1343* (Oxford, 2000).

Frame, Robin, *The Political Development of the British Isles, 1100–1400* (Oxford, 1990).

Gillingham, John, *The English in the Twelfth Century: Imperialism, National Identity, and Political Values* (Woodbridge, 2000).

Kennedy, Ruth and Simon Meecham-Jones (eds.), *Authority and Subjugation in Writing of Medieval Wales* (New York, 2008).

Leckie, R. William, *The Passage of Dominion: Geoffrey of Monmouth and the Periodization of Insular History in the Twelfth Century* (Toronto, 1981).

Smith, Brendan (ed.), *Ireland and the English World in the Late Middle Ages: Essays in Honour of Robin Frame* (New York, 2009).

Tatlock, J. S. P., *The Legendary History of Britain* (Berkeley, CA, 1950).

Chapter 6: The idea of sanctity and the uncanonized life of Margery Kempe

Beckwith, Sarah, *Christ's Body: Identity, Culture, and Society in Late Medieval Writings* (1993).

Blumenfeld-Kosinski, Renate and Timea Szell (eds.), *Images of Sainthood in Medieval Europe* (Ithaca, NY, 1991).

Brown, Peter, *The Cult of the Saints: Its Rise and Function in Latin Christianity* (Chicago, IL, 1981).

Bynum, Caroline Walker, *The Resurrection of the Body in Western Christianity, 200–1336* (New York, 1995).

Caciola, Nancy, *Discerning Spirits: Divine and Demonic Possession in the Middle Ages* (Ithaca, NY, 2003).

Coletti, Theresa, "*Paupertas est donum Dei*: Hagiography, Lay Religion, and the Economics of Salvation in the Digby *Mary Magdalene*," *Speculum* 76 (2001), 337–78.

French, Katherine, *People of the Parish: Community Life in a Late Medieval Diocese* (Philadelphia, PA, 2000).

Kieckhefer, Richard, *Unquiet Souls: Fourteenth-Century Saints and Their Religious Milieu* (Chicago, IL, 1984).

Kinane, Karolyn Ann, "Sanctity Deferred: The Problem of Imitation in Early English Saints Lives," Ph.D. thesis, University of Minnesota, 2005.

Kleinberg, Aviad M., *Prophets in Their Own Country: Living Saints and the Making of Sainthood in the Later Middle Ages* (Chicago, IL, 1992).

Krug, Rebecca, *Reading Families: Women's Literate Practice in Late Medieval England* (Ithaca, NY, 2002).

Lochrie, Karma, *Margery Kempe and the Translations of the Flesh* (Philadelphia, PA, 1991).

Murray, Alexander, *Reason and Society in the Middle Ages* (Oxford, [1978] 1986).

Newman, Barbara, "What Did it Mean to Say 'I Saw'? The Clash between Theory and Practice in Medieval Visionary Culture," *Speculum* 80 (2005), 1–43.

Salih, Sarah, *Versions of Virginity in Late Medieval England* (Rochester, NY, 2001).

Sanok, Catherine, *Her Life Historical: Exemplarity and Female Saints' Lives in Late Medieval England* (Philadelphia, PA, 2007).

Smith, Julia M. H., "The Problem of Female Sanctity in Carolingian Europe *c.* 780–920," *Past and Present* 146 (1995), 3–37.

Staley, Lynn, *Margery Kempe's Dissenting Fictions* (University Park, PA, 1994).

Swanson, Robert N., *Religion and Devotion in Europe, c. 1215–c.1515* (Cambridge, 1995).

Toynbee, Margaret, *Saint Louis of Toulouse and the Process of Canonisation in the Fourteenth Century* (Manchester, 1929).

Vauchez, Andre, *The Laity in the Middle Ages: Religious Beliefs and Devotional Practices*, ed. Daniel E. Bornstein, trans. Margery J. Schneider (Notre Dame, IN, 1993).

Voaden, Rosalynn, *God's Words, Women's Voices: The Discernment of Spirits in the Writing of Late-Medieval Women Visionaries* (Woodbridge, 1999).

Warren, Nancy Bradley, *Spiritual Economies: Female Monasticism in Later Medieval England* (Philadelphia, PA, 2001).

Waters, Claire M., *Angels and Earthly Creatures: Preaching, Performance, and Gender in the Later Middle Ages* (Philadelphia, PA, 2004).

Weinstein, Donald and Rudolph M. Bell, *Saints and Society: The Two Worlds of Western Christendom, 1000–1700* (Chicago, IL, 1982).

Winstead, Karen, *Virgin Martyrs: Legends of Sainthood in Late Medieval England* (Ithaca, NY, 1997).

Wogan-Browne, Jocelyn, *Saints' Lives and Women's Literary Culture, c. 1150–1300: Virginity and its Authorizations* (Oxford, 2001).

Chapter 7: Visual texts in post-Conquest England

Recent studies of works discussed

Bloch, R. Howard, *A Needle in the Right Hand of God: The Norman Conquest of 1066 and the Making and Meaning of the Bayeux Tapestry* (New York, 2006).

Gameson, Richard (ed.), *The Study of the Bayeux Tapestry* (Woodbridge, 1997).

Geddes, Jane, *The St. Albans Psalter: A Book for Christina of Markyate* (2005).

Haney, Kristine, *The St. Albans Psalter: An Anglo-Norman Song of Faith* (New York, 2002).

Hart, Cyril, "The Bayeux Tapestry and Schools of Illumination at Canterbury," *Anglo-Norman Studies* 22 (2000), 117–67.

Panayotova, Stella, *The Macclesfield Psalter* (2008).

Sandler, Lucy Freeman, "In and Around the Text: The Question of Marginality in the Macclesfield Psalter," in Stella Panayotova (ed.), *The Cambridge Illuminations: The Conference Papers* (2007), pp. 105–14.

General and theoretical studies

Alexander, J. J. G. (gen. ed.), *A Survey of Manuscripts Illuminated in the British Isles*, 7 vols. (1975–96).

Alexander, J. J. G. and Paul Binski (eds.), *Age of Chivalry: Art in Plantagenet England, 1200–1400* (1987).

Binski, Paul, *Becket's Crown: Art and Imagination in Gothic England, 1170–1300* (New Haven, CT, 2004).

Camille, Michael, "Seeing and Reading: Some Visual Implications of Medieval Literacy and Illiteracy," *Art History* 8 (1985), 26–49.

Image on the Edge: The Margins of Medieval Art (Cambridge, MA, 1992).

"The Gregorian Definition Revisited: Writing and the Medieval Image," in Jerome Baschet and Jean-Claude Schmitt (eds.), *L'image: fonctions et usages des images dans l'occident médiéval* (Paris, 1996), pp. 89–107.

Hageman, Mariëlle and Marco Mostert (eds.), *Reading Images and Texts as Forms of Communication* (Turnhout, 2005).

Hahn, Cynthia, *Portrayed on the Heart: Narrative Effect in Pictorial Lives of Saints from the Tenth through the Thirteenth Century* (Berkeley, CA, 2001).

Hamburger, Jeffrey F. and Anne-Marie Bouché (eds.), *The Mind's Eye: Art and Theological Argument in the Middle Ages* (Princeton, NJ, 2006).

Kendrick, Laura, *Animating the Letter: The Figurative Embodiment of Writing from Late Antiquity to the Renaissance* (Columbus, OH, 1999).

Kessler, Herbert, *Studies in Pictorial Narrative* (1994).

Levy, Bernard S. (ed.), *The Bible in the Middle Ages: Its Influence on Literature and Art* (Binghamton, NY, 1992).

Lewis, Suzanne, *Reading Images: Narrative Discourse and Reception in the Thirteenth-Century Illuminated Apocalypse* (New York, 1995).

Pächt, Otto, *The Rise of Pictorial Narrative in Twelfth-Century England* (Oxford, 1962).

Rudolph, Conrad (ed.), *A Companion to Medieval Art: Romanesque and Gothic in Northern Europe* (Oxford, 2006).

Schapiro, Meyer, *Words and Pictures: On the Literal and the Symbolic in the Illustration of a Text* (The Hague, 1973).

Sears, Elizabeth and Thelma K. Thomas (eds.), *Reading Medieval Images: The Art Historian and the Object* (Ann Arbor, MI, 2002).

Chapter 8: Literacy, schooling, universities

General materials on schools and literacy

Arnold, D. O., "Thomas Sampson and the Orthographia Gallica," *Medium Ævum* 6 (1937), 193–209.

Aston, Margaret, *Lollards and Reformers: Images and Literacy in Late Medieval Religion* (1984).

Bush, Jonathan A. and Alain Wijffels (eds.), *Learning the Law: Teaching and the Transmission of Law in England 1150–1900* (1999).

Catto, J. I. (ed.), *The Early Oxford Schools, The History of the University of Oxford: Vol. I* (Oxford, 1984).

Catto, J. I. and Ralph Evans (eds.), *Late Medieval Oxford, The History of the University of Oxford: Vol. II* (Oxford, 1992).

Clanchy, M. T., "Moderni in Education and Government in England," *Speculum* 50 (1975), 671–88.

From Memory to Written Record, 2nd edn. (Oxford, 1993).

Copeland, Rita, *Rhetoric, Hermeneutics and Translation in the Middle Ages: Academic Traditions and Vernacular Texts* (Cambridge, 1991)

Courtenay, William J., *Schools and Scholars in Fourteenth-Century England* (Princeton, NJ, 1987).

Emden, A. B., *A Biographical Register of the University of Oxford to A.D. 1500*, 3 vols. (Oxford, 1957–59).

A Biographical Register of the University of Cambridge to 1500 (Cambridge, 1963).

Galloway, Andrew, "The Rhetoric of Riddling in Late-Medieval England: The 'Oxford' Riddles, the *Secretum Philosophorum*, and the Riddles in *Piers Plowman*," *Speculum* 70 (1995), 69–105.

Green, Richard F., *Poets and Princepleasers: Literature and the English Court in the Late Middle Ages* (Toronto, 1980).

Hudson, Anne, *The Premature Reformation: Wycliffite Texts and Lollard History* (Oxford, 1988).

Hunt, R. W., *The History of Grammar in the Middle Ages: Collected Papers*, ed. G. L. Bursill-Hall (Amsterdam, 1980).

Irvine, Martin, *The Making of Textual Culture:."Grammatica" and Literary Theory, 350 to 1100 AD* (Cambridge, 1994).

Leader, Damian (ed.), *A History of the University of Cambridge: Vol. 1: The University to 1546* (Cambridge, 1989).

Legge, M. Dominica, "William Kingsmill – a Fifteenth-Century Teacher of French in Oxford," in *Studies in French Language and Medieval Literature Presented to Professor Mildred K. Pope* (Manchester, 1939), pp. 241–46.

Mann, Jill, "'He Knew Nat Catoun': Medieval School-Texts and Middle English Literature," in Jill Mann and Maura Nolan (eds.), *The Text in the Community: Essays on Medieval Works, Manuscripts, Authors, and Readers* (Notre Dame, IN, 2006), pp. 41–74.

Miner, John N., *The Grammar Schools of Medieval England: A. F. Leach in Historiographical Perspective* (Montreal, 1990).

Minnis, Alastair, *Medieval Theory of Authorship: Scholastic Literary Attitudes in the Later Middle Ages* (1984).

Moran[-Cruz], Jo Ann H., *The Growth of English Schooling 1340–1548: Learning, Literacy, and Laicization in Pre-Reformation York Diocese* (Princeton, NJ, 1985).

Murray, Alexander, *Reason and Society in the Middle Ages* (Oxford, [1978] 1985).

Orme, Nicholas, *English Schools in the Middle Ages* (1973).

Education in the West of England, 1066–1548 (Exeter, 1976).

From Childhood to Chivalry: The Education of the English Kings and Aristocracy 1066–1530 (1984).

Medieval Schools from Roman Britain to Renaissance England (New Haven, CT, 2006).

Parkes, Malcolm B., "The Literacy of the Laity," in *Scribes, Scripts and Readers: Studies in the Communication, Presentation and Dissemination of Medieval Texts* (1991), pp. 275–97.

Post, Gaines *et al.*, "The Medieval Heritage of a Humanistic Ideal: 'Scientia donum dei est, unde vendi non potest,'" *Traditio* 11 (1955), 195–234.

Reynolds, Suzanne, *Medieval Reading: Grammar, Rhetoric and the Classical Text* (Cambridge, 1997).

Richardson, H. G., "Business Training in Medieval Oxford," *American Historical Review* 46 (1941), 259–80.

Rickert, Edith, "Chaucer at School," *Modern Philology* 29 (1932), 257–74.

Rothwell, William, "The Teaching of French in Medieval England," *Modern Language Review* 67 (1968), 37–46.

"The Trilingual England of Geoffrey Chaucer," *Studies in the Age of Chaucer* 16 (1994), 45–67.

"Henry of Lancaster and Geoffrey Chaucer: Anglo-French and Middle English in Fourteenth-Century England," *Modern Language Review* 99 (2004), 313–27.

Russell, J. Stephen, *Chaucer and the Trivium: The Mindsong of the Canterbury Tales* (Gainesville, FL, 1998).

Southern, R. W., *Scholastic Humanism and the Unification of Europe,* 2 vols. (Oxford, 1995–2001).

Stock, Brian, *The Implications of Literacy: Written Language and Models of Interpretation in the Eleventh and Twelfth Centuries* (Princeton, NJ, 1983).

Turner, Ralph V., "Who Was the Author of *Glanvill?* Reflections on the Education of Henry II's Common Lawyers," *Law and History Review* 8 (1990), 97–127.

Weisheipl, James A., "Curriculum of the Faculty of Arts at Oxford in the Early Fourteenth Century," *Mediaeval Studies* 26 (1964), 143–85.

Wormald, Patrick, *The Making of English Law: King Alfred to the Twelfth Century* (Oxford, 1999).

Wright, Laura, "Bills, Accounts, Inventories: Everyday Trilingual Activities in the Business World of Later Medieval England," in D. A. Trotter (ed.), *Multilingualism in Later Medieval Britain* (Cambridge, 2000), pp. 149–56.

Zieman, Katherine, *Singing the New Song: Literacy and Liturgy in Late Medieval England* (Philadelphia, PA, 2008).

More specialized studies in book history (books being the major evidence for medieval schooling)

Cavanaugh, Susan H., "A Study of Books Privately Owned in England 1300–1450," Ph.D. thesis, University of Pennsylvania, 1980.

"Royal Books: King John to Richard II," *The Library* 6th series 10 (1988), 304–16.

Coates, Alan, *English Medieval Books: The Reading Abbey Collection from Foundation to Dispersal* (Oxford, 1999).

Doyle, A. I., "English Books In and Out of Court from Edward III to Henry VII," in V. J. Scattergood and J. W. Sherborne (eds.), *English Court Culture in the Later Middle Ages* (1983), pp. 163–81.

Jayne, Sears R., *Library Catalogues of the English Renaissance* (1956; reprinted Winchester, 1983).

Ker, N. R., *Medieval Libraries of Great Britain: A List of Surviving Books,* 2nd edn., Royal Historical Society Guides and Handbooks 3 (1964).

Watson, Andrew G., *MLGB: Supplement to the Second Edition*, RHS Guides and Handbooks 15 (1987).

Krochalis, Jeanne E., "The Books and Reading of Henry V and his Circle," *Chaucer Review* 23 (1988), 50–77.

Powicke, F. M., *The Medieval Books of Merton College* (Oxford, 1931).

Sharpe, Richard (gen. ed.), *Corpus of British Medieval Library Catalogues*, currently 13 vols. (1990–).

Whitwell, Robert J., "The Libraries of a Civilian and Canonist and of a Common Lawler, an. 1294," *Law Quarterly Review* 21 (1905), 393–400.

Chapter 9: Anglo-Latin literature in the later Middle Ages

For orientation in the field of medieval Anglo-Latin literature, fundamental is Ralph J. Hexter, "*Latinitas* in the Middle Ages: Horizons and Perspectives," *Helios* 14 (1987), 69–92, replying to (the ecumenicist views of) Daniel Sheerin, "*In media Latinitate*," *Helios* 14 (1987), 51–67. Also, Michael Richter, "A Socio-linguistic Approach to the Latin Middle Ages," *Studies in Church History* 11 (1975), 69–82; Joseph Farrell, *Latin Language and Latin Culture from Ancient to Modern Times* (Cambridge, 2001), though it has very little on properly medieval developments; and W. Martin Bloomer, "Marble Latin: Encounters with the Timeless Language," in *The Contest of Language: Before and Beyond Nationalism*, ed. *idem* (Notre Dame, IN, 2005), pp. 207–26.

On the origins of Latin and the invention of Roman literature, stimulating and instructive is T. J. Cornell, *The Beginnings of Rome: Italy and Rome from the Bronze Age to the Punic Wars (c. 1000–264 BC)* (1995), pp. 41–46, on the languages, and pp. 57–77, on the foundation legends; also, Thomas N. Habinek, *The Politics of Latin Literature: Writing, Identity, and Empire in Ancient Rome* (Princeton, NJ, 1998); and W. Martin Bloomer, *Latinity and Literary Society at Rome* (Philadelphia, PA, 1997).

The essential basis for medieval Anglo-Latin research now is Richard Sharpe, *A Handlist of the Latin Writers of Great Britain and Ireland before 1540* (1997; reprinted with additions and corrections Turnhout, 2001). For guides to various Latin uses in addition to the literary ones, see *Medieval Latin: An Introduction and Bibliographical Guide*, eds. F. A. C. Mantello and A. G. Rigg (Washington, DC, 1996); and on Latin–vernacular relations, see Jocelyn Wogan-Browne, Nicholas Watson, Andrew Taylor, and Ruth Evans, *The Idea of the Vernacular: An Anthology of Middle English Literary Theory, 1280–1520* (University Park, PA, 1999).

For a survey of the period in question here, see A. G. Rigg, *A History of Anglo-Latin Literature 1066–1422* (Cambridge, 1992). For such writers as can be conceived as historians, there is a great deal of useful information and analysis in Antonia Gransden, *Historical Writing in England c. 550–c. 1307* (1974) and *Historical Writing in England c. 1307 to the Early Sixteenth Century* (1982). For the post-Roman, pre-Norman period, see Michael Lapidge, *Anglo-Latin Literature 600–899* (1996), esp. perhaps the compendious "Anglo-Latin Literature," pp. 1–35, and *Anglo-Latin Literature 900–1066* (1993). On the immediately post-medieval Anglo-Latin (susceptible of various definitions), see esp. J. W. Binns, *Intellectual Culture in Elizabethan and Jacobean England: The Latin Writings of the Age* (Leeds, 1990); also, Leicester Bradner, *Musae Anglicanae: A History of Anglo-Latin Poetry 1500–1925* (New York, 1940); and Carlson, *English Humanist Books: Writers and Patrons, Manuscript and Print 1475–1525* (Toronto, 1993). For orientation, see Peter Burke, "'Heu

Domine, Adsunt Turcae': A Sketch for a Social History of Post-Medieval Latin," in ed. *idem* and Roy Porter, *Language, Self, and Society: A Social History of Language*, (Cambridge, 1991), pp. 23–50; reprinted in *The Art of Conversation* (Ithaca, NY, 1993), pp. 34–65; or "Latin: A Language in Search of a Community," in *Languages and Communities in Early Modern Europe* (Cambridge, 2004), pp. 43–60.

On Geoffrey of Monmouth, still fundamental is Robert W. Hanning, *The Vision of History in Early Britain: From Gildas to Geoffrey of Monmouth* (New York, 1966), though see also (among a great deal of important recent work on the post-Conquest period) John Gillingham, "The Context and Purposes of Geoffrey of Monmouth's *History of the Kings of Britain*," *Anglo-Norman Studies* 13 (1990), 99–118, and "The Beginnings of English Imperialism," *Journal of Historical Sociology* 5 (1992), 393–409; Siân Echard, *Arthurian Narrative in the Latin Tradition* (Cambridge, 1998); and Kellie Robertson, "Geoffrey of Monmouth and the Translation of Insular Historiography," *Arthuriana* 8 (1998), 42–57. On the hagiographical consequence, see esp. David Townsend, "Anglo-Latin Hagiography and the Norman Transition," *Exemplaria* 3 (1991), 385–433; also, S. J. Ridyard, "*Condigna Veneratio*: Post-Conquest Attitudes to the Saints of the Anglo-Saxons," *Anglo-Norman Studies* 9 (1986), 179–206. On the 1191 exhumation, see Antonia Gransden, "The Growth of the Glastonbury Traditions and Legends in the Twelfth Century," *Journal of Ecclesiastical History* 27 (1976), 337–58, esp. 349–58. On the moment of the 1399 "Record and Process," see A. G. Rigg, "Anglo-Latin in the Ricardian Age," in A. J. Minnis, Charlotte C. Morse, and Thorlac Turville-Petre (eds.), *Essays on Ricardian Literature in Honour of J. A. Burrow* (Oxford, 1997), pp. 121–41; also, Carlson, "The Invention of the Anglo-Latin Public Poetry (*circa* 1367–1402) and its Prosody, especially in John Gower," *Mittellateinisches Jahrbuch* 39 (2004), 389–406. Of particular influence has been Paul Strohm, "Saving the Appearances: Chaucer's 'Purse' and the Fabrication of the Lancastrian Claim," in *Hochon's Arrow: The Social Imagination of Fourteenth-Century Texts* (Princeton, NJ, 1992), pp. 75–94. On the 1513 literary-historical episode, see esp. John Scattergood, "A Defining Moment: The Battle of Flodden and English Poetry," in Jennifer Britnell and Richard Britnell (eds.), *Vernacular Literature and Current Affairs in the Early Sixteenth Century* (Aldershot, 2000), pp. 62–77.

Chapter 10: The vernaculars of medieval England, 1170–1350

Manuscripts

For Old English works in twelfth- and early thirteenth-century manuscripts fundamental is Neil Ker, *Catalogue of Manuscripts Containing Anglo-Saxon* (Oxford, 1957). A number of twelfth-century manuscripts, however, are described in more detail by Orietta Da Rold at the draft Catalogue of the AHRC-funded Project, "The Production and Use of English Manuscripts, 1060 to 1200": www.le.ac.uk/english/em1060to1220. See also Tony Hunt, *Teaching and Learning Latin in Thirteenth-Century England*, 3 vols. (Cambridge, 1991), and, as a case-study of a manuscript discussed here, Oliver M. Traxel, *Language Change, Writing and Textual Interference in Post-Conquest Old English Manuscripts: The Evidence of Cambridge University Library, Ii. 1. 33* (Frankfurt, 2004).

Close study of particular manuscripts is often highly rewarding. On London, British Library, Harley 978, see Alan Coates, *English Medieval Books: The Reading Abbey Collections from Foundation to Dispersal* (Oxford, 1999), pp. 72–76, 162–63 and Andrew Taylor, *Textual Situations: Three Medieval Manuscripts and Their Readers* (Philadelphia, PA, 2002).

On London, British Library, Cotton Tiberius A.iii, see Helmut Gneuss, "Origin and Provenance of Anglo-Saxon Manuscripts: The Case of Cotton Tiberius A.iii," in P. R. Robinson and Rivkah Zim (eds.), *Of the Making of Books: Medieval Manuscripts, Their Scribes and Readers, Essays Presented to M. B. Parkes* (Aldershot, 1997), pp. 13–48; Tracy-Anne Cooper, "The Pragmatic Handbook of an Eleventh-Century Archbishop: Cotton Tiberius A.iii," *Anglo-Norman Studies* 28 (2006), 47–64.

The whole of Oxford, Bodleian Library, Digby 86 is available in facsimile: *Facsimile of Oxford, Bodleian Library, MS Digby 86*, ed. Judith Tschann and M. B. Parkes, EETS s.s. 16 (Oxford, 1996). Many of these texts in Digby 86 are printed by E. Stengel, *Codicem manu scriptum Digby 86 in Bibliotheca Bodleiana asservatum* (Halle, 1871); T. Erickson (ed.), *Le Lai du Cor*, Anglo-Norman Text Society (1973). Published studies on the manuscripts in their entirety are necessarily rather superficial: see, for example, John Frankis, "The Social Context of Vernacular Writing in the Thirteenth Century: The Evidence of the Manuscripts," in P. R. J. Coss and Simon D. Lloyd (eds.), *Thirteenth-Century England* (Woodbridge, 1986), pp. 175–84; Neil Cartlidge, "The Composition and Social Context of Oxford, Jesus College MS 29 (II) and London, British Library, MS Cotton Caligula A. ix," *Medium Ævum* 66 (1997), 250–69; Marilyn Corrie, "The Compilation of Oxford, Bodleian Library, MS Digby 86," *Medium Ævum* (1997); John Scahill, "Trilingualism in Early Middle English Miscellanies: Languages and Literature," *Yearbook of English Studies* 33 (2003), 18–32.

On London, British Library, Harley 2253, see Susanna Fein (ed.), *Studies in the Harley Manuscript: The Scribes, Contents, and Social Contexts of British Library MS Harley 2253* (Kalamazoo, MI, 2000). A full edition of the French, Latin, and English contents is promised by Fein; meantime, many of the English lyrics (but not the political lyrics) are available in G. L. Brook (ed.), *The Harley Lyrics: The Middle English Lyrics of MS. Harley 2253* (Manchester, [1956] 1968); for a few others, see Carleton Brown, *English Lyrics of the XIIIth Century* (Oxford, 1932), which includes lyrics from many other manuscripts. A full facsimile is available: *Facsimile of British Museum MS. Harley 2253*, introduction N. R. Ker, EETS (1965); snippet facsimiles and editions of the English lyrics are available at the Wessex Parallel Web Texts: www.soton.ac.uk/~wpwt/harl2253/harley.htm. Harley 2253 was written by three scribes, one of whom, as Carter Revard has meticulously proven, came from Ludlow in Shropshire ("Richard Hurd and MS Harley 2253," *Notes and Queries* 224 [1970], 199–202). See now Carter Revard, "Oppositional Thematics and Metanarrative in MS Harley 2253, Quires 1–6," in Wendy Scase (ed.), *Essays in Manuscript Geography: Vernacular Manuscripts of the English West Midlands from the Conquest to the Sixteenth Century*, Medieval Texts and Cultures of Northern Europe 10 (Turnhout, 2007), pp. 95–112.

Editions and studies of literary texts

W. W. Skeat (ed.), *Ælfric's Lives of Saints*, EETS os 76, 82, 94, 114 (1889–1900; reprinted as 2 vols., 1966); Ian Short, "Language and Literature," in Christopher Harper-Bill and Elisabeth van Houts (eds.), *A Companion to the Anglo-Norman World* (Woodbridge, 2003), pp. 191–213; Ian Short, "Patrons and Polyglots: French Literature in Twelfth-Century England," *Anglo-Norman Studies* 14 (1991), 229–49; Elaine Treharne, "The Life of English in the Mid-Twelfth Century: Ralph D'Escures' Homily on the Virgin Mary," in Ruth

Kennedy and Simon Meecham-Jones (eds.), *Literature of the Reign of Henry II* (2006), pp. 169–86; Nancy F. Partner, *Serious Entertainments: The Writing of History in Twelfth-Century England* (1977); Peter Damian-Grint, *The New Historians of the Twelfth-Century Renaissance* (Woodbridge, 1999). Margaret Laing's *Catalogue of Sources for a Linguistic Atlas of Early Medieval English* (Cambridge, 1993) lists all the English texts in medieval manuscripts from the twelfth to the fourteenth centuries. An excellent starting place for studying the Katherine Group texts, which include saints' lives and meditations (*Saint Katherine, Saint Margaret, Saint Juliana, Hali Meiðhad* and *Sawles Warde* – the Katherine Group; *On Ureisun of ure Louerde, On Lofsong of ure Lefdi*, and the *Wohunge of ure Lauerd* – the Wooing Group), is Bella Millett with George B. Jack and Yoko Wada, *Ancrene Wisse, the Katherine Group, and the Wooing Group, Annotated Bibliographies of Old and Middle English Literature 2* (Cambridge, 1996); Geoffrey Shepherd (ed.), *Ancrene Wisse: Parts Six and Seven* (1959; rev. edn. Exeter, 1985); A. Ewert (ed.), *Marie de France: Lais* (Oxford, 1944); Glyn Burgess and Keith Busby (eds. and trans.), *The Lais of Marie de France* (1986); Bella Millett (ed.), *Ancrene Wisse: A Corrected Edition of the Text in Cambridge, Corpus Christi College, MS 402, with Variants from Other Manuscripts: Drawing on the Uncompleted Edition by E. J. Dobson*, with a Glossary and Additional Notes by Richard Dance, EETS OS 325 and 326 (Oxford, 2005–6); Judith Weiss, "Structure and Characterisation in *Havelok the Dane*," *Speculum* 44 (1969), 247–57; David Staines, "*Havelok the Dane*: A Thirteenth-Century Handbook for Princes," *Speculum* 51 (1976), 602–23; Neil Cartlidge, "In the Silence of a Midwinter Night: A Re-evaluation of the *Visio Philiberti*," *Medium Ævum* 75 (2006), 24–45; T. Davies (ed.), *Medieval English Lyrics: A Critical Anthology* (1963), p. 317; Seth Lerer, "Medieval English Literature and the Idea of the Anthology," *PMLA* 118 (2003), 1251–67.

A new series of translations of Anglo-Norman texts as well as continental French texts written in England, including romances, saints' lives, and other narratives, is now available in the Medieval and Renaissance Texts and Studies series, published by the Arizona Center for Medieval and Renaissance Studies, Arizona State University, Tempe.

General introductory works

English is by far the best-served of the literary languages, and there is a vast array of research tools available in this area. Starting points for all serious scholars of Middle English are the *Index of Middle English Verse* by Carleton Brown and Rossell Hope Robbins (New York, 1943), its *Supplement* by Robbins and John L. Cutler (Lexington, KY, 1965), and the *Manuscript Index to the Index of Middle English Verse* by Richard Hamer (1995), as well as the multi-volume *Indexes of Middle English Prose* and *Manual of the Writings in Middle English 1050–1500*, the last with full lists of criticism. Volumes in the latter two series continue to appear, as do volumes in a new series, *Annotated Bibliographies of Old and Middle English Literature* (Cambridge).

Other general studies and guides relevant to this period include Phillip Pulsiano and Elaine Treharne (eds.), *Blackwell Companion to Anglo-Saxon Literature* (Oxford, 2001); Alan Lupack, *The Oxford Guide to Arthurian Literature and Legend* (Oxford, 2007); Elizabeth Archibald and Ad Putter, *The Cambridge Companion to the Arthurian Legend* (Cambridge, 2008); M. T. Clanchy, *From Memory to Written Record: England 1066–1307*, 2nd edn. (Oxford, 1993); Bella Millett's important website on textual mouvance at www.soton.ac.uk/~wpwt/mouvance/mouvance.htm; David Wallace (ed.), *The Cambridge History of Medieval English Literature* (Cambridge, [1999] 2002); Thomas J. Farrell (ed.), *Bakhtin* and *Medieval Voices* (Gainesville, FL, 1995); Thorlac Turville-Petre, *England the Nation: Language, Literature, and National Identity, 1290–1340* (Oxford, 1996); Joyce Coleman, *Public Reading and the Reading Public in Late Medieval England and France* (Cambridge, 1996).

For Anglo-Norman, the major works are Johan Vising, *Anglo-Norman Language and Literature* (1923); Dominica Legge, *Anglo-Norman Literature and Its Background* (Oxford, 1963); and Ruth J. Dean with Maureen B. M. Bolton, *Anglo-Norman Literature: A Guide to Texts and Manuscripts*, Anglo-Norman Texts Society Occasional Publications 3 (1999).

For Latin, see above, Chapter 9.

Chapter 11: English literary voices, 1350–1500

Much of the scholarship on later Middle English is part of that for earlier Middle English; see the further reading for Chapter 10, and for readings of literature in historical and cultural contexts see the further reading for the Introduction. The major works in late medieval English literature have extensive bibliographies and current guides, many included in the series mentioned for Chapter 10. Student editions of such works often provide the best introduction to the wider range of scholarly materials:

Bevington, David, *Medieval Drama* (Boston, MA, 1975).
Chaucer, Geoffrey, *The Riverside Chaucer*, 3rd edn., gen. ed. Larry D. Benson (Boston, MA, 1987).
  The Canterbury Tales: Fifteen Tales and the General Prologue, eds. V. A. Kolve and Glending Olson (New York, 2005).
  Troilus and Criseyde, ed. Stephen Barney (New York, 2006).
  Dream Visions and Other Poems, ed. Kathryn Lynch (New York, 2007).
Gower, John, *The Major Latin Works*, trans. Eric W. Stockton (Seattle, WA, 1962).
  Mirour de l'Omme (The Mirror of Mankind), trans. William Burton Wilson, rev. Nancy Wilson Van Baak (East Lansing, 1992).
  Confessio Amantis, ed. Russell Peck, with Latin translations by Andrew Galloway, 3 vols. (Kalamazoo, MI, 2003–6).
  The Minor Latin Works, ed. R. F. Yeager (Kalamazoo, MI, 2005).
  The French Balades, ed. R. F. Yeager (Kalamazoo, MI, 2010).
Hoccleve, Thomas, *The Regement of Princes*, ed. Charles R. Blyth (Kalamazoo, MI, 1999).
  My Compleinte and Other Poems, ed. Roger Ellis (Exeter, 2001).
Julian of Norwich, *The Showings of Julian of Norwich*, ed. Denise N. Baker (New York, 2005).
Kempe, Margery, *The Book of Margery Kempe*, trans. Barry Windeatt (Harmondsworth, 1985).
  The Book of Margery Kempe, ed. Barry Windeatt (Woodbridge, 2004).
Langland, William, *The Vision of Piers Plowman: A Critical Edition of the B Text*, ed. A. V. C. Schmidt, 2nd edn. (1995).
  Piers Plowman: A New Annotated Edition of the C-Text, ed. Derek Pearsall (Exeter, 2008).
Lydgate, John, *Fall of Princes*, ed. Henry Bergen, 4 vols., EETS 121–24 ([1924–27] 1964–67).
Malory, Sir Thomas, *Le Morte d'Arthur*, ed. Stephen Shepherd (New York, 2003).
Pearl poems – (Sir Gawain and the Green Knight, Cleanness, Patience, Pearl, and, in this edition only, St. Erkenwald): The Complete Works of the Pearl Poet, eds. Malcolm Andrew, Ronald Waldron, and Clifford Peterson, trans. Casey Finch (Berkeley, CA, 1993).

St. Erkenwald, ed. Ruth Morse (Cambridge, 1975).

Selections from English Wycliffite Writings, ed. Anne Hudson (Cambridge, 1978)

In addition, a very wide range of further Middle English literature is available from TEAMS, in print (Kalamazoo, MI), and free online at: www.lib.rochester.edu/camelot/teams/tmsmenu.htm#menu. More scholarly editions appear regularly from EETS, many older texts of which are available online at: http://quod.lib.umich.edu/c/cme.

Recent critical approaches and other introductory materials are collected in some of the many companions and guides available that center on later medieval English literature:

Brown, Peter (ed.), *The Blackwell Companion to Chaucer* (Oxford, 2002).

    (ed.), *Blackwell Companion to Medieval English Literature and Culture* (Oxford, 2007).

Corrie, Marilyn (ed.), *A Concise Companion to Middle English Literature* (Oxford, 2009).

Galloway, Andrew, *Medieval Literature and Culture* (2006).

Lerer, Seth (ed.), *The Yale Companion to Chaucer* (New Haven, CT, 2007).

Scanlon, Larry (ed.), *Cambridge Companion to Medieval English Literature, 1100–1500* (Cambridge, 2009).

Strohm, Paul (ed.), *Middle English: Oxford Twentieth-century Approaches to Literature* (Oxford, 2007).

Turville-Petre, Thorlac, *Reading Middle English Literature* (Oxford, 2007).

Chapter 12: Literary reformations of the Middle Ages

Primary

Andrewes, Lancelot, *Lancelot Andrewes: Selected Sermons and Lectures*, ed. Peter McCullough (Oxford, 2005).

Bevis of Hamton: The Romance of Sir Beues of Hamtoun, ed. Eugen Kölbing, EETS ES 46, 48, 65, reprinted 1 vol. (New York, 1978).

Brewer, Derek (ed.), *Chaucer: The Critical Heritage*, 2 vols. (Boston, MA, 1978).

Bunyan, John, *The Pilgrim's Progress and Grace Abounding*, ed. Roger Sharrock (1966).

Drayton, Michael, *The Works of Michael Drayton*, ed. J. William Hebel, 5 vols. (Oxford, 1961).

Guy of Warwick: The Romance of Guy of Warwick, ed. Julius Zupitza, EETS ES 42, 49, 59, reprinted 1 vol. (New York, 1966).

Herbert, George, *The Works of George Herbert*, ed. F. E. Hutchinson (Oxford, 1941).

Jonson, Ben, *Ben Jonson*, eds. C. H. Herford and Percy and Evelyn Simpson. 11 vols., corrected edn. (Oxford, 1954).

Lydgate, John, *Lydgate's Fall of Princes*, ed. Henry Bergen, 4 vols. EETS ES 121–24 (1924–27).

Marlowe, Christopher, *The Complete Works of Christopher Marlowe*, ed. Fredson Bowers, 2nd edn., 2 vols. (Cambridge, 1981).

Mirror for Magistrates, The, ed. Lily B. Campbell (New York, 1938).

Murray, James A. H. (ed.), *The Romances and Prophecies of Thomas of Erceldoune*, EETS OS 68 (1875).

Nichols, John (ed.), *The Progresses and Public Processions of Queen Elizabeth*, 3 vols. (1823, reprinted New York, n.d.).

Percy Folio: Bishop Percy's Folio Manuscript: Ballads and Romances, eds. John W. Hales and Frederick J. Furnivall, 3 vols. (1868).

Raby, F. J. E. (ed.), *The Oxford Book of Medieval Latin Verse* (Oxford, 1959).

Shakespeare, William, *The Riverside Shakespeare*, gen. ed. G. Blakemore Evans, 2nd edn. (Boston, MA, 1997).

Spenser, Edmund, *The Faerie Queene*, ed. A. C. Hamilton, 2nd edn. (New York, 2000).

Vaughan, Henry, *Henry Vaughan: The Complete Poems*, ed. Alan Rudrum (1976).

Secondary

Cooper, Helen, *The English Romance in Time: Transforming Motifs from Geoffrey of Monmouth to the Death of Shakespeare* (Oxford, 2004).

Duffy, Eamon, *The Voices of Morebath: Reformation and Rebellion in an English Village* (New Haven, CT, 2001).

Field, Rosalind and Alison Wiggins (eds.), *Guy of Warwick: Icon and Ancestor* (Cambridge, 2007).

Gillespie, Stuart and Neil Rhodes (eds.), *Shakespeare and Elizabethan Popular Culture* (2006).

King, Andrew, *The Faerie Queene and Middle English Romance: The Matter of Just Memory* (Oxford, 2000).

Lewis, C. S., *The Discarded Image: An Introduction to Medieval and Renaissance Literature* (Cambridge, 1964).

McKisack, May, *Medieval History in the Tudor Age* (Oxford, 1971).

Parry, Graham, *The Trophies of Time: English Antiquarians of the Seventeenth Century* (Oxford, 1995).

Weimann, Robert, *Shakespeare and the Popular Tradition in the Theater: Studies in the Social Dimension of Dramatic Form and Function* (Baltimore, MD, 1978).

Chapter 13: Re-creating the Middle Ages

Alexander, Michael, *Medievalism: The Middle Ages in Modern England* (New Haven, CT, 2007).

Barczewski, Stephanie L., *Myth and National Identity in Nineteenth-Century Britain: The Legends of King Arthur and Robin Hood* (Oxford, 2000).

Biddick, Kathleen, *The Shock of Medievalism* (Durham, NC, 1998).

Chandler, Alice, *A Dream of Order: The Medieval Ideal in Nineteenth-Century English Literature* (Lincoln, NE, 1970).

Davis, Kathleen and Nadia Altschul, *Medievalisms in the Postcolonial World: The Idea of "The Middle Ages" Outside Europe* (Baltimore, MD, 2009).

Fay, Elizabeth, *Romantic Medievalism: History and the Romantic Literary Ideal* (New York, 2002).

Harty, Kevin, *The Reel Middle Ages: Films about Medieval Europe* (Jefferson, NC, 1999).

Hutner, Gordon and Larry Scanlon (eds.), *Medieval America*, special issue of *American Literary History* 22(4) (2010).

Simmons, Clare A., *Reversing the Conquest: History and Myth in 19th-Century British Literature* (New Brunswick, NJ, 1990).

Utz, Richard and Tom Shippey (eds.), *Medievalism in the Modern World: Essays in Honour of Leslie Workman* (Turnhout, 1998).

Index